LANGUAGE, GENDER AND SOCIETY

Edited by

Barrie Thorne
Michigan State University, East Lansing

Cheris Kramarae
University of Illinois, Urbana

Nancy Henley
University of California, Los Angeles

HEINLE & HEINLE PUBLISHERS

A Division of Wadsworth, Inc.
Boston, Massachusetts 02116

Library of Congress Cataloging in Publication Data

Main entry under title:

Language, gender, and society.

   Bibliography: p.
   Includes index.
   1. Language and languages--Sex differences--
Addresses, essays, lectures. 2. Communication--Sex
differences--Addresses, essays, lectures. I. Thorne,
Barrie. II. Kramarae, Cheris. III. Henley, Nancy.
P120.S48L36   1983   401'.9   82-22537
ISBN 0-8384-2937-8

Cover design by Diana Esterly

First printing: October 1983

Printed in the U.S.A.

11 12 13

Dedicated, in a spirit of sisterhood,

to our mothers:

Alison Comish Thorne, Deda Rae Gamble, Estella Ziegenhein Main

and to our sisters:

Avril, Sandra, Glee, Donna, Edyth, Dorothy

PREFACE

The format of this book resembles *Language and Sex: Difference and Dominance,* but the material is almost all new. In the years since that volume was published (1975) the field it helped to inaugurate has expanded enormously. To return to the metaphor we used then: We are now beyond the first crest, and riding high on waves of interest in the complex relationship between women, men, and language. In the last decade the research has extended into many named disciplines; e.g., anthropology, child development, education, folklore, psychology, linguistics, literature, literary criticism, sociology, and speech communication. And the field, which had its genesis in the women's movement, is continually enlivened by feminist writing and activism. Those of us working in this field have made contact with each other across disciplinary boundaries and national borders and among universities, colleges, publishing houses, journals, and other arenas of learning and action. Together we have created spaces in which our concerns have flourished—in special conferences, in sessions of annual meetings and informal gatherings, and in courses and workshops; through style sheets and guidelines for nonsexist language now circulating widely as tools for social change; through collaborative work on journal issues and anthologies and through *Women and Language News,* which reports on ongoing research, conferences, and new publications. We especially thank Pat Nichols, Pamela Tiedt, and Sharon Veach at Stanford University, the founders and people who made *WLN* a publication that has helped to support an expanding international network.[1]

Cheris Kramarae has joined the editors of the 1975 volume, adding her background in speech communication to that of the other two editors—Barrie Thorne's sociolinguistics and Nancy Henley's psycholinguistics. Most of the essays in this volume are by authors who were not included in the earlier volume; the rest of the essays, by authors who were, represent advances in knowledge and theory. The greatest change, however, is in the size and organization of the annotated bibliography: so much has been written and published since 1974 that it is difficult to keep up with it, let alone incorporate it all in a book of limited size.

We would like to thank the following people who helped supply citations or critical comments on drafts of the bibliography: Carolyn Burke, Frank de Caro, Rayna Green, Joseph J. Hayes, Lee Jenkins, Sally McConnell-Ginet, Wendy Martyna, Namascar Saktini, Muriel Schulz, and Candace West. We received special help with citations from other countries from Helga Andresen, Dédé Brouwer, Marinel Gerritsen, Ingrid Guentherodt, Marlis Hellinger, Cordula Mathias, Anke Meyer, Tove Beate Pedersen, Sheila Ramsey, Irene Tatarnikova, Senta Trömel-Plötz, Jyotsna Vaid, Fritjof Werner, and Susan Wobst. Janice Hill and Sharon Tuckman helped us sort out files. We received help with computer work from Kuniko Akatagawa, Lucy Holley, Judy Page, Steven Steinberg, and, especially, Steve Goldman. Barrie Thorne's work was facilitated by support from the College Scholar program (Sociology Department and College of Social Science) and by All University Research Grants, Michigan State University. Cheris Kramarae received research assistant support from the Department of Speech Communication, University of Illinois. We also want to thank Peter, Andrew, Abigail, Dale, Brinlee, and Jana.

We are pleased we are able to bring this exciting work to a larger audience, to share the stimulation of new ideas, information, directions in theory, and fresh thinking about previous received truths.[2] Eight years have intervened between the publication of *Language and Sex* and *Language, Gender and Society.* We cannot at this point predict a third volume, but we look forward to what the field will have revealed to us by 1990, and hope, with the other authors, that these investigations will contribute to the elimination of sex bias, not only in language but in society as a whole.

Barrie Thorne
Cheris Kramarae
Nancy Henley

September 1982

NOTES

1. *Women and Language News* is now edited by Cheris Kramarae and Paula Treichler at the University of Illinois. (*WLN,* 244 Lincoln Hall, 702 S. Wright, Univ. of Illinois, Urbana, IL 61801)

2. One change we have made in this volume is to capitalize *Black* in the essays and the bibliography, following the argument by Catharine A. MacKinnon (in *Signs,* 7, no. 3 [1982], 516) and Geneva Smitherman that *Black* refers, not merely to skin pigmentation, but to a heritage, a social creation, and often a personal identity in ways at least as meaningful as do ethnic identities which are conventionally capitalized.

ACKNOWLEDGMENTS

The editors wish to thank the individuals and publishers mentioned below for permission to reprint their copyrighted materials:

Wendy Martyna, "Beyond the He/Man Approach: The Case for Nonsexist Language." Slightly expanded and revised version of a paper which appeared in *Signs: Journal of Women in Culture and Society,* Vol. 5, No. 3, 1980, pp. 482–93. Used by permission of the author and publisher, The University of Chicago Press. Copyright © 1980 by the University of Chicago. All rights reserved.

Sally McConnell-Ginet, "Intonation in a Man's World." Revised version of a paper which appeared in *Signs: Journal of Women in Culture and Society,* Vol. 3, No. 3, 1978, pp. 541–59. Used by permission of the author and publisher, The University of Chicago Press. Copyright © 1978 by the University of Chicago. All rights reserved.

Pamela M. Fishman, "Interaction: The Work Women Do." Revised version of a paper which appeared in *Social Problems,* Vol. 25, No. 4, 1978, pp. 397–406. Used by permission of the author and publisher. Copyright © 1978 by the Society for the Study of Social Problems.

Jack W. Sattell, "Men, Inexpressiveness, and Power." Revision of "The Inexpressive Male: Tragedy or Sexual Politics?" which appeared in *Social Problems,* Vol. 23, No. 4, 1976, pp. 469–77. Used by permission of the author and publisher. Copyright © 1976 by the Society for the Study of Social Problems.

CONTENTS

SEX SIMILARITIES AND DIFFERENCES IN LANGUAGE, SPEECH, AND NONVERBAL COMMUNICATION: AN ANNOTATED BIBLIOGRAPHY

COMPILED BY CHERIS KRAMARAE, BARRIE THORNE, AND NANCY HENLEY

SELECTED PAPERS

INTRODUCTION

We selected the essays in this collection in order to represent something of the variety of topics in and approaches to the study of language and gender. The essays are arranged according to the same general outline as the bibliography which follows.

"Language, Gender and Society: Opening a Second Decade of Research," the introductory essay, provides an overview of this rapidly expanding field, tracing its development, especially in the last decade. In it we emphasize the changes in thinking that have taken place: about relations between language structure and language use, the move from the study of isolated variables to the study of usage in social context, and reconceptualizations of sex and gender. We argue that increased attention to woman–woman talk involves an important redirection of research on language and gender. This overview, written by authors from several disciplines—sociology, speech communication, and psychology—reflects the strongly interdisciplinary nature of the field.

The overview discusses the nine essays that follow. The first two, by psychologists, examine *sex bias* as it exists in everyday language and usage. Wendy Martyna ("Beyond the He/Man Approach: The Case for Nonsexist Language") and Donald MacKay ("Prescriptive Grammar and the Pronoun Problem") review important research, including their own, showing the effects of masculine "generics" on cognition, attitudes, and behavior.

Sex differentiation and its perception in language use is the topic of the next two essays, both by linguists. Patricia Nichols ("Linguistic Options and Choices for Black Women in the Rural South") shows the importance of social context in linking gender with language use. Sally McConnell-Ginet ("Intonation in a Man's World"), examining research on intonation patterns, notes that the same patterns may be evaluated differently when used by a woman than when used by a man; intonation differences influence, and are influenced by, our perception and indeed our whole thinking about the sexes.

The next three essays, all by sociologists, focus on *conversation interaction* and social power. Pamela Fishman ("Interaction: The Work Women Do") analyzes recurring patterns in the household conversations of three heterosexual couples; she concludes that the conversations were under male control but mainly produced by female work. Candace West and Don Zimmerman ("Small Insults: A Study of Interruptions in Cross-Sex Conversations between Unacquainted Persons") analyze patterns of interruption in mixed-sex conversations in natural and experimental settings. Jack Sattel ("Men, Inexpressiveness, and Power") reinterprets a phenomenon which has been termed a "tragedy of American society"; he argues that men exercise and maintain power over women—and over other men—through withholding self-disclosure.

"Consciousness as Style; Style as Aesthetic" by Julia Penelope and Susan Wolfe, both in English language studies, speaks of *genre and style,* arguing that there is a unique perspective and style in women's writing, particularly in the language of feminist writers.

The final essay, "Men's Speech to Young Children," by psychologists Jean Berko Gleason and Esther Blank Greif, deals with *children and language.* The authors explore the social contexts of both language and gender, comparing the speech that fathers, mothers, and women and men day-care teachers address to young children.

All of these essays make it clear that complex analysis of gender in the context of settings, roles, and other social identities can yield more insight than can an abstract search for sex differences.

NOTES ON THE AUTHORS

Pamela M. Fishman is a sociologist living in Brooklyn, New York, working as a writer for Prospect Park.

Jean Berko Gleason is in the Department of Psychology, Boston University.

Esther Blank Greif is in the Department of Psychology, Boston University.

Nancy Henley is in the Department of Psychology and Women's Studies Program, University of California, Los Angeles.

Cheris Kramarae is in the Department of Speech Communication, University of Illinois, Urbana.

Donald G. MacKay is in the Department of Psychology, University of California, Los Angeles.

Wendy Martyna is in the Department of Psychology, University of California, Santa Cruz.

Sally McConnell-Ginet is in the Department of Modern Languages and Linguistics, Cornell University, Ithaca, New York.

Patricia C. Nichols is in the Department of English, San José State University, California.

Julia Penelope (Stanley) is in the Department of English, University of Nebraska, Lincoln.

Jack W. Sattel is in the Department of Sociology, Normandale Community College, Bloomington, Minnesota.

Barrie Thorne is in the Department of Sociology, Michigan State University, East Lansing.

Candace West is in the Department of Sociology, University of California, Santa Cruz.

Susan J. Wolfe is in the Department of English, University of South Dakota, Vermillion.

Don H. Zimmerman is in the Department of Sociology, University of California, Santa Barbara.

LANGUAGE, GENDER AND SOCIETY:
OPENING A SECOND DECADE OF RESEARCH*

Barrie Thorne, Cheris Kramarae, and Nancy Henley

The title of this book, *Language, Gender and Society,* anchors themes crossing many fields of inquiry. The essays and the annotated bibliography illustrate the array of theories, questions, and findings which make up the substance of the field. The rapid expansion of research on the sexual differentiation of language and speech is documented by the bibliography, which includes over five times as many items as the version compiled almost ten years ago (Henley & Thorne, 1975).

In annotating these references and organizing them into categories, we have sometimes felt like women at sewing machines, trying to pull together workable seams from the yards of material at hand. This overview, while it stands independently, can also be seen as a companion to the bibliography. In discussing the origins and development of the field, we first follow the language seams, noting the very different questions about relationships between language and gender which have been pursued, for example, by linguists, conversation analysts, folklorists, and poets. We also discuss the challenges that inter-disciplinary feminist work poses to traditional approaches to language, and to gender, the other anchor-point of this field. *Sex* and *gender,* like language, are more problematic than many have initially supposed, and we discuss the changes in conceptualization that have accompanied the development of this field, including a deepened understanding of the social organization of gender, and a shift from earlier emphasis on mixed-sex talk to closer attention to women's speech with one another. Women's language has emerged not only as a vital research topic but also as a basis for rethinking conventional models of language use and for sorting out questions of value and social change.

*We want to thank Wendy Martyna, Sally McConnell-Ginet, Patricia Nichols, Avril Thorne, and Candace West for their helpful comments on an earlier draft of this essay.

THE ORIGINS OF INTEREST IN LANGUAGE AND THE SEXES

When we began research on language and gender a decade ago, we traced the origins of this field to early 20th-century anthropologists who, drawing on earlier reports of travelers and missionaries, described separate "men's and women's languages" in societies removed from Western cultures (see the annotated bibliography, Sec. IV-G). In his influential book, *Language: Its Nature, Development and Origin,* Otto Jespersen (1922) reviewed cross-cultural reports and added a series of speculations about Western women's supposed preferences for refined, euphemistic, and hyperbolic expression, and men's alleged greater use of slang and innovations.

When the women's movement of the late 1960s spurred unprecedented interest in relationships of women, men, and language, feminists turned to earlier sources like Jespersen, pursuing their leads, but also questioning their sexist pronouncements. In the process, we often ended up addressing questions we ourselves had not posed. Feminist researchers have struggled to move from the shadow of stereotypes and continual outside criticism of this sort of work, and to create our own lines of inquiry.

In the course of this work we have discovered other historical origins: the writings of earlier feminists such as Charlotte Carmichael Stopes (1908) who wrote a treatise on the use of *man* in British law, and its effect on women's freedom, and Elsie Clews Parsons (1913) who discussed sex-linked taboos on language use and observed that there was a linguistic double-standard which assumed "the superiority of man." In 1946, Mary Beard, the historian, discussed the problematic "generic masculine" (Beard, 1946). Discoveries of this kind have brought us both exhilaration at the discovery of foremothers and anger at the erasure of their work and the loss of their company at earlier times in our education.

VARIED APPROACHES TO LANGUAGE

It is notable that until the impetus of the contemporary women's movement, linguists and sociolinguists who were alert to other sources of difference did not attend to sex-based language variation. As Thomas Kuhn (1962) observed in studying the development of scientific paradigms, knowledge is strongly affected by external forces. Social movements—in this case the feminist movement—have often pushed disciplines into interests researchers long avoided.

The actions and articulations of the women's movement, and women's lived experiences, have raised questions not only about the sexual differentiation of language and speech but also about ways language aids the construction of a male supremacist society. Because of traditional scholarly neglect and trivialization of issues of gender, researchers whose work is cited in the bibliography have often worked at the edges of academic disciplines. They have used traditional theories and research tools, but have also revised and challenged them, for example, by connecting research on sexism in language structure with questions about language use, by rethinking empirical research on sex differences in speech, and by developing significant insight into the social contexts of both language and gender.

Relations between Language Structure and Language Use

Language structure traditionally has been distinguished from language use, as in the classic division between *langue* (the code, abstracted from context) and *parole* (actual speech). Building on such distinctions, those researching gender and language initially separated research on sexism in language (with a focus on structure) from inquiry into ways women and men use the code. (The first sections of our bibliography continue to reflect this division.) However, as research on gender and language has developed, more connections have been drawn between sexism in the code and the ways speakers make use of it (Spender, 1980).

Hundreds of essays have pointed to varied ways in which language aids the defining, deprecating, and excluding of women (see Sec. II of the bibliography). For example, women tend to be defined by their relation to men ("Miss/Mrs." or "Harold's widow"), while men are given autonomous and varied linguistic status. For almost 100 years many states required wives to change their names to their husbands' (Stannard, 1977). In many other ways, the available and "approved" titles, pronouns, lexicons, and labels reflect the fact that women (as well as other subordinates)[1] have been named by others.

Men's extensive labeling of women as parts of body, fruit, or animals and as mindless, or like children—labels with no real parallel for men—reflects men's derision of women and helps maintain gender hierarchy and control. Researching terms for sexual promiscuity, Julia Penelope Stanley (1977) found 220 terms for a sexually promiscuous woman and only 22 terms for a sexually promiscuous man. She notes that there is no linguistic reason why the first set is large and the latter small. Many of the terms Stanley categorizes are used not only among men to discuss women and to address women they know but also to address unknown women in public. As Carol Brooks Gardner (1981) describes, many men consider women to be "open persons" when they are in public streets. The address rights of women and men are different enough, Gardner suggests, so that men can remark on parts of a woman's body, call her "honey" or obscenities, threaten her, and yet often fail to recognize how offensive these remarks are to the woman. Gardner's analysis connects patterns in the language code—the asymmetry of labels and names applied to women and men—with asymmetries in ways men and women use language in daily interaction.

Males are clearly more visible than females in language content and use. For example, computer analysis of 100,000 words from children's schoolbooks (Graham, 1973) found male pronouns to outnumber female ones by almost four to one. This ratio was not primarily due to the use of masculine words in generic context; 97 percent of the uses of *he* referred to male humans or animals, or to persons presumed male (*sailor, farmer*), and men were referred to specifically seven times as often as women. Despite the infrequent use of the masculine "generic"[2] compared with specific masculine reference, the masculine "generic" has a high occurrence in our lives compared with many other sources of influence. Donald MacKay (1980) has estimated that in the course of a lifetime a highly educated American is exposed to generically used *he* a million times.[3]

The use of *man* to refer to people in general or *he* to refer to sex-indefinite antecedents is a paramount example of the invisibility of women in language. Many grammarians and linguists claim that this form is innocuous in its omission of women and girls and that it includes the female in its meaning. However, there is ample research evidence that the masculine "generic" does not really function as a generic. In various studies words like *he* and *man* in generic contexts were presented orally or in writing to people who were asked to indicate their understanding by drawing, bringing in, or pointing out a picture, by describing or writing a story about the person(s) referred to, or by answering yes or no when asked whether a sex-specific word or picture applies to the meaning (Silveira, 1980, summarizes fourteen of these studies). In all of these studies, women and girls were understood to be included significantly less often than men and boys, a finding true for both female and male subjects.[4] Female subjects, even though they tend not to include women in their interpretation, still are more likely to interpret the masculine "generic" generically than are males, and less likely to use the form themselves in producing language. As would be expected, both women and men report that they usually image males when they read or hear the masculine "generic." Moreover, Wendy Martyna (1978) found women had less imagery of any sort with this form, suggesting that females may suppress imagery in order to be connected to their language. These sex differences again point to the interplay of language structure and use.

The work of Martyna (1978; in this volume) and MacKay (1980; in this volume) exemplifies the contribution that psychological empirical research can make to this field of study. Both have carried out extensive studies of the comprehension and production of generic forms, Martyna with a large number of subjects covering a broad range of age groups, and with particular interest in imagery; MacKay with theoretical contributions to linguistic understanding of pronoun comprehension, and special attention to testing alternatives to the masculine "generic." Currently psycholinguists are examining related topics, such as the effect of the usage on attitudes toward women and its differential effect on the self-esteem of females and males; the comparative difficulty in the cognitive processing of the masculine and the sex-neutral generic; and the changes, if any, speakers report making in their use of this form and their difficulty with and readiness to make changes.

Some have characterized the feminist concern with sexist bias in language as Whorfian, i.e., as accepting the Sapir/Whorf hypothesis (Whorf, 1956) that language shapes our perceptions, determining not only how we think about things but even what we can conceive (for discussion of this hypothesis, see Hymes, 1964; Brown, 1965). This hypothesis, currently out of vogue largely owing to the work of Rosch (1974), has a range of interpretation, from weak to strong. No one would question that how something is worded can make a great difference in how it is understood; writers of fiction and of advertising copy and constructors of psychological scales live by that understanding. Whether or not language limits our thinking in ways that make it impossible to conceive of some things has not been shown. It does seem clear that language can make thinking of things in specific ways more difficult or easy. Little attention to the Whorfian question has been given by those interested in questions of language and gender, though some work has begun on this issue (e.g., Schneider & Foss, 1977; Shimanoff, 1977). The question seems ripe for new investigation drawing on language and gender research.

The study of the sexual differentiation of language and speech has never been a detached, armchair enterprise; efforts to change language are closely interwoven with the research of the last decade. These efforts include protests against sexist language, experiments with alternative forms (such as truly inclusive pronouns), the development and distribution of style sheets for nonsexist language (Miller & Swift, 1980), women's efforts to name their experience through creating words like *sexism* and *male chauvinism,* and other acts of naming discussed by Julia Penelope and Susan Wolfe (in this volume). Some researchers have studied processes of deliberate language change. For example, Barbara Bate (1978) explored ways in which different members of a university faculty changed, or resisted changing, their use of sexist language. This is another example of research exploring relationships between language structure and use.

Although critics of research on language and sex portray "generic" pronouns as the entire issue (and write trivializing articles on, e.g., "personhole" covers), the issues are in fact more sweeping. Feminists (e.g., Daly, 1978; Rich, 1979; Spender, 1980) have examined language as a symbolic system closely tied to patriarchal social structure. They argue that language is deeply partriarchal, that the "theft of language" is part of women's condition of relative powerlessness (Rich, 1979), and that women need to rework traditional forms in order to create women-centered language and meaning. This approach—which connects language structure, use, and experience—has emerged in the United States, not primarily in the work of linguists or sociolinguists, but in the writings of poets and radical feminists, as described by Penelope and Wolfe (in this volume). In drawing close ties between symbolic structure and experience and evoking the transformative power of aesthetics, the voices of Mary Daly, Susan Griffin, Adrienne Rich, and others are resonant with those of contemporary French feminists such as Hélène Cixous, Julia Kristeva, Luce Irigaray, and Monique Wittig (Stanton, 1980; also see Sec. VI-C of the bibliography). All of these theorists regard language both as critical restraint *and* as release.

Although there are crucial differences among these French feminists, they share an intellectual and political tradition anchored in existentialism, Lacanian psychoanalysis and post-structuralism. They locate women's oppression in the production of discourse and meaning; language, they argue, is deeply phallogo-centric, constituting men as subjects and women as "absence" or "other." French feminists seek to inscribe women's experiences in language and thought, not through altering specific usages such as sexist pronouns (which the French might see as minor efforts at repair), but through "rupturing discourse," e.g., through "writing from the body" (Cixous, 1976) or through effecting an epistemological shift to a lesbian subject (Wittig, 1980).[5] Recent translations of French feminist writing on language (e.g., Marks & deCourtivron, 1981; Guadin et al., 1982; *Signs,* 1982) will no doubt lead to fruitful encounters between the French tradition, which is abstract and theoretical, relating language to the unconscious and to the body, and the more pragmatic and empirical approaches, attentive to everyday uses of speech, which dominate thinking about gender and language in the United States.

Sex Differences and Similarities in Speech: From Isolated Variables to Social Context

Over the last decade, empirical evidence has accumulated to provide complex understanding of the ways in which women and men speak, at least in white, middle-class, heterosexual segments of U.S. society.[6] Adding sex to the list of variables studied by sociolinguists, much of the research of the early 1970s relied on the tools of traditional linguistics, looking for sex differences in word choice, syntax, phonetics, or suprasegmentals. Stereotyped statements of linguists such as Jespersen (1922) and others who have written (or joked) about women's speech (while typically assuming men's speech to be the standard) generated questions like the following: Do women have a more limited vocabulary than men do, or do they use more—or different—adjectives and adverbs? Are women more apt to leave their sentences unfinished? Do they enunciate more properly? Do they use lots of "superficial" words? Are their sentences longer, or shorter, then men's? Do they use more questioning, or uncertain intonation?

Research pursuing questions of this kind has been important in modifying and carefully refuting stereotyped claims. But when it lacked theoretical guidance, such work eventually seemed to have little purpose beyond checking (and perhaps unwittingly perpetuating) stereotypes about the sexes, especially women, and their ways of speaking.[7] The results of these studies of isolated variables are, not surprisingly, very complex and often contradictory. There are two areas where recurring sex differences have been found. Women more often choose "correct" phonetic variations (such as the suffix -*ing* rather than -*in*)— "correct" in being traditionally associated with grammar books and middle-class upward mobility (see bibliography, Sec. IV-C). And, as Sally McConnell-Ginet (in this volume) carefully explores, women tend to use a wider range of pitch and more variable intonation than men. No consistent sex differences have been found in amount of vocabulary or choice of adjectives and adverbs, although in different social groups the sexes may use somewhat different lexicons (see Sec. IV-B). Finally, no consistent sex differences have been found in the use of syntactic forms such as patterns of question-asking (see Sec. IV-B).

The complex findings that emerge from research of this kind are illustrated by studies of men's and women's use of tag questions. In an influential series of speculations about "women's language," Robin Lakoff (1975) claimed that women more often use tag questions ("Hilda arrived, didn't she?"). Two studies—one of college students assigned to discussion groups (McMillan et al., 1977) and the other of heterosexual couples conversing at home (Fishman, 1980)—did find that women used more tag questions than men. However, Baumann (1976) found that in a classroom setting women and men used about the same number of tag questions. Lapadat and Seesahai (1977) found that in informal conversations men used twice as many tag questions as women; Johnson (1980) found, in analyzing meetings of engineers and designers in a corporation, that the male leader used the majority of tag questions; and Dubois and Crouch (1977) found men participants in a professional conference used thirty-three tag questions, while women used none. It is hard to draw conclusions from all of this, except that the initial claim was phrased too simply. The study of isolated variables almost invariably leads to further questions about the effects of setting, topic, roles, and other social factors that may interact with gender. It also raises questions about language function and use (McConnell-Ginet, 1980). For example, Lakoff claims that tag questions convey uncertainty; Fishman demonstrates women's use of tags to elicit response from uncommunicative male conversational partners; Johnson describes tags as devices used to sustain interaction; and Dubois and Crouch observe that tag questions may be used in an overbearing way, to forestall opposition.

A review of the literature shows that very few expected sex differences have been firmly substantiated by empirical studies of isolated variables. Some popular beliefs about differences between the sexes appear to have little basis in fact, and in a few cases research findings actually invert the stereotypes. For example, women are said to be more talkative than men, but studies of mixed-sex groups tend to find the reverse—that men talk more than women (see bibliography, Sec. V-B).

The persistence of gender stereotypes has led to research specifically on perceptions and evaluations of speech (see Sec. III). Researchers have found that in some cases similar speech by females and males is perceived differently—for example, an infant's cry was interpreted as anger when listeners were told the baby was a boy, and as fear when they were told it was a girl (Condry & Condry, 1976). McConnell-Ginet (in this volume) observes that the same intonation patterns may be evaluated differently when used by a woman than when used by a man—our hearing is sex-typed. Patricia Bradley (in press) found that in small decision-making groups the use of qualifying phrases adversely affected judgments of women, but not of men, speakers. And another study found that students judged women professors, but not most men professors, as more likable *and* as less competent the more they generated student participation in class (Macke et al., 1980).

There have been other redirections of research. Recognizing that findings of sex difference have been over-reported (especially those which accord with polarized gender stereotypes), researchers increasingly use the phrase "sex similarities and differences." Our theories, however, remain whetted on difference, and we need further theoretical work to integrate findings of both similarity and difference. In addition, in traditional research, difference is too often located not in social structure but in women. As subordinates, women are more often conceptualized in a singular condition, while men are allowed individualism which transcends gender. This pattern is evident in the asymmetric contrast between "women's language" and "neutral" (or male) language which is found, for example, in Jespersen (1922) and Lakoff (1975).

Units of language study—phonemes, words, contrasts of pitch—which are taken from linguistics often seem too small, and counting and correlating methods too abstracted from context, to yield meaningful understanding of patterned relationships between gender and language. In the first phase of language/gender research, many of us were eager to piece together an overall portrayal of differences in the speech of women and men. We invented notions like *"genderlect"* to provide overall characterizations of sex differences in speech (Kramer, 1974; Thorne & Henley, 1975). The "genderlect" portrayal now seems too abstract and overdrawn, implying that there are differences in the basic codes used by women and men, rather than variably occurring differences, and similarities, in the frequency with which women and men use specific features of a shared code (McConnell-Ginet, 1980). "Genderlect" implies more homogeneity among women, and among men—and more difference between the sexes—than is, in fact, the case.

The most fruitful research on gender and speech has conceptualized language not in terms of isolated variables, nor as an abstracted code, but within contexts of actual use. For example, although they often focus on one aspect of speech such as interruptions, questions, false starts, or the initiation of topics (see Sec. V of the bibliography), conversation analysts look at such features within the give-and-take of actual talk. Pamela Fishman (in this volume) analyzes recurring patterns in the household conversations of three heterosexual couples. Although the women tried more often than the men to initiate conversations, the women succeeded less often because of minimal responses from their male companions. In contrast, the women pursued topics the men raised, asked more questions, and did more verbal support work than the men. Fishman concludes that the conversations were under male control but mainly produced by female work. Candace West and Don Zimmerman (in this volume) analyze patterns of interruptions in mixed-sex conversations in natural and in experimental settings. They discuss patterns (greater male interruption) found across situations, while also attending to the variable influence of setting. In general, researchers have focused more on some speech settings, e.g., experimental laboratories, classrooms, and conferences, than on others. Section V-F of the bibliography cross-lists studies by setting, and makes clear how little we know about the possible effects of situation on female and male speech.

Attending to social context, researchers have increasingly conceptualized language use in terms of strategies. For example, Penelope Brown (1976:247) argues that linguistic analyses too often reify rules rather than regard humans as "rational actors oriented toward communicative goals and employing strategies to achieve those goals." When women or men speak, they intend to do certain things, such as create rapport or assert or resist control, and, given the different positions of the sexes in society, speech strategies may vary by sex (Kramarae, 1981). Several papers in this volume analyze the speech strategies of men and women which emerge from their structured positions of inequality. Men exercise and maintain power over women through withholding self-disclosure (Sattel) and response to the topics women raise (Fishman) and through interrupting women more than women interrupt men (West & Zimmerman). Women's speech strategies—for example, their "interaction work" (Fishman, in this volume) and styles of "politeness" (Brown & Levinson, 1978; Lakoff, 1975)—may be understood, at least in part, as ways of coping with greater male power. McConnell-Ginet (in this volume) also uses the notion of speech strategies to analyze the different intonation patterns used by women and men.

Although gender and power structures are closely tied (Henley, 1977), there are dimensions to gender other than power. Roger Abrahams (1975) compares the speech of Black men, who seek to establish reputations in the world of the street, with the talk of Black women, oriented to maintaining respectability in the home. Research on women's and men's use of speech genres such as gossip, insults, joking, and storytelling has also been sensitive to speech strategies (Borker, 1980; see Sec. VI-A of the bibliography). Folklorists sensitive to gender have begun to locate storytelling, gossiping, insults, joking, and chatting in relation to sexual divisions of labor, offering valuable information about their use to create intimacy or distance, and to define group values, as well as to control or subvert the control of others.[8]

RETHINKING SEX AND GENDER

Approaches to sex and gender, as well as to language, have shifted as the field has developed. Initially, researchers treated gender as an unproblematic independent variable, reporting correlations between sex of speaker and specific items of speech, such as choice of phonetic variant or frequency of display of the categories Robert Bales (1950) devised for the study of small group interaction. When sex differences were found, it was often implied that "sex" accounted for the findings in a self-explanatory way. Description was thereby mistaken for explanation. The approach also assumed that gender is best understood as an individual attribute, essence, or perhaps "role" (e.g., the "male instrumental role" versus the "female expressive role" in the Bales tradition, critically reviewed in Meeker and Weitzel-O'Neill, 1977). Even when the speech of women and men was not found to be dichotomous, these polarized, stereotyping conceptions of gender were rarely recast (Kessler & McKenna, 1978).

Within the last decade, largely due to the contributions of feminist theory (the only theoretical tradition to take gender as a basic category of analysis), a more sophisticated understanding of sex and gender has emerged. It has become apparent that gender is not a unitary, or "natural" fact, but takes shape in concrete, historically changing social relationships. Abstracted, dichotomous frameworks have been supplanted by insight into social arrangements of gender, including the social construction of gender divisions (involving the cultural suppression of similarities between women and men, partly through verbal and nonverbal display); sexual divisions of labor which allocate women and men to different positions, activities, and social networks; and the social regulation of sexuality, which is closely intertwined with gender.[9]

Gender, like language, has been returned to its social contexts, and we have moved beyond a first, probably necessary, stage of work, in which we sought correlations between frequency of a linguistic feature and the sex of speaker or spoken to. Thus, Pat Nichols (in this volume) shows the importance of social context in linking gender with language use. In a study of language varieties spoken by Black residents of a rural coastal area and a nearby river island in South Carolina, she traces the different social networks and educational and work opportunities tied to gender, race, age, and locale. It is these different networks and opportunities—and not the sex of speakers, viewed abstractly— that account for syntactic variation within as well as across gender groups. Jean Berko Gleason and Esther Blank Greif (in this volume) also explore the social contexts of both gender and language, comparing the speech that fathers, mothers, and women and men day-care teachers address to young children. Gender modulates the performance of situated roles; for example, male parents and male teachers use more imperatives than women in either role. But overall, the major lines of difference lie not between the sexes, but between the speech of teachers (of both sexes) and that of parents. Complex descriptions of relationships among speakers—sensitive to gender in the context of setting, roles, and other social identities such as age, class, or ethnicity—yield more insight than an abstract search for isolated sex differences.

BREAKING CATEGORIES OPEN: THE EXAMPLE OF SILENCE

Overviews necessarily look backwards, patterning and joining work that has already been done. Questions, however, look forward, bursting open previous seams. To illustrate the convergence of different lines of inquiry we turn from speech to silence. Poets, theorists, and sociolinguists have recognized, as Adrienne Rich (1978:17) has written, that silence

is a presence/it has a history   a form   Do not confuse it   with any kind of absence.

What are the forms and experiences of silence in the separate and connected worlds of women and men? Those who have looked at the effects of gender on perceptions of speech have observed that women may be stereotyped as talkative because they are *expected* to be more silent than men (Kramer, 1974), and in mixed-sex conversations women *are* more silent, with men tending to take more and longer turns at talk (see bibliography, Sec. V-B). We now understand some of the mechanisms, such as interruption and inattention to the topics women raise, which men use to construct women's silence in mixed-sex talk. Women's use of silence as a subversive strategy has also been explored, especially by literary critics (see bibliography, Sec. VI-B and VI-C). Women's presence is muted in the content as well as the form of talk through sexist constructions like the "generic" *he* and the ignoring of women's literary, musical, and political contributions. There have been studies (e.g., Kramarae, 1981) exploring reasons for the relative absence of women's voices in public discourse. Men, especially those with class and race privilege, remain the chief gatekeepers of language: the editors, publishers, rhetoricians, dictionary-makers, broadcasters, high-status educators. In a related vein, Tillie Olsen (1979) writes of "unnatural silences" due to circumstances of sex, race, and social class which systematically obstruct literary creativity and remove the voices of the oppressed from poetry and fiction. There has been a revaluation of arenas of speech and writing where these voices have been found—gossip, storytelling, chit-chat, diaries, and letters (see bibliography, Sec. VI-A). Focusing on deep structures of meaning, French feminist theorists argue that practices of signification mark women as negation, as silence. They, like U.S. writers such as Adrienne Rich and Audre Lorde (1980), believe that a central task of feminism is to bring women to speech, to inscribe women into language. The process of breaking silence, of coming to speech on one's own rather than patriarchal terms, is a source of magnificent writing about women and language, much of it in poetry (see bibliography, Sec. VI-C). The shift to woman as subject marks an important redirection of research on language and gender.

CENTERING ON WOMEN'S TALK

The shift to woman as subject has been inspired by, and has helped to inspire, closer attention to women's use of language, especially with one another. A focus on women with women breaks with a past where women and their talk have largely been defined by and in terms of men.[10] This definition persisted in the first phase of concerted research on gender and communication; questions were imaged primarily in terms of mixed-sex conversations, with patterns of same-sex talk used mainly as comparison, to highlight the distinctive features of talk between men and women.

Early in the last decade, largely due to the revaluing of women and their bonds—a gift of the feminist movement—we realized that little was published about the somewhat separate talking and nonverbal worlds of women with women. There was far more information about male-male interaction, for example, from small groups research conducted only with male subjects (Jenkins, 1980; Jenkins & Kramer, 1978) and the work of sociologists who studied male adolescent peer groups (Labov, 1972). Research on communication among women has begun to lift the heavy weight of stereotypes ("clucking hens") which have so often been applied to the talk of groups of women.[11] There is imaginative new research on women's gossip, humor, and story-telling as verbal art (see bibliography, Sec. VI-A). And there are more studies of the speech and nonverbal patterns used by groups of women and girls. These studies point to recurring patterns which distinguish talk among women from that in mixed-sex or all-male groups: mutuality of "interaction work" (active listening, building on the utterances of others), collaboration rather than competition, flexible leadership rather than the strong dominance patterns found in all-male groups (Aries, 1976; Kalčik, 1975; Goodwin, 1980). In their paper in this volume, Penelope and Wolfe describe a "discursive, conjunctive style" in the language of feminist writers, a style akin to speech among women.

Research on women's speech with women has just begun, and it should be emphasized that we may well know less than we think about women's (and men's)[12] language use. But the work has already challenged existing frameworks of analysis. For example, research centering on women's talk has suggested alternative models for understanding the choreographies of conversation. Carole Edelsky (1981) found that women participate more actively when the "floor" of talk is not of the one-turn-at-a-time model described by conversation analysts, but is more informal and collaborative, with people often speaking at the same time. The collaborative forms of storytelling which Susan Kalčik (1975) describes in a women's consciousness-raising group depart from the conventional models of narrative which more sharply distinguish speaker from audience (Jenkins, 1982).

Talk among women provides a fresh vantage point on the adequacy of models of inquiry and on the questions of change which are so closely intertwined with research on language and the sexes. Explicitly or implicitly, it has often been suggested that women should adopt "masculine" forms, that they should speak with more forcefulness and assertion (see bibliography, Sec. V-G). However, as we have focused on the strategies and styles which women more frequently use—forms which are highlighted by studies of all-female groups—we have come to reassess their value.

The collaborative patterns which are central to talk among women—drawing out other speakers, supportive listening and head nods, mutual sharing of emotions and personal knowledge, respect for one another's conversational space—are weak or "powerless" only when contrasted with their opposites. For example, open, sharing behaviors become weak only when another person in an interaction refuses to reciprocate them. Being sensitive to another's need—inviting them to take turns at talk, drawing out the topics they raise—is heard as ineffectual only when this sensitivity is not reciprocated. Revealing emotions is a disadvantage only when others are being reserved and refusing to share or to show emotion. The "powerlessness" of the speech patterns women more often use exists only relative to the power of so-called masculine patterns. When only women are told to change their behavior, and essentially to adopt "male forms," the characteristics of male speech are ignored, and the assumption of power as domination is reproduced.

A feminist definition of power—power as energy, effective interaction, or empowerment—contrasts with and challenges the assumption of power as domination or control (Hartsock, 1981). The feminist challenge, Nancy Hartsock observes, is to develop forms based on this alternative vision as a way of transforming institutions based on dominance. This vantage point suggests an alternative strategy for transforming gender asymmetries in talk. This strategy affirms rather than denies the patterns often found in women's talk, using them to transform the larger world of speech, empowering subordinates and challenging the communication patterns used by dominants.

Mischa Adams (1980) provides an example of this process in a discussion of telling moments when women and men have transformed stereotyped inter-actions. She describes a graduate seminar in which the women were rendered silent, while the professor and most of the male students monopolized talk, controlling the floor through eye contact, interruption, and throwing the floor only to one another. Those who were squeezed out analyzed these patterns and set out to change them, not by adopting the dominant discourse, but by empowering one another. They arrived early and sat in a way that diffused eye contact around the group; they built on one another's comments in the discussion, giving the mutual gift of "interaction work"; they invited the silent to speak. Rather than overvaluing and imitating the dominant style (monopoly of turn-space, interruptions, topic control), they used collaborative patterns to draw in, and empower, more participants.

A second example of feminist transformation of language, again starting from women's experiences, comes from literature: Adrienne Rich's efforts to create a new language which transcends the patriarchal legacy of received forms. As Joanne Feit Diehl (1980) observes, this is a bold, even heroic venture, but Rich does not undertake it with the aggressive ways of patriarchal discourse. She uses a "gentle poetics," speech close to women's experiences and intimate conversation, language which is empowering rather than dominating.

This visionary concluding theme suggests fresh questions and vantage points which attend the opening of the second decade of feminist research on language. It is clear that the study of language and gender is now well established, with a distinctive subject matter which cuts across diverse disciplines and methodologies and pushes the boundaries of mainstream work. The questions which animate the field have emerged, in increasingly central ways, from women's experiences both inside and outside of male traditions. The research continues to be deeply political, seeking not only to illuminate, but also to change relations between women, men, and language.

NOTES

1. A related topic is the development of Black naming practices in the U.S. Most Blacks brought by slavers to this country were named by the people who bought them, although they were not given the owner's last name. While they used their assigned names when dealing with owners and overseers, slaves used African names among family and friends. After the Civil War, many Blacks, to represent their changed social conditions, changed their names, often to names based on African naming practices (Paustian, 1976).

2. What grammarians have called the *generic masculine* has been variously relabeled the "pseudo-generic," the "false generic," and "prescriptive *he.*" We use the term *masculine "generic"* to indicate generic reference in masculine form, and also to question whether the masculine *is* generic when so used.

3. Overall, the findings to date from the study of the masculine "generic" support MacKay's (1980) conclusion that this form has the advantages of the best propaganda in its potential for influence: frequency of occurrence, covertness, and association with high prestige sources.

4. Lest readers think this exclusion is a creation of feminists' insistence that the masculine "generic" excludes women, the finding turned up at least as early as 1971, too early for any significant effects on the college students who were studied.

5. French feminists and U.S. radical feminists such as Mary Daly, Adrienne Rich, and Audre Lorde (1980) have theorized deep relationships between sexuality and speech. Their writings have enlivened U.S. feminist theory, which has attended to men's control of women's labor, bodies, and consciousness (Kelly, 1979), but has less fully taken up issues of language.

6. There has been remarkably little research on the intersections of gender, race, social class, and sexualities. "White," "middle and upper-middle-class," "heterosexual," and even "college student" remain unmarked categories in much of the work cited in the bibliography. Calling attention to this skew in knowledge, in Section VIII of the bibliography we have cross-referenced all items explicitly dealing with variations of race, ethnicity, sexualities, and social class. In addition, Section VII, on children and language, suggests relationships between gender and age. These topics are all overdue for more extensive theoretical and empirical research.

7. Past research on gender and child language acquisition has also been shaped by evaluative claims -- in this case, that girls have an edge of "verbal superiority." The findings, in fact, are inconclusive and self-contradictory (Macauley, 1978 and other references in Sec. IV-E of the bibliography). Klann-Delius (1981) argues that questions of "better" or "worse" have been misleading, that possible difference, and not deficit, is the issue. She also calls for more careful specification of areas of similarity and difference in the processes by which girls and boys acquire language.

8. Past academic "small group" researchers who focused on the interaction of men in the military and in business often considered talk only as an aid in establishing *categories* of interaction, such as systems of competition and hierarchies. Such inattention to speech and to other everyday small group activities diminishes the value of this research to communication theory (Jenkins, 1980). The material in this volume offers many correctives for theories of small group interaction, discourse, and the ethnography of speaking.

9. Gayle Rubin (1975) analyzes gender divisions, sexual divisions of labor, and sexualities as interrelated components of "sex/gender systems," which vary by culture and are historically changing. While *sex* technically refers to biological phenomena, such as hormones and chromo-

somes, and *gender* to social and cultural phenomena, the two words are often used interchangeably, and, given the complex interactions of biology and culture, that ambiguity doesn't seem problematic. The term *sex and gender* also usefully suggests that sexuality is intricately related to gender. Adrienne Rich (1980), like Rubin, shows close connections between compulsory heterosexuality and gender arrangements.

10. Elaine Showalter (1981) describes a related shift in feminist literary criticism, from revisionary readings of male texts to "gynocritics," or sustained investigation of women writers and female experience. Jessie Bernard (1981) effects the same change of vision in *The Female World,* which explores the social structure and culture (including language) of the worlds of women which are somewhat separate from those of men.

11. The revaluing of women's experience and the challenging of stereotyped assumptions have led to renaming, which opens fresh perspectives on traditional topics in sociolinguistics. Suzanne Roff-Lowe suggests that what has been called women's "linguistic insecurity" may rather be seen as "linguistic flexibility" (Nichols, in this volume). And Sally McConnell-Ginet (in this volume) uses "dynamism," rather than "instability" (a term found in earlier literature) to characterize women's intonation patterns. (Also see Henley, 1977: 71, 76).

12. The feminist interests which have animated research on language and gender have weighted inquiry more towards the speech of women than that of men. However, studies of patriarchal language, research on mixed-sex and all-male groups, and efforts to specify male experience in contexts of gender rather than as spuriously universal have enhanced our understanding of relationships of men to language.

REFERENCES

Abrahams, Roger. 1975. Negotiating respect: Patterns of presentation among Black women. *Journal of American Folklore,* 88, 58–80.

Adams, Mischa B. 1980. *Communication and gender stereotype.* Unpublished Ph.D. dissertation, Univ. of Calif., Santa Cruz.

Aries, Elizabeth. 1976. Interaction patterns and themes of male, female, and mixed groups. *Small Group Behavior,* 7, 7–18.

Bales, Robert F. 1950. *Interaction process analysis.* Reading, Mass.: Addison-Wesley.

Bate, Barbara. 1978. Nonsexist language use in transition. *Journal of Communication,* 28 (1), 139–49.

Baumann, Marie. 1976. Two features of "women's speech." In Betty Lou Dubois & Isabel Crouch (eds.), *The sociology of the languages of American women.* San Antonio, Texas: Trinity Univ., 33–40.

Beard, Mary. 1946. *Woman as force in history.* New York: Macmillan.

Bernard, Jessie. 1981. *The female world.* New York: The Free Press.

Borker, Ruth. 1980. Anthropology: Social and cultural perspectives. In Sally McConnell-Ginet, Ruth Borker, & Nelly Furman (eds.), *Women and language in literature and society.* New York: Praeger, 26–44.

Bradley, Patricia. In press. The folklinguistics of women's speech: An empirical examination. *Communication Monographs.*

Brown, Penelope. 1976. Women and politeness: A new perspective on language and society. *Reviews in Anthropology,* 3, 239–49.

Brown, Penelope & Stephen Levinson. 1978. Universals in language usage: Politeness phenomena. In Esther Goody (ed.), *Questions and politeness: Strategies in social interaction.* Cambridge: Cambridge Univ. Press, 56–289.

Brown, Roger. 1965. *Social psychology,* ch. 7. New York: The Free Press.

Cixous, Hélène. 1976. The laugh of the Medusa. *Signs,* 1, 875–94.

Condry, John & Sandra Condry. 1976. Sex differences: A study of the eye of the beholder. *Child Development,* 47, 812–19.

Daly, Mary. 1978. *Gyn/Ecology: The metaethics of radical feminism.* Boston: Beacon Press.

Diehl, Joanne Feit. 1980. "Cartographies of Silence": Rich's *Common Language* and the woman poet. *Feminist Studies,* 6, 530–47.

Dubois, Betty Lou & Isabel Crouch. 1977. The question of tag questions in women's speech: They don't really use more of them, do they? *Language in Society,* 4, 289–94.

Edelsky, Carole. 1981. Who's got the floor? *Language in Society,* 10, 383–421.

Fishman, Pamela M. 1980. Conversational insecurity. In Howard Giles, W. Peter Robinson & Philip M. Smith (eds.), *Language: Social psychological perspectives.* New York: Pergamon Press, 127–32.

——— 1983. Interaction: The work women do. In this volume.

Gardner, Carol Brooks. 1981. Passing by: Street remarks, address rights, and the urban female. *Sociological Inquiry,* 50, 328–56.

Gaudin, Collette et al. (eds.). 1982. *Feminist readings: French texts/American contexts.* Yale French Studies, Number 62.

Gleason, Jean Berko & Esther Blank Greif. 1983. Men's speech to young children. In this volume.

Goodwin, Marjorie Harness. 1980. Directive-response speech sequences in girls' and boys' task activities. In Sally McConnell-Ginet, Ruth Borker, and Nelly Furman (eds.), *Women and language in literature and society.* New York: Praeger, 157–73.

Graham, Alma. 1973. The making of a nonsexist dictionary. *Ms.,* 2 (Dec.), 12–16.

Hartsock, Nancy. 1981. Political change: Two perspectives on power. In *Quest* Staff and Book Committee (eds.), *Building feminist theory.* New York: Longman, 3–19.

Henley, Nancy. 1977. *Body politics: Power, sex, and nonverbal communication.* Englewood Cliffs, N.J.: Prentice-Hall.

Henley, Nancy & Barrie Thorne. 1975. Sex differences in language, speech, and nonverbal communication: An annotated bibliography. In Barrie Thorne & Nancy Henley (eds.), *Language and sex: Difference and dominance.* Rowley, Mass.: Newbury House.

Hymes, Dell, ed. 1964. *Language in culture and society,* parts 3 & 4. New York: Harper & Row.

Jenkins, Lee & Cheris Kramer. 1978. Small group process: Learning from women. *Women's Studies International Quarterly,* 1, 67–84.

Jenkins, Mercilee M. 1980. Toward a model of human leadership. In Cynthia L. Berryman & Virginia A. Eman (eds.), *Communication, language and sex.* Rowley, Mass.: Newbury House, 149–58.

——— 1982. Stories women tell: An ethnographic study of personal experience narratives in a women's rap group. Paper given at the 10th World Congress of Sociology, Mexico City.

Jespersen, Otto. 1922. *Language: Its nature, development and origin.* London: Allen & Unwin.

Johnson, Janet L. 1980. Questions and role responsibility in four professional meetings. *Anthropological Linguistics,* 22, 66–76.

Jones, Ann Rosalind. 1981. Writing the body: Toward an understanding of *l'écriture féminine.* *Feminist Studies,* 7, 247–63.

Kalčik, Susan. 1975. ". . . like Ann's gynecologist or the time I was almost raped": Personal narratives in women's rap groups. *Journal of American Folklore,* 88, 3–11.

Kelly, Joan. 1979. The doubled vision of feminist theory. *Feminist Studies,* 5, 216–27.

Kessler, Susan J. & Wendy McKenna. 1978. *Gender: An ethnomethodological approach.* New York: Wiley.

Klann-Delius, Gisela. 1981. Sex and language acquisition—Is there any influence? *Journal of Pragmatics,* 5, 1–25.

Kramarae, Cheris. 1981. *Women and men speaking.* Rowley, Mass.: Newbury House.

Kramer, Cheris. 1974. Women's speech: Separate but unequal? *Quarterly Journal of Speech,* 60, 14–24.

Kuhn, Thomas S. 1962. *The structure of scientific revolutions.* Chicago: Univ. of Chicago Press.

Labov, William. 1972. *Language in the inner city: Studies in the Black English vernacular.* Philadelphia: Univ. of Penn. Press.

Lakoff, Robin. 1975. *Language and woman's place.* New York: Harper & Row.

Lapadat, Judy & Maureen Seesahai. 1977. Male versus female codes in informal contexts. *Sociolinguistics Newsletter,* 8 (3), 7–81.

Lorde, Audre. 1980. Poetry is not a luxury. In Hester Eisenstein & Alice Jardine (eds.), *The future of difference.* Boston: G.K. Hall, 125–27.

Macauley, Ronald K.S. 1978. The myth of female superiority in language. *Journal of Child Language,* 5, 353–63.

MacKay, Donald G. 1980. On the goals, principles, and procedures for prescriptive grammar: Singular *they. Language in Society,* 9, 349–67.

——— 1983. Prescriptive grammar and the pronoun problem. In this volume.

Macke, Anne Statham & Laurel Walum Richardson, with Judith Cook. 1980. *Sex-typed teaching styles of university professors and student reactions.* Columbus, Ohio: The Ohio State Univ. Research Foundation.

Marks, Elaine & Isabelle deCourtivron (eds.), 1981. *New French feminisms.* New York: Schocken.

Martyna, Wendy. 1978. What does "he" mean? Use of the generic masculine. *Journal of Communication,* 28 (1), 131–38.

——— 1983. Beyond the "he/man" approach. The case for nonsexist language. In this volume.

McConnell-Ginet, Sally. 1980. Linguistics and the feminist challenge. In Sally McConnell-Ginet, Ruth Borker, & Nelly Furman (eds.), *Women and language in literature and society.* New York: Praeger, 3–25.

——— 1983. Intonation in a man's world. In this volume.

McMillan, Julie R., A. Kay Clifton, Diane McGrath, & Wanda S. Gale. 1977. Women's language: Uncertainty or interpersonal sensitivity and emotionality? *Sex Roles,* 3, 545–59.

Meeker, B. F. & P. A. Weitzel-O'Neill. 1977. Sex roles and interpersonal behavior in task-oriented groups. *American Sociological Review,* 42, 91–105.

Miller, Casey & Kate Swift. 1980. *The handbook of nonsexist writing.* New York: Lippincott & Crowell.

Nichols, Patricia C. 1983. Linguistic options and choices for Black women in the rural South. In this volume.

Olsen, Tillie. 1979. *Silences.* New York: Delacorte Press.

Parsons, Elsie Clews. 1913. *The old-fashioned woman: Primitive fancies about the sex.* New York: G.P. Putnam's Sons.

Paustian, P. Robert. 1976. The evolution of personal naming practices among American Blacks. *Names,* 24, 177–91.

Penelope (Stanley), Julia & Susan J. Wolfe. 1983. Consciousness as style; Style as aesthetic. In this volume.

Rich, Adrienne. 1978. Cartographies of silence. In *The dream of a common language: Poems 1974–1977.* New York: W.W. Norton, 16–20.

——— 1979. *On lies, secrets, and silence.* New York: W.W. Norton.

——— 1980. Compulsory heterosexuality and lesbian existence. *Signs,* 5, 631–60.

Rosch, Eleanor. 1974. Linguistic relativity. In Albert Silverstein (ed.), *Human communication: Theoretical explorations.* New York: Halsted, 95–121.

Rubin, Gayle. 1975. The traffic in women: Notes on the "political economy" of sex. In Rayna R. Reiter (ed.), *Toward an anthropology of women.* New York: Monthly Review Press, 157–210.

Sattel, Jack W. 1983. Men, inexpressiveness, and power. In this volume.

Schneider, Michael & Karen A. Foss. 1977. Thought, sex and language: The Sapir-Whorf hypothesis in the American women's movement. *Bulletin: Women's Studies in Communication,* 1 (no. 1), 1-8.

Shimanoff, Susan. 1977. Man equals human: Empirical support for the Whorfian hypothesis. *Bulletin: Women's Studies in Communication,* 1 (no. 2), 21–27.

Showalter, Elaine. 1981. Feminist criticism in the wilderness. *Critical Inquiry,* 8, 179–206.

Signs. 1981. Special section on French feminist theory. *Signs,* 7, 5–86.

Silveira, Jeanette. 1980. Generic masculine words and thinking. In Cheris Kramarae (ed.), *The voices and words of women and men.* Oxford: Pergamon Press, 165–78. Also *Women's Studies International Quarterly,* 3, no. 2/3.

Spender, Dale. 1980. *Man made language.* London: Routledge & Kegan Paul.

Stanley, Julia Penelope. 1977. Paradigmatic woman: The prostitute. In David L. Shores (ed.), *Papers in language variation.* Birmingham: Univ. of Alabama Press.

Stannard, Una. 1977. *Mrs. man.* San Francisco: Germainbooks.

Stanton, Domna. 1980. Language and revolution. In Hester Eisenstein & Alice Jardine (eds.), *The future of difference.* Boston: G.K. Hall, 73–87.

Stopes, Charlotte Carmichael. 1908. *The sphere of "man": In relation to that of "woman" in the constitution.* London: T. Fisher Unwin.

Thorne, Barrie & Nancy Henley. 1975. Difference and dominance: An overview of language, gender, and society. In Barrie Thorne & Nancy Henley (eds.), *Language and sex: Difference and dominance.* Rowley, Mass.: Newbury House, 5–42.

West, Candace & Don H. Zimmerman. 1983. Small insults: A study of interruptions in cross-sex conversations between unacquainted persons. In this volume.

Whorf, Benjamin Lee. 1956. *Language, thought and reality.* Cambridge, Mass.: M.I.T. Press.

Wittig, Monique. 1980. The straight mind. *Feminist Issues,* 1, 103–111.

BEYOND THE HE/MAN APPROACH:
THE CASE FOR NONSEXIST LANGUAGE*

Wendy Martyna

Time calls it "Ms-guided" (Kanfer, 1972), a syndicated columnist, "linguistic lunacy" (Van Horne, 1976). *T. V. Guide* (1971) wonders what the "women's lib redhots" with "the nutty pronouns" are doing. The media still haven't gotten the message: the case against sexist language was not constructed as comic relief for critics of women's liberation. A clear understanding of the sexist language issue continues to elude the popular press, despite the increasingly serious treatment given to most other feminist isssues. And the media is not alone in its misunderstanding. Despite the acceleration of academic attention to feminist concerns, the same misinterpretations of the sexist language issue often characterize the reactions of both Harvard professors and advice columnists.

This discussion separates the strands of argument often tangled in current approaches to the issue, whether these approaches appear in the popular media, academic journals, or feminist publications. The arguments against sexist language have been mistranslated more often than not. Those mistranslations have then been responded to by opponents of language change. Clarifying these, and synthesizing the case against sexist language, can help to offset the continuing, annoying trivialization of this issue, which has constituted a major roadblock on the path toward a language that speaks clearly and fairly of both sexes.

The *he/man* approach to language involves the use of male terms to refer both specifically to males and generically to human beings ("A Man for All Seasons" is specific; "No man is an island" is generic). The *he/man* approach

*This work is dedicated to the memory of Kate De Pierri, who was a contemporary in spirit, energy, and commitment, despite the fifty years between us. Early encouragement, much appreciated, came from Catharine Stimpson, Barrie Thorne, Nancy Henley, Cheris Kramarae, and Adrienne Rich. Valuable resources were provided by Mary Ritchie Key, Virginia Valian, Simon Klevansky, Patti Leasure, LeeAnn Slinkard, and the many generous people who are part of the "women-and-language grapevine." I am particularly grateful for the critical readings of earlier drafts given by Len Erickson, Herb Clark, Sandra Bem, Leigh Star, and Terri Daly. This is a slightly expanded and revised version of a paper which appeared in *Signs: Journal of Women in Culture and Society*, 1980, 5, 482–93.

has received most attention in current debates on sexist language, due not only to its ubiquity but also to its status as one of the least subtle of sexist forms. In linguistic terms, some have characterized the male as an unmarked, and the female as a marked, category. The unmarked category represents both maleness and femaleness, while the marked represents femaleness only (Clark & Clark, 1977). Thus, the male in Lionel Tiger's *Men in Groups* excludes the female in Phyllis Chesler's *Women and Madness,* while the male in Thomas Paine's *Rights of Man* is supposed to encompass the female in Mary Wollstonecraft's *Rights of Woman.* What would the world be like if the male were instead the marked category? Dorothy Sayers (1947) imagines this arrangement:

> In any book on sociology he would find, after the main portion dealing with human needs and rights, a supplementary chapter devoted to "The position of the male in the perfect state." His newspaper would assist him with a "Men's corner" . . . people would write books called, "History of the male" or "Males of the Bible" or "The psychology of the male." If, after a few centuries of this kind of treatment, the male was a little self-conscious, a little on the defensive, and a little bewildered about what was required of him, I should not blame him. If he traded a little upon his sex, I could forgive him. If he presented the world with a major social problem, I would scarcely be surprised.

The outlines of the *he/man* debate are evident in an exchange of letters in the *Harvard Crimson* in 1971. The Harvard Linguistics faculty (1971) criticized an attempt by a theology class to eliminate sexist language from its discussions:

> The fact that the masculine is the unmarked gender in English . . . is simply a feature of grammar. It is unlikely to be an impediment to change in the patterns of the sexual division of labor towards which our society may wish to evolve. There is really no cause for anxiety or pronoun-envy on the part of those seeking such changes.

Virginia Valian and Jerrold Katz (1971) countered by posing this hypothetical situation:

> In culture R the language is such that the pronouns are different according to the color of the people involved, rather than their sex . . . the unmarked pronoun just happens to be the one used for white people. In addition, the colored people just happen to constitute an oppressed group. Now imagine that this oppressed group begins complaining about the use of the "white" pronoun to refer to all people. Our linguists presumably then say, "Now, now, there is really no cause for anxiety or pronoun-envy." It isn't a question of linguistics, but of how the people involved feel.

These exchanges attracted *Newsweek*'s attention, whose article ("Pronoun Envy") (1971) was seen by the students as "a prime example of the use of trivialization by the media as a way of attacking and exploiting feminist activities" (Culpepper-Hough & Cox, 1972).

The students' claim: the generic masculine is both ambiguous and discriminatory. The linguists' claim: it is simply a feature of grammar, unrelated to the issue of sex discrimination. The students' counter-response: it is more than a feature of grammar, but a factor which both reflects and maintains societal sexism. This 1971 scenario has been enacted many times in the years since, the cast varying, but the plot and dialogue remaining familiar. William James noted three stages a new idea moves through: it is first attacked as absurd; then admitted to be true, but seen as obvious and insignificant; and finally, seen as so important that its adversaries claim they discovered it. If James is correct, then the controversy over sexist language now sits somewhere between stages one and two.

RESISTANCE TO CHANGE

Comments on the *he/man* issue vary in their subtlety. Among the most blatant are personal attacks on those who attack the generic masculine. One writer (Mayer, 1975: 20–21) describes the editor who had altered his sexist prose as "an ardent Amazonian." He later burst out: "Women are irrational, all women; when some women threaten to disembowel me unless I say 'personhole-cover,' I am surer even than I was that all women are irrational."

Trivializations of the movement for sexist language appear in a wide range of locations, from *Time*'s article on "sispeak," (Kanfer, 1972) to a nationally syndicated columnist's critique of the "libspeak tantrum" (Mayer, 1975).

This reaction to sexist language appears more striking when contrasted to the popular response to racist language. The U.S. Secretary of Agriculture, Earl Butz, left office following public outcry over his racist remarks (which the media refused to repeat, "even in this liberated age" [Felton, 1976]). Butz's remarks were equally sexist, but he apologized only to the Black male members of Congress, not the females; and it was his racism, not his sexism, which caused his censure. Public reaction to Billy Carter's "witticisms," often as racist and sexist as Butz's remarks, illustrate this same contrast. Sexist language is popularly treated as a source of humor more often than outrage. Pauli Murray (1970) has called this ridicule of women "the psychic counterpart of violence against blacks," and Naomi Weisstein (1973) speaks of this humor as "a weapon in the social arsenal constructed to maintain . . . sex inequalities, . . . showing that women can't be taken seriously."

If pronouns are as amusingly insignificant as some consider them to be, we should expect no outcry were the situation reversed, and the female pronoun became the generic. Yet when the female pronoun has been used to refer to both sexes, as in the teaching profession, males have lobbied for use of the male pronoun, arguing that use of *she* is responsible, in part, for their poor public image and low salaries (Fenner, 1974). The injustice of a generic *she* seems more apparent to some than the inequity of a generic *he*. The first is seen as unfair and exclusionary; the second as "simply a feature of grammar."

Resistance to language change has also involved more sophisticated lines of argument. The first centers on the meaning of *he*. The generic masculine does not need replacement, argue some, for *he* can include *she* (or *man* can embrace *woman*, as grammar teachers are fond of saying). Frank M. (1976) argues this position in a letter to "Dear Abby":

I'm tired of the ignorance of those who insist that the word *man* applies only to males. My dictionary has several definitions, of which the first two are: 1) human being, person . . . 2) the human race. So why don't we stop all this asinine change of words?

Others argue over intentions rather than dictionary meanings, claiming that the generic masculine includes both sexes because they intend it to. Anthony Burgess (1976), for example, says that his use of *he* and *man* is neutral, and that it is women who "force chauvinistic sex onto the word." A poetic opponent of language change argues the neutrality of *he* and *man*: "Women whose lib has caused such paranoia / Take every remark, as a slur, to their lawyer . . . / These wopeople who are constantly vexed / Feel every word is biasedly sexed. / But not every phrase has evil intent / And usually nothing degrading is meant" (Yablok, 1977).

Yet the question of what *he* and *man* really mean is fully answered neither by turning to dictionary definitions, nor by consulting the intentions of its users. Good intentions are not enough, unfortunately, to guarantee generic meaning will be conveyed. And guided tours through Latin and Old English are not enough to guarantee that the generic masculine is used clearly and fairly today. Further, the denotations found in dictionaries do not always reveal the connotations that *he* and *man* can carry.

Others who resist language change neither deny that sexist language can serve as a symbol of sexist society, nor that sexist society needs to be changed. What they do disclaim is that the one has much to do with the other. The need, they say, is to change the sources, rather than the symbols, of sexism in society. Nina Yablok (1977) puts forth in rhyme: "If I had my choice, if I had my druthers / I'd take equal rights. Leave equal words to the others." And to Stefan Kanfer (1972), the hope for a nonsexist language reveals "a touching, almost mystical trust in words." Another columnist makes the same point less gently, chastising "those few distracted feminists who have foolishly imagined they would improve their condition by remodeling words like old hats" (Smith, 1975).

Another line of resistance concerns the very possibility of language change. Defenders of the *he/man* approach place such change on a continuum ranging from difficult to impossible. Robin Lakoff (1975: 45), whose work has encouraged a greater awareness of sexist language, has nevertheless argued that pronouns are "too common, too thoroughly mixed throughout the language, for the speaker to be aware each time he uses them. It is realistic only to hope to change those linguistic uses of which speakers themselves can be made aware, as they use them."

Others are deterred by the difficulty, rather than the impossibility, of language change. One writer (Devol, 1977), referring to "the ugly and awkward *he or she* forms," says: "They may be only a passing fad, but they offend the traditional eye." Eye trouble isn't the only complaint. To William Buckley (1976), the "distortions ring in the ear."

This pessimism about language change is at least partly due to a mis-representation of the causes for optimism. A common view seems to be that feminists have failed to take into account the complexities of language change, viewing it as a relatively quick and easy process. In fact, those who advocate nonsexist language do not pretend that change will be either quick, easy, or unopposed.

Much resistance to change arises from a confusion over *what* will be changed, as well as *why* there should be change. The widespread worry is that both specific and generic forms of *he* and *man* will be eliminated should language change go according to feminist plan. Some writers manifest a mania for manipulating each *man* in our language into a *person,* and then mentioning the menace such manipulations pose. Russell Baker (1973), for example, would have substituted *person* for each *man* in that sentence, as he did in his satire of "Nopersonclature." Despite the many suggestions to the contrary, we don't have to begin language change by renaming N.O.W. the National Organization for Wopeople. The many fears of retitling such works as "Four Horsemen of the Apocalypse" and "A Man for All Seasons" are similarly unfounded: those *man's* are specific, not generic. Sexism, not *sex,* is under attack.

The fear of losing all sex-specific terms in the language has led to the characterization of a nonsexist language as "sexually obscure" (Shenker, 1971), "a unisex tongue . . . a dull tongue and a false one" (White, 1974), and "a spaying of the language" (McCabe, 1977). One member of the California State Assembly opposed a move to replace "assemblyman" with "assembly member." "That takes the masculinity out of it!" he declared (*Los Angeles Times,* 1977). A Los Angeles City Council member said he would rather be known as "council jerk" than the proposed "council member." "We've gone too far," he objected. "This is a lot of stupid junk. Pretty soon you won't know who is a man and who is a woman" (*Los Angeles Times,* Oct. 10 and Oct. 17, 1974). And a city official in northern California objects to being called *chairperson* because, as she says, "You have to admit the term 'chairperson' isn't very sexy" (*Palo Alto Times,* Nov. 9, 1977).

Not only a "sex-less" language, but an ungrammatical one, is feared by those who oppose language change. William Buckley, Jr. (1976) is among those refusing to substitute singular *they* for generic *he.* Those who issue guidelines for nonsexist language, he says, "want us to validate improper usage." Anyone who uses a singular *they,* in Buckley's view, "should not be hired as a professional writer."

Misinterpretations of what will be changed, and why, have led many to fear that the *he/man* approach will be replaced by a "sex-less" and "ungrammatical" language. Yet the nonsexist language I and others envision will be humanized rather than "de-sexed." It will be a language which neither obscures nor emphasizes the differences between the sexes, one which is clearly committed to expressing both maleness and femaleness, rather than a maleness that is supposed to encompass us all.

ARGUMENTS FOR CHANGE

Those who oppose the generic masculine are concerned with both equal rights *and* equal words. Nonsexist language would not only reflect a move toward a nonsexist ideology; it would function in itself as one form of social equality. Eliminating the ambiguity and sex-exclusiveness of the *he/man* approach would enable us to more clearly and fairly communicate about the sexes. Attempts to change the language are not attempts to change society in its entirety; they are attempts to change the language, as one aspect of society.

The New York State Supreme Court housed a confrontation in 1976 between those who differ on this question of equity. Ellen Cooperman's petition to change her name to "Cooperperson" was denied by the Court, on grounds it would set a precedent for other "ludicrous changes (Mannings becoming Peoplings)," and expose the women's movement to ridicule. She considered her petition as personally and politically important, arguing that "Cooperman" reflects "the pervasiveness of linguistic male predominance," and is among those factors complicating women's efforts to achieve self-identity (Cooperperson, 1976). Her view is shared by many others who testify to the importance of the *he/man* issue. For example, Susan Sontag (1973: 186) sees language as "the most intense and stubborn fortress of sexist assumptions," one which "crudely enshrines the ancient bias against women."

Marge Piercy (1973: 56) speaks poetically of the psychological force that sexist language can exert: "The state owns me and hangs a man's name on me / like the tag hung on dogs, my name is, property of . . . / The language betrays us and rots in the mouth / with its aftertaste of monastic sewers on the palate. / Even the pronouns tear my tongue with their metal plates." For Mary Daly (1973: 6–7) "the liberation of language is rooted in the liberation of women," for in a sexist world, "symbol systems and conceptual apparatuses have been male creations . . . and function to falsify our own self-image and experiences."

Research has begun to suggest the behavioral implications of sexist language. Sandra Bem and Daryl Bem (1973), for instance, have assessed the impact of sex-biased job advertisements, finding that sex-unbiased ads encourage more high school females to apply for male-related jobs. Most such studies have focused on the psychological impact of broad gender cues. While there is ample data to suggest that manipulating such cues has psychological impact, we have not yet assessed the particular contribution the generic masculine makes in creating these cues. The data on the way the generic *he* encourages a male rather than neutral interpretation, however, suggest that role is considerable.

Cognitive confusion is another consequence of the generic masculine, one particularly relevant for the academic disciplines. Joan Huber (1976: 89), for example, has characterized the use of *he* and *man* as "an exercise in doublethink that muddles sociological discourse." She cites a recent sociology text which proclaims: "The more education an individual attains, the better his occupation is likely to be, and the more money he is likely to earn." The statement is accurate only if the individual is male. The American Anthropological Association (1974: 12) is among many scholarly associations to caution its members that use of the generic masculine is "conceptually confusing."

Ambiguity results when generic and specific meanings are not easily separable; exclusion results when context prohibits a generic interpretation. Watch what context does to the supposedly generic *he* used by Paul Meehl (1967) to describe this hypothetical researcher. *He* produces a long list of publications, but little contribution to the enduring body of knowledge, and "his true position is that of a potent-but-sterile intellectual rake, who leaves in his merry path a long train of ravished maidens, but no viable scientific offspring."

Startled laughter often greets such sentences as "Menstrual pain accounts for an enormous loss of manpower hours," or "Man, being a mammal, breastfeeds his young." We do a double take when hearing of the gynecologist who was awarded a medical award for "service to his fellow man." C. S. Lewis (1960: 11) captures the importance of these startled reactions:

> In ordinary language the sense of a word . . . normally excludes all others from the mind . . . . The proof of this is that the sudden intrusion of any irrelevant sense is funny. It is funny because it is unexpected. There is a semantic explosion because the two meanings rush together from a great distance; one of them was not in our consciousness at all till that moment. If it had been, there would be no detonation.

To avoid this "semantic explosion," we are cautioned by writers' manuals to avoid a generic *he* when the issue of sex "is present and pointed," as in "The pool is open to both men and women, but everyone must bring his or her own towel" (Bernstein, 1965: 351). Similarly, we avoid a generic *he* when the female meaning is predominant. An investigation of psychology textbooks found that hypothetical professors, physicians, and psychologists were referred to as *he*, while hypothetical nurses, teachers, and librarians were *she* (American Psychological Assn., 1975). If *he* includes *she*—if *man* embraces *woman*— why these shifts to the female pronoun?

Empirical explorations of how we comprehend the generic masculine also indicate its sex-exclusiveness. My studies of pronoun usage show striking sex differences in both the use and understanding of the generic masculine. Females use *he* less often than do males, and turn more frequently to alternatives such as *he or she* and *they*. Males have an easier time imagining themselves as members of the category referenced by generic *he*. Seven times as many males as females say they see themselves in response to sex-neutral sentences referring to a "person" or "human being." In general, males appear to be using and understanding *he* in its specific more often than generic sense. Females both avoid the use of *he* and respond to its use with a more generic than specific interpretation. To do otherwise would be to encourage self-exclusion (Martyna, 1978a; 1978b).

Context, many say, should be sufficient to decide whether a specific or generic meaning of *he* and *man* is intended. Yet my empirical explorations demonstrate that even in clearly generic contexts (e.g., "When someone is near a hospital, he should be quiet"), *he* is ambiguous, allowing both specific and generic interpretations to be drawn (Martyna, 1978a; 1978b). My research does not argue that *he cannot* function generically, but that it allows both specific and generic interpretation, even in a context which should force a generic inference. Moreover, our encounters with *he* rarely take place in clearly generic contexts. In educational materials, for instance, the sex-specific *he* appears five to ten times for every single generic *he* (Tittle et al., 1974; Graham, 1973). The generic masculine thus appears amidst a profusion of references to specific males. Based on this predominantly sex-specific usage, our best guess when encountering a *he* is that it will not contain an implicit *she*.

The confusion and exclusion caused by the generic masculine have striking social implications. Although one legal scholar notes the "useful function" ambiguity can perform, "By virtue of its lack of precision" (Lewis, 1972) the ambiguity of *he* and *man* is far from useful for those who are included by inference only. A member of Canadian Parliament, Simma Holt, challenged the equity of the Federal Interpretation Act, which reads: "Words importing male persons include female persons and corporations." Holt was reassured that the Act creates no injustice, for females are explicitly included within the definition of the generic masculine. Doubting that assurance, Marguerite Ritchie surveyed several hundred years of Canadian law, and discovered that the ambiguity of the generic masculine has allowed judges to include or exclude women, depending on the climate of the times and their own personal biases. As she concludes: "Wherever any statute or regulation is drafted in terms of the male, a woman has no guarantee that it confers on her any rights at all" (Ritchie, 1975: 702). Legal controversy over the generic masculine has arisen in the United States as well; involving, for example:

- administration of a scholarship fund set up for "worthy and ambitious young men" (Cusick, 1975)
- dispute over a Kiwanis Club admission of women, despite bylaws specifying "men" as members (O'Hearn, 1974)
- the appeal of a murder conviction in which the self-defense instructions to the jury were phrased in the generic masculine, thus "leaving the jury with the impression that the objective standard to be applied is that applicable to an altercation between two men" (*State of Washington* v. *Yvonne Wanrow,* 1977)
- sex-biased application of the legal notion of "a reasonable man" (Collins, 1977)

The implicit equation of maleness with humanness in our language leads to striking social and psychological implications, striking in part because of the silence that has surrounded them in most discussions of sexist language. The personal testimonies and research studies described in this section offer both subjective and objective testimony to the injustice of the generic masculine. What has been seen as "pronoun envy" is instead a protest against social and psychological exclusion; what has too often been taken in jest was never intended to be funny.

PROSPECTS FOR LANGUAGE CHANGE

Language change may be difficult, but it is not impossible. Some prominent individuals, for example, have made striking changes in their language use. Millions were listening when Harry Reasoner apologized for referring, on a previous broadcast, to the "men" of the judiciary committee. In response to the many objections he had received, he not only apologized, but also asked indulgence for future language offenses he might inadvertently commit (Ward, 1975). A variety of government agencies, feminist groups, professional associations, religious organizations, educational institutions, publishing firms, and media institutions have also endorsed language change, issuing guidelines or passing regulations concerning sexist language.[1] Initial empirical studies suggest considerable language changes among university faculty and politicians (Purnell, 1978; Bate, 1978).

The strongest argument for the possibility of language change is that substantial numbers of language-users have already managed to construct detours around generic *he* and *man*. There are many examples of similarly successful language changes. Ann Bodine (1975) surveys instances of socially motivated language change in England, Sweden, and Russia; Paul Friedrich (1972) investigates the Russian example in detail, exploring how pronominal change resulted from a growing concern for social equality.

Many guidelines for nonsexist language encourage either the replacement of the generic masculine with sex-inclusive or sex-neutral forms, or rewriting to avoid the need for a singular pronoun or noun. Maija Blaubergs (1978) and Barbara Bate (1978) have both categorized the many proposed alternatives to sexist language forms. The two main ones are sex-inclusive forms (such as *he or she* and *women and men*) and sex-neutral terms (such as *chairperson* and *humanity*). Since 1970, several new pronouns, including *tey, co,* and *E,* have been suggested.[2]

Despite claims to the contrary, *they* has long been in use as an alternative to *he.* Ann Bodine (1975) helps to set the issue of grammaticality in perspective. She notes that while *he* involves a disagreement in gender, *they* involves a disagreement in number, and it was the prescriptive grammarians of the 18th century who determined that number should take precedence over gender. "Despite almost two centuries of vigorous attempts to analyze and regulate it out of existence," Bodine claims, "singular *they* is alive and well." Research on pronoun use confirms Bodine's observation (Martyna, 1978a; Langendoen, 1970).

The difficulty of changing the language is not denied by those of us who argue the possibility of change; it is instead contrasted with the difficulty of *not* changing. While awkwardness may result from the *he or she* construction, this awkwardness is seen by many as far less troublesome than the ambiguity and sex-exclusiveness of the *he/man* approach. C. S. Lewis (1960: 6) spoke of a "momentary aphasia" that can be produced from "prolonged thought *about* the words which we ordinarily use to think *with.*" But in his view, "[this] is to be welcomed. It is well that we should become aware of what we are doing when we speak, of the ancient, fragile, and (well used) immensely potent instruments that words are." Transition times are frequently troublesome. Awkwardness will surely decline as we continue to create a language that speaks more fairly and clearly of us all. Someday, in fact, the *he/man* approach may itself seem so awkward that we will wonder how we managed, all those years, to refer to she's as *he,* to women as *men.*

Why the persistent misrepresentation and misunderstanding of the sexist language issue? The simplest explanation is anti-feminism, both an opposition to feminist claims and a refusal to take them seriously. Yet this, by itself, is not enough. Why should this issue remain a source of ridicule when other feminist claims have come to be treated seriously? Why do some feminists, both female and male, consider the fight for "equal words" to be misdirection of energy?

While a resistance to feminism is surely one explanation of the confusion and controversy, the other may be a resistance to those aspects of social change that are seen as more symbolic than real. There seems to be a general cultural reluctance to acknowledge the power of language in our lives, an insistence that language is of symbolic rather than actual importance. We chant in childhood, "Sticks and stones can break my bones, but words can never hurt me," yet we carry our psychological scars long after the bruises and scrapes have healed. We may still be in the midst of a cultural reaction against early preoccupation with the magical power of words.

The importance of this kind of "magic" was suggested by the Sapir-Whorf hypothesis (Carroll, 1956), which states that language can determine our thought and behavior patterns, and that different languages can shape different world views. It is usually assumed that feminist argument is grounded in the Sapir-Whorf hypothesis. Michael Schneider and Karen Foss (1977: 3) worry that "feminists inadvertently have helped to perpetuate and diffuse an outdated, oversimplified, and basically inaccurate view of the relationship between thought and language." In its strongly stated form, this hypothesis has seen little empirical support and strong theoretical criticism since its formulation in the 1920s and 1930s. Yet it has come to be generally accepted in its moderate version: that language may influence, rather than determine, thought and behavior patterns. The moderate version of the Sapir-Whorf hypothesis is reflected in the feminist move for nonsexist language. The issue is not what *can* be said about the sexes, but what can be *most easily* and *most clearly* said, given the constraints of the *he/man* approach and other forms of sexist language.

What can be done to resolve the controversy over sexist language?

A dual strategy, involving both research and action, can be most effective in accelerating the language changes already in progress. The many research projects, articles, and course offerings described in *Women and Language News,*[3] a national newsletter, reflect the increasing interdisciplinary and international interest in language and sexism. These theoretical and empirical approaches contribute to our understanding of the nature and consequences of sexist language and lend a credibility to feminist claims that contrasts sharply with their popular trivialization. Such approaches need to be translated into other persuasive forms. An advertisement sponsored by the Business Council for the United Nations Decade for Women exemplifies this translation. It displays a phone message form with "Mr. _____ " and "Please call him" encircled. "Hey Mister, your slip is showing," it reads. "A little thing, right? But the thinking behind it hurts. Change it. And together we'll change the world."

Action, as well as research, is essential for language change efforts to succeed. Pressure on government agencies and the media, for example, can involve letter-writing campaigns, public advertisements, popularization of research results, workshops for those with power to effect language change, and organized demands for guidelines and regulations encouraging nonsexist language use.

Despite the misinterpretations of the sexist language controversy, the movement toward nonsexist language has begun. That movement has been slowed by the confusion characterizing most approaches to the issue—a confusion obscuring both the importance and the extent of language change. This synthesis of the sexist language controversy can help us to be clear about past confusion, and to be effective in crafting future change.

Mary Beard is among those who would have celebrated these signs of change, having articulated the importance of sexist language long before this decade's attention to the issue. As she recognized, these issues "are fundamental for precision in thought and its communication," and "involve [our] judgments on everything human" (Beard, 1946: 60). Edward Sapir (1933) was equally aware of the psychological implications of language. "All in all," he claimed, "it is not too much to say that one of the really important functions of language is to be constantly declaring to society the psychological place held by all of its members." Those of us who argue for language change would agree. Our goal is to revise the character of that declaration, so that our language comes to suggest the equal humanity of *all* its users.

NOTES

1. For example, American Psychological Association (1977); Scott, Foresman and Company (1974).

2. See Miller and Swift (1972) (*tey*); Orovan (1971) (*co*); Fenner (1974) (*ne*); MacKay (1978) (*E*); and Baron (1981), who discusses thirty-five different proposals.

3. *Women and Language News,* 244 Lincoln Hall, 702 S. Wright, Univ. of Illinois, Urbana, Il. 61801.

REFERENCES

American Anthropological Association. 1974. *Newsletter* (January), 12.

American Psychological Association. 1975. Guidelines for nonsexist use of language: Task force on issues of sexual bias in graduate education. *American Psychologist* (June), 682-84.

——— 1977. Guidelines for nonsexist language in APA journals. *Publication Manual Change Sheet 2*. Washington, D.C.: A.P.A.

Baker, Russell. 1973. Nopersonclature. *New York Times* (March 4).

Baron, Dennis E. 1981. The epicene pronoun: The word that failed. *American Speech*, 56, 83–97.

Bate, Barbara. 1978. Nonsexist language use in transition. *Journal of Communication*, 28 (1), 139–49.

Beard, Mary. 1946. *Woman as force in history*. New York: Macmillan.

Bem, Sandra & Daryl Bem. 1973. Does sex-biased job advertising "aid and abet" sex discrimination? *Journal of Applied Social Psychology*, 3 (1), 6–18.

Bernstein, Theodore. 1965. *The careful writer: A modern guide to English usage*. New York: Atheneum.

Blaubergs, Maija. 1978. Changing the sexist language: The theory behind the practice. *Psychology of Women Quarterly*, 2 (3), 244–61.

Bodine, Ann. 1975. Androcentrism in prescriptive grammar: Singular *they*, sex-indefinite *he* and *he or she*. *Language in Society*, 4, 129–46.

Buckley, William F. 1976. Unsex me now. *National Review* (May 28), 583.

Burgess, Anthony. 1976. Dirty words. *New York Times Magazine* (August 8).

Carroll, J. B. (ed.). 1956. *Language, thought and reality: Essays of Benjamin Whorf*. Cambridge, Mass.: M.I.T. Press.

Clark, Herbert & Eve Clark. 1977. *Psychology and language: An introduction to psycholinguistics*. New York: Harcourt Brace Jovanovich.

Collins, Ronald K. L. 1977. Language, history, and the legal process: A profile of the "reasonable man." *Camden Law Journal*, 8 (2), 312–23.

Cooperperson, Ellen. 1976. What's in a name? Sexism. *New York Times* (November 21), 26.

Culpepper-Hough, Emily & Harvey Cox. 1972. Letter to the editor. *Newsweek* (January 10).

Cusick, Frederick. 1975. Law students win their case—against a will. *Daily Hampshire Gazette* (March 1), Northampton, Mass.

Daly, Mary. 1973. *Beyond God the father: Toward a philosophy of women's liberation*. Boston: Beacon Press.

Devol, Edward. 1977. The he-she dilemma built into the tongue. *San Francisco Chronicle* (February 13).

Felton, David. 1976. Butz is just a 4-letter word. *Rolling Stone* (November 18).

Fenner, M. S. 1974. After all: Proposal for unisex pronoun. *Today's Education*, 63 (summer), 110.

Frank M. 1976. "Dear Abby." *Los Angeles Times* (August 17), 4.

Friedrich, Paul. 1972. Social context and semantic feature: The Russian pronominal usage. In J. Gumperz & D. Hymes (eds.), *Directions in sociolinguistics*. New York: Holt, Rinehart and Winston.

Graham, Alma. 1973. The making of a nonsexist dictionary. *Ms.*, 2 (Dec.), 12–16.

Harvard Linguistics Faculty. 1971. Pronoun envy. *Harvard Crimson* (November 16).

Huber, Joan. 1976. On the generic use of male pronouns. *The American Sociologist*, 11 (May), 89.

Kanfer, Stefan. 1972. Sispeak: A Ms-guided attempt to change herstory. *Time*, 100 (October 23), 79.

Lakoff, Robin. 1975. *Language and woman's place*. New York: Harper & Row.

Langendoen, D. Terence. 1970. *Essentials of English grammar*. New York: Holt, Rinehart and Winston.

Lewis. C. S. 1960. *Studies in words*. London: Cambridge University Press.

Lewis, Ovid. 1972. Law, language and communication. *Case Western Reserve Law Review*, 23, 316.

Los Angeles Times. 1974a. Council acts to desex job titles. (October 10), 1.

———— 1974b. Council OK's dropping of job sex titles. (October 17), 5.

———— 1977. Assembly moves to desex titles. (January 14), 3.

MacKay, Donald G. 1978. Birth of a word. Dept. of Psychology, Unpublished paper. Univ. of California, Los Angeles.

Martyna, Wendy. 1978a. What does "he" mean? Use of the generic masculine. *Journal of Communication,* 28 (1), 131–38.

———— 1978b. Using and understanding the generic masculine: A social psychological approach to language and the sexes. Ph.D. dissertation, Stanford Univ.

Mayer, Milton. 1975. On the siblinghood of persons. *The Progressive* (September), 20–21.

McCabe, Charles. 1977. Spaying the language. *San Francisco Chronicle* (May 24).

Meehl, Paul. 1967. Theory testing in physics: A methodological paradox. *Philosophy of Science,* 34, 103–15.

Miller, Casey & Kate Swift. 1972. De-sexing the English language. *Ms.,* 1 (spring).

Murray, Pauli. 1970. Testimony before U.S. Congress, House, Special Subcommittee on Education of the Committee on Education and Welfare, *Discrimination against women,* 91st Congress, 2d session, on section 805 of H.R. 16098.

Newsweek. 1971. Pronoun envy. (December 6).

O'Hearn, B. W. 1974. N.Y. Kiwanis Club admits first woman. *Middletown Connecticut Press* (January 23).

Orovan, Mary. 1971. Humanizing English. Mimeographed, Hackensack, N.J.

Palo Alto Times. 1977. Chairperson title brings objections. (November 9).

Piercy, Marge. 1973. Doing it differently. In *To be of use.* New York: Doubleday.

Purnell, Sandra. 1978. Politically speaking, do women exist. *Journal of Communication,* 28 (1), 150–56.

Ritchie, Marguerite. 1975. Alice through the statutes. *McGill Law Journal,* 21.

Sapir, Edward. 1963 (orig., 1933). David Mandelbaum (ed.), *Selected writings of Edward Sapir in language, culture, and personality.* Berkeley, Calif.: Univ. of California Press.

Sayers, Dorothy. 1947. The human-not-quite-human. *Unpopular Opinions.* New York: Harcourt, Brace.

Schneider, Michael & Karen Foss. 1977. Thought, sex and language: The Sapir-Whorf hypothesis in the American women's movement. *Bulletin: Women's Studies in Communication,* 1 (1), 3.

Scott, Foresman and Company. 1974. *Guidelines for improving the image of women in textbooks.* Glenview, Ill.: Scott, Foresman.

Shenker, Israel. 1971. Is it possible for a woman to manhandle the King's English? *New York Times* (August 29).

Smith, Jack. 1975. Vive la difference. *Los Angeles Times* (October 16).

Sontag, Susan. 1973. The third world of women. *Partisan Review,* 40 (2).

T.V. Guide. 1971. As we see it. (July 17), 1.

Tittle, Carol, Karen McCarthy, & Jane Steckler. 1974. *Women and educational testing.* Princeton, N.J.: Educational Testing Service.

Valian, Virginia & Jerrold Katz. 1971. The right to say "he." *Harvard Crimson* (November 24).

Van Horne, Harriet. 1976. Women's movement foolishly assaults the English language. *Rocky Mountain News* (February 19), 51, Denver, Colo.

Ward, Jean. 1975. Attacking the King's English: Implications for journalism in the feminist critique. *Journalism Quarterly* (winter), 699–705.

Washington, State of, v. Yvonne Wanrow. 1977. Supreme Court of Washington (559 Pacific Report, 2d series), 548–59.

Weisstein, Naomi. 1973. Why we aren't laughing—anymore. *Ms.,* 2 (5).

White, E. B. 1974. Quoted in Blake Green, A new English: Unbiased or unsexed? *San Francisco Chronicle* (October 11), 23.

Women and Language News, 244 Lincoln Hall, 702 S. Wright, Univ. of Illinois, Urbana, Ill. 61801.

Yablok, Nina. 1977. A woperchild joins the arguthing. *New York Times* (March 30).

PRESCRIPTIVE GRAMMAR
AND THE PRONOUN PROBLEM *

Donald G. MacKay

How did sexism in language come about, and how can it be changed? The prescriptive grammar taught in our schools and followed in our publishing houses is relevant to both issues. The prescription of *he* to mean "he or she" clearly illustrates the role of prescriptive grammar in perpetuating sexist language. The original prescription began about 250 years ago and, according to Bodine (1975), is attributable to bias on the part of male prescriptivists. But historical prejudice seems hardly enough to account for its continuation in over 85% of the grammar textbooks recently used in the American educational system (Bodine, 1975). Rather, the persistence of the prescription seems attributable to a set of sophisticated and seemingly plausible assumptions which serve to perpetuate it.

The present study examines some recent evidence bearing on these assumptions and concludes that the prescription of *he* to mean "he or she" is defective. Some directions for further research which seems needed to correct this defect are suggested, as well as a general principle for guiding prescriptive grammar, which may help prevent defective prescriptions in the future.

At least thirteen assumptions have been used to bolster the prescriptive use of *he*. They are discussed below under five standard headings in the psychology and sociology of language: *production* (how prescriptive *he* is used), *comprehension* (how prescriptive *he* is understood), *learning* (why people learn prescriptive *he*), *language and cognition* (effects of prescriptive *he* on thought), and *language change* (the best change to make in the case of prescriptive *he*). Most of the assumptions appear repeatedly in print, and Martyna (1980) provides excellent examples from the writing of journalists. However, the assumptions are seldom stated in an explicit or formal manner, and they vary in the extent to which they are held and in the generality of their claims; some apply almost exclusively to prescriptive *he*, while others are applicable to any word. Some of the assumptions even contradict one another, since they have, until now, appeared piecemeal throughout the literature rather than as a collection.

*The author gratefully acknowledges the support of NIMH Grant 19964-08, and thanks Dr. D. Burke for comments on an earlier version of this manuscript.

THE PRODUCTION ASSUMPTIONS

The Generic Assumption:

This is the assumption that *he* consistently refers to generic or sex-indefinite antecedents (as recommended in prescriptive grammars), a usage that has been called "generic *he*." In fact, however, generic *he* is not used consistently to mean "he or she" and is more accurately labeled "prescriptive *he*," as in the present study. Martyna (1978a) showed that, in context, speakers consistently use prescriptive *he* only when referring to predominantly male antecedents (e.g., *doctor, lawyer*), not when referring to predominantly female antecedents (e.g., *nurse, secretary*) as in "A nurse must answer her calls." (See Panel 1.) As the Association for Women in Psychology Ad Hoc Committee on Sexist Language (1975) points out, this inconsistency in use suggests that speakers find prescriptive *he* inadequate for making generic reference to predominantly female antecedents and that, in gereral, generic *he* is not being used generically.

Panel 1: A summary of Martyna (1978a): What does "he" mean? Use of the generic masculine.

Martyna (1978a) examined whether college students use prescriptive *he* consistently when referring to generic antecedents in an experimental situation designed to elicit normal usage without normal awareness. Each of forty Stanford students (twenty males and twenty females) heard a series of forty-eight incomplete sentences. To direct attention away from the true purpose of the experiment, only eighteen of the incomplete sentences were "experimental" fragments, such as "When an artist becomes famous." Both filler and experimental fragments were randomly intermixed for each subject and none contained a pronoun. However, the experimental fragments contained a generic noun which was either male-related (e.g., *doctor*), female-related (e.g., *nurse*), or neutral (e.g., *person*).

The subjects' task was to complete each sentence as quickly as possible, and say it aloud. Example completions for the three types of fragments (italicized) are as follows: *"Before a judge can give a final ruling,* he must weight the evidence." *"When a person loses money,* he is apt to feel bad." *"After a nurse has completed training,* she goes to work." Following this sentence completion task, Martyna asked the subjects to describe any images that had come to mind as they were thinking up their completion for each fragment.

The results showed that subjects usually used a pronoun in completing the fragments, and the pronoun used varied with the nature of the antecedent: usually *he* for fragments containing male-related nouns such as *doctor*, usually *she* for fragments containing female-related nouns such

---

as *nurse*, and any one of various pronouns (*he, he or she*, and *they*) for fragments containing neutral nouns such as *person*.

In a second, otherwise identical, experiment, the same subjects were presented with sentences typed on index cards and wrote out their completions. Alternatives to the prescriptive use of *he* appeared more often in this second "visual" experiment, but in both experiments women were more likely than men to use alternatives to prescriptive *he* And both experiments showed differences between men and women in reported imagery while completing sentences using prescriptive *he*: males usually reported imaging a male, whereas women usually reported an absence of imagery for sentences they completed using prescriptive *he*.

These findings indicate that prescriptive *he* is not used consistently as a generic term, meaning "he or she," but is routinely replaced by *she, they,* and *he or she,* depending on whether it is spoken or written, and on who is doing the talking or writing, and what is being talked about. Martyna therefore concluded that "*he* deserves to live out its days doing what it has always done best—referring to *he* and not *she.*"

The Dictionary Assumption:

This is the assumption, that the way a word is used, as reflected in the dictionary, justifies its prescription. The assumption is patently false; usage may be the *result* of the prescription. For example, current use of prescriptive *he* may reflect 250 years of prior prescription and cannot justify its prescription for the future.

Moreover, dictionaries cannot be relied on to provide accurate representations of how words are used. Dictionaries often depict not current but past usage, or the dictionary maker's view of how words ought to be used. A comparison of dictionary entries for *he* and *she* provides an example. Dictionaries invariably list two senses of *he*, a specific male sense and a "generic human" sense. But for some reason most dictionaries list only the specific female sense of *she* and fail to note that speakers almost invariably use *she* rather than *he* to refer to supposedly generic classes such as *nurse* or *secretary* (see Martyna, 1978a).

THE COMPREHENSION ASSUMPTIONS

The Pronominal Surrogate Assumption:

This is the assumption that pronouns simply stand for their antecedents and that prescriptive *he* designates a sex-indefinite antecedent, such as *person* or *pedestrian,* without excluding women or adding new meaning of its own.

A long line of experiments, including Kidd (1971), Moulton, Robinson, and Elias (1978), Martyna (1978b), MacKay and Fulkerson (1979), and MacKay

(1980b) have tested and conclusively refuted the pronominal surrogate assumption. The findings of MacKay and Fulkerson (1979) illustrate the quality and strength of the available evidence against this assumption. In the main experiment, ten men and ten women, U.C.L.A. students, listened to sentences such as "When a botanist is in the field, he is usually working" and responded as quickly as possible either YES (the sentence could refer to one or more females) or NO (the sentence could not refer to one or more females). As in Martyna (1978a), most of the sentences were "fillers," randomly mixed with a small number of "experimental" sentences which contained a prescriptive *he* referring to either a "male-related" antecedent (*engineer, doctor*), a "female-related" antecedent (*model, secretary*), or a "neutral" antecedent (*student, musician*). To establish these three categories, eighty pilot subjects (forty males and forty females) estimated the percentage of males and females employed in these and twenty-seven other occupations. The judgments of males vs. females did not differ and were in close agreement with the *actual* percentages of men and women in these categories as determined by the U.S. Department of Commerce (1976).

We sought to find out how accurately and quickly subjects would respond that the sentences containing prescriptive *he* could refer to a female. A YES answer was scored as correct, and a NO answer as incorrect. Accuracy was very low. The results showed that 95% of the subjects made errors (on 91% of the trials), responding NO, that sentences containing prescriptive *he* could not refer to a female. Females made as many errors as males, and it made no difference whether the prescriptive *he* referred to a predominantly male, female, or neutral antecedent. In contrast, the same subjects responded that sex-specific "filler" sentences such as "An old housekeeper cleaned her carpet before sunrise" could refer to a female much more accurately (i.e., with YES; there were 2% errors on the average). Correct responses to other filler sentences such as "His aunt came to the party" indicated that the subjects were not responding *only* to the pronouns in the sentences.

Three control experiments confirmed that prescriptive *he* was responsible for the exclusion of women in the experimental sentences. One was identical to the main experiment except that subjects responded YES if a sentence could refer to *one or more males* and NO if not. Responses were fast and accurate (99% correct) for sentences containing prescriptive *he*.

The second control experiment was identical to the first except that the pronoun *she* was substituted for prescriptive *he* in the experimental sentences. This change of pronoun changed the response pattern from 99% YES to 3% YES, indicating that *she* excludes men in the comprehension of sex-indefinite antecedents and is even more inadequate than *he* for conveying the "he or she" concept.

The third control experiment was identical to the main study except that the experimental sentences were rewritten to omit prescriptive *he*. Thus a sentence such as "When a botanist is in the field, he is usually working" was changed to

"A botanist who is in the field is usually working." With this seemingly minor change, errors (i.e., answers of NO, the sentence could not refer to females) dropped to 43%, and an effect of antecedent class appeared (68% errors for predominantly male antecedents, 42% for neutral antecedents and 19% for female antecedents), along with an effect of subject sex (males made more errors than females). These findings suggest that adding prescriptive *he* dramatically increases the exclusion of women and washes out effects of subject sex and nature of the antecedent.

MacKay and Fulkerson (1979) summarized their results in a new model of pronoun comprehension which suggests that listeners who encounter the pronoun *he* search the sentence for a noun assumed with high probability to be male. Listeners also assume that antecedents of *she* are likely to be female. Contrary to the pronominal surrogate assumption, they *do not* infer that *he* means "he or she" just because its antecedent happens to be a generic noun such as *person*.

The Context Assumption:

This is the assumption that prescriptive *he* is one of many ambiguous words which carry out multiple semantic duties but are nevertheless readily interpreted on the basis of situation or sentence context. For example, when listening to a gasoline commercial, we don't confuse a *tank* for gasoline with a *tank* for military destruction. Similarly, under the context assumption, we don't confuse prescriptive *he* in contexts referring to people with specific *he* referring to men. An experiment by MacKay (1980b) refuted the context assumption using large-scale paragraphs of the sort encountered in the everyday experience of university students. Ten U.C.L.A. students (five males and five females) read two paragraphs containing prescriptive *he* referring to neutral antecedents (e.g., *person, writer*). After reading each paragraph, they answered three multiple choice questions. One of the questions indirectly (and unbeknownst to the subjects) assessed comprehension of prescriptive *he* and its antecedents. In reference to a textbook paragraph about a beginning writer, the question tapping comprehension of prescriptive *he* was: "The beginner discussed in the paragraph is (a) *male;* (b) *female;* (c) *either male or female.*" The issue was whether subjects would usually choose alternative (c), indicating generic comprehension of prescriptive *he* in this context.

Only 20% of the subjects consistently chose alternative (c); 80% of the subjects made errors on 63% of the trials, responding (a) *male,* rather than (c) *either male or female.* Women made exactly as many errors as men, and none of the errors involved choosing (b) *female.* Such findings contradict the assumption that the context will resolve the ambiguity of prescriptive *he.* They also indicate that the "he or she" concept is highly unavailable when *he* is used as a generic pronoun. However, the "he or she" concept became highly available to refer to a totally unfamiliar neologism. Thirty additional subjects read the same paragraphs with prescriptive *he* replaced by a neologism they had never before encountered (*E, tey,* or *e*). They made only 10% errors on the critical question (i.e., 90% chose *either male or female* as the referent). Moreover, the neologisms were as good as prescriptive *he* in other respects; they neither slowed the overall reading time nor diminished comprehension of the main content of the paragraphs.

The Neutralization Assumption:

Linguists generally characterize prescriptive *he* as an example of neutralization, a hypothetical process postulated in several other areas of English grammar (see Clark & Clark, 1977). For example, it is assumed that to ask how *tall* someone is in neutral contexts such as "How tall is the boy?" simply requests information without presupposing or biasing the nature of the response. More generally it is assumed that "unmarked" members or polar pairs such as *tall-short* allow neutral interpretations. Likewise, *he* is posited to be the unmarked member of the *he-she* pair and its use is assumed to be neutral when the sex of its referent is unknown, indeterminate, or irrelevant.

The neutralization assumption as applied to prescriptive *he* is false: the experiments discussed above by MacKay and Fulkerson (1979) and MacKay (1980b) indicate that prescriptive *he* is not neutral and leads neutral antecedents such as *person, pedestrian,* or *writer* to be interpreted as masculine (see also Kidd, 1971; Martyna, 1978b). The available evidence for this conclusion is in fact so forceful as to call into question the original claims concerning neutralization in other polar pairs such as *tall-short.*

THE LEARNING ASSUMPTIONS

The learning assumptions deal with why people learn to use prescriptive *he* in the first place and how people can presumably learn to use and interpret it generically in the future.

The Typicality Assumption:

Under the typicality assumption, speakers use *he* to refer, for example, to *a doctor,* thereby signaling that doctors are typically male, and they use *she* for *a nurse* to signal that nurses are typically female. The typicality assumption has an obvious but generally overlooked extension; namely that some form *other than he* would be needed to signal the fact that classes such as *writer* are about 50% male and 50% female. In fact, however, the pronominal prototype assumption is incorrect even as it stands. MacKay and Fulkerson (1979) found that subjects could accurately judge the percentage of males and females in occupational classes such as *doctor, nurse,* and *writer* and that neither natural nor experimental experience with prescriptive *he* in association with these classes affected such judgments. Contrary to the pronominal prototype assumption, adults determine the composition of occupational classes through experience with or knowledge about people in these classes, and not through language conventions such as the use of prescriptive *he*.

The Semantic Flexibility Assumption:

Under the semantic flexibility assumption, the meaning of a word is highly flexible and can be established by declaration. In the case of nouns, the strategy of proposing and adopting a special purpose definition for a common noun in some new domain of use is remarkably common (see Britton, 1978). For example, psychologists defined and used the word *reinforcement* in a manner remote from its original dictionary definition, and this special purpose definition has become widely learned and accepted. People likewise experience no difficulty in learning new meanings for old words such as *Blacks*. If this is true in general, then it should be possible to teach people the "he or she" meaning of prescriptive *he*. Indeed, this is what our prescriptive grammar, our educational system, and our publishing establishments have been attempting to do for the last 250 years, and the fact that people don't now interpret prescriptive *he* generically indicates that these large scale and long term efforts have failed.

Why is *he* semantically inflexible? One reason is the incompatibility of its primary vs. prescribed meanings. Primary and secondary meanings are compatible in successful cases of semantic flexibility such as the psychological use of the term *reinforcement*. But the primary meaning of *he* is diametrically opposed to its secondary "he or she" meaning: the primary meaning excludes women whereas the prescribed meaning is intended to include them. Incompatible primary and secondary meanings interfere with one another and a prescription such as "*true* will henceforth and in certain contexts mean *false*" could be expected to meet with a comparable lack of success.

The Teachability Assumption:

It is sometimes assumed that additional efforts, such as footnotes in the preface of books and journals, would suffice to teach the generic interpretation of prescriptive *he*. This assumption overlooks both the interference of incompatible meanings and the difficulties of defining words while speaking. These difficulties seem especially serious since children almost certainly encounter and presumably often acquire prescriptive *he* from spoken language (Nilsen, 1977).

THE LANGUAGE AND COGNITION ASSUMPTIONS

The following assumptions are central to the issue of the damage done by prescriptive *he*; they focus on the relation between language and other aspects of cognition, including thought, feelings, attitudes, and level of aspiration.

The Thought is Sexist Assumption:

Under the "thought is sexist" assumption, the fact that people systematically misinterpret prescriptive *he* as referring to a male rather than a generic *person* or *writer* indicates that people have male-specific notions of "person" or "writer." Thus, *thought* is sexist, not *language,* and this becomes an argument against language change.

The findings of MacKay and Fulkerson (1979) contradict this argument, by showing that subjects have quite accurate concepts for *person* or *writer,* even though prescriptive *he* influences these concepts during "on-line" processing of a sentence. After reading sentences containing prescriptive *he* referring to *a nurse, a doctor, a writer,* etc., subjects' estimates of the proportion of women within these occupations were in close agreement with the actual percentages of women in these categories.

The Language Independence Assumption:

This postulate, that language and thought are independent of one another, contradicts the Sapir-Whorf hypothesis that language influences thought. Recent evidence suggests that both positions may be correct, and that language influences some types of thought but not others.

The two main types of thought are *descriptive* and *evaluative;* most of the current literature on language and cognition deals with descriptive thought or judgments about observable aspects of the real world. Judgments of the shape or color of objects are prime examples of descriptive thought. Contrary to the Sapir-Whorf hypothesis, Rosch (1973) found that monolingual speakers of Dani think about the colors and shapes of objects in the same way as do speakers of English, a language which codes shapes and colors quite differently from Dani.

Judgments concerning the sex ratio of occupational classes provide another example of descriptive thought. Under the Sapir-Whorf hypothesis, one might expect prescriptive *he* to call up a male image so often in association with categories such as, say, *professor,* as to cause us to underestimate the proportion of professors who are female. But as noted above, MacKay and Fulkerson (1979) found no evidence for this version of the Sapir-Whorf hypothesis.

On the other hand, MacKay (1979) found that prescriptive *he does* influence evaluative thought, i.e., subjective or personal judgments concerning the *value* of concepts or events. The subjects in this experiment read one of four paragraphs containing identical information about self-actualization. The only difference was that one paragraph used prescriptive *he* to refer to "a self-actualized person," the second used plural *they* to refer to "self-actualized persons," the third used specific *he* to refer to "Mike Scott, a self-actualized person," and the fourth used specific *she* to refer to "Mary Scott, a self-actualized person." The main issue was whether female subjects would find the paragraph containing prescriptive *he* to be less relevant to their personal lives than the paragraph containing the plural *they.*

Female subjects who had expressed sympathy for the women's movement in a questionnaire found the paragraph containing prescriptive *he* less personally relevant and more difficult to comprehend than the otherwise identical paragraph containing the plural *they*. It was as if they felt excluded from paragraphs containing prescriptive *he* and resented the peripheral status of women implied by its use. The otherwise identical paragraphs referring to a specific female ("Mary Scott") or a specific male ("Mike Scott") reinforced this conclusion. These women found the "Mary Scott" paragraph more personally relevant and easier to comprehend than the "Mike Scott" paragraph. They also felt that the author of the prescriptive *he* version was more likely to be male than the author of any other version of the paragraph.

A second, otherwise identical experiment with subjects who had expressed less sympathy toward the women's liberation movement confirmed that prescriptive *he* influences attitudes but suggested that the precise nature of its effects depends on already existing attitudes of the perceiver. In this experiment, women found the prescriptive *he* version more personally relevant than the plural *they* or the "Mary Scott" version. Two underlying beliefs showed up in their answers to the questionnaire: that women in general are peripheral or unimportant, but that they (the subjects) personally are unlike other women and are capable of both self-fulfillment and success in a "man's world." They therefore found the prescriptive *he* paragraph more personally relevant than the "Mary Scott" paragraph because they were interested in "male-oriented" messages signalled by the use of prescriptive *he* and were uninterested in messages about another woman, a class they generally had little desire to identify with. In line with this interpretation, these women, like the pro-feminist women in the first experiment, felt that the author of the prescriptive *he* paragraph was more likely to be male than the author of any of the other paragraphs.

Such findings relate to issues raised by Shepelak (1977) as to whether women would avoid participating in activities commonly designated with prescriptive *he* and whether people would identify with women less because of the preponderance of prescriptive references to males rather than females. The answer to both issues seems to be that some would and others wouldn't, depending on their cognitive framework for dealing with oppression, in this case the oppression of being excluded from the category "person" in paragraphs containing prescriptive *he* (see also Bate, 1975). One is the *feminist* framework represented by the women who expressed sympathy for the women's movement. Under this framework, persons, male or female, are considered different but equal and implications to the contrary are resented. Another is the *assimilation* framework whereby goals ascribed for males are accepted, valued, and sought after while goals ascribed for females are rejected. A third is the *conformist* framework whereby women value and pursue goals ascribed for females. Women adopting this framework may be more likely to accept the connotation of prescriptive *he* that women, including themselves, are peripheral and to reject motives such as ambition and adventurousness which conflict with the more passive orientation assigned to them as women.

A complete evaluation of the effects of prescriptive *he* therefore requires an evaluation of the cognitive styles that people develop for handling it. In particular, one must weigh the psychological costs of the conformist style which entails lower self-esteem for the women who adopt it, and of the assimilation style which entails a loss of sisterhood among women and condescension toward women in general.

The Triviality Assumption:

According to this assumption, prescriptive *he* is a trivial problem, incurs no serious social or psychological consequences, and is "less in need of changing" than other aspects of sexist language (Lakoff, 1973: 75).The frequency of prescriptive *he* alone suffices to question the triviality assumption. Over the course of a lifetime, repetition of prescriptive *he* exceeds 1,000,000 in the experience of educated Americans (see MacKay, 1980a), but the consequences of that many shaping trials are beyond the ken of present-day psychology. Until such consequences can be determined, the assumption that prescriptive *he* is trivial and should be ignored or should take second place to other problems in sexist language must be dismissed as unfounded.

The fact that prescriptive *he* influences attitudes (MacKay, 1979) also cannot be ignored or considered trivial, since prescriptive *he* has all the characteristics of a highly effective propaganda technique: *repetition* (the frequency of prescriptive *he* implies repetition beyond all extant propaganda techniques), *early age of acquisition* (prior to age 6, according to Nilsen, 1977), *covertness* (use of prescriptive *he* is not usually intended as an open attempt to maintain or alter attitudes), *association with high prestige sources* (especially university textbooks), and *indirectness* (its message is presented indirectly as if it were a matter of common and well-established knowledge).

Although the full impact of prescriptive *he* remains to be explored, effects on attitudes related to achievement motivation, perseverance, and level of aspiration seem likely. McArthur and Eisen (1976) found that stories about male vs. female protagonists performing certain activities influenced the achievement motivation (desire to excel in these activities) of male vs. female children. Montemayor (1975) found analogous results for both the performance and rated attractiveness of an activity. Prescriptive *he* could have similar effects on a much larger scale and may even contribute to the fact that *before* attending school, boys aspire to traditionally male occupations and girls aspire to traditionally female occupations (see Beuf, 1974).

Another area for further study concerns the possibility of subtle but nontrivial effects of perscriptive *he* on the emotional state or feelings of both men and women. Adamsky (1981) found that women reported feelings of importance, power, and superiority when use of prescriptive *he* was changed to *she*. This finding suggests that repeated everyday experience of prescriptive *he* may contribute to the feelings of importance, power, and superiority which are common among men, and the feelings of unimportance, powerlessness, and inferiority which are common among women (see Feigen-Fasteau, 1975). The possibility of such effects cannot be ignored or considered trivial.

Prescriptive *he* also has specific effects on behavior which contradict the triviality assumption. Bem and Bem (1973) found that high school women were less likely to respond to job advertisements containing prescriptive *he* than to otherwise similar advertisements using *she* instead of *he* as the generic pronoun. This finding suggests that use of prescriptive *he* can aid and abet sex discrimination in the job market.

THE LANGUAGE CHANGE ASSUMPTIONS

So far none of the assumptions underlying the prescription of *he* to mean "he or she" has proven correct. The production data indicated that dictionaries are inaccurate, that prescriptive *he* is not being used generically, and that even if it were, this would not justify its prescription. The comprehension data indicated that prescriptive *he* is not a neutral or unmarked term which simply stands in place of its antecedents. Even within large-scale paragraph contexts, *he* polarizes the interpretation of neutral antecedents, so that sentences containing prescriptive *he* are usually taken to refer to males rather than to both sexes. The learning data indicated that whatever the teaching technique, speakers are unlikely to learn to use and interpret prescriptive *he* generically. Moreover, prescriptive *he* serves no socially justifiable function and has serious social and psychological consequences. Such facts provide a compelling case for language change. The following assumptions concern processes of language change, with reference to prescriptive *he* (see also Martyna, 1980; Blaubergs, 1978).

The Immutable Assumption:

It is often assumed that pronouns are part of a "closed class" (see Clark & Clark, 1977) and that introducing a new pronoun or changing existing pronouns is impossible. The history of English directly refutes the immutability assumption: three new third person pronouns (*it, she,* and *they*) have been introduced into English, and the system of second person pronouns (which once included *thee, thou, thine,* and *thy*) has been radically changed as a result of egalitarian forces (see Bodine, 1975).

The Ease of Change Assumption:

Diametrically opposed to the immutability assumption is the belief that language change is quick and easy, given a genuine need for a new word. For example, Bodine (1975) argued that it is unnecessary for speakers of English to consciously attempt to change the language or alter the use of prescriptive *he;* we only need to ignore prescriptive grammar and the problem of *he* will be solved by unpremeditated accommodation through the singular use of *they* as in "Someone lost their sweater."

Singular *they* is useful in certain contexts, especially to refer to indefinite pronouns in short sentences such as the one above. But contrary to the ease of change assumption, singular *they* has made no noticeable inroads into formal writing (see Greene, 1978), even though the need for an alternative to prescriptive *he* has been recognized for almost a century (Converse, 1884). Moreover, a series of systematic analyses by MacKay (1980a, summarized in Panel 2) suggests that singular *they* suffers from a number of problems as a general substitute for prescriptive *he* and that given only unpremeditated accommodation, the problem of prescriptive *he* is likely to continue indefinitely.

Panel 2: A summary of MacKay (1980a): On the goals, principles and procedures for prescriptive grammar.

MacKay (1980b) describes the goal of prescriptive grammar (to predict which among a set of alternative forms or rules will prove most useful for future speakers to teach, learn, and use) and outlines three basic procedures for accomplishing this goal. The procedures are illustrated for a single hypothetical prescription: the substitution of singular *they* for prescriptive *he*. The first procedure illustrates how to determine the costs and benefits of this prescription for readers encountering singular *they* in representative contexts of current use. The second procedure evaluates the relative frequency with which these costs and benefits are likely to be encountered. The third evaluates the relative disruptiveness of the costs and advantageousness of the benefits.

Projected benefits of this particular prescription included neutral connotation (unlike prescriptive *he,* connotations of singular *they* are neutral with regard to sex); naturalness (singular *they* often sounds more natural than any other alternative for reference to corporate and indefinite nouns and to indefinite pronouns such as *everybody*); simplicity (singular *they* is readily substituted for prescriptive *he* without requiring retroactive changes or false starts); retrievability (as a high frequency pronoun, *they* is readily retrieved for production).

Projected costs of the prescription included covert referential ambiguity (e.g., when *their* is substituted for *his* in "If a scholar has no faith in his principles, how can he succeed?," the *their* could refer either to "a scholar's own principles" or to "principles of some as yet unknown or indeterminant persons"); overt referential ambiguity (e.g., *they* substituted for *he* in the above sentence could refer to either *principles* or *scholar,* both overt components within the sentence); loss of imageability, impact, and memorability; loss of precision (singulars such as *he, she,* and *it* refer precisely to one and only one entity, whereas plurals such as *they* refer vaguely to any number of entities greater than one, and the prescriptive use of *they* as a singular would extend this vagueness to *any* number of entities, one or more); distancing and dehumanizing connotations (because of the frequent association of *they* with abstract and nonhuman entities).

Other projected costs included long-lasting and potentially disruptive side effects on other areas of the language (e.g., the normal plural function of *they* may suffer, due to the loss in precision that would ensue if *they* succeeded as a singular). Moreover, some of the projected costs were found to be frequent and highly disruptive. It was concluded that if these findings generalize to other language contexts (such as speaking and listening), this prescription should not be endorsed.

An interesting subsidiary result indicated that prescriptive *he* was used more frequently in referring to *man* (the species) than to other antecedents such as *child.* This increased density of prescriptive *he's* suggested that frequent association with *he* may have altered the originally intended generic meaning of the word *man.* This result suggests that proposals for solving the problem of prescriptive *he* must simultaneously consider proposals for solving the species *man* problem and vice versa.

Another variant of the ease of change assumption is found in Clark and Clark (1977: 554): "when people lack a word for a useful concept, they soon find one." Contrary to this view of lexical innovation, we have yet to find an agreed-upon neologism to replace prescriptive *he*, despite the dozens of proposals since Converse (1884). Changing prescriptive *he* has been neither quick nor easy and may require the combined resources of the institutions which were in some measure responsible for the problem in the first place: our prescriptive grammar, educational system, and publishing establishments.

CONCLUSIONS

Since the prescription of *he* to mean "he or she" is defective, what is now needed is a new prescription to stand in its place: one which will be written into prescriptive grammars, taught in our schools, and followed in our publishing systems so as to bring about a permanent change in the language. This new and as yet unformulated prescription must be easy to teach and to learn and must take into consideration the traditional literary standards (for, say, clarity, style, and economy) of our educational and publishing systems. Since this new prescription must be agreed upon and widely accepted, it must be demonstrated to be the best available solution, based on solid evidence rather than on assumptions, as in the case of prescriptive *he*.

Two different programs of research seem required to formulate and support the new prescription; both programs can make use of the theoretical framework and techniques outlined in Panel 2 for predicting the costs and benefits of alternative recommendations and for evaluating the relative disruptiveness of the negative characteristics.

The goal of Program I is to establish an immediate, short-term prescription by determining the costs and benefits of already available alternatives such as *he or she,* singular *they*, pluralization, and use of specific rather than generic examples. Each of these available alternatives has assets in some contexts and flaws in others; by determining the precise nature of those contexts, it will be possible to determine which alternative works best in which context. The prescription resulting from this "cost-benefit by context" analysis will take the form "use *he or she* in context x, singular *they* in context y, and not *he* in any generic context." This multi-alternative, multi-context prescription will undoubtedly be more complex and difficult to learn than, say, "use *he* to mean 'he or she'," and should be considered a tentative but necessary first step.

The goal of Program II is to establish a simpler and more permanent prescription, which may entail determining the best possible neologism for expressing the *he or she* concept. Any neologism suffers a major disadvantage in the short run: people will have to accept and learn to use it. In the long run, however, neologisms have major advantages over available alternatives. For example, unlike recycled words such as singular *they* and prescriptive *he,* a neologism automatically signals that a new and distinctive meaning is being expressed. MacKay (1980b) showed that already existing neologisms are readily comprehended to mean "he or she" even when encountered for the first time without explanation. By clearly signaling the "he or she" meaning, neologisms also call attention to the problem of prescriptive *he,* which is important for creating the desire to change a long-standing habit. Program II must therefore determine in detail the short-term and long-term costs and benefits of neologisms *per se.*

Program II must also determine and perhaps help invent the best possible neologism. MacKay (1980b) showed that E (capitalized) is easier to learn, produce, and comprehend than *tey* or *e* (lower case), but how do we know whether this set includes the *best possible* alternative? What is required is an iterative approach involving the following cycle of steps: First investigate already existing neologisms to determine what characteristics an ideal solution should have. Next, invent alternatives which incorporate those ideal characteristics and test them against the old to determine which is best. Repeat until the best fit solution is found. Then compare this best possible neologism (Program II) against available alternatives (Program I) to determine the best possible way of expressing the "he or she" concept. Finally, introduce the resulting prescription into prescriptive grammar for implementation in our educational and publishing systems. If this final goal can be achieved, we will reform prescriptive grammar and establish a new standard for future prescriptions: *to prescribe*

*forms with the greatest benefit and the least cost, where benefits facilitate
communication (including learning, comprehension, and use of the language
over very long periods of time) and costs make communication more difficult
(relative to all other means of expressing the same concept).*

REFERENCES

Adamsky, Catheryn. 1981. Changes in pronominal usage in a classroom situation. *Psychology of Women Quarterly,* 5, 661–69.

Association for Women in Psychology Ad Hoc Committee on Sexist Language. 1975. Eliminating sexist language: The can, should and how to. Paper presented to the Open Forum at the meeting of the American Psychological Association, Chicago, Ill.

Bate, Barbara. 1975. Generic man, invisible woman: Language, thought and social change. *Michigan Papers in Women's Studies,*2, 1–13.

Bem, Sandra & Daryl Bem. 1973. Does sex-biased job advertising "aid and abet" sex discrimination? *Journal of Applied Social Psychology,* 3 (1), 6–18.

Beuf, Ann. 1974. Doctor, lawyer, household drudge. *Journal of Communication,* 24, 142–49.

Blaubergs, Maija S. 1978. Changing sexist language; The theory behind the practice. *Psychology of Women Quarterly,* 2, 244–61.

Bodine, Ann. 1975. Androcentrism in prescriptive grammar: Singular "they," sex-indefinite "he" and "he or she." *Language in Society,* 4, 129–46.

Britton, B. K. 1978. Lexical ambiguity of words used in English text. *Behavior Research Methods and Instrumentation,* 10, 1–7.

Clark, Herbert & Eve V. Clark. 1977. *Psychology and language: An introduction to psycholinguistics.* New York: Harcourt Brace Jovanovich.

Converse, Charles C. 1884. A new pronoun. *The Critic and Good Literature,* 4, 55.

Feigen-Fasteau, Marcel. 1972. *The male machine.* New York: Delta.

Greene, Wendy. 1978. A survey of sex-indefinite pronouns: Anyone can use "they" if they try. *Women and Language* News, 4, 5.

Kidd, Virginia. 1971. A study of the images produced through the use of a male pronoun as the generic. *Movements: Contemporary Rhetoric and Communication,* 1, 25–30.

Lakoff, Robin. 1973. Language and woman's place. *Language in Society,* 2, 45–79.

MacKay, Donald G. 1979. Language, thought and social attitudes. In Howard Giles, W. Peter Robinson, & Philip M. Smith (eds.), *Language: Social psychological perspectives.* 1980. New York: Pergamon Press, 89–96.

——— 1980a. On the goals, principles, and procedures for prescriptive grammar. *Language in Society,* 9, 349-67.

——— 1980b. Psychology, prescriptive grammar and the pronoun problem. *American Psychologist,* 35, 444-49.

MacKay, Donald & David Fulkerson. 1979. "On the comprehension and production of pronouns." *Journal of Verbal Learning and Verbal Behavior,* 18, 661–73.

Martyna, Wendy. 1978a. What does "he" mean? Use of the generic masculine. *Journal of Communication,* 28 (1), 131–38.

——— 1978b. Using and understanding the generic masculine: A social-psychological approach. Ph.D. dissertation, Stanford Univ. Stanford, Calif.

——— 1980. Beyond the "he/man" approach: The case for nonsexist language. *Signs,* 5, 482–93. In this volume.

McArthur, Leslie & S. Eisen. 1976. Achievements of male and female storybook characters as determinants of achievement behavior by boys and girls. *Journal of Personality and Social Psychology,* 33, 467–73.

Montemayor, Raymond. 1974. Sexism in children's books and elementary teaching materials. In A. P. Nilsen, H. Bosmajian, H. L. Gershuny, & J.P. Stanley (eds.), *Sexism and language.* Urbana, Ill.: National Council of Teachers of English.

Moulton, Janice, George M. Robinson, & Elias Cherin. 1978. Psychology in action: Sex bias in language use: "Neutral" pronouns that aren't. *American Psychologist,* 33, 1032–36.

Nilsen, Alleen Pace. 1977. Sexism in children's books and elementary teaching materials. In Alleen Pace Nilsen, Haig Bosmajian, H. Lee Gershuny, and Julia P. Stanley (eds.), *Sexism and language.* Urbana, Ill.: National Council of Teachers of English, pp. 161–79.

Rosch, Eleanor. 1973. Natural categories. *Cognitive Psychology,* 4, 328–50.

Shepelak, Norma. 1977. Does "he" mean "she" too?: The case of the generic anomaly. Paper presented at the Fourth National Conference on Feminist Psychology, St. Louis, Mo.

United States Department of Commerce Census Bureau. 1976. *Civilian labor force by sex.* Berkeley, Calif.: Univ. of California Press.

LINGUISTIC OPTIONS AND CHOICES
FOR BLACK WOMEN IN THE RURAL SOUTH*

Patricia C. Nichols

All of us learn to speak as members of larger social groups, and these groups have well-defined webs of speaking relationships before we enter them as members. Wittgenstein (1969) and other philosophers have debated the question of "private language" and have argued persuasively that there can be no such entity. Language exists and is experienced as a communal activity. Thus, when we ask questions about women's use of language, we must ask also, *which* women as members of *which* social groups. "Women's language" is as much a myth as "private language."

Here I examine the language use of women in an all-Black speech community in coastal South Carolina, an area which has had the longest sustained inhabitation by Afro-American families in the history of the country. The language use of these women will be compared with that described for women of largely North European descent, living in urban communities in North America and Europe. It becomes apparent that women use language in ways that reflect the options available to them within their particular speech communities. In some circumstances they exhibit linguistically innovative behavior; in others, conservative. They make choices in the contexts of particular social networks rather than as some generalized response to the universal condition of women.

Most of the Black population of coastal South Carolina is descended directly from slaves brought to the Carolina colony between 1670 and the Revolutionary War, some from the Caribbean but most from West Africa itself. By 1776, over half the population of South Carolina was of African descent. If contemporary Afro-Americans were to trace the immigration patterns of their ancestors, most would discover that a Carolina port was the original place of entry into North America. Historian Peter Wood has called Sullivan's Island in the Charleston

*A preliminary report on this research was presented at the Conference on the Sociology of the Languages of American Women, organized by Betty Lou Dubois and Isabel Crouch and held at New Mexico State University, Jan. 16–17, 1976. For slightly different versions of that paper, see Nichols (1976 and1978). I am indebted to Dubois and Crouch for providing the initial forum for discussion of many of the ideas found in the present paper. A Woodrow Wilson Dissertation Fellowship in Women's Studies (1974–75) provided partial funding for research on the South Carolina speech community.

harbor, where incoming slaves were usually quarantined, the "Ellis Island" of Black Americans (Wood, 1974: xiv). Many of these incoming Africans were shipped to rural Georgetown County, the site of the present study. (See the map of Coastal South Carolina, Figure 1.) Georgetown was the center of a large and prosperous rice-growing industry, and white landowners there used large numbers of slaves in the cultivation, harvest, and probably overall management of this subtropical crop. By 1830 the Georgetown district had an overwhelmingly Black population, with a ratio of nine Blacks to one white. Blacks continued to be in the majority until well into the 20th century; only with the 1970 census did whites slightly outnumber Blacks. The vigor of the Black population is attested to by the extent of their participation in local politics. Georgetown County was the last in the state to lose its elected Afro-American legislators after the reconstruction period which followed the Civil War and the first to regain local elected officials with the civil rights movement of the 1950s.

In rural parts of Georgetown County, transportation was a difficult matter, and connection with the wider society was somewhat tenuous until the later part of the 20th century. The linguistic and cultural patterns in this area still reflect the common West African heritage. (See Joyner, 1977, on folklife of the Waccamaw Neck.) For my study, I selected an area of the county which is undergoing extensive social change and which provides an ideal situation for observation of changing language patterns associated with this social change. In

Figure 1   Coastal South Carolina and Georgia

general, young and middle-aged women are changing their language use at a faster pace than men in their age groups, but some older women are slower to change than men.

A *speech community* shares "rules for the conduct and interpretation of speech, and rules for the interpretation of at least one linguistic variety" (Hymes 1972: 54). The language shared by the Black population in this area of the county comprises a speech continuum which ranges from an English creole known as *Gullah* or *Geechee* on the one end, to a variety of Black English in the center, to a regionally standard variety of English at the other end. Gullah developed historically from a pidgin based on both English and a number of West African languages, spoken by the earliest West African migrants to this region. As the breakdown of institutionalized segregation makes possible the formation of friendships and occupational contacts across ethnic lines in a wide variety of situations, many Blacks are choosing to speak the regional variety of standard English and are abandoning the older creole patterns. In general, the language use of individual speakers encompasses different portions of the speech continuum and reflects individual life experiences and choices. For some speakers, the range extends from Gullah to Black English, with a sprinkling of standard syntactic patterns. For others, the range extends from Black English to the regionally standard English, with variable usage depending on the social context. Members of the same household often encompass the entire speech continuum in their daily language use.

For six months during 1974 and 1975 I studied the speech of Blacks in the Waccamaw Neck area of Georgetown County, using both participant-observation and quantitative sociolinguistic methods. Influenced by the concept of "action anthropology," developed initially by Sol Tax (1958) and his associates on the Fox Project in Iowa, and extended by Piddington (1960) and others, I sought to act in some functional capacity within the community, and obtained a job as an unpaid classroom aide in the elementary school attended by most of the children in the area. Working in a single classroom in a situation where the children changed classes hourly, I observed daily more than 100 children at the fourth, fifth, and sixth grade levels. As I came to know the children, I was invited into homes and attended church services and social events in the community, observing and participating in a wide range of speech events. Since the school was integrated, the fact that I was a white woman was more readily accepted than might have been the case ten years earlier when schools were still rigidly segregated along ethnic lines. At this particular school, approximately half of the staff and ten percent of the student body were white. The language of the white children ranged along a continuum from a dialect of nonstandard English known as Appalachian Speech (Wolfram & Christian, 1976) to a regionally standard dialect of English. While in some social contexts white children used features of speech characteristic of their Black playmates, there were sharp differences between the speech of Black and white children at the nonstandard end of the continua. At the standard end, the speech of the two groups was much more similar. The speech of the Black children encompassed the creole to standard continuum described above.

After working in the school for three months, I volunteered to teach a writing class one evening a week on an all-Black river island, home of one cohesive group of children in the elementary school. Introduced to island residents at a weekly church service, I offered to teach the class and described its purpose. About twenty young people signed up for the class and attended regularly throughout the winter months, writing assigned compositions and reading them to each other. On the days I taught the class, I went over to the the island early and visited in homes to obtain recorded interviews for a quantitative study of the island residents' speech. Several similar interviews were conducted on the mainland as well. A total of sixteen recorded interviews form the basis for the following quantitative description of male and female speech of Blacks in one portion of the rural South. These quantitative data supplement and confirm findings made as participant-observer in numerous speech situations within the community during the five months of fieldwork.

Both economically and linguistically, island residents contrast with Black mainland residents. A small educated elite on the mainland, comprised of teachers, preachers, political figures, businessmen, and school board members, used the regionally standard dialect in their public lives; in their homes they often used the dialect of Black English. This group had been landowners for several generations, and held considerable political power in the county, electing one of the state's first Black magistrates after the voter registration drives associated with the civil rights movement of the 1950s. A larger mainland group was much poorer, having held land no more than one generation. This mainland group had little education and, for the most part, was confined to domestic and laboring jobs. The most heavily creolized language in the entire Black speech community was found in this portion of the population.

In contrast, the island residents had been largely independent of the powerful white landowners in the county since the end of the Civil War, when an ex-slave acquired land from his former owner. Although the majority of land on the island was still owned by whites, no permanent resident of the island was white. The majority of Black residents had gradually acquired land over the past hundred years, until virtually all Blacks living on the island belonged to some household which owned land there. Communal rice farming had been the basis of the economy up until three decades ago, when floods ruined the crop several years in a row. By the 1950s, motorized transportation was widely available, and many island residents took jobs off the island as construction workers and as domestic laborers. Operating from a stronger economic base, island residents were generally wider traveled than the poorer mainland group, and thus had wider exposure to a variety of dialects. The speech of island residents was less creolized than that of the poorer mainland group, but less standardized than that of the educated elite on the mainland. All but one island-born adult could read and write, and many had completed high school. Most of the men held jobs as bricklayers, carpenters, or electricians in the construction industry. Women worked as domestics in mainland homes and motels, as sales clerks, and—in one case—as a mail carrier. A few island women were teachers, but they no longer lived on the island because of the difficult daily commute over two miles of river. A decade earlier, the island had had its own elementary school, staffed by island teachers, but this had closed as the county consolidated small schools into larger ones. Children now commuted daily to mainland schools, as did the adults to their mainland jobs.

Because of their wide contacts off the island, residents generally had exposure to a wide range of language use. Within this community of some 200 residents, however, certain sub-groups were making different choices from the range of linguistic options available to them. These differences were strongly evident among young people who attended the weekly writing class. Because the population of the island was comprised of one social class and one ethnic group, the major social differences among them were age and sex.

In the age group from fifteen to twenty-five, members of the writing class differed most sharply in their language use along sex lines. Of basically the same age and family background, these young people showed different levels of competence in the use of standard written English. Sisters were uniformly better able to use conventional spelling, punctuation, and sentence structure than were their brothers. Young men attended the class in equal numbers with young women and often had insightful things to say about the topics assigned for composition, but their use of standard English was much less sure than that of the young women in the group.

Observing the daily performance of younger children from the island in the elementary classroom, I noted that the sex difference in language use began to be apparent at about the age of ten. One young island woman gave supporting evidence for this observation, from her own memory of "running with her brothers" in daily activities on the island until the age of ten. At that age, her mother told her that she was now a "young lady," with responsibilities that involved participating in certain activities within the home and spending less time outside with the boys. From tape-recorded stories told by island children of six to twelve years of age, I was able to document the change toward standard English on the part of all island children attending the mainland school, with girls showing more rapid movement in this direction than boys. Letters written to me by boys and girls who were ten at the time of the study show maintenance of this sex difference. Girls who were ten at that time used some creole constructions in their letters; now at the age of sixteen, some of them are writing in standard English, with no indication of their original creole language variety. Boys of the same age have become more standard in their writing, but their language use still reflects original creole language constructions in syntax and morphology.

Recorded interviews of island adults showed similar patterns of language use among the young and middle-aged women, while older women spoke more like the men in their age group. From observation of the daily activities of island adults, I determined that their ages fell into three social groupings: older adults over sixty-five who no longer worked outside the home and remained on the island most of the day; middle-aged adults between thirty and fifty who had growing families and commuted daily to jobs on the mainland; young adults between fifteen and twenty-five, usually not yet married, who engaged in frequent school and social activities with each other. All adults on the island participated in weekly interaction with each other at the regular island church services and meetings; most interacted with smaller groups on the daily boat rides to and from the mainland and on walks from the boat landing to their homes.

I recorded individual speakers in natural conversation with me in their own homes, often in the presence of other family members and friends, and always with the full knowledge and consent of the participants. In these conversations, men and women of the three different age groups were represented from the island population, and from the two older groups in the mainland population. The recorded interviews were supplemented by extensive observation and participation in speech events within the island and the mainland communities, and in groups which included both children and adult speakers as participants. Notes were taken on as many of these events as possible, where recording was not feasible. Examples of written language use were obtained from the younger portion of island and mainland populations, in the form of short essays in the island writing class and in the form of letters from many of the mainland children after completion of the initial field work.

From a total of twenty-two interviews, twelve from the community on the river island and four from the community on the mainland were selected for close analysis of the occurrence of linguistic variables. Three morphosyntactic variables were chosen for analysis: (1) the third person singular pronoun; (2) a complementizer or infinitive marker; (3) a locative pronoun meaning "position at." From observations in this contemporary Black speech community, as well as from earlier studies of Gullah made by Turner (1949) and Cunningham (1970), I determined that use of standard forms for these variables would constitute innovative behavior for the communities under study and would represent language change in the direction of the standard. For a more detailed linguistic analysis, see Nichols (1976).

Examples of the older creole usage for these variables are as follows:

I. third person singular pronouns
    ee - "he, she, it, his, her, its"
    um - "him, her, it"
    1. *ee* must-a hide in them-wood or something. (he)
    2. Miss Hassell had—*ee* had all kinds of flowers. (she)
    3. and *ee* was foggy, and they couldn't see. (it)
    4. he took *ee* mother 'long with um. (his)
    5. but I ain't see she fuh tell *um* nothing. (her)
    6. I ain't know fuh get *um* off. (it)

II.   complementizer
      fuh - "to"
      7. I come *fuh* get my coat.
III. locative preposition
      to - "at"
      8. Can we stay *to* the table?

For each speaker, the total possible frequency for each of the three selected grammatical variables was tabulated and compared with his or her actual use of creole and nonstandard variants during the course of the interview. Table 1 shows these figures for island men and women in the three age groups. Included, as well, are figures for four older men and women in the lower socioeconomic group on the mainland.

Table 1

Speaker	Preposition %	Preposition N	Pronouns %	Pronouns N	Complementizer %	Complementizer N	Overall c/ns %	Sex groups c/ns %f	Sex groups c/ns %m
Mainland									
old adults									
1f	100	(7)	39	(87)	66	(12)	68		
2f	90	(20)	79	(101)	65	(26)	78		
3m	70	(10)	15	(103)	20	(5)	35		
4m	50	(4)	47	(15)	0	(3)	32		
Total:							53	73	34
Island									
old adults									
5f	57	(7)	14	(50)	43	(7)	38		
6m	67	(6)	3	(68)	0	(7)	23		
7m	70	(10)	23	(96)	11	(28)	35		
8m	70	(10)	39	(66)	6	(30)	39		
Total:							34	31	37
middle adults									
9f	0	(1)	0	(19)	0	(7)	0		
10f	25	(4)	0	(48)	0	(7)	8		
11m	30	(10)	14	(125)	0	(24)	15		
12m	86	(7)	6	(49)	0	(11)	31		
Total:							8	4	23
young adults									
13f	100	(2)	0	(5)	0	(3)	33		
14f	0	(15)	0	(114)	0	(36)	0		
15m	100	(4)	40	(5)	17	(12)	52		
16m	100	(1)	8	(66)	17	(12)	42		
Total:							32	17	47

N = number of possible occurrences; f = female speaker; m = male speaker; c = creole variants; ns = nonstandard variants

The data in Table 1 are presented in terms of the percentage of creole and nonstandard variants used by individual speakers, age groups, and males and females within a given age group. The higher the percentage, the more creolized the speech. For island residents, men and women in the oldest age group use approximately the same percentage of creolized speech. Young and middle-aged women use the least, making their speech the most standard in the group and, in terms of the norms of the speech community, the most innovative. Young men use the most creolized speech of all island residents, making them the most conservative members of the group. This fact is particularly interesting in view of the close family relationships between several speakers, represented in Table 1. In the young adult group, Speaker 13 and Speaker 15 are sister and brother; Speaker 9 and Speaker 11 in the middle-aged group are their mother and father, respectively. The other two young adults, Speaker 14 and Speaker 16, are also sister and brother; their father is Speaker 12 in the middle-aged group. The two men in the middle-aged group are next-door neighbors on the island, but Speaker 12 is much less widely traveled; his more heavily creolized speech reflects that fact.

In general, the amount of travel and exposure to a wide range of language varieties affects the percentage of creolized speech *within gender groups,* but not across them. Of the two young adult females, both have attended the mainland high school, but Speaker 14, with no creole and nonstandard variants, holds a job after school as a sales clerk in a mainland store. In this job she interacts with tourists from all over the east coast. Of the two young adult males, Speaker 15 still attended high school at the time of the study, while Speaker 16 had completed it. Speaker 16 sometimes worked as a waiter in a mainland restaurant and often helped his mother with a mail delivery route as well; he shows slightly less creolized speech than his younger friend. Despite his extensive exposure to mainland speech varieties, however, Speaker 16 shows far more creolized speech than his sister, Speaker 14. The same is true, to a lesser extent, for the husband and wife pair, Speakers 9 and 11. Although he has traveled and lived off the island to a far greater extent than his wife, Speaker 11 uses some creole and nonstandard variants while his wife uses none. We may conclude, then, that exposure to other language varieties has some effect on individual speech patterns, but membership in a particular gender group is the more influential factor, for the young and middle-aged groups.

In the older age group on the island, men and women use approximately the same degree of creolized speech. This is true, despite the fact that one of the women, Speaker 6, had both a mother and an aunt who had attended college, while one of the men, Speaker 8, had had no schooling at all and was illiterate. All speakers in this group had worked off the island for some portion of their lives, and all except Speaker 5 had lived in mainland communities for portions of their lives. While members of this group had all had exposure to other speech varieties, this exposure seemed to have no gender-related effect on their language use, as was the case for young and middle-aged adults.

This difference between the age groups is related to social changes which have had a greater influence on the younger adults than on the older generation. Only in the adult lifetimes of the middle-aged women have jobs beyond those of domestic or farm laborer and teacher been available to Black women in the rural South. The newly available jobs of sales clerk and mail carrier entail extensive interaction with a diverse tourist population which visits the South Carolina coast between March and Novermber each year. Older women often worked in motels as maids for this same tourist population, but these jobs required little language interaction. Men of all age groups, on the other hand, work at jobs that require little use of standard English. Older men had worked in lumber camps in a nearby town; middle-aged men now hold jobs as carpenters and bricklayers in the construction industry, and their sons often work with them. Only Speaker 16 of the younger adult males has taken a job that requires some interaction with a diverse public, and his language use in island contexts has not changed toward the standard variety. Men from the island often work with each other on their mainland jobs, while the jobs of island women tend to be isolated from other island women and from other members of the larger Black speech community. The island speech patterns, therefore, are more likely to be maintained in male work groups than in the isolated female jobs characteristic of the contemporary community.

In contrast, among mainland adults from the poorer socioeconomic group, females have occupational patterns that lead to maintenance of older speech patterns. In this segment of the mainland population, older adults rarely had any formal schooling, and most could neither read nor write. As illiterates, women were much more confined to their immediate communities than were men. As shown by Table 1, older mainland women use more than twice as many creole and nonstandard variants as older mainland men, showing the highest percentage of these forms of all speakers interviewed. Speaker 1 and Speaker 3 had been born on the same original plantation and both had worked there for a portion of their lives. The male, Speaker 3, however, had attended the plantation school and was much more widely traveled than the woman, Speaker 1—working in town as a laborer in the local steel mill during his middle years. She, on the other hand, had been confined to jobs in the immediate vicinity of the plantation, working a farm laborer, as a domestic in homes of white landowners, and as a cook in a seafood cannery. Both had acquired land on or near the original plantation. Speaker 2 and Speaker 4 had worked on another plantation in the area for all of their adult lives, living in homes provided by the owner. The woman, Speaker 2, had been born on this plantation as the daughter of a former slave and had lived there all her life, working in the owner's house as a domestic. The man had moved to the plantation as a young man in his twenties and had lived there ever since, caring for the horses and farm equiment. Neither was widely traveled.

Language use patterns within the Black speech community suggest that, where educational and occupational opportunities are limited, women will show more conservative linguistic behavior than men in their group. When these opportunities begin to expand, they do so along sex-segregated lines. White-collar jobs in sales, nursing, and elementary school teaching are opening up primarily for women, in part because of the low salaries associated with such jobs. Somewhat paradoxically, such jobs are also ones that require knowledge and use of standard English, even heavy investment in higher education. Blue-collar jobs in construction work traditionally have been more available to men than to women. While paying far more than the white-collar jobs held by many women, these blue-collar jobs now open to Black men require little or no use of the standard language variety, either in speaking or writing. Thus, when occupational opportunities begin to expand, men and women must engage in different kinds of preparation in order to take advantage of them. Why might women adopt innovative linguistic patterns associated with the new white-collar jobs, even though the income produced at these jobs is so much less than that of men in jobs requiring no linguistic adjustment or formal education investment?

The answer to why women adopt innovative linguistic behavior lies, I think, in the incentives provided by the new occupational opportunities. Data from the 1970 census indicate that the median salary for Black women in rural South Carolina is less than half that for Black men. Almost all Black women in the area work for a good portion of their lives, and the incentive to prepare for the best-paying jobs available is great. Families often make great sacrifices to send daughters to college, recognizing the importance of their earning power to the family; one middle-aged man from the island had paid for the education of two sisters through his work in construction. Men, on the other hand, have little incentive to attend college or even to take academic courses in high school seriously. As one young man from the island explained, men can make more laying brick than women can make teaching school. He saw little sense in attending college except for something "big," like becoming a doctor. For related reasons, men have little incentive to learn the standard language variety. For young island men, the choice of the creole language variety of their childhood is one which reinforces their sense of group identity and a way of life important to them, and it is in no way incompatible with the present occupational choices available to them.

For the island community, the long history of land ownership provides an economic base which enables women to take advantage of expanded job opportunities requiring heavy investment in formal education. While island men are supportive of their efforts in this direction, these men have far less incentive to change either their linguistic patterns or their traditional educational goals in a similar way.

OTHER STUDIES OF WOMEN'S SPEECH

One of the most widely held beliefs about the language behavior of women is that they are more sensitive to and make greater use of standard-prestige features than men. (See Lakoff, 1975, for a recent expression of this belief.) In the United States, "standard-prestige" English is generally taken to be that variety used by news broadcasters on the major networks; other English-speaking nations have slightly different standards. The use of features characteristic of the standard-prestige variety of English has generally been taken to represent conservative linguistic behavior, in contrast to the present study where the use of standard English represents innovative behavior, in terms of the norms of the speech community.

Some recent sociolinguistic studies have found that women who are conservative in some aspects of their speech may be innovative in other aspects, presenting a paradox for the researcher who tries to explain their behavior (Labov, 1972; Trudgill, 1974). Labov and Trudgill have labeled them "linguistically insecure,"[1] while Shuy has suggested that women must remain for linguists "one of the mysteries of the universe" (Shuy, 1970). More recently, in addressing the place of women in linguistic change, Labov (1978) argued that the cases where women are innovative and lead in change represent changes in the system, while cases where men lead in change represent isolated retrograde movement. All of these explanations are inadequate, primarily because they assume that women behave as some sort of universal speech group, rather than as members of specific speech communities who make choices in terms of the linguistic options available to them within those communities.

A major flaw common to most sociolinguistic studies of the past two decades is the assumption that women are automatically members of the same social class as their husbands (or father, if they have no husband). That unquestioned assumption underlies methods used by sociolinguists to study language use in urban communities throughout the United States and Europe (Labov, 1966; Levine & Crockett, 1967; Shuy, Wolfram, & Riley, 1968; Wolfram, 1969; Nordberg, 1973). Although Trudgill (1972; 1974) does include information on individual women's occupational and educational status in his description of sex-differentiated language use in Norwich, England, he fails to provide information on the distribution of men and women by social class. Thus we have no way of knowing at which social rank women are using these standard-prestige features. In other studies, the finding that wives use more standard language than their husbands (or than other men considered to be in the same class as their husbands) has been taken as "proof" that women use more standard language than men.

As early as 1951, sociologists were questioning the widely held assumption that husbands and wives are equal socially. In a now-classic essay on women as a minority group, Hacker (1951: 64) observed that marriage may not represent the point of minimum social distance, but almost the reverse: ". . . a dominant group member may be willing to marry a member of a group which, in general, he would not wish admitted to his social club." Watson and Barth (1964) and Acker (1973) have questioned the unexamined assumptions, underlying all current models of social stratification, that the occupation of head of household is a major index of an entire family's social class and that the family is the primary social unit. Haug (1973) analyzed data from the 1970 U.S. census on working couples, and she suggests that the common practice of using only the husband's occupation as a major indicator of social class may have resulted in the misclassification of as many as one-third of all families in the United States. Particularly at the lower end of the social scale, women tend to hold jobs which are higher on the social scale than those held by their husbands. We have seen this tendency reflected in the job patterns for young and middle-aged women in the Black speech community. Haug also found that, among working couples, women more often than not outrank men educationally. Except for the very oldest generation, more than half the wives in her study had more education than their husbands.

Haug's study and others summarized in Acker (1980) call into question the relevance of traditional social stratification models for the lives of women. Acker (1980: 33) concludes that "stratification theory has been a theory of white males," observing that the concept of *class* has been built on under-standings of the socioeconomic world as lived by men. Linguistic studies that assign women to social classes based on questionable sociological models will reveal little about the comparative language use of women and men.

For the linguist seeking to correlate language use with social position, a model of social interaction that focuses more sharply on life experiences that necessitate language use would seem to be most appropriate. Where a particular occupation falls on some scale of prestige or desirability matters less for language use than the kind and extent of language use characteristic of that occupation. Social network theory, used by Bott (1956) to study differences between families of ostensibly the same social classes and by Gal (1978) to study differences in men and women's language shift in a farming village, seems to provide a more adequate model for the study of sex-differential language use than does traditional social stratification theory. Sankoff and Laberge (1978) have attempted to modify traditional occupational rankings to take account of the "linguistic market," or the extent to which the standard language variety is used within occupational groups. Whether such a modification of social stratification theory proves more feasible than the ethnographic approach of social network theory is a matter for future exploration. What seems clear is that future studies of sex-differentiated language can no longer rely on traditional sociological models of social class if their results are to have any validity.

Even within the traditional stratification framework, a few linguistic studies have contradicted the general finding that women use more standard-prestige features than men in their groups. In a study of the Black working class of Washington, D. C., Fasold (1972) found either no difference, or slightly greater use of standard forms by males. Wolfram and Christian (1976) found little difference in the use of standard forms in the Appalachian Mountains of West Virginia, although women avoided socially stigmatized features to some extent. In a recent study of white speech in an Alabama city and countryside, Feagin

(1979) found no difference for upper class urban speakers, but some expected and some unexpected differences for working class speakers. Teenagers in this class showed the expected differences, with girls using more standard speech than boys. The speech of rural men was slightly more nonstandard than that of rural women, as expected, but urban working class women used more non-standard speech than men in their group. Feagin suggests that lack of exposure to prestige forms might account for the less standard speech of urban working class women. Another explanation might be that advanced for the Black community described here: like poor women in the inner city of Washington, in the mountains of West Virginia, and in the swamps of South Carolina, poor women in Alabama have had little opportunity or incentive to *use* standard-prestige forms in the course of their daily activities.[2]

CONCLUSION

Linguists have long understood that the interaction of language and social life has important consequences for linguistic behavior (Ferguson, 1959; Hymes, 1967, 1973). Hymes observes that inequality among speakers arises because some speakers participate in social situations not available to other speakers. If men and women have differentiated social roles within society, we must expect language use to reflect that fact. If their life experiences are sharply different, their speech will be different. However, the ways and extent to which they differ can be expected to vary from social group to social group. In some speech communities, men or sub-groups of men may exhibit more conservative linguistic behavior than women; in others, the reverse may be true. The linguistic choices made by both men and women are always constrained by the options available to them, and these options are available always and only in the context of a group which shares rules for the use and interpretation of language. To speak of "women's language" outside that context is linguistically naive.

NOTES

1. The term "linguistic flexibility" to describe the linguistic behavior in question has been suggested by Suzanne Roff-Lowe.

2. I am currently studying the language use of an all-white rural community in South Carolina, located approximately twenty miles from the Black speech community described here. In this community, also undergoing large-scale social change (in this case associated with the influx of a more widely traveled population from a nearby military base), I am finding older women to speak more like men in their age group, while younger women use considerably more standard speech than the young men with whom they played as children.

REFERENCES

Acker, Joan. 1973. Women and social stratification: A case of intellectual sexism. *American Journal of Sociology,* 78, 936–45.

——— 1980. Women and stratification: A review of recent literature. *Contemporary Sociology,* 9, 25–39.

Bott, Elizabeth. 1956. Urban families: Conjugal roles and social network. *Human Relations,* 8, 345–84.

Cunningham, Irma A. E. 1970. *A syntactic analysis of Sea Island creole (Gullah).* Ph. D dissertation, Univ. of Michigan, Ann Arbor.

Fasold, Ralph. 1972. *Tense marking in Black English: A linguistic and social analysis.* Washington, D.C.: Center for Applied Linguistics.

Feagin, Crawford. 1979. *Variation and change in Alabama English: A sociolinguistic study of the white community.* Georgetown Univ. Press.

Ferguson, Charles A. 1959. Diglossia. *Word,* 15, 325–40.

Gal, Susan. 1978. Peasant men can't get wives: Language change and sex roles in a bilingual community. *Language in Society,* 7, 1-16.

Hacker, Helen Mayer. 1951. Women as a minority group. *Social Forces,* 30, 60–69.

Haug, Marie R. 1973. Social class measurement and women's occupational roles. *Social Forces,* 52, 86–98.

Hymes, Dell. 1967. Models of the interaction of language and social setting. *Journal of Social Issues,* 23, 8–28.

——— 1972. Models of the interaction of language and social life. In J. Gumperz & D. Hymes (eds.), *Directions in sociolinguistics.* New York: Holt, Rinehart, and Winston.

——— 1973. On the origins and foundations of inequality among speakers. *Daedalus,* 102, 59–86.

Joyner, Charles Winston. 1977. *Slave folklife on the Waccamaw Neck: Antebellum Black culture in the South Carolina lowcountry.* Ph.D. dissertation, Univ. of Pennsylvania, Philadelphia.

Labov, William. 1966. *The social stratification of English in New York City.* Washington, D.C.: Center for Applied Linguistics.

——— 1972. *Sociolinguistic patterns.* Philadelphia: Univ. of Pennsylvania Press.

——— 1978. The role of women in linguistic change. Paper given at the annual meeting of the Linguistic Society of America, Boston, December 28–30, 1978.

Lakoff, Robin. 1975. *Language and woman's place.* New York: Harper & Row.

Levine, Lewis & Harry J. Crockett, Jr. 1967. Speech variation in a Piedmont community: Postvocalic *r.* In S. Lieberson (ed.), *Explorations in sociolinguistics.* Bloomington: Indiana Univ. Press.

Nichols, Patricia C. 1976. Black women in the rural South: Conservative and innovative. In B. L. Dubois & I. Crouch (eds.), *Papers in Southwest English, IV: The sociology of the languages of American women.* San Antonio, Texas: Trinity Univ.

——— 1978. Black women in the rural South: Conservative and innovative. *International Journal of the Sociology of Language,* 17, 45–54.

Nordberg, Bengt. 1973. Contemporary variation as a stage in a long-term phonological change. Rapport NR 28, Forskningskommitten I Uppsala· för Modern Svenska. Uppsala Univ., Uppsala, Sweden.

Piddington, Ralph. 1960. Action anthropology. *Journal of the Polynesian Society,* 69, 199–213.

Sankoff, David & Suzanne Laberge. 1978. The linguistic market and the statistical explanation of variability. In David Sankoff (ed.), *Linguistic variation: Models and methods.* New York: Academic Press.

Shuy, Roger. 1970. Sociolinguistic research at the Center for Applied Linguistics: The correlation of language and sex. International Days of Sociolinguistics. Rome: Instituto Luigi Sturzo, 849–57.

Shuy, Roger, Walt Wolfram, & William K. Riley. 1968. *Field techniques in an urban language study.* Washington, D.C.: Center for Applied Linguistics.

Tax, Sol. 1958. The Fox Project. *Human Organization,* 17, 17–19.

Trudgill, Peter. 1972. Sex, covert prestige and linguistic change in the urban British English of Norwich. *Language in Society,* 1, 179–95.

——— 1974. *The social differentiation of English in Norwich.* Cambridge: Cambridge Univ. Press.

Turner, Lorenzo D. 1949. *Africanisms in the Gullah dialect.* Chicago: Univ. of Chicago Press.

U. S. Bureau of the Census. 1973. Subject reports: Negro population. *1970 Census of Population.*

Watson, Walter & Ernest Barth. 1964. Questionable assumptions in theory of social stratification. *Pacific Sociological Review,* 7, 10–16.

Wittgenstein, Ludwig. 1969. *Philosophical investigations,* 3rd ed. Translated by G. E. M. Anscombe. New York: Macmillan. (First published in 1953.)

Wolfram, Walt. 1969. *A sociolinguistic description of Detroit Negro speech.* Washington, D.C.: Center for Applied Linguistics.

Wolfram, Walt & Donna Christian. 1976. Appalachian speech. Center for Applied Linguistics.

Wood, Peter H. 1974. *Black majority: Negroes in colonial South Carolina from 1670 through the Stono Rebellion.* New York: Alfred A. Knopf.

INTONATION IN A MAN'S WORLD*

Sally McConnell-Ginet

"If one were to examine the literature on men's and women's speech, one would conclude that it was a rare phenomenon, found mostly among extinct American Indian tribes. It has been reported mostly by linguists who were also anthropologists, for cases in which the grammar or phonology of the language could be stated only by taking it into account. Working out from ordinary linguistics then, one would have to conclude that in most societies men and women talk alike. That is a strange conclusion to arrive at, if language is a social instrument, given the importance of role differentiation along sexual lines in most times and places and it is a false conclusion of course." (Hymes, 1971: 69).

When Dell Hymes made these comments, the literature on women's and men's way of speaking could probably have been read in a fortnight. Since that time, there has been an explosion in the study of sex-differentiated linguistic behavior, and few people interested in language use any longer assume that women and men "talk alike" in most societies. We are still, however, at a very early stage in our understanding of how women and men speak, why they speak as they do, and the importance of language use for women in "a man's world." We have only recently begun to realize that social constraints on speech behavior may restrict women's and men's options and that such constraints function in the control of women. Recent investigations in this area are largely the product of feminist scholars' concern to understand how talk works to create and maintain sex-stereotyping and male dominance.[1] Our speech not only reflects our place in culture and society but also helps to create that place.

"Ordinary linguistics," as Hymes calls it, provides theories and descriptions of structured language systems—e.g., an account of the regular syntactic relation between English declaratives ("Joan *ate* the spinach with gusto") and interrogatives ("*Did* Joan *eat* the spinach with gusto?") or of the processes involved in pronunciation of "want to" as "wanna." Such general features of English are part of the system acquired by both women and men, although one

*This is a revised version of a paper which appeared in *Signs: Journal of Women in Culture and Society,* Spring 1978, 3, 541–59. I want to thank Cheris Kramarae and Barrie Thorne for their helpful suggestions on this version.

sex might, for example, more frequently choose to use an interrogative form or a verbal contraction in certain contexts. If women always said "wanna" and men "want to," we would speak of sex differences in a low-level phonetic rule for speech production, but if each sex understood the equivalence of the forms, the basic structural systems underlying women's and men's linguistic knowledge would be identical. What I call "extraordinary" linguistics—the explicit and detailed characterization of the actual utterances of people situated in real social contexts—relies on standard linguistic accounts of the language systems in which those utterances are cast. In other words, we can't make much progress in describing socially significant differences in language use (the case of present interest to us being the interaction of language and sex) without a framework within which we can say explicitly what it is that "differs."[2]

Intonation—the tune to which we set the text of our talk—functions prominently in stereotypes of female and male speech in American English. In "ordinary linguistics," intonational structures are far less well understood than, for example, syntactic structures. This is connected to the fact that members of the speech community have a less well-developed and clearly articulated conscious awareness of tunes than of texts. Our writing system, for example, ignores intonation. (A small caveat is in order: punctuation and italics are sometimes rough indicators of intonational features.) We also don't find parents "correcting" children's intonational patterns as they sometimes do syntax or word choices. This somewhat peripheral status of intonation in the linguistic system may help to explain why speech melodies seem to be sex-typed. Over and above literal message content, tunes and their variations do apparently convey (cultural) values of femininity and masculinity as well as other traits that are culturally linked to gender (emotionality, for example).

Although not all aspects of how speech melodies are performed are relevant to describing the structured language systems, some certainly are. What we do know about the linguistic structure of intonation in American English also makes plausible the hypothesis that the basic intonational system might be used differently by women and men. Analysts agree that intonational patterns in American English are frequently used to convey "illocutionary force"— whether, for example, the speaker is framing an utterance as a question or as an assertion—and certain other aspects of the speaker's "attitude." Thus, intonational choices will be among the primary indicators of a speaker's aims and of the speech strategies used to pursue those aims. Given a sociocultural system in which women and men are in different social networks and positions and in which their behavior is differently evaluated, we might predict that intonational usage would be an important constituent of sex-differentiated "styles" of speaking.[3] This applies whether such "styles" are normative ideals, disparaged stereotypes, or attested actualities. Many actual sex differences in favored strategies of language use in particular contexts are due to male dominance of women; they often represent women's attempts to "cope" with social restrictions. Women's lives consist of more than their relations to men, however, and thus women's ways of talking will be influenced by factors unconnected to male dominance. Intonational studies help shed light on the complex interaction of language and women's experience.

A single speech melody can be performed as part of a number of quite different strategies and thus its occurrence is not definitive evidence of any particular strategic orientation. Similarly, there can be many different reasons for performing a particular melody in a certain way, for selecting one "variant" rather than another. A major thesis of this paper is that most discussions of intonational usages have assumed an androcentric perspective. The significance attributed to women's tunes has typically failed to take into account the complex range of possibilities that emerge when women's experiences and their viewpoints are seriously considered.

This androcentric perspective is manifest in two distinct but related ways. First, male-created stereotypes of what women are like are relied on both to shape beliefs about what tunes occur and to interpret and evaluate the tunes that are actually heard. Second, frameworks for analyzing the significance of particular speech melodies do not take account of women's distinctive experiences; in particular, there is a tendency to assume that men's behavior is paradigmatic of human behavior. On the one hand, women are seen as fundamentally unlike men—"feminine" speech melodies are heard as signaling women's instability (often, incompetence) and as symbolic of their devalued "naturalness." On the other hand, such interpretations rest on the untenable assumption that women's and men's life histories are identical, that there are no differences in the ways they have come to speak as they habitually do and have come to adopt the strategies they typically employ.

Women's speech is discounted in a man's world primarily on the basis of "how" it is said—the tunes used (and other features of "style"). The substance of female texts—"what" is said—is frequently ignored or (mis)interpreted in light of hearers' assessments of the significance of the forms in which those texts are delivered. The problem, of course, is not in the melodies or their performers but in the interpreters.

The following section reviews both empirical research and anecdotal suggestions about how the sexes "sound" and, in particular, how both women and men use and interpret intonational patterns. The final section sketches a framework for explaining these observations and for further refining and testing specific hypotheses about the interaction of intonation and speaker/hearer gender.

INTONATION: "IT'S NOT WHAT SHE SAYS BUT HOW SHE SAYS IT"

Many distinct pheonomena are included under everyday uses of the term "intonation" (often equated, in nontechnical discussions, with "tone of voice"). Intonation does not characterize segments of sound but is perceived as a rhythmic structure "overlaid" on a complete utterance. The main perceptual cues are pitch and volume changes over the course of an utterance. The language system does not recognize absolute values of pitch, volume, and duration but rather a number of abstract relational patterns, each of which can be "realized" in different registers, in different volumes, and at different rates. These *variants*—alternative ways of performing basic intonational contours—play a role (only partly conventionalized) in communication. What variant is used may tell us, for example, where the speaker is from, or whether she just woke up, or whether he is lecturing to a class or talking to a friend, or how interested in the conversation the speaker wishes to appear.

Sex differences in speech are basically of two kinds. The first is what I have just called *variation:* alternative ways of uttering the "same" linguistic unit. For intonation, this amounts to different ways of playing a single tune. The English intonational pattern which is commonly called the "question intonation" ends with a pitch rise to a point higher than earlier pitch levels in the sentence. There are, however, many variations possible on this one basic pattern. We might investigate whether women tend to make this final pitch rise relatively larger than men (rising more tones) in certain contexts. When answering the phone, perhaps she says

$$H^{e^{l^{l^{o}}}}$$

whereas he says

$$H^{e^{l^{lo}}}$$

These are different versions or *variants* of the general pattern often notated as "Hello ↑," a pattern some analysts call "high-rise" to indicate that it may occur on utterances that are not questions.

The second kind of sex difference that can be manifest in speech involves different *selection* among the basic structural units—that is, different uses of the common system. By this I mean that women and men might tend to choose somewhat different strategies for speaking in roughly comparable situations. For example, a women might more often than a man answer the phone with a "Hello ↑." He might, however, tend to prefer "Hello ↓" (the fall or "neutral" intonation). These two intonational contours or tunes are quite distinct linguistically—they are *not* variations on a single melodic frame but different tunes altogether. To use one rather than the other is to engage in a different linguistic action; to act differently in roughly comparable situations is to pursue different strategies.

To put it slightly differently, we can think of the intonational system as including a "dictionary" of meaningful tunes, an inventory of meaningful contours. Two people with the same internal dictionary can nonetheless have different patterns of usage. Where different pronunciations of a single intonational "word" occur in different frequencies in the speech of two individuals, their usage reflects *variation*-based differences. Where the frequency of occurrence of particular "words" differs in some context, then the difference is *selection*-based. Frequencies of " ↑ " compared to " ↓ " reflect selection; the "slope" of the rising (or falling) contour is subject to variation. (The distinction is by no means always easy to draw, but I confine attention to clear cases.)

Since any basic linguistic unit can be acquired by any speaker, all intonational (and other) differences in the speech of the sexes with a physiological explanation are variation-based. There are probably a few such differences. Adult men tend to be larger than adult women and thus their basic instrument for speech is pitched in a somewhat lower register. The larger vocal cords tend to vibrate more slowly, producing sounds which are lower in fundamental frequency (measured in units called hertz, abbreviated Hz) and thus heard as lower pitched. There is actually considerable overlap between the physiologically determined pitch ranges of adult female and male voices, but individuals seldom use in speech the full gamut of pitches they are capable of producing.

Still, although certain components of intonational differences between the sexes are a function of anatomical differences, it is clear that *sociocultural factors* also contribute significantly to establishing parameters of variation. Overt *speech stereotypes* of "feminine" or "masculine" speech (either believed typical of women and men, respectively, or desirable for them) rely most heavily on variants. This is probably because distinctions among variants do not alter overt referential meaning and are thus readily available as explicit signals of social meaning. What variants a speaker favors (within the range anatomical constraints permit) will depend on a number of factors: e.g., which variants are most frequently heard and under what situations, or which variants are favored by the people with whom one identifies.

Even dimensions of variation that are quite constrained by individual physical characteristics can be affected by social and cultural factors. For example, different cultures settle on different parts of the possible pitch range for actual use in speaking by each sex. The studies of H. T. Hollien and his colleagues suggest that the speaking pitches of American males are, on the average, lower than those of some of their European counterparts by more than differences in size would predict.[4] Devereux (1949) observes that the Mohave pay no attention to the male "voice change" at the time of puberty and that men do not shift pitch when imitating women. In our own culture, however, high-pitched voices are devalued and labeled "shrill" if they are loud. The fact that our speech melodies are sung in different registers, then, reflects not simply the biological fact of our different physical size but is also a product of our "learning" to sound like women and men, although we have relatively little information on exactly how this works.[5]

If average speaking pitch is an important cue to speaker sex, reflecting both biologically based differences and cultural stereotypes overlaid on that biological base, it is apparently *not* the primary cue for stereotyping speaker's gender. Sachs, Lieberman, and Erickson (1973), Sachs (1975), and Coleman (1976) show clearly that pitch is not crucial to the identification of speaker sex and that other vocal tract characteristics play an important role. Sachs and her colleagues first played recordings of elicited sentence imitations from pre-adolescent children to judges and found sex of child quite reliably assigned although overall the average fundamental frequency was higher for the boys' voices than for the girls. Matching girls and boys for height and weight (as a rough guide to probable vocal tract size and fundamental range), they found that vowel formant structure differed significantly for voices judged most reliably as "girl-like" or "boy-like." In subsequent studies, Sachs found judges able to discriminate sex on the basis of isolated vowels and of backwards speech but less reliably than from sentences, which suggests that intonational characteristics may also be operative.

Support for this hypothesis is provided by Bennet and Weinberg who found that "monotonicity had a deleterious effect on the perception of femaleness and an enhancing effect on the perception of maleness" (1979: 183) for judges (all female) of children's speech. Fichtelius, Johansson, and Nordin (1980) isolated intonational features by filtering speech to eliminate segmental information. The result is a signal in which words are no longer recognizable but rhythmic and pitch features of the original speech signal—the "suprasegmental" or "melodic" characteristics—are unaffected. Although they are tentative in reporting results on the basis of their limited study of Swedish-speaking children, they note that "[t]he acoustic variable showing the greatest covariation with the respondents' judgment of sex as well as the speakers' actual sex is the number of large frequency variations per time unit" (1980: 223). Again, both actual and perceived femaleness correlate with changing frequencies; i.e., with non-monotonicity.

Perhaps even more startling is Terango's (1966) finding that adult males whose speech was heard as "effeminate" by judges had, on the average, slightly *lower*-pitched voices than a matched group of males whom judges heard as non-remarkably "masculine" in their speech. Terango did find significant acoustic differences between the two sets of voices: the group heard as effeminate used a significantly wider *range* of speaking pitches and changed pitch more frequently.

My own informal observations suggest that when they imitate female speech, males (including young boys) emphasize intonational contours. Mimicry of female tunes shows pronounced and rapid pitch shifts (and probably also exaggerated shifts in intensity levels). Central to the stereotype of "feminine" speech is the use of a relatively wide pitch range with frequent and rapid long glides. To imitate a woman by using an extreme version of this sort of pattern may be seen as a hostile act, and Austin suggests that to imitate a man by assuming the "swoopy" patterns of the feminine stereotype is an extreme example of "derogatory imitation, one of the most infuriating acts of aggression one person can commit on another" (1965: 36).

Male intonational patterns do not seem to be imitated in a derogatory way, either in mocking of females or males. There are two possible reasons: (1) male intonations are heard as neutral—just as both sexes wear pants yet only women wear dresses, some patterns are heard as female while the rest are "unmarked" for sex; (2) men lose by sounding woman-like, whereas women do not lose (perhaps they even gain in some contexts) by sounding man-like.[6] This does not mean that the male patterns are necessarily highly valued. Nonetheless, there is an asymmetry in imitative behavior to be explained.

Impressionistic accounts of men who are self-consciously rejecting a prescribed masculine role often refer to the use of special intonations. Newton says of a female inpersonator: "The impression of femininity is conveyed more by the intonation, stress, and pronunciation than by the pitch itself. This intonation is parodying sweetness, rather mincing. It is a convincing imitation of affected female speech style" (1972: 72). Crystal (1971), a leading authority on English intonation, claims: "Intuitive impressions of effeminacy in English, for example, . . . are mainly [based on] non-segmental [features]: a 'simpering' voice, for instance, largely reduces to the use of a wider pitch-range than normal (for men), with *glissando* effects between stressed syllables, a more frequent use of complex tones (e.g. the fall-rise and the rise-fall), the use of breathiness and huskiness in the voice, and switching to a higher (falsetto) register from time to time" (1971: 189). From the Terango study and other accounts of speech effeminacy and derogatory imitation, we can hypothesize that certain intonational variants are stigmatized markers of "feminine" speech, indicating in male usage either overt flaunting of the code for sex-appropriate behavior (presenting oneself as "gay," for example) or a derogatory imitation of women. Informal observation in the language laboratory indicates that male students are sometimes loath to reproduce patterns in a second language that involve the long and rapid glides (especially if reversed on a single syllable) that they associate with female or effeminate speech in American English.[7]

Comparing male speech perceived as effeminate to characterizations of global differences in female/male speech suggests the likely intonational cues for judgments of speakers on a femininity/masculinity dimension. Overall, without reference to particular contexts or to individual differences, female and effeminate male speech are apparently distinguished from "ordinary" male speech in the following ways: the male pitch range is narrower than the female/effeminate and shows slower and less frequent pitch shifts. Amplitude changes—linked to loudness—are not mentioned but are probably also important, with female/effeminate speech registering more and greater shifts in amplitude. We can call this cluster of factors *dynamism* and say that female and effeminate male intonational variants are characteristically more dynamic than typical male patterns. By this I mean that we "hear" dynamism as "feminine," that dynamism is an especially salient cue to speaker gender.[8]

But do women (as a group) actually show different patterns of intonational variation from men? Is the stereotype of female speech a reflection (albeit exaggerated and distorted) of actual female speech melodies? The answer seems to be affirmative within a relatively small amount of systematically collected data. Takefuta, Jancosek, and Brunt (1972) had twelve female and twelve male speakers record ten sentences each, reading each sentence with different intonations, and found a significantly greater pitch shift in the female reading voices. Other reading studies suggest similar results, although it is unclear what the relation of oral reading styles is to ordinary speech.

Brend (1975), a linguist working in a tradition begun by Pike's (1946) landmark study of American English intonation, is one of the few to have addressed the question of sex differences in intonation from a linguist's perspective. She does not specify how her data were obtained nor whether she considered the interaction of sex with other sociolinguistic variables to arrive at her findings. Following Pike, she characterizes the patterns purportedly used by women as "polite and cheerful," "unexpectedness and surprise," "hesitation" (a pattern Pike suggests can indicate endearment, especially if used by a woman), "incomplete and unexpected." She summarizes her results as follows:

> Men consistently avoid certain intonation levels or patterns. They very rarely, if ever, use the highest level of pitch that women use. That is, it appears probable that most men have only three contrastive levels of intonation, while many women, at least, have four. Men avoid final patterns which do not terminate at the lowest level of pitch, and use a final, short upstep only for special effects . . . Although they also use short down-glides . . . they seem in general to avoid the one-syllable long pitch glides, and completely avoid the reverse glides on one syllable. (Brend, 1975: 86–87

Brend's way of describing the differences implies that the sexes have different language systems. In particular, the suggestion that few men but many women use four contrastive levels (implying distinct inventories of basic units) is probably more accurately put in terms of sex-preferred modes of variation. Some of the differences she points to, however, almost surely do involve sex-preferences in selections among available basic tune-forms. The variation-based differences noted by Brend fit with the dynamic complex already described.

Intonational tunes are a major means by which speakers express their emotional involvement in a particular exchange, their attitudes, and their general "stance" in the discourse. Bolinger (1970) has noted the difficult interpretive problem created by the fact that the same acoustic features can result either from a speaker's conscious manipulations or from internal phenomena not under the speaker's control. Thus, when we are judging data from groups of speakers who show differences in the intonational features associated with the expression of emotion, it is impossible to identify causal factors.

Keeping this in mind, it is noteworthy that the dynamic complex associated with the speech of women and effeminate males is also associated with emotional expressiveness. The degree of perceived emotion is strongly correlated with pitch range (at least for male speakers): the greater the range of pitches used, the greater degree of expressed emotion hearers perceive.[9] Thus, when compared as a group to men, women may well (simply on the basis of their dynamic pitch patterns) be heard as emotional. The patterns themselves may originate quite independently of their use in emotional expression, serving other purposes and having other causes. However, to be emotional is (in part) to express one's emotion. It is possible that part of women's *being* emotional in our culture derives from our *sounding* emotional. And we sound emotional because our everyday "tunes"—the patterns we use in ordinary circumstances where no extremes of emotion are felt or expressed—show a degree of dynamism found in men's tunes only in extraordinary circumstances of heightened emotional expression. Of course, the problem is that the culture does not simply categorize us as emotionally expressive (a positive and useful trait whose lack handicaps many males as well as some females) but also views us as unstable and unpredictable.

Whether or not expressed emotionality really bears any relation to the "predictability" of one's behavior is one unanswered question. Even were that relation to exist it would not imply a deficiency (unpredictability) to overcome; after all, behaving predictably is not necessarily desirable. However, though emotional expressiveness and its possible concomitants might not be handicaps were androcentric biases eliminated, the fact remains that one's intonational patterns are not really adequately expressive of emotions if they are heard in reference to a presumptive "ideal" that inadequately reflects usage of the entire speech community. The young male apparently "learns" to "sound masculine" (as he learns to "sound cool") whereas the culture believes that the young female is destined by her biological endowment to be at the mercy of inner psychic upheavals which produce her dynamic tunes. To some extent, such a belief simply reflects ignorance of the fact that intonational patterns are basically cultural constructs (different cultures using their own distinctive patterns and "meanings"), although they are "internalized" very early and not easily subject to conscious modification.

To make matters more complicated, intonation does have a "natural" base as well. The quickened breathing and muscular tension that accompany certain kinds of heightened emotion can have an effect on our speech melodies: increased fluctuations in respiration and muscular activity will produce more dynamic tunes. And many of the culture-specific "meanings" associated with particular melodies represent conventionalized metaphors that refer to the nonlinguistic ("natural") significance associated with certain features of melodies. For example, to keep the voice level, to speak in a "flat" monotone, requires suppression of certain "natural" physical impulses. It is thus a "natural" indicator of "control" over one's internal mechanisms. By extension, the style can come to signify "control" more generally and can be thus heard and evaluated that way. As Bolinger (1964) puts it, intonation is "around the edge of language." Because of this interplay between the natural and cultural "meanings," intonation is readily available and perhaps especially effective as a cultural symbol of woman's perceived greater "naturalness," one important aspect of which is the "free expression of her emotions."[10] This is easily perceived by male-dominated culture as a failure to control emotion and a reflection of her innate inferiority to the male. Of course, one could equally well emphasize the positive side of dynamic and expressive communicative behavior and suggest that many males apparently fail to achieve the expressive versatility of most females.

The connection of the female/male dynamic intonational stereotype with stereotyped emotionally expressive behavior could conceivably be explained as either physiologically based (e.g., due to purported inner homeostatic mechanisms that keep most males on a more even keel than most females) or socioculturally based (due to learned sex-typing of other kinds of emotionally expressive behavior such as crying) or both.[11] Note that I refer to "purported" homeostatic mechanisms; Barrie Thorne has reminded me that there is evidence from male pathology that it's not some inner "even keel" but a bottling-up or repression. It is still, of course, possible that females have a tendency to more internal volatility and that males are handicapped by a tendency toward internal stagnation. My own guess is that the contribution of biological factors is likely to be minuscule here. Whatever the ultimate finding on that score, it is clear that society and culture have played an enormous role in shaping our emotional expressiveness. The point of interest in the present discussion is that women *are* (culturally) emotional because they sound that way.

Dynamism, by and large, seems to derive from variation-based differences in women's speech compared to men's, although it is possible that selection-preferences also contribute to the general dynamic picture. (There are too little data to even begin to decide just what factors are involved.) Because of the significance attached to variants (e.g., as expressive of emotionality), however, it is quite possible for speakers to include variation-preferences as well as unit-selections as part of a particular strategic orientation toward speech. In particular, dynamism can be used as a positive resource for speakers. To sound highly emotional might enable one to attain ends not reachable by calm behavior if one is a subordinate, such as a child interacting with an adult or a woman with a man. And of course certain situations promote the expression of emotion: the care of a child puts greater demands on emotional expressiveness than repairing telephone lines.

In addition to dynamism as a dimension on which female intonations are said to differ from male, it is said that the sexes tend to favor different endings (often called "terminals" by linguists) for their tunes. According to Brend (1972), men avoid final patterns that do not terminate at the lowest level, using rising terminals only for special effects (whatever that might mean—they certainly do use such patterns). Pike (1946) also suggested that women were primary users of many patterns with final rise. In her informal descriptions, Eble (1972) mentions the "'whining, questioning, helpless' patterns, which are used predominantly by women." To use a rising terminal rather than a falling terminal is, as discussed above, to select a different basic "tune." A syntactic analogy is the choice between issuing directives in an interrogative form ("Would you put out the garbage?") or an imperative form ("Put out the garbage"). We impute different intended structural messages on the basis of the selection of units. Patterns of such differences indicate strategic orientations. The difficulty, of course, is determining what the intended messages are, since intonational "words" can either provide a "frame" for the text they carry or can have a meaning that is superimposed on (and largely independent of) that text. The discussion of a particular example that follows will illustrate these points.

The English high-rise or so-called "question" intonational pattern, as noted earlier, ends with a rising terminal that reaches a level higher than earlier parts of the utterance. Lakoff (1975) has claimed that women are more likely than men to use what she calls an "inappropriate question intonation," as in the following:

Husband: When will dinner be ready?
Wife: Six o'clock?

Lakoff claims that the wife's rising terminal indicates her failure to make a statement when discourse requires it, thus signaling uncertainty or lack of self-assertiveness. However, as was argued in McConnell-Ginet (1975), there are many alternative functions that this high-rise tune can be serving. The wife in the scenario may be heard as both stating and questioning. Her unexpressed question may be "why do you need to know?" or "are you listening to me?" or "do you want to eat earlier?" or any of a host of other possibilities. Or, less specifically than questioning, she may be simply indicating desire for a continuation of the discourse. Ladd (1980) argues that we need not appeal to "implicit" questioning but should understand the high-rise as conveying non-finality or incompleteness (of which tentativeness, doubt, and questioning are simply special instances).

Men certainly do use the high-rise intonational pattern to respond to questions for which they have the answer, and there is no evidence that such uses are heard as "effeminate" or even particularly hesitant or indecisive. Not surprisingly, those who favor this tune for virtually all utterances are probably heard as somewhat hesitant and non-assertive.[12] Although there may be more women than men with this habit, the reasons are unlikely to be found in the pattern's being associated with "femininity." If there are sex differences in this usage, they will arise because one sex has more need or liking than the other for this particular communicative ploy: accompanying one explicit speech act (roughly, declaring) with another, which is implicit questioning, or more generally, requesting some additional input from the other party to the exchange.

Do women and men actually tend to answer *Wh*-questions with different contours? (*Wh*-questions include "*when* will dinner be ready?," "*where* do you live?," "*what's* your name?") The answer seems to depend, as one might expect, on the nature of the communicative context. Edelsky (1979) compared use of high-rise, fall, and another pattern which she calls fall-rise. This fall-rise, called "low-rise" in McConnell-Ginet (1978), is heard as having a definite rising terminal, but it is not perceived as at all "incomplete" or "questioning" like the high-rise. Acoustically, its final rise usually stops at a point below some earlier high in the utterance. Schematically, we can contrast the three patterns as follows:

A. Hel$_{lo}$ Fall

B. Hel$_{lo}$ Fall-Rise or Low-Rise

C. Hel^{lo} High-Rise ("Question")

Edelsky's female and male subjects were not differentiated in their use of the high-rise. In contrast, pilot studies I have been conducting (McConnell-Ginet, 1978, gave a preliminary report) show women using more high-rise and more low-rise. Edelsky's study had interviewers approach people in a student union and ask "Where were you born?" or "What's your favorite color?," whereas our interviewers asked (in front of a campus landmark) "What building is this?" The Edelsky questions were survey in type; ours were the kind one expects from strangers. Whether or not this difference in the communicative context explains the different findings, it is clear that we need considerably more data from real communicative exchanges if we are to have any real insight into "how she says it" or, for that matter, "how he says it."

In addition, we need more systematic study of how tunes are interpreted. Edelsky's research has begun this by investigating the contribution of the three contours to evaluation of persons using them in response to the "Where were you born?" question. She found high-rise and fall associated with stereotypically "feminine" and "masculine" qualities, respectively, with the low-rise in between. For instance, judges heard a high-rise response as sociable whereas the fall was self-centered. (The study used the matched-guise technique so that, unbeknownst to experimental subjects, judgments were made of the same voice with different tunes.) How do judges arrive at such evaluations? My conjecture is that they figure out what sort of strategy would lead someone to speak "like that" in the hypothetical situation. Then they evaluate people on the basis of their opting for that strategy (and, thus, for that mode of speaking). This is, of course, an unsubstantiated claim which requires considerable elaboration and investigation. It is important, however, to consider somewhat more carefully than we have in the past the possible bases on which judges evaluate speech samples.[13] It is also improtant to find more direct tests of what speakers intend and hearers attribute to uses of particular tunes in a given situation.

Clarion calls to "further research" are easier to sound than to obey. One of the reasons intonation continues to baffle linguistic investigators—we still cannot adequately characterize "how she said it"—is that the tunes of speech shade into one another rather than being sharply distinguished like the sounds of speech. Traditional linguistic research—"ordinary linguistics" in Hymes's terms—deals with discrete entities, i.e., with "either-or" oppositions rather than "more-or-less" gradations. Where continuously varying parameters are significant, it is helpful to supplement human observations with instrumental measurements. We can also take advantage of such sophisticated machines as speech synthesizers to subject explicitly formulated hypotheses to controlled tests. I do not suggest that technology yields insight nor that carefully collected data are the magic key to understanding the role of intonation in women's and men's lives. But I do argue that, in order to understand the ways in which "how she said it" can work for and against her, we need to widen our descriptive base. Women certainly do not at all times in all places "talk in italics," to use Lakoff's phrase. We need to know when, where, and why does someone "talk like a woman," and, an obvious but often overlooked question, who talks "like a woman?" We also need to know how sex differences in intonation develop and what their consequences are for women's and men's lives.[14]

TOWARD A THEORY OF SEX DIFFERENCES IN INTONATION

"Ordinary linguistics" leaves unanswered many of the most interesting questions about the function of language in people's lives. Linguists have recently, however, expanded the horizons of "ordinary linguistics." This expansion is partly due to social and political pressures (originating in the civil rights movement of the 1960s and continuing in the women's movement) to understand how language is used to support the status quo and to serve the interests of the powerful. Such understanding can suggest strategies to change the status quo and can be used to increase appreciation of speech styles of subordinates. Even apart from such practical concerns, however, many linguists have begun to see that the "ordinary" linguistic practice of abstracting from the social context and focusing on a mythic "ideal" speaker in splendid isolation from other human beings, though a necessary part of linguistic analysis, is not enough to explain how language works. Unless language is put back into the social setting from which it is extracted for initial analysis, the processes of language change, for example, cannot be properly understood.[15] But even an expanded and "extraordinary" linguistics will not be able to answer all the issues raised by examining sex differences in language use. We must turn to other disciplines such as psychology, sociology, anthropology, and, more generally, women's studies scholarship. Because it requires sophistication in all these areas, a "general" theory of intonation (in a man's world or anywhere else) awaits future collaborative research. The following outlines a preliminary theoretical perspective on sex differences in intonation.

1. In oral communication speech melodies are primary cues of speaker sex.

2. The speech community explicitly associates certain intonational patterns with the speech of women. These patterns function as part of a cultural

stereotype and can be used in derogatory imitation directed against women or men. The negative connotations of the stereotype are the products of misogyny in an androcentric culture. But "feminine" patterns can also be adopted by males to express a rejection of socially imposed canons of sex-appropriate behavior. American English speakers do not appear to exploit a masculine intonational stereotype for purposes of negative imitation or rejection of gender identification by females; stereotyped tunes are "feminine" only (more precisely, "non-masculine").[16] Sex-stereotyped tunes are not universal, however: what is perfectly ordinary for men in one language may sound effeminate in another.

3. In addition to the overt stereotypes, there are certain general features of intonation that correlate with speaker sex. To present oneself as feminine or masculine, one shifts speech melodies (probably not consciously) toward the extremes identified with female and male speech respectively. It is not the sex of the other conversational participants that determines how strongly feminine or masculine a speech style will be used, but the speaker's need or desire for a particular mode of self-presentation. A woman may wish to deemphasize or emphasize her sex in working with male colleagues, and she may wish to express her "solidarity" with or dissimilarity to female colleagues.[17] These factors are not necessarily articulated in a conscious way, and some uses of particular tunes may be attributable to a particular individual's idiosyncratic habits. Hence, it is difficult (in some cases, impossible) to determine the speaker's attitudes and aims from the evidence of her (or his) tunes. However, clear-cut cases (where nonlinguistic knowledge can inform us of participants' attitudes toward and interests in a particular interaction) can permit us to identify the intonational markers of speaker sex that function as gender symbols for the speech community.

4. Our culture, overtly espousing sexual egalitarianism and providing many shared spheres of activity, predisposes us to believe that learned behavior is androgynous and that actual sex differences in behavior must be due to biological rather than social and cultural factors. The belief that intonation directly reflects internal states promotes its use to mark gender. Because certain features of intonation are in fact affected by a speaker's internal state, those features are often (incorrectly) believed to be consistently reliable indicators of speakers' attitudes and emotions.

5. Intonational "habits" are established without conscious consideration of available options and perhaps partly in unreflective response to available models.[18] The differences in dynamic range that have been observed in some studies probably arise chiefly from male efforts to "restrict" range. The extreme of "masculine" intonation in American English is a complete monotone,[19] whereas there are (theoretically) no limits at the other end of the scale. Masculine speech melodies can thus be heard as metaphors for control, for "coolness," and feminine speech melodies as uncontrolled, untamed by culture. The association of feminine and masculine extremes with the full disclosure of

emotion and with its repression, respectively, reflect the general connection of the masculine extreme with constraint.

6. The "feminine" habit of keeping pitch and loudness changing may serve the important function of attracting and holding the listener's attention. Women may need this device more than men because of (1) their relative powerlessness (dynamic rendition of the text is invaluable in holding the listener's attention if one lacks the authority to require that attention) and (2) their frequent contact with young children who are not yet socialized to attend reliably to verbal signals.[20] If these suggestions are viable, increased or relatively great dynamism should be a feature of "powerless" speech and also of interaction with young children.

7. Because the primary linguistic function of intonation is to indicate how an utterance "fits" in a discourse—what the speaker is doing by means of uttering a particular text in a particular context—women and men will typically use different patterns for equivalent situations because they have different strategies for speech action. In speech as in other areas women and men frequently "act" differently, because of differences in their early socialization and their access to power and because of the general expectations attached to their social positions. In a particular case one may not know the complex of causes of a person's intonational strategies—some people "wheedle" because of a vocal habit established in early childhood, others because they calculate that it is most likely to bring the ends they desire, still others because no other means of attaining their goals has occurred to them. Specific tunes are virtually *never* selected at a conscious level. It should be noted that a particular individual may have one strategy or general communicative goal in mind yet be interpreted by her (or his) addressee as motivated by some quite different factor. This possibility of miscommunication is a consequence of the fact that the same forms serve multiple functions.

This sketch of a theory of sex differences in intonation raises rather than answers questions.[21] For example, if subsequent investigation should establish that women are hurt by their use of intonational patterns that male culture devalues, ought we try to train ourselves in new melodic habits or strategies? Not necessarily. To accept the values set by the man's world is to continue residence in woman's place. Recognition of the positive values of some now generally negatively valued tunes can help women (and other subordinated speakers) develop their own speech powers as they choose. Women's tunes probably can be interpreted to keep her in her place: on her back and out of power. But views of women's intonational styles as uncontrolled (uncontrollable) and ineffectual (lacking in authority) can be challenged once the androcentric origins of these views are clearly understood.

NOTES

1. See, for example, the essays in this book and in the earlier Thorne and Henley (1975). In addition to such studies, my own approach to the study of language in social life owes much to such work as that in Ervin-Tripp (1973), Goffman (1969), Labov (1972), and Gumperz and Hymes (1972).

2. For further discussion of these issues, see McConnell-Ginet (1979), which is a reply to Kean (1979).

3. Brown (1980) develops the notion of sex-typed "styles" as generated by strategies women and men develop from their distinct social experiences, drawing on the detailed and very interesting theory of universals of politeness in Brown and Levinson (1978).

4. See Majewski, Hollien, and Zalewski (1972); Hollien and Jackson (1973); Hollien and Shipp (1972); also relevant is Michel, Hollien, and Moore (1965).

5. Aronovitch (1976) found little correlation between personality judgments and average pitch, but his study was not designed to allow isolation of pitch from other variables. That high pitch tends to be devalued, especially if combined with relative loudness, is suggested by the unquestioned assumption of von Raffler-Engel and Buckner (1976) that women's high-pitched voices are intrinsically unpleasant if loud.

6. That the second explanation has force is suggested by the fact that male subjects, asked to read a passage "as you think a woman would" in one of the studies reported in McConnell-Ginet (1978), were very reluctant to do so; whereas women were much more cooperative in reading "as you think a man would" (and tended to comply by monotonizing their reading voice). Cheris Kramarae (personal communication) notes that courtship is a context where women might lose by sounding "like a man." Barrie Thorne (personal communication) observed monotonic intonation in the speech of a fourth-grade girl who had been disparagingly described by another girl as "like a boy." The comment mentioned "looks" but Thorne noted that the girl in question had long hair and suggested that the impression of "like a boy" might well have been based in part on "sounds," even though only "looks" got noted explicitly by the other girl.

7. Suggested to me by Richard Leed, Professor of Slavic Linguistics at Cornell University, on the basis of his experience with students learning Russian.

8. Both Bennett and Weinberg (1979) and Terango (1966) provide significant empirical support for this view of our perception of dynamism.

9. See, e.g., Huttar (1968) and Soron (1964). Literature on intonational expression of emotion is voluminous but not methodologically very sound. See, however, Uldall (1960), Greenberg (1969), and Reardon (1971). See also the section on intonation and emotion in Bolinger (1972). A problem often ignored is that the specific import of a tune depends on the text it carries and the context in which it occurs, a point made in Ladd (1980). See also Gunter (1974) and Liberman and Sag (1974).

10. See Ortner (1974) for discussion of connections between nature/culture and female/male dichotomies. Liberman (1975) suggests that certain "global" features of intonational patterns can play a role as incompletely conventionalized vocal symbols.

11. There are people who automatically assume sex differences in behavior are our anatomical destiny. See Aronovitch (1976) for mention of some psychologists' belief in "physiological differences in homeostatic mechanisms" leading to "less emotional balance in the female than in the male." Whether or not biological differences are involved, the important point is the significance of cultural and social influences and the existence of great individual variation among individuals of each sex.

12. My mail indicates that women's supposed "timidity" is indeed a popular explanation of the high-rise on declaratives. In response to a quotation from me in a recent newspaper article suggesting that the high-rise is a way of asking a question whose content is not made explicit, I received a number of letters from people who wanted to "help" with my research, suggesting that the explanation was women's "fear of asserting themselves." My guess is that people are more likely to

offer the "fear" account if a woman's usage is involved than if interpreting the high-rise pattern on a man's declarative. The classic study of how the same behaviors are differently labeled if ascribed to female rather than to male is Condry and Condry (1976).

13. Sachs (1975: 167) addresses the issue of the basis of speech evaluations. Drawing on research by Frederick Williams and his colleagues, she suggests the possibility that judges label speech on the basis of social stereotypes. Although her discussion deals primarily with the characterization of the speech rather than with attributes imputed to the speaker on the basis of the speech (the subject of most research on evaluation of women's speech), similar questions are involved. For examples of attribution to women of personal characteristics on the basis of their speech, see Giles et al. (1980), who report on the contribution of a regional accent to people's "first impressions" of a woman's attitudes and behavioral style. They also found that women with different outlooks on feminist issues "sounded" different to judges. What features of speech were involved we don't know, but it is at least plausible that intonational characteristics play a role.

14. For several years I have been conducting exploratory research with the help of a number of Cornell University students to test some of the hypotheses presented in this paper. We have acoustic data from reading studies and from naturalistic observation that support the "dynamism" hypothesis above. We have also used the "matched-guise" technique first described in Lambert et al. (1960) to test contribution of different contours to judgments of speakers' traits, and our results are similar to those reported in Edelsky (1979). Our goal eventually is to devise more direct tests of conveyed meaning and to use synthetic speech to manipulate particular acoustic variables more systematically. I have been assisted in this research by Dr. Susan Hertz, who has developed the Cornell speech synthesis system; David Walter, phonetics laboratory technician; and the following undergraduate research assistants: Susan Costello, Lisa Fine, Elizabeth Kaplan, Jennifer Klein, Cynthia Putnam, and Daniel Segal. McConnell-Ginet (1978) reported some initial results, but the research is really still in early stages and will not be ready for publication for several more years.

15. See Weinreich, Labov, and Herzog (1968) for this viewpoint. I want to emphasize again that the view that abstraction from the social context is inadequate does *not* imply that such abstraction is dispensable as a component of linguistic analysis. See Kean (1979) and McConnell-Ginet (1979) for further discussion.

16. Barrie Thorne has raised the possibility that some women may also announce a rejection of socially imposed canons of sex-appropriate behavior through their linguistic choices. However, the asymmetry in intonation seems similar to that between dresses (a "feminine" mode of clothing, carrying a strong message when worn by men) and pants (though not "feminine" by any means, their being worn by a woman need not convey any special message about attitudes toward sexual norms). For a woman to eschew markedly "feminine" practices is not equivalent to a man's adopting these same practices.

17. Using the stereotypical "feminine" tunes is only one way available to women to "bond" with one another. Barrie Thorne (personal communication) observes extensive use of the high-rise intonation in California among feminists speaking to one another. As she suggests, it probably functions as an invitation to others to speak, emphasizing the collectivity of the group and underscoring a speaker's desire not to present herself as a "heavy." There is much to be learned about how we deal with one another as women and how those "dealings" are changing as feminism transforms the contexts in which they occur.

18. See account in Lieberman (1967: 45–46) of a thirteen-month-old girl and a ten-month-old boy who used higher fundamental frequencies when "talking to mother" than when "talking to father," presumably in imitation of their parents' speech. Very young children also show intonational "style-shifting": the use of certain varieties of speech melody to mark the nature of an interaction; see Weeks (1970).

19. I have observed some adolescent males using an extremely monotonic style, especially in peer interactions, and decreased dynamism in adolescent males has been noted by many observers though never, so far as I know, systematically studied. For adult male speech, it appears to be the case that any variation in dynamism is seen as significant, whereas female speech is already presupposed to be dynamic. See Aronovitch (1976) for this interpretation of his results (esp. 218).

20. See, for example, Kaplan (1970), a study which found infants attended to pitch shifts and suggested that intonation plays an important role in aiding the child's language acquisition.

21. In addition to the works already cited, my own understanding of English intonation has drawn much from Crystal (1969). Future studies must also take account of Waugh and van Schooneveld (1979), a collection of new essays on current research on intonation.

REFERENCES

Aronovitch, Charles D. 1976. The voice of personality: stereotyped judgements of their relation to voice quality and sex of speaker. *Journal of Social Psychology,* 99, 207–20.

Austin, William. 1965. Some social aspects of paralanguage. *Canadian Journal of Linguistics,* 2, 31–39.

Bennett, Suzanne & Bernd Weinberg. 1979. Sexual characteristics of pre-adolescent children's voices. *Journal of the Acoustical Society of America,* 65, 179–89.

Bolinger, Dwight. 1964. Around the edge of language: Intonation. *Harvard Educational Review,* 34, 282–93. Reprinted in Bolinger, 1972.

———1970. Relative height. In P. R. Leon, G. Faure, & A. Rigault (eds.), *Prosodic feature analysis.* Montreal: Marcel Didier. Reprinted in Bolinger, 1972.

——— (ed.). 1972. *Intonation.* Harmondsworth, Middlesex, England: Penguin Books.

Brend, Ruth M. 1972. Male-female intonation patterns in American English. *Proceedings of the Seventh International Congress of Phonetics Sciences, 1971.* The Hague: Mouton. Reprinted in Barrie Thorne & Nancy Henley (eds.), *Language and sex: Difference and dominance.* Rowley, Mass.: Newbury House, 1975.

Brown, Penelope. 1980. Why and how are women more polite: Some evidence from a Mayan community. In Sally McConnell-Ginet, Ruth Borker, & Nelly Furman (eds.), *Women and language in literature and society.* New York: Praeger.

Brown, Penelope & Stephen Levinson. 1978. Universals of language usage: Politeness phenomena. In Esther Goody (ed.), *Questions and politeness: Strategies in social interaction. Cambridge Papers in Social Anthropology,* 8, 56–311. Cambridge: Cambridge Univ. Press.

Coleman, Ralph O. 1976. A comparison of the contributions of two voice quality characteristics to the perception of maleness and femaleness in the voice. *Journal of Speech and Hearing Research,* 19, 168–80.

Condry, John & Sandra Condry. 1976. Sex differences: A study of the eye of the beholder. *Child Development,* 47, 812–19.

Crystal, David. 1969. *Prosodic systems and intonation in English.* Cambridge: Cambridge Univ. Press.

——— 1971. Prosodic and paralinguistic correlates of social categories. In Edwin Ardener (ed.), *Social anthropology and language.* London: Tavistock.

Devereux, George. 1949. Mohave voice and speech mannerisms. *Word,* 5, 268–72. Reprinted in Dell Hymes (ed.), 1964, *Language in culture and society.* New York: Harper & Row.

Eble, Connie C. 1972. How the speech of some is more equal than others. Paper given at Southeastern Conference on Linguistics.

Edelsky, Carole. 1979. Question intonation and sex roles. *Language in Society,* 8, 15–32.

Ervin-Tripp, Susan. 1973. *Language acquisition and communicative choice.* Stanford, Calif.: Stanford Univ. Press.

Fichtelius, Anna, Iréne Johansson, & Kerstin Nordin. 1980. Three investigations of sex-associated speech variation in day school. In Cheris Kramarae (ed.), *The voices and words of women and men.* Oxford: Pergamon Press, 219–26. Also in *Women's Studies International Quarterly,* 3 (2/3), 219–26.

Giles, Howard, Philip Smith, Caroline Brown, Sarah Whiteman, & Jennifer Williams. 1980. Women's speech: The voice of feminism. In Sally McConnell-Ginet, Ruth Borker, & Nelly Furman (eds.), *Women and language in literature and society.* New York: Praeger.

Goffman, Erving. 1969. *Strategic interaction.* Philadelphia: Univ. of Pennsylvania Press.

Greenberg, S. Robert. 1969. An experimental study of certain intonational contours in American English. *UCLA Working Papers in Phonetics,* 13, Los Angeles, Calif.

Gumperz, John J. & Dell Hymes (eds.). 1972. *Directions in sociolinguistics.* New York: Holt, Rinehart & Winston.

Gunter, Richard. 1974. *Sentences in dialog.* Columbia, S.C.: Hornbeam Press.

Hollien, Harry & B. Jackson. 1973. Normative data on the speaking fundamental frequency characteristics of young adult males. *Journal of Phonetics,* 1, 117–20.

Hollien, Harry & T. Shipp. 1972. Speaking fundamental frequency and chronological age in males. *Journal of Speech and Hearing Research,* 15, 155–59.

Huttar, George. 1968. Relations between prosodic variables and emotions in normal American English utterances. *Journal of Speech and Hearing Research,* 11, 481–87.

Hymes, Dell. 1971. Sociolinguistics and the ethnography of speaking. In E. Ardener (ed.), *Social anthropology and language.* London: Tavistock.

Kaplan, Eleanor L. 1970. Intonation and language acquisition. *Papers and Reports on Child Language Development,* 1, 1–21.

Kean, Mary-Louise, 1979. Comment on McConnell-Ginet's "Intonation in a Man's World." *Signs: Journal of Women in Culture and Society,* 5, 367–71.

Labov, William. 1972. *Sociolinguistic patterns.* Philadelphia: Univ. of Pennsylvania Press.

Ladd, D. Robert. 1980. *The structure of intonational meaning: Evidence from English.* Bloomington: Univ. of Indiana Press.

Lakoff, Robin. 1975. *Language and woman's place.* New York: Harper & Row.

Lambert, Wallace E., R. C. Hodgson, & Stephen Fillenbaum. 1960. Evaluational reactions to spoken languages. *Journal of Abnormal and Social Psychology,* 60, 44–51.

Liberman, Mark. 1975. The intonational system of English. Doctoral dissertation, M.I.T., Cambridge, Mass.

Liberman, Mark & Ivan Sag. 1974. Prosodic form and discourse function. *Papers from the 10th Regional Meeting of the Chicago Linguistic Society.* Department of Linguistics, Univ. of Chicago.

Lieberman, Philip. 1967. *Intonation, perception, and language.* Cambridge, Mass.: M.I.T. Press.

Majewski, W., H. Hollien, & J. Zalewski. 1972. Speaking fundamental frequency characteristics of Polish adult males. *Phonetica,* 25, 119–25.

McConnell-Ginet, Sally. 1975. Our father tongue. *Diacritics,* 5, 44–50.

——— 1978. Intonation in the social context: Language and sex. Paper presented at the 9th International Congress of Sociology, Uppsala, Sweden.

——— 1979. Reply to Kean. *Signs: Journal of Women in Culture and Society,* 5, 371–72.

Michel, J., H. Hollien, & P. Moore. 1965. Speaking fundamental frequency characteristics of 15, 16 and 17-year-old girls. *Language and Speech,* 9, 46–51.

Newton, Esther. 1972. *Mother Camp: Female impersonators in America.* Englewood Cliffs, N.J.: Prentice-Hall.

Ortner, Sherry B. 1974. Is female to male as nature is to culture? In Michelle Zimbalist Rosaldo & Louise Lamphere (eds.), *Woman, culture and society.* Stanford, Calif.: Stanford Univ. Press.

Pike, Kenneth. 1946. *The intonation of American English.* Ann Arbor: Univ. of Michigan Press.

Reardon, R. C. 1971. Individual differences and the meanings of vocal emotional expressions. *Journal of Communication,* 21, 72–82.

Sachs, Jacqueline. 1975. Cues to the identification of sex in children's speech. In Barrie Thorne & Nancy Henley (eds.), *Language and sex: Difference and dominance.* Rowley, Mass.: Newbury House.

Sachs, Jacqueline, P. Lieberman, & Donna Erickson. 1973. Anatomical and cultural determinants of male and female speech. In Roger W. Shuy & Ralph W. Fasold (eds.), *Language attitudes: Current trends and prospects.* Washington, D.C.: Georgetown Univ. Press.

Soron, Henry I. 1964. On relationships between prosodic features and lexical content of speech. *Journal of the Acoustical Society of America,* 36, 1048.

Takefuta, Y., E. Jancosek, & M. Brunt. 1972. A statistical analysis of melody curves in intonations of American English. *Proceedings of the Seventh International Congress of Phonetic Sciences, 1971.* The Hague: Mouton.

Terango, Larry. 1966. Pitch and duration characteristics of the oral reading of males on a masculinity-femininity dimension. *Journal of Speech and Hearing Research,* 9, 590–95.

Thorne, Barrie & Nancy Henley. (eds.). 1975. *Language and sex: Difference and dominance.* Rowley, Mass.: Newbury House.

Uldall, Elizabeth. 1960. Attitudinal meanings conveyed to intonational contours. *Language and Speech,* 3, 233–34.

von Raffler-Engel, Walburga & Janis Buckner. 1976. A difference beyond inherent pitch. In Betty Lou Dubois & Isabel Crouch (eds.), *The sociology of the languages of American women.* San Antonio, Texas: Trinity Univ.

Waugh, Linda R. & C. H. van Schooneveld (eds.). 1979. *The melody of language: Intonation and prosody.* Baltimore, Md.: Univ. Park Press.

Weeks, T. 1970. Speech registers in young children. *Papers and Reports on Child Language Development,* 1, 22–42.

Weinreich, Uriel, William Labov, & Marvin Herzog. 1968. Empirical foundations for a theory of language change. In Winfred Lehmann & Hakov Malkiel (eds.), *Directions for historical linguistics.* Austin: Univ. of Texas Press.

INTERACTION: THE WORK WOMEN DO*

Pamela M. Fishman

The oppression of women in society is an issue of growing concern, both in academic fields and in everyday life. Despite research on the historical and economic bases of women's position, we know little about how hierarchy is routinely established and maintained in daily experience. This essay analyzes conversations between women and men in their homes, demonstrating how verbal interaction helps to construct and maintain the hierarchical relations between men and women.

Weber (1969: 152) provided the classic conception of power as the ability of one actor in a social relationship to impose their will on another. Recently, Berger and Luckmann (1967: 109) have discussed power from a perspective which specifies an important way of "imposing one's will" on others. They define power as a question of potentially conflicting definitions of reality; that of the most powerful will be "made to stick." Imposing one's will can be much more than forcing someone else to do something. Power may also involve the ability to impose one's definition of what is possible, what is right, what is rational, what is real. Power is a product of human activities, just as the activities are themselves products of the power relations in the socioeconomic world.

Power usually is analyzed macrosociologically; it cannot be solely a result of what people do within the immediate situation in which it occurs. What people do in specific interactions expresses and reflects historical and social structural forces beyond the boundaries of their encounters. Power relations between men and women are the outcome of the social organization of their activities in the home and in the economy. Power can, however, be analyzed microsociologically, which is the purpose of this paper. Power and hierarchical relations are not abstract forces operating on people. Power must be a human accomplishment, situated in everyday interaction. Both structural forces and interactional activities are vital to the maintenance and construction of social reality, including hierarchies.

Recent work on gender and the English language shows that the male-female hierarchy is inherent in the words we use to perceive and name our world: the use of the generic "man" to refer to the human species (Stanley, 1977); the addition

*This is a revised version of a paper which appeared in *Social Problems,* 1978, 25, 397–406.

of suffixes ("authoress," "actress," "stewardess") when referring to female practitioners (Miller & Swift, 1976); the asymmetrical use of first and last names (women are more often called by their first, men by their last, even when they are of equal rank) (see McConnell-Ginet, 1978, for a full discussion). These and other studies document the male-dominated reality expressed through our language.

Much less attention has been directed toward how male-female power relations are expressed through the dynamics of conversation.[1] To complement other language and gender studies, we need more analyses of the interactional production of a particular reality through people's talk.

Conversational activity is significant for intimates. Berger and Kellner (1970) have argued that at present, with the increasing separation of public and private spheres of life, intimate relationships are among the most important reality-maintaining settings. They apply this argument specifically to marriage. The process of daily interaction in the marital relationship is ideally

> . . . one in which reality is crystallized, narrowed, and stabilized. Ambivalences are converted into certainties. Typifications of self and other become settled. Most generally, possibilities become facticities (1970: 64).

In these relationships, in these mundane interactions, much of the essential work of sustaining the reality of the world goes on. Intimates often reconstruct their separate experiences, past and present, with one another. Specifically, the couple sustain and produce the reality of their own relationship, and more generally, of the world.

Although Berger and Kellner have analyzed marriage as a reality-producing setting, they have not analyzed the interaction of marriage partners nor the differences and inequalities which may be involved in the reality-construction process. I shall focus here on the interactional activities that constitute the everyday work done by intimates and the different activities of the partners which emerge. It is through this work that people produce their relationship to one another, their relationship to the world, and those patterns normally referred to as social structure.

WORK IN INTERACTION[2]

Sometimes we think of interaction as work. At a party or meeting where silence lies heavy, we recognize the burden of interaction and respond to it as work. The many books written on "the art of conversation" call attention to the tasks involved in interaction. It is not simply an analogy to think of interaction as work. Rather, it is an intuitive recognition of what must be accomplished for interaction to occur.

Interaction requires at least two people. Conversation is produced not simply by their presence, but also by the display of their continuing agreement to pay attention to one another. That is, all interactions are potentially problematic and occur only through the continual, turn-by-turn, efforts of the participants.

Sacks and his followers (Sacks et al., 1974; Schegloff & Sacks, 1974; Schegloff, 1972) have sought to specify how conversationalists accomplish such things as beginnings and endings. They have ignored, however, the interaction between intimates. Schegloff and Sacks (1974: 262) characterize intimates in home situations as "in continuing states of incipient talk." Thus, they contend that their analysis of the activities involved in opening and closing conversations, and in keeping conversation going, do not apply to intimate conversations. But this perspective disregards the many conversations that do not begin with greetings nor end with good-bye's. If one sees a movie with friends, conversation afterwards does not begin anew with greetings. In social gatherings lulls occur and conversation must begin again. In any setting in which conversation is possible, attempts at beginning, sustaining, and stopping talk still must be made. And these attempts must be recognized and oriented to by both parties for them to move between states of "incipient" and "actual" conversation.

In a sense, every remark or turn at speaking should be seen as an *attempt* to interact. It may be an attempt to open or close a conversation. It may be a bid to continue interaction, to respond to what went before, and elicit a further remark from one's partner. Some attempts succeed; others fail. For an attempt to succeed, the other party must be willing to do further interactional work. That other person has the power to turn an attempt into a conversation or to stop it dead.

DATA

The data for this study come from fifty-two hours of tape-recorded conversation between intimates in their homes. Three heterosexual couples agreed to place tape recorders in their apartments. They had the right to censor the material before I heard it. The apartments were small, so that the recorders picked up all conversation from the kitchen and living room as well as the louder portions of talk from the bedroom and bath. The tapes could run for a four-hour period without interruption. Though I had timers to switch the tapes on and off automatically, all three couples insisted on doing the switching manually. The segments of uninterrupted recording vary from one to four hours.

The three couples had been together for various amounts of time—three months, six months, and two years. All were white and professionally oriented, between the ages of twenty-five and thirty-five. One woman was a social worker and the other five people were in graduate school. Two of the women were avowed feminists and all three men as well as the other woman described themselves as sympathetic to the women's movement.

The tape recorders were present in the apartments from four to fourteen days. I am satisfied that the material represents natural conversation and that there was no undue awareness of the recorder. The tapes sounded natural to me, like conversations between my husband and myself. Others who read the transcripts agree. All six people reported that they soon began to ignore the tape recorder; they were apologetic about the material, calling it trivial and uninteresting, just the ordinary affairs of everyday life. Furthermore, one couple forgot the recorder sufficiently to begin making love in the living room while the recorder was on. That segment and two others were the only ones the participants deleted before handing the tapes over to me.

METHOD

I began the research in order to explore the ways in which power was reflected and maintained in daily interactions. I had some ideas of what to look for, but generally my categories and concepts developed out of the conversations on the tapes. For example, I did not start the analysis with the conception of interactional work, but as I noticed the frequency of questions on the tapes and began to think about how they functioned conversationally, I came to the notion of work.

The frequency counts reported in the body of the paper are from twelve and a half hours of transcribed tapes. Five hours of the transcripts were the first ones I did and these were selected for two reasons. First, when I started the research I was looking for examples of decision-making and references to Garfinkel's (1967) "essential features" of conversation. I transcribed segments which showed either of these. Second, I also had the sense while listening to the tapes that some of the conversations were "good" ones and others were "bad." I transcribed some of each in hope that I could find what was going on conversationally that led me to those vague evaluations. The identification of conversational strategies and the conception of conversational work came out of my analysis of these first five hours.

The remaining seven and a half hours were transcribed with no motive but that of transferring more of the tapes to paper. They represent all the talk on one side of tape from each of the three couples.[3] I then used these to double-check the frequency counts of the strategies I had by then specified (the variation has not been significant). The analysis of topic initiations which comes later in this paper was based on all the transcripts.

PRELIMINARY EVIDENCE

Some evidence of the power relations between couples appeared while I was still in the process of collecting the tapes. During casual conversations with the participants after the taping, I learned that in all three couples the men usually set up the tape recorders and turned them on and off. More significantly, some of the times that the men turned the recorders on, they did so without the women's knowledge. The reverse never occurred.

To control conversation is not merely to choose the topic. It is a matter of having control over the definition of the situation in general, which includes not only what will be talked about, but whether there will be a conversation at all and under what terms it will occur. Control over specific details of the situation can be important. The addition of a tape recorder in the home is an example of a change in a routine situation. The men clearly had and actively maintained unilateral control over this new feature in the situation.

This research also raised the issue of a typically private interaction becoming available to a third party, the researcher. The men more often played back the tapes for possible censoring, and they made the only two attempts to exert control over the presentation of the data to me. One case involved the "clicks" that are normally recorded when the recorder is turned off. Since more than one time segment was often on the same side of a tape, I relied on the clicks, as well as my sense of the conversations, to know when a new time segment began. One man carefully erased nearly all the clicks on the tapes, making it difficult to separate out recordings at different time periods. (He said he wanted to make the recording sound smoother.)

The second instance was a more explicit illustration of male censorship. Early on, I made the error of asking a couple to help transcribe a segment of their tape. The error was doubly instructive. First, I saw that the participants could rarely hear or understand the problem areas any better than I even though they had been "on the spot" and were hearing their own voices. Second, the man kept wanting to know why I was interested in the segment, repeatedly guessing what I was looking for. At the time, I only knew that it was an example of decision-making and did not know specifically what I wanted. He never accepted this explanation. He became irritated at my continued attempt at literal transcription and kept insisting that he could give me the sense of what occurred and that the exact words were unimportant. He continued the attempt to determine the meaning of the interaction retrospectively, with constant references to his motives for saying this or that. It took hours to withdraw from the situation, as he insisted on giving me the help that I had requested.

The preliminary data suggest that the men are more likely than the women to control conversation. The men ensured that they knew when the tape recorder was on and, thus, when their interaction was available to a third party. They were unconcerned, however, whether the women also knew. Further, in at least two cases they attempted to control my interpretation of the tapes.

FINDINGS: INTERACTIONAL STRATEGIES

Textual analysis revealed how interactants do the work of conversation. There are a variety of strategies to insure, encourage, and subvert conversation. The differential use of these strategies by women and men suggests that there is inequality in talk between the sexes. Conversation is more problematic for women, who work harder to make it happen. Talk seems less problematic for men, who exert control over when and how it will occur. As these findings indicate, there are specific ways to see this inequality in action.

While there are problems with generalizing from three couples to male-female conversations overall, I do so for a number of reasons. First, this work suggests many areas for further study: Will other researchers find the same patterns among other heterosexual couples? Do these patterns appear in other hierarchical relations, like bosses and workers, teachers and students? Are there male-female conversational differences in larger groups and are the patterns similar or different? What will we find in video-taped interactions? Second, while the findings are based on the conversations of three couples, they have been confirmed many times by my own informal observations and by reports from other people of their experience. Finally, the findings are helpful. Since the strategies are quite concrete, they can be noticed in conversation. They are cues by which people, and particularly women, can figure out what is happening in their own interactions.

Asking Questions

There is an overwhelming difference between female and male use of questions as a resource in interaction. At times I felt that all women did was ask questions. In the transcripts the women asked two and a half times the questions that the men did.

Other research (Lakoff, 1975) suggests that women ask more questions than men. Lakoff has interpreted women's question-asking as an indication of their insecurity, a linguistic signal of an internal psychological state resulting from the oppression of women. But a psychological analysis is unnecessary to explain why women ask more questions than men. Since questions are produced in conversations, we should look first to how questions function there.

Questions are interactionally powerful utterances. They are among a class of utterances, like greetings, treated as standing in a paired relation; that is, they demand a next utterance. Questions are paired with answers (Sacks, 1972). They "deserve" answers. The absence of a response is noticeable and may be complained about. A question does work in conversation by opening a two-part (Q–A) sequence. It is a way to insure a minimal interaction—at least one utterance by each of the two participants. By asking questions, women strengthen the possibility of a response to what they have to say.

Once I had noted the phenomenon of questions on the tapes, I attended to my own speech and discovered the same pattern. I tried, and still do try, to break myself of the "habit" and found it very difficult. Remarks kept coming out as questions before I could rephrase them. When I did succeed in making a remark as a statement, I usually did not get a response. It became clear that I asked questions not merely out of habit nor from insecurity but because it was likely that my attempt at interaction would fail if I did not.

Asking "D'ya Know"

In line with the assumption that children have restricted rights to speak in the presence of adults, Harvey Sacks (1972) describes a type of question used extensively by children as a conversational opening: "D'ya know what?" As with other questions, it provides for a next utterance. The next utterance it engenders is itself a question, which provides for yet another utterance. The archetype is, "D'ya know what?" "What?" "Blahblah (answer.)." Sometimes, of course, the adult answers with an expectant look or a statement like, "Tell me what." Whatever the exact form of the first response, initial questions like "D'ya know what?" set off a three-part sequence, Q–Q–A, rather than a simple Q–A sequence.

Sacks points out that the children's use of this device is a clever solution to their problem of insuring rights to speak (at the same time, their use of this strategy acknowledges those restricted rights). In response to the "What?" the children may say what they wanted to say in the first place. Finding such three-part "D'ya know" sequences in interaction informs us both about the work of guaranteeing interaction and the differential rights of the participants. This device was used twice as often by the women.

Attention Beginnings

The phrase, "this is interesting," or a variation thereof, occurs throughout the tapes. Ideally, the work of establishing that a remark is interesting is accomplished by both interactants. The first person makes a remark; the second person orients to and responds to the remark, thus establishing its status as something worthy of joint interest or importance. All this occurs without the question of its interest ever becoming explicit.[4] The use of "This is really interesting" as an introduction shows that the user cannot assume that the remark itself will be seen as worthy of attention. At the same time, the user tries single-handedly to establish the interest of their remarks. The user is saying, "Pay attention to what I have to say, I can't assume that you will." The women used twice as many attention beginnings as the men.

There are also many instances of "y'know" interspersed throughout the transcripts. While this phrase does not compel the attention of one's partner as forcefully as "this is interesting" does, it is an attempt to command the other person's attention. The women said "you know" five times as often as the men (for further analysis of this phrase, see Fishman, 1980).

Minimal Response

Another interaction strategy is the use of the minimal response, when the speaker takes a turn by saying "yeah," "umm," "huh," and only that. Women and men both do this, but they tend to use the minimal response in quite different ways. The male usages of the minimal response displayed lack of interest. The monosyllabic response merely filled a turn at a point when it needed to be filled. For example, a woman would make a lengthy remark, after which the man responded with "yeah," doing nothing to encourage her, nor to elaborate. Such minimal responses operate to discourage interaction.

The women also made this type of minimal response at times, but their most frequent use of the minimal response was as "support work." Throughout the tapes, when the men are talking, the women are particularly skilled at inserting "mm's," "yeah's," "oh's," and other such comments throughout streams of talk rather than at the end. These are signs from the inserter that she is constantly attending to what is said, that she is demonstrating her participation, her interest in the interaction and the speaker. How well the women do this is also striking— seldom do they mistime their insertions and cause even slight overlaps. These minimal responses occur between the breaths of a speaker, and there is nothing in tone or structure to suggest they are attempting to take over the talk.

Making Statements

Finally, I would like to consider statements, utterances that do nothing to insure their own success or the success of the interaction. Of course, a statement does some interactional work: it fills a turn and provides for a response. However, such statements display an assumption on the part of the speaker that the attempt will be successful as is; it will be understood, the statement is of interest, there will be a response. It is as if speakers can assume that everything is working well; success is naturally theirs.

In the transcribed material, the men produced over twice as many statements as the women, and they almost always got a response, which was not true for the women. For example: many times one or both people were reading, then read a passage aloud or commented on it. The man's comments often engendered a lengthy exchange, the woman's seldom did. In a discussion of their respective vitas, the man literally ignored both long and short comments from the woman on her vita, returning the conversation after each remark of hers back to his own. Each time, she turned her attention back to his vita "as directed."

TOPIC INITIATION

Women use many of these strategies so frequently because conversations are generally more problematic for them than for men. This can be seen by looking at what happens to the topics women and men introduce into conversation.[5]

I considered an utterance to be a topic initiation if it addressed itself to a different subject from the utterance preceding it, or if it reinitiated a topic after an outside interruption, like a phone call, or after a very lengthy silence. In the latter case, I relied on a sense from the tapes that the topic had been dropped and the next mention of it was thus a reintroduction.

Using this method on the transcripts, I found that there were seventy-six topics raised. The women initiated forty-seven of them, the men twenty-nine. That is, the women raised between one and a half and two times more topics than did the men.

However, raising a topic does not insure that it gets talked about. Introducing a topic is an attempt to get a conversation going, not a guarantee that it will occur. In order for the topic to be successful, to turn into an actual conversation, both participants must work to make it happen. They both must orient to the topic and to one another. Not only must one person raise the topic, the other person must respond, and at least some of those responses must contribute to the topic's elaboration. At minimum, the two people need to take turns speaking, thus displaying their mutual orientation to each other and to the topic at hand.

Table 1 shows what happened to the topics raised by women and men. Of the forty-seven topics initiated by the women, seventeen succeeded, while twenty-eight of the twenty-nine topics raised by the men succeeded. Thus, while the women made 62% of all the attempts to introduce topics, they only raised 38% of the topics which evolved into conversation.

Table 1.   Topic Success and Failure

	Success	Failure	Uncertain	Total
M	28	0	1	29
F	17	28	2	47
Total	45	28	3	76

Clearly, the women had much more trouble getting conversations going than the men did. We cannot explain the women's failures on the basis of the content of the topics, since what the women and men wanted to talk about was quite similar—an article in the paper, something that happened during the day, friends, dinner, work. Topics introduced by the women failed because the men did not respond with the attention necessary to keep the conversation going.

In contrast, the men's topics succeeded not because they were inherently more interesting but because the women upheld their part of the conversations. The women responded regularly and in non-minimal ways; they displayed orientation by taking conversational turns. Topics men initiated succeeded because both parties worked to turn the initial attempt into an actual conversation.

Topics fail not only through the extreme case of nonresponse of the other party. Many topics continue to be pushed by the raiser over some period of time, yet the topic fails conversationally because there is no joint development of it. The increasing use of conversational devices like question-asking and attention beginnings is one sign that a topic is in trouble. Similarly, we can trace topic failure by noting the use of minimal responses (see above) which do nothing to develop the topic or to express interest.

The structure of pauses in the conversation is another indication of the failure of a topic. In a developing conversation, the pauses between one person's utterance and the other person's response are often a second or less, and seldom more than three seconds. (There are exceptions to this, such as when a person's pause displays appreciation of a poem or thinking about what has been said. Such displays are normally clear in the utterance following the pause.) Long pauses between turns at speaking usually indicate minimal attention and interest on the part of the responder. It is as if the responder is thinking, "Oh, yeah. I have to say something here." Minimal responses, which are good ways of saying something without saying anything particular, often follow long pauses.

Another indication that the topic is in trouble occurs when a person pauses in the midst of an utterance. Internal pauses often increase when the speaker's utterances have been continually met by minimal responses or long pauses from the other party. The number of "you know's" also increases in these circumstances, and one often finds internal pausing and "you know" together.[6]

CONCLUSIONS

There is an unequal distribution of work in conversation. We can see from the differential use of strategies that the women are more actively engaged in insuring interaction than the men. They ask more questions and use more attention beginnings. Women do support work while the men are talking and it is the women who generally do active maintenance and continuation work in conversations. The men, on the other hand, do much less active work when they begin or participate in interactions. They rely on statements, which they assume will get responses. They much more often discourage interactions initiated by women than vice versa.

These data suggest several general patterns of female-male interactional work. Compared with the men, the women tried more often and succeeded less often in getting conversations going, whereas the men tried less often and seldom failed in their attempts. Both men and women regarded topics introduced by women as tentative; many of these were quickly dropped. In contrast, topics introduced by the men were treated as topics to be pursued; they were seldom rejected. The women worked harder than the men in conversation because they had less certainty of success with the topics they raised. The women did much of the necessary work of interaction, starting conversations and then working to maintain them.

The failure of the women's attempts at interaction is not due to anything inherent in their talk, but to the failure of the men to respond, to do interactional work. The success of the men's attempts is due to the women doing interactional work in response to remarks by the men. Thus, the definition of what is appropriate or inappropriate conversation becomes the man's choice. What part of the world the interactants orient to, construct, and maintain the reality of, is his choice, not hers. Yet the women labor hardest in making interactions go.

As with work in its usual sense, there appears to be a division of labor in conversation. The people who do the routine maintenance work, the women, are not the same people who either control or benefit from the process. Women are the "shitworkers" of routine interaction, and the "goods" being made are not only interactions, but, through them, realities.

This analysis of the detailed activity in everyday conversation suggests other dimensions of power and work. Two interrelated aspects concern women's availability and the maintenance of gender. While women have difficulty generating interactions, they are almost always available to do the conversational work required by men and which is necessary for interactions. Appearances may differ by case: sometimes women are required to sit and "be a good listener" because they are not otherwise needed. At other times women are required to fill silences and keep conversation moving, to talk a lot. Sometimes they are expected to develop others' topics, and at other times they are required to present and develop topics of their own.

Women are required to do their work in a very strong sense. Sometimes they are required in ways that can be seen in interaction, as when men use interactional strategies such as attention beginnings and questions, to which the women fully respond. There are also times when there is no direct situational evidence of "requirement" from the man, and the woman does so "naturally." "Naturally" means that it is morally required to do so and a highly sanctionable matter not to. If one does not act "naturally," then one can be seen as crazy and deprived of adult status. We can speculate on the quality of doing it "naturally" by considering what happens to women who are unwilling to be available for the various jobs that the situation requires. Women who successfully control interactions are often derided and doubt is cast on their femininity. They are often considered "abnormal"—terms like "castrating bitch," "domineering," "aggressive," and "witch" may be used to identify them. When they attempt to control conversations temporarily, women often "start" arguments. Etiquette books are filled with instructions to women on how to be available. Women who do not behave are punished by deprivation of full female status. One's identity as either male or female is the most crucial identity one has. It is the most "natural" differentiating characteristic there is.

Whereas sociologists generally treat sex as an "ascribed" rather than as an "achieved" characteristic, Garfinkel's (1967, ch. 5) study of a transsexual describes one's gender as a continual, routine accomplishment. He discusses what the transsexual Agnes has shown him, that one must continually give off the appearance of being female or male in order for your gender to be unproblematic in a given interaction. Agnes had to learn these appearances and her awareness of them was explicit. For "normally sexed" people, it is routine.

To be identified as female, women are required to look and act in particular ways. Talking is part of this complex of behavior. Women must talk like a female talks; they must be available to do what needs to be done in conversation, to do the shitwork and not complain. But all the activities involved in displaying femaleness are usually defined as part of what being a woman *is*, so the idea that it is work is obscured. The work is not seen as what women do, but as part of what they are. Because this work is obscured, because it is too often seen as an aspect of gender identity rather than of gender activity, the maintenance and expression of male-female power relations in our everyday conversations are hidden as well. When we orient instead to the activities involved in maintaining gender, we are able to discern the reality of hierarchy in our daily lives.

The purpose of this study has been to begin an exploration of the details of concrete conversational activity of couples in their homes from the perspective of the socially structured power relationship between males and females. From such detailed analysis we see that women do the work necessary for interaction to occur smoothly. But men control what will be produced as reality by the interaction. They already have, and they continually establish and enforce, their rights to define what the interaction, and reality, will be about.

NOTES

1. A notable exception is the work on interruptions in conversation by West (1979), West and Zimmerman (1977), and Zimmerman and West (1975). Other conversational research can be found in Dubois and Crouch (1976).

2. Throughout this paper, I use the terms interaction and conversation interchangeably, although I do not mean to suggest that conversation covers all the essential components of interaction.

3. The discrepancy between the possible twelve hours of tape and the actual seven and a half hours of transcript represents long periods of silence.

4. The notion that joint expression of interest is a necessary feature of conversation is discussed by Garfinkel (1967: 38–42).

5. The following is a synopsis of material in Fishman, 1978.

6. See Fishman, 1980, for a full dicussion of pause structures.

REFERENCES

Berger, Peter & Hansfried Kellner. 1970. Marriage and the construction of reality. In Hans Peter Dreitzel (ed.), *Recent sociology, No. 2*. London: Macmillan, 50–72.

Berger, Peter & Thomas Luckmann. 1967. *The social construction of reality*. New York: Anchor Books.

Dubois, Betty Lou & Isabel Crouch (eds.). 1976. *The sociology of the languages of American women*. San Antonio, Texas: Trinity Univ.

Fishman, Pamela M. 1978. What do couples talk about when they're alone? In Douglas Butturff & Edmund L. Epstein (eds.), *Women's language and style*. Akron, Ohio: L & S Books, 11–22.

——— 1980. Conversational insecurity. In Howard Giles, Peter Robinson, & Philip M. Smith (eds.), *Language: Social psychological perspectives*. New York: Pergamon Press, 127–32.

Garfinkel, Harold. 1967. *Studies in ethnomethodology*. Englewood Cliffs, N.J.: Prentice-Hall.

Lakoff, Robin. 1975. *Language and woman's place*. New York: Harper & Row.

McConnell-Ginet, Sally. 1978. Address forms in sexual politics. In Douglass Butturff & Edmund L. Epstein (eds.), *Women's language and style*. Akron, Ohio: L & S Books, 23–35.

Miller, Casey & Kate Swift. 1976. *Words and women*. New York: Anchor Press.

Sacks, Harvey. 1972. On the analyzability of stories by children. In John Gumperz & Dell Hymes (eds.), *Directions in sociolinguistics: The ethnography of communication.* New York: Holt, Rinehart and Winston, 325–45.

Sacks, Harvey, Emanuel Schegloff, & Gail Jefferson. 1974. A simplest systematics for the organization of turn-taking for conversation. *Language, 50,* 696–735.

Schegloff, Emanuel. 1972. Sequencing in conversational openings. In John Gumperz & Dell Hymes (eds.), *Directions in sociolinguistics: The ethnography of communication.* New York: Holt, Rinehart and Winston, 346–80.

Schegloff, Emanuel, & Harvey Sacks. 1974. Opening up closings. In Roy Turner (ed.), *Ethnomethodology.* Middlesex, England: Penguin Education, 197–215.

Stanley, Julia. 1977. Gender-marking in American English: Usage and reference. In Aileen Pace Nilsen, Haig Bosmajian, H. Lee Gershuny, & Julia Stanley (eds.), *Sexism and language.* Urbana, Ill.: National Council of Teachers of English, 43–74.

Weber, Max. 1969. *The theory of social and economic organization.* New York: The Free Press.

West, Candace. 1979. Against our will: Male interruptions of females in cross-sex conversation. In Judith Orsanu, Mariam K. Slater, & Leonore Loeb Adler (eds.), *Language, sex and gender* (Annals of the New York Academy of Sciences, Vol. 327), 81–97.

West, Candace & Don H. Zimmerman. 1977. Women's place in everyday talk: Reflections on parent-child interaction. *Social Problems, 24,* 521–29.

Zimmerman, Don & Candace West. 1975. Sex roles, interruptions and silences in conversation. In Barrie Thorne & Nancy Henley (eds.), *Language and sex: Difference and dominance.* Rowley, Mass.: Newbury House, 105–29.

SMALL INSULTS:
A STUDY OF INTERRUPTIONS IN CROSS-SEX CONVERSATIONS BETWEEN UNACQUAINTED PERSONS*

Candace West and Don H. Zimmerman

The exercise of power in interactions between women and men is perhaps most effective when it is muted, if not euphemized. Thus, while smiles, sociable chitchat, pats on the back, and the use of first names commonly communicate closeness and friendliness, such expressions can play an invidious part in exchanges between the sexes. For example, the smiles women offer men have been interpreted as gestures of appeasement (Firestone, 1970: 90; Goffman, 1979: 48), men's greater license to touch women has been linked to the expression of dominance (Henley, 1973, 1977), and gender-associated address terms have been analyzed as forms of "sexual politics" (McConnell-Ginet, 1978). Fishman's (1977, 1978a, 1978b) analyses of talk between cross-sex, intimate couples find that a couple's conversational topic is essentially the man's choice. Females, notes Fishman, must ask more questions, fill more silences, and use more attention-getting beginnings than their male partners.

Interruptions in conversation also appear to have micropolitical significance (Eakins & Eakins, 1978; Octigan & Niederman, 1979; Leet-Pellegrini, 1980). A compelling "for instance" is provided by Eakins and Eakins (1978), who report that male faculty members contribute more interruptions to departmental faculty meetings than females. In their study, the "most interrupted" female was a faculty member who did not yet hold a Ph.D. degree, while the "least interrupted" male was the chairman of the department.

Our own early research (Zimmerman & West, 1975) on same-sex and cross-sex exchanges in natural settings found that interruptions were initiated very rarely in same-sex conversations, where they appeared in symmetrical distributions between individual speakers. But in cross-sex conversations, the pattern was grossly asymmetrical: males initiated all but two of the forty-eight

*This is a revised version of a paper presented at the American Sociological Association's annual meetings, San Francisco, Sept. 4–8, 1978. The authors would like to acknowledge the many helpful comments of Wendy Martyna, Sharon Veach, Thomas P. Wilson, and the editors of this volume. We alone are responsible for any deficiencies in the paper.

interruptions we observed, and interrupted more in every exchange in our collection. In a subsequent study (West & Zimmerman, 1977) we compared these eleven cross-sex exchanges with five parent-child interactions recorded in a physician's office. Finding that parents interrupted children on twelve of the total fourteen occasions, we noted that females and young children apparently receive similar treatment in conversations with males and with adults (see also Greif, 1980). We suggested that repeated interruption by one's conversational partner might be not only a consequence of one's lesser status but also a way of establishing and maintaining that status differential (West & Zimmerman, 1977).

Since our original sampling procedure was non-random, we are concerned with whether the generality of our findings extends beyond the particular conversations we happened to record. Many of the conversations between adults, for example, were conducted among friends relaxing in a variety of locations (such as drugstores, coffee shops, and other public places in a university community);[1] both the casual settings and degree of familiarity between speakers may have contributed to our findings. As Goffman observes:

> When a set of persons are on familiar terms and feel that they need not stand on ceremony with one another, then inattentiveness and interruptions are likely to become rife, and talk may degenerate into a happy babble of disorganized sound. (Goffman, 1967: 40)

Given that our 1975 study included cross-sex exchanges between familiar, and in some cases, intimate pairs conversing casually under relaxed circumstances, it is possible that conversationalists' ritual ease with one another might have influenced our results.

In this essay we compare findings of our previous research with similar data from cross-sex interactions between previously unacquainted persons in a laboratory setting. Although these conditions are markedly different from those which our original results were produced, essentially the same pattern of interruption emerged. This result lends plausibility to our suggestion that the patterns we observe are a basic feature of interaction between males and females in our culture.[2]

We begin with a brief consideration of the concept of interruption, followed by a discussion of our research design and methods. In addition to comparing the findings of our present research to those of our original study, we analyze additional evidence bearing on the issue of whether or not women "invite" interruptions (e.g., by talking too much or by failing to struggle against them). We conclude with a discussion of the notion that the interruption is a device for exercising power and control in conversation.

INTERRUPTIONS

We define interruptions as violations of speakers' turns at talk (West & Zimmerman, 1977; Zimmerman & West, 1975).[3] This definition is based on a model of turn-taking in conversation advanced by Sacks, Schegloff, and Jefferson (1974). Sacks et al. argue that "one party at a time" is the preferred order of conversational interaction from the viewpoint of speakers. Appropriate turn-taking places, which Sacks et al. term unit-types, include possibly complete words, phrases, clauses, or sentences, depending on their context.

Sacks et al. represent the mechanism for speaker transition as an ordered set of rules speakers employ to produce a normatively constrained order of conversational interaction. For each possible turn-transition place (i.e., completion of a unit-type as outlined above), these rules provide, in order of priority, that: (1) a current speaker may select a next speaker at talk (e.g., by using a term of address), and, if not choosing to do so, (2) a next speaker may self-select, and, if not, (3) the current speaker may continue. The exercise of any of the options recycles the entire rule-set back to the first option.

Sacks et al. suggest that each speaker, on initiating speech, is allocated at least one unit-type before the transition between turns ought properly to occur (1974: 702–4). But, since speakers also orient to minimizing gaps between turns at talk, they operate under tight constraint according to the model's provisions. On the one hand, they must be oriented to achieving turn-transition as close as possible to the actual completion of a current speaker's unit-type; on the other hand, they must avoid simultaneous speech occurrences (1974: 704–6). The delicate timing involved in honoring these constraints often produces a brief stretch of simultaneous speech initiated by a next speaker just as a current speaker arrives at a possible turn-transition place. Sacks et al. (1974: 706–8) note the routine occurrence of these brief simultaneities in the proximity (e.g., within a syllable) of possible completion points. We term this type of simultaneity an *overlap*, and view it as largely produced by constraints of the turn-taking system.

In contrast to overlaps, *interruptions* do not appear to have a systemic basis in the provisions of the turn-taking model. An interruption involves a "deeper intrusion into the internal structure of a speaker's utterance" than an overlap, and penetrates well within the syntactic boundaries of a current speaker's utterance (West & Zimmerman, 1977: 523). Defined operationally, candidate interruptions are incursions initiated more than two syllables away from the initial or terminal boundary of a unit-type.[4] Given that conversationalists can precisely time the placement of their speech relative to that of their co-participants (Jefferson, 1973), such "deep" incursions are difficult to dismiss as "errors" produced by systemic constraints of the Sacks et al. model. Indeed, it is in terms of the model that interruptions can be viewed as *violations* of turn-taking rules (which provide that the proper place for transition between speakers is at the terminal boundary of a possible unit-type). We intend the term *interruption* to refer only to those deep incursions that have the potential to disrupt a speaker's turn, although actual disruption (e.g., diversion of activity within a turnspace to address the intrusion, including yielding the turnspace to the interrupter) is a product of further interaction between the parties (Jefferson & Schegloff, 1975; West, 1979).

Thus, it is important to distinguish interruptions from other instances of simultaneity which appear to ratify, or otherwise contribute to, the talk of a current speaker. Jefferson (1973), for example, analyzes the emphatic "YEAH" interjected by a speaker, to display recognition of that which is in-the-course-of-being-said. "Saying the same thing at the same time," an instance of precision-timing, exhibits "independent knowledge" by the hearer of what the speaker is about to say (Jefferson, 1973). Intrusions such as these display active listening or intense involvement in the conversation. Interruptions, in contrast, have no such facilitative warrant. Instead, these incursions have the potential to disrupt turns at talk, disorganize the ongoing construction of conversational topics, and violate the current speaker's right to be engaged in speaking. In the following excerpts, drawn from our earlier data (West & Zimmerman, 1977: 527), we see the potential effects of interruption:[5]

> Female: Both really (#) it just strikes me as too 1984ish y'know to sow your
>   seed or whatever (#) an' then have it develop miles away not caring
>   i ⌈ f   ⌉
> Male: ⌊ Now: : ⌋ it may be something uh quite different (#) you can't
>   make judgments like that without all the facts being at your disposal

Or:

> Female: So uh you really can't bitch when you've got all those on the
>   same day (4.2) but I uh asked my physics professor if I couldn't
>   chan ⌈ ge that ⌉
> Male: ⌊ Don't ⌋ touch that
> (1.2)
> Female: What?
> (#)
> Male: I've got everything jus'how I want it in that notebook (#) you'll
>   screw it up leafin' through it like that.

Here we observe interrupted speakers dropping out and interrupters using the usurped turns to pursue their own agendas.[6]

In summary, what we have called "overlaps" (Sacks et al. use the term to refer to all instances of simultaneity) are (1) events occurring in the immediate vicinity of possible turn-transition places; and (2) those brief utterances (e.g., "yeah," "right") or longer incursions (e.g., "saying the same thing at the same time") which have some facilitative warrant.

But interruptions cannot be explained by the operation of the turn-taking system, and reflect the influence of factors exogenous to the management of turn-taking per se. One such factor is, of course, the gender of conversationalists.

DESIGN AND METHODS

The research reported below is based on five cross-sex conversations recorded in a laboratory setting. Subjects of the study were white first-year and second-year university students (five males and five females) between the ages of eighteen and twenty-one. We recruited students from large, lower division sociology courses who were all, by design, previously unacquainted with one another. Randomly paired, they were brought together in the laboratory and told to "relax and get to know one another" prior to discussion of a pre-selected topic ("bicycle safety on campus"). Conversationalists wore microphones from cords hung around their necks, and, with their knowledge and consent, they were audiotaped and videotaped through a one-way mirror. The audio portion of the initial twelve minutes in which speakers were free to talk about matters of their own choosing was fully transcribed, yielding 107 pages of transcript for purposes of our present analysis. In these transcripts, we identified instances of interruption as we have defined it.

We used unacquainted persons as subjects for the following reasons. First, in the original study, the majority of conversation pairs were previously acquainted, and it is possible that the pattern of male-initiated interruption we observed might have been affected by unknown factors peculiar to the catch-as-catch-can sample. Using randomly paired strangers reduces the plausibility of this alternative hypothesis. Beyond this issue, we surmised that the formality of the laboratory setting and the notion that people meeting for the first time are more likely to "stand on ceremony" (i.e., exhibit regard for the ritual order of interaction) might inhibit interruption, if interruption is seen as an act of impoliteness (cf. Goffman, 1967: 33–40). In addition, we analyzed only the initial twelve minutes of conversation—a brief enough interval to assume that interactants were still on their "best behavior" and a relatively small window through which we might observe a pattern originally located in longer sequences of talk.

Thus, we argue that reproduction of a similar pattern of predominantly male-initiated interruption under these conditions offers evidence for the robustness of the phenomenon, at least in a university community.

FINDINGS

Our earlier study of acquainted conversationalists found marked asymmetries in initiations of interruptions between persons in cross-sex dyads (Zimmerman & West, 1975). The exchanges we analyzed were selected from longer stretches of talk by excerpting all topically coherent segments exhibiting two or more instances of silence or simultaneous speech, without regard for who overlapped whom. In other words, those segments were selected precisely because of the silence and simultaneity they contained. Three-fourths of our total data were recorded unobtrusively in drugstores, coffee shops, and other public places in a university community; the remainder were taped in private dwellings. Nine of the eleven cross-sex exchanges ensued between previously acquainted persons, whose relationships with one another ranged from casual acquaintanceship to intimacy (Zimmerman & West, 1975: 111–12).

In that study, the cross-sex transcripts displayed gross asymmetries. Forty-six out of forty-eight, or 96% of the interruptions were done by males to females. Ten of our eleven cross-sex interactions exhibited interruptions, ranging from a low of two to a high of thirteen and averaging 4.2 per transcript. And, in every conversation, the male interrupted the female more frequently than the converse.

Give the marked asymmetry in the initiation of interruptions, we concluded that "men deny equal status to women as conversational partners" and that "just as male dominance is exhibited through male control of macro-institutions in society, it is also exhibited through control of at least a part of one micro-institution" (Zimmerman & West, 1975: 125).

As Table 1 reveals, our second study reproduces the findings of our earlier research. A total of twenty-eight interruptions were observed, of which twenty-one or 75% were male-initiated—a lesser proportion than in the first study, but still three times more frequent overall than female-initiated interruption.[7] Each of the five cross-sex exchanges exhibited interruption, ranging from a low of four to a high of eight and averaging 5.6 such events per transcript. Moreover, as was the case in the first study, males interrupted females more often in each of the five conversations, ranging from 63% (five of eight) to 100% (four of four). While the number of events is small, the consistency of the pattern is remarkable; the probability of males initiating more interruptions in all five conversations by chance is .03125 (binomial test). Thus, observations made three years later than the first study and employing more stringent procedures yield essentially the same finding.[8]

Table 1.   Interruptions in 5 Cross-Sex Conversations Between Unacquainted Persons

| Conversation[a] | Amount of interruption | | |
	Male-initiated interruptions	Female-initiated interruptions	Total
DYAD 1	75%	25%	100% (4)
DYAD 2	100	0	100 (4)
DYAD 3	67	33	100 (6)
DYAD 4	83	17	100 (6)
DYAD 5	63	37	100 (8)
Total	75% (21)	25% (7)	100% (28)

[a]Listed in order of increasing interruptions.

WHY DO MEN INTERRUPT?

Clearly, our earlier results cannot be explained away as a function of intimacy between cross-sex conversational partners. As we have seen, males interrupt females more often even when parties to talk are previously unacquainted. What then accounts for such findings?

As in so many other domains of sexual inequality (e.g., the sex-segregated labor force, the income differential between "men's" and "women's" occupations), gender is often invoked to justify or rationalize one or another aspect of what Goffman (1977) refers to as "the arrangement between the sexes." For example, there is the notion (ventured in classrooms and at professional conferences) that women "invite" interruption by men through somehow seeming to tolerate it or failing to struggle against it. This argument presumes, of course, that lack of evidence of a "fight" may be interpreted as "asking for" intrusion into one's conversational turnspace. However, West (1979) has shown that the pattern of females' responses to deep interruption contradicts this notion. In a study of cross-sex speakers' negotiations of who shall drop out of simultaneous speech and who shall continue, females were no more likely to drop out than were males when their turns were interrupted. The turnspace was more often ceded to the interrupter than to the interrupted party, regardless of the intruder's gender.[9]

Another explanation for males' disproportionate interruption of females focuses on the amount of talk women are thought to do in cross-sex exchanges. Here, the idea is that women are so "gabby" that men may be forced to interrupt them "simply to get a word in edgewise." Certainly, this issue is clouded by our stereotypes regarding the amount of talk in which women *ought* to engage (see Kramer, 1975: 48).

Existing empirical research on how much women actually talk, compared with men, contains a number of unfortunate ambiguities. Brownell and Smith (1973) note that amount of speech in a sentence, length of response, average total number of words produced, time periods of speech, and mean number of words per pause have all been used as indices of "amount of speech." Some studies have employed noninteractional research designs to obtain measurements (e.g., Gall et al., 1969; Swacker, 1975); others (e.g., Strodtbeck, 1951; Soskin & John, 1963) have examined taped discussions. While the evidence is not conclusive, the literature suggests that men talk as much or more than women when the sexes converse (Argyle et al., 1968; Bernard, 1972; Hilpert et al., 1975; Kenkel, 1963; Strodtbeck & Mann, 1956; Wood, 1966).

To be sure, the pertinent issue for our own studies is not just the amount of speech produced (by whatever criterion), but its relationship to conversational control. For example, Komarovsky cautions that the dominant partner in a marriage may not be the most talkative partner: "He doesn't say much" (says his wife) "but he means what he says and the children mind him." (1967: 353). However, Eakins and Eakins' (1978: 26) analysis of departmental faculty meetings finds that the number of turns taken (like the number of interruptions initiated) increases with status in the department (e.g., rank or length of tenure), and that "males, without exception, spoke longer per turn." Males' longer turns, we note, may be a function of many things—among them, less frequent interruption by females.

With these considerations in mind, we reanalyzed our cross-sex exchanges between unacquainted persons to see what—if any—relationship existed between amount of talk and interruption. One possible procedure for assessing this relationship might be a simple count of the total number of syllables, words, or unit-types uttered by males in comparison with females. However, this method is clearly unsatisfactory if the "hypothesis" (of greater female talkativeness) is construed to mean that males interrupt females because they want to say something and females, by virtue of their talkativeness, do not afford them the opportunity to do so. To support this hypothesis, one would have to relate the *local* amount of speech to the occurrence of interruption; that is, show that males tend to interrupt females when the latter talk on "at length." At the very least, then, we would expect that males' interruptions would occur later in the females' turns than the converse, since implicit in the notions of males' interrupting to "get a word in edgewise" is the male's "justifiable impatience" with not being able to speak. If interruption is to be warranted on such grounds, it should come "late," rather than "early," in the female's turn. Consequently, as a rough measure of "amount of speech" we counted the number of syllables to onset of interruption (including the syllable interrupted if such be the case) beginning with the initiation of the interrupted speaker's turn. Vocalizations such as "Mm" and "Uh" were counted as syllables. Clearly, we might count words or even unit-types as measures of "talking too much," a point to which we return below.

The hypothesis stated above receives no support; indeed the opposite appears to be true. Males interrupt females, on the average, 12.1 syllables ($s=11.9$) from the beginning of their turns. Females interrupt males (albeit less frequently) an average of 25.4 syllables ($s=14.2$) into their turns. If anything, this finding suggests that it is females, not males, who interrupt to "get a word in edgewise." Moreover, using either words to onset or unit-type to onset—units obviously related, though imperfectly, to syllables to onset—we get substantially the same results.[10] By none of these measures does females' alleged "gabbiness" account for males' intrusions into their turns.

Below, we discuss some implications of these findings in relation to issues of power and control in the larger context of institutional arrangements in our society.

DISCUSSION

Our conversations between unacquainted persons were collected three years after the earlier materials were assembled. In the years between 1972 and 1975, much has been made of the anticipated consequences of the feminist movement and changing attitudes toward women's and men's roles. Whatever changes may have occurred, we have found—under conditions which constitute a conservative test—a pattern of male-initiated interruption in conversations between strangers which is substantially similar to our earlier findings. Assuming this to be the case, some people may, nevertheless, say that inequality in the arena of turn-allocation (and the associated opportunity to develop a coherent string of utterances within a given turn) is trivial compared to the inequality that exists in the larger societal context. When viewed from a perspective encompassing the fate of women in the various institutional domains of society, the many small insults women suffer in face-to-face interaction do perhaps seem trivial. Yet, we would argue that the gestures of power[11]—minor in import viewed one by one—are an integral part of women's *placement* in the social scheme of things. These daily gestures are constant "reminders" which help constitute women's subordinate status. Let us consider this point in more detail.

Interruptions in cross-sex conversation are only one aspect of the relationship between men and women in this society. A fuller picture can be obtained only through study of a broad range of circumstances which, in turn, hinge on large-scale institutional arrangements.

Everyday encounters do not merely reproduce larger institutional arenas. Social occasions are the habitat of a variety of situated identities and located activities which occur within the context of a larger society, and are distinguishable from it. Yet, if these occasions do not simply mirror the patterns of more massive institutional activity, they are not immune to the influence of what Goffman has termed "externally realized matters" which

> . . . are given some official place and weight in most encounters, figuring as avowed elements in the situation, even if only as determinants of the terms of address employed, as when two customers are treated alike except that one is called Sir and the other Miss. (1961: 29)

Thus, for example, when male and female subjects encounter one another for the first time in the somewhat unusual but nevertheless institutionalized setting of the laboratory, they take into account the circumstances they share, and their identities as subjects and students to fill the time with talk and to "get acquainted." Beyond the fact that participants could presumably recognize the sex category of their partner, sexual categorization was not in any obvious manner "built in" to the structure of the encounter in the way "subject" and "student" apparently were (the use of these identities as resources for talk was ubiquitous in all five exchanges—see Zimmerman and Maynard, 1979). Nevertheless, the distributional evidence prompts the inference that sex category was salient in the interaction and employed in and through the management of talk.[12] As Goffman has observed in a different context:

> A man may spend his day suffering under those who have power over him, suffer this situation at almost any level of society, and yet on returning home each night regain a sphere in which he dominates. And wherever he goes beyond the household, women can be there to prop up his show of competence. . . . Wherever the male goes, apparently, he can carry a sexual division of labor with him. (1977: 315)

Assuming for the moment the generality of our findings, it also appears that whenever males and females talk, there are discernible echoes of "a sexual division of labor," and a quite portable one at that.

Throughout the research we discuss in this paper, we have relied on the work of Sacks, Schegloff, and Jefferson (1974) to furnish a model of conversational structure which provides a theoretical context for interpreting the phenomenon of interruption. The model Sacks et al. have developed is an abstract and general system of rules by which conversational exchanges are finely and deeply ordered. It is analytically independent of, but simultaneously sensitive to, whatever systems of variables (speaker identity, social situation, etc.) may function as the input for the particular *use* by participants of turn-taking options. Consequently, the study of the effect of exogenous variables such as gender is a study of how such characteristics are transformed by participants into particular conversational events. Put another way, if particular developments in conversation, including the placement of the onset of speech, have the standing of events or actions, they are, in the first instance, events or actions accomplished through participants' use of conversational procedures. If we suppose that the system of options which comprise the mechanism of turn-allocation are *oriented to* (Sacks et al., 1974: 723–24) by conversationalists, the accomplishment of routine turn-taking furnishes a "seen-but-unnoticed" array of ordinary events which stand as a background against which violations and the consequences of such violations are made visible as possible "troubles." Interruption as a violation of turn-taking procedures is thus not a non-event, but a "happening" in the context of an ordered system for managing turn-transition. The intrusion may of course be ignored, or it may furnish the particulars of a complaint. However, it may also be subject to attempts to contest it in its course, or to repair the problems it may have occasioned—e.g., ambiguity concerning which of two or more simultaneous stretches of speech is to achieve implicativeness for the next utterance (cf. Jefferson & Schegloff, 1975). It is thus something more than an analyst's construct.[13]

If interruptions were randomly distributed across social categories of speakers, one could assume that their occurrence stems from purely local circumstances, i.e., factors peculiar to a given conversation. We have developed evidence that interruptions are not random relative to one type of social category, namely gender.[14] Moreover, we argue that the fact that females find themselves subject to interruption more frequently than males in cross-sex conversations is not merely an indicator of a power differential, e.g., of the relative power to control one's turn at talk. The asymmetry in the initiation of interruption, insofar as it is a stable feature of the verbal interaction between men and women in this society, *constitutes* a power differential readily found in both ordinary and extraordinary settings in which men and women come together to talk (but see Beattie, 1981). It is, in other words, a way of "doing" power in face-to-face interaction, and to the extent that power is implicated in what it means to be a man vis-à-vis a woman, it is a way of "doing" gender as well (cf. Zimmerman & West, 1977).

APPENDIX

The transcript techniques and symbols were devised by Gail Jefferson in the course of research undertaken with Harvey Sacks. Techniques are revised, symbols added or dropped as they seem useful to work. There is no guarantee or suggestion that the symbols of transcripts alone would permit the doing of any unspecified research tasks: they are properly used as an adjunct to the tape-recorded materials.

Transcribing Conventions

Mary: I don' ⌈know⌉ John: ⌊You⌋ don't	Brackets indicate that the portions of utterances so encased are simultaneous. The left-hand bracket marks the onset of simultaneity, the right-hand bracket indicates its resolution.
A: We:::ll now	Colons indicate that the immediately prior syllable is prolonged.
A: But -	A hyphen represents a cutting off short of the immediately prior syllable.
CAPS or <u>underscoring</u>	Both of these are used to represent heavier emphasis (in speaker's pitch) on words so marked.
A: "Swat I said= B: =But you didn't"	Equal signs are used to indicate that no time elapses between the objects "latched" by the marks. Often used as a transcribing convenience, it can also mean that a next speaker starts at precisely the end of a current speaker's utterance.
(1.3)	Numbers in parentheses indicate the seconds and tenths of seconds ensuing between speaker turns. They may also be used to indicate the duration of pauses internal to a speaker's turn.
(#)	Score sign indicates a pause of about a second; that it wasn't possible to discriminate precisely.
(word)	Single parentheses with words in them indicate that something was heard, but the transcriber is not sure what it was. These can serve as a warning that the transcript may be unreliable.
((softly))	Double parentheses enclose "descriptions" not transcribed utterances.

A: I (x) I did   Parentheses encasing an "x" indicate a hitch
                                 or stutter on the part of the speaker.

A: Oh Yeah?   Punctuation marks are used for intonation, not
                                 grammar.

( )   Empty parentheses signify untimed pauses.

°So you did.   The degree symbol represents softness, or
                                 decreased amplitude.

.hh hh eh-heh   These are breathing and laughing indicators.
                                 A period followed by "hh's" marks an inhala-
                                 tion. The "hh's" alone stand for exhalation.
                                 The "heh's" are laughter syllables.

NOTES

1. One or the other of the authors carried a tape recorder and taped what could be heard by virtue of normal access available to any member of the public. Thus, the "sample" was based on availability or opportunity (Zimmerman & West, 1975: 111–12).

2. Other research, conducted before and after our 1975 study, appears to support this inference. Studies by Argyle et al. (1968), Eakins and Eakins (1976), McMillan et al. (1977), Natale et al. (1979), Octigan and Niederman (1979), and Willis and Williams (1976) suggest that the pattern of male-initiated interruption (variously defined) is fairly stable. Leet-Pellegrini (1980), examining opening and closing portions of laboratory interactions between cross-sex dyads, did not observe a simple pattern of predominantly male-initiated interruption but instead reported a more complex pattern resulting from the three-way interaction of gender, expertise, and time (i.e., movement from opening to closing segments). Moreover, Beattie (1981) reports no significant asymmetry in interruptions between males and females in tutorial groups of three to six students and a tutor. He found that students tended to interrupt their tutor more frequently than the converse. Beattie's definition of interruption differs from ours, and it is therefore difficult to compare his research with our own, although he attempts to align his definition (after Ferguson, 1977) with ours for this purpose (Beattie, 1981: 31). An experimental study by Leffler et al. (1980) reports that people in "teacher" roles interrupt more than when they are cast in "student" roles, with the overall effect of status being greater than that of gender. However, West (1980) found that, in a medical setting, male physicians interrupt their patients more frequently than the converse, but that this pattern is *reversed* when the physician is a female. The interaction of gender, situation, and other social identities is clearly an important agenda for future studies of interruption patterns and other language behaviors.

3. Edelsky (1981) raises some provocative questions concerning the wisdom of confining analysis to a turn-taking framework rather than exploring parallel modes of organizing discourse. Her argument is lengthy and complex and thus difficult to summarize (much less discuss and evaluate) in an endnote. Should her use of the notion of "floor" prove useful, it may help to specify more precisely the conditions under which phenomena such as interruptions occur (and the linkage of interruption and other verbal instrumentalities of power to gender, status, and other related variables).

4. In our original study we defined interruption as the onset of simultaneous speech prior to the last *word* that could define the possible terminal boundary of a unit-type (Zimmerman & West, 1975: 114). We came to reconsider this definition on theoretical grounds, i.e., on the contrast between the notion of interruption and the idea of system-induced simultaneity (Sacks et al., 1974: 702–6).

We revised our earlier definition along more stringent lines, viewing "overlaps" as those simultaneities occurring within the first or last syllable of unit-types; "shallow interruptions" as simultaneities occurring within the second or second-to-last syllable, or between first and second or next-to-last and last syllable of unit-types; and "deep" interruptions as those onsets of simultaneity more than two syllables away from the beginning or end of a unit-type. We decided to consider only "deep" interruptions on the conservative assumption that onsets more than two syllables away from a unit-type boundary were least likely to be due to systemic reasons. The interruptions referred to in the body of this paper are, in these terms, "deep" interruptions.

Since we have shifted our definition between the original study and the laboratory investigation, obvious questions of comparability occur. We handled this problem by analyzing our laboratory results using both definitions, although for presentational purposes we shall present our findings employing the "deep" interruption criterion in the text and relegate to an endnote the results employing the earlier definition. As it turns out, the pattern of interruption remains robust in the face of the definitional switch, the only consequence being a reduction in the number of simultaneities classified as (deep) interruption. See endnote 7 below for further discussion.

5. The transcribing conventions used for our data are presented in the Appendix to this paper. Brackets are used to encase those positions of speakers' utterances that are simultaneous.

6. Of course, not all interruptions "succeed," and the one interrupted may not yield. See also note 13.

7. As noted in note 4, the laboratory study employed a more stringent definition of interruption than the original research. Results reported in Table 1 use the later definition. Classifying the simultaneities observed in the laboratory using the original definition ("prior to last lexical constituent") yields a larger number of interruptions (fifty-six versus twenty-eight) but the proportion of male-initiated interruptions is exactly the same, that is, 75%. Moreover, as was the case using the later definition ("more than two syllables") males interrupted more frequently in each of the five dyads (in the order presented in Table 1: 80%; 100%; 83%; 75%; 56%).

8. Five female-female pairs and five male-male pairs were also recorded in the laboratory setting. For these unacquainted conversationalists, we found that interruption tended toward symmetry in six of the ten dyads. But, in two of the male-male exchanges and two of the female-female exchanges, interruptions were distributed asymmetrically between conversational partners. The four asymmetrical exchanges also contained the largest frequency of interruptions per dyad in our same-sex collection.

9. This comparison was not possible in our earlier study since there were only two interruptions of men initiated by women. Thus, the 1975 study may have portrayed women as more helpless in the face of interruption by a male than now appears warranted.

10. Using "words" as the unit of measure, average words to onset for male-initiated interruptions was 10.0 (s=8.7); the figure for female-initiated interruptions was 21.0 (s=12.9). Using "unit-types," the respective means are 1.67 (s=.84) and 2.43 (s=.73). In both cases, we counted the word or unit-type in progress at the time of interruption in calculating the value for each interruption.

11. Interruption is viewed as a form of dominance in studies by Argyle et al. (1968); Courtwright et al. (1979); Leet-Pellegrini (1980); Rogers and Jones (1975); and Willis and Williams (1976). For a broader perspective on the micro-politics of language and body behavior, see Henley (1977: 19–21).

12. On this matter, we should consider the accountability of certain features of those with whom we come into contact. One feature of any conversational exchange is that it is a potentially describable event. While one might characterize a conversation as about "nothing," one cannot so easily evade being able to say something about the person or persons one talked to. The sex, age, and race of the one spoken to are, we suspect, accountable features of persons, i.e., a shared and enforceable social accounting scheme. Insofar as this is so, we might be tempted to say that matters such as gender are always "noticeable" and "salient" in ways that other, more remotely situated identities may not be.

13. Comparisons of resolutions and retrievals of overlaps and interruptions reveal consistent differences in their consequences for subsequent conversation. For example, in the case of interruption (including now *both* shallow and deep interruptions [see note 4] in the fifteen same-sex and cross-sex laboratory dyads [N=295]), the restitution of states of simultaneity involved dropping out by one or both parties almost 30% of the time. Overlaps (N=498), in contrast, resulted in speakers dropping out in little more than 7% of the instances. Moreover, in the case of overlap speakers were more likely to finish their utterances within a state of simultaneous speech (49% versus 25%). Speakers also retrieved interrupted utterances (e.g., by repeating them "in the clear") more often than they retrieved portions of overlapped talk (34% versus 14%).

These findings suggest that our theoretical distinctions between overlap and interruption have empirical basis in the actual practices of conversationalists (Jefferson & Schegloff, 1975).

14. Thus far, we have been in a situation in which the activities of pursuing and understanding the phenomenon of interruption have limited the scope of the generalizations we might attempt. The detailed transcription necessary for our analyses has tended to reduce the number of dyads studied; the convenience of laboratory recording (among other things) has moved research from natural to contrived settings. As with most laboratory studies, the availability of students as subjects might lead to a focus on a particular population—one that is generally young, white, and affluent in an institutional setting and in a stage of life that might be characterized as a deferral of adulthood.

But power and the exercise of control constitute significant aspects of many recurring interactions in which women are engaged, such as those between bosses and employees, Blacks and whites, husbands and wives, or doctors and patients (West, 1980). Indeed, the proportion of cross-sex conversations between peers, such as college students of approximately equal age and status, is probably insignificant in comparison with the totality of talk between the sexes. At issue in further research is the matter of being male or female: whether and how this takes precedence—however subtly—over the realization of, and interaction with, the variety of situated identities we inhabit in everyday life.

REFERENCES

Argyle, Michael, Mansur Lalljee, & Mark Cook. 1968. The effects of visibility on interaction in a dyad. *Human Relations,* 21, 3–17.

Beattie, Geoffrey W. 1981. Interruption in conversational interaction, and its relation to the sex and status of the interactants. *Linguistics,* 19, 15–35.

Bernard, Jessie. 1972. *The sex game.* New York: Atheneum.

Brownell, Winifred & Dennis R. Smith. 1973. Communication patterns, sex, and length of verbalization in speech of four-year-old children. *Speech Monographs,* 40, 310–16.

Courtwright, John A., Frank E. Millar, & Edna Rogers-Millar. 1979. Domineeringness and dominance: Replication and expansion. *Communication Monographs,* 46, 179–92.

Eakins, Barbara & Gene Eakins. 1976. Verbal turn-taking and exchanges in faculty dialogue. In Betty Lou Dubois & Isabel Crouch (eds.), *The sociology of the languages of American women.* San Antonio, Texas: Trinity Univ., 53–62. Study also reported in Eakins & Eakins, 1978.

——— 1978. *Sex differences in human communication.* Boston: Houghton Mifflin.

Edelsky, Carole. 1981. Who's got the floor? *Language in Society,* 10, 383–421.

Ferguson, Nicola. 1977. Simultaneous speech, interruptions and dominance. *British Journal of Social and Clinical Psychology,* 16, 295–302.

Firestone, Shulamith. 1970. *The dialectic of sex.* New York: Bantam.

Fishman, Pamela. 1977. Interactional shitwork. *Heresies,* no. 2, 99–101.

——— 1978a. Interaction: The work women do. *Social Problems,* 25, 397–406. Reprinted in this volume.

—— 1978b. What do couples talk about when they're alone? In Douglas Butturff & Edmund L. Epstein (eds.), *Women's language and style*. Akron, Ohio: L & S Books, 11–22.

Gall, Meredith D., Amos K. Hobby, & Kenneth H. Craik. 1969. Non-linguistic factors in oral language productivity. *Perceptual and Motor Skills*, 29, 871–74.

Goffman, Erving. 1961. *Encounters*. Indianapolis: Bobbs-Merrill.

—— 1967. *Interaction ritual*. Garden City, N.Y.: Anchor/Doubleday.

—— 1977. The arrangement between the sexes. *Theory and Society*, 4, 301–31.

—— 1979. *Gender advertisements*. New York: Harper & Row.

Greif, Esther Blank. 1980. Sex differences in parent-child conversations. *Women's Studies International Quarterly*, 3, 253–58.

Henley, Nancy. 1973. The politics of touch. In Phil Brown (ed.), *Radical psychology*. New York: Harper & Row, 421–33.

—— 1977. *Body politics*. Englewood Cliffs, N.J.: Prentice-Hall.

Hilpert, Fred, Cheris Kramer, & Ruth Ann Clark. 1975. Participants' perceptions of self and partner in mixed-sex dyads. *Central States Speech Journal*, 26, 52–56.

Jefferson, Gail. 1973. A case of precision timing in ordinary conversation: Overlapped tag-positioned address terms in closing sequences. *Semiotica*, 9, 47–96.

Jefferson, Gail & Emanuel Schegloff. 1975. Sketch: Some orderly aspects of overlap in natural conversation. Unpublished manuscript, Dept. of Sociology, Univ. of California, Irvine.

Kenkel, William F. 1963. Observational studies of husband-wife interaction in family decision-making. In Marvin Sussman (ed.), *Sourcebook in marriage and the family*. Boston: Houghton Mifflin, 144–56.

Komarovsky, Mirra. 1967. *Blue-collar marriage*. New York: Vintage.

Kramer, Cheris. 1975. Women's speech: Separate but unequal? In Barrie Thorne & Nancy Henley (eds.), *Language and sex: Difference and dominance*. Rowley, Mass.: Newbury House, 43–56.

Leet-Pellegrini, Helena N. 1980. Conversational dominance as a function of gender and expertise. In Howard Giles, W. Peter Robinson, & Philip M. Smith (eds.), *Language: Social psychological perspectives*. Oxford: Pergamon, 97–104.

Leffler, Ann, Dair Gillespie, & Joseph C. Conaty. 1980. Top dogs and space hogs: The effects of status differentiation on nonverbal behavior. Unpublished paper, Dept. of Sociology, Univ. of Utah.

McConnell-Ginet, Sally. 1978. Address forms in sexual politics. In Douglas Butturff & Edmund L. Epstein (eds.), *Women's language and style*. Akron, Ohio: L & S Books, 23–35.

McMillan, Julie R., A. Kay Clifton, Diane McGrath, & Wanda S. Gale. 1977. Women's language: Uncertainty or interpersonal sensitivity and emotionality? *Sex Roles*, 3, 545–59.

Natale, Michael, Elliot Entin, & Joseph Jaffe. 1979. Vocal interruptions in dyadic communication as a function of speech and social anxiety. *Journal of Personality and Social Psychology*, 37, 865–78.

Octigan, Mary & Sharon Niederman. 1979. Male dominance in conversations. *Frontiers*, 4, 50–54.

Rogers, William T. & Stanley E. Jones. 1975. Effects of dominance tendencies on floor holding and interruption behavior in dyadic interaction. *Human Communication Research*, 1, 113–22.

Sacks, Harvey, Emanuel Schegloff, & Gail Jefferson. 1974. A simplest systematics for the organization of turn-taking for conversation. *Language*, 50, 696–735.

Soskin, William F. & Vera P. John. 1963. The study of spontaneous talk. In Roger Barker (ed.), *The stream of behavior*. New York: Appleton-Century-Crofts.

Strodtbeck, Fred L. 1951. Husband-wife interaction over revealed differences. *American Sociological Review*, 16, 468–73.

Strodtbeck, Fred L. & Richard D. Mann. 1956. Sex role differentiation in jury deliberations. *Sociometry*, 19, 3–11.

Swacker, Margery. 1975. The sex of the speaker as a sociolinguistic variable. In Barrie Thorne & Nancy Henley (eds.), *Language and sex: Difference and dominance*. Rowley, Mass.: Newbury House, 76–83.

West, Candace. 1979. Against our will: Male interruptions of females in cross-sex conversation. In Judith Orsanu, Mariam K. Slater, & Leonore Loeb Adler (eds.), *Language, sex and gender (Annals of the New York Academy of Sciences,* Vol. 327), 81–97.

——— Forthcoming. When the doctor is a lady: Power, status and gender in physician-patient exchanges. In Ann Stromberg, ed., *Women, health and medicine.* Palo Alto: Mayfield.

West, Candace & Don H. Zimmerman. 1977. Women's place in everyday talk: Reflections on parent-child interaction. *Social Problems,* 24, 521–29.

Willis, Frank N. & Sharon J. Williams. 1976. Simultaneous talking in conversation and sex of speakers. *Perceptual and Motor Skills,* 43, 1067–70.

Wilson, Thomas P. & Don H. Zimmerman. 1979/80. Ethnomethodology, sociology and theory. *Humboldt Journal of Social Relations,* 7, 52–87.

Wood, Marvin M. 1966. The influence of sex and knowledge of communication effectiveness on spontaneous speech. *Word,* 22, 112–37.

Zimmerman, Don H. & Douglas Maynard. 1979. The initiation of topics in conversational study of the social organization of relationships. Paper given at the meeting of the American Sociological Association, August, Boston.

Zimmerman, Don H. & Candace West. 1975. Sex roles, interruptions and silences in conversations. In Barrie Thorne & Nancy Henley (eds.), *Language and sex: Difference and dominance.* Rowley, Mass.: Newbury House, 105–29.

——— 1977. Doing gender. Paper given at the meeting of the American Sociological Association, September, Chicago.

MEN, INEXPRESSIVENESS, AND POWER*

Jack W. Sattel

"Another thing I learned—if *you* cry, the audience won't. A man can cry for his horse, for his dog, for another man, but he cannot cry for a woman. A strange thing. He can cry at the death of a friend or a pet. But where he's supposed to be boss, with his child or wife, something like that, he better hold 'em back and let *them* cry."—John Wayne, in one of his last interviews.

Much of the recent commentary on men and sex roles in this society has focused on the inability of males to show affection, tenderness, or vulnerability in their dealings with both other men and women. John Wayne may be dead, but the masculine style stressing silent strength and the masking of emotions is still very much alive. What are the origins and dynamics of such "male inexpressiveness"? How do the strictures against masculine self-disclosure connect to the other roles men and women play in this society?

In their initial thinking about American sex roles, sociologists didn't question the social processes that gave rise to the expectations that men would be relatively unemotional and constrained in the amount of intimacy they displayed and expected from others. For example, in an influential early theoretical statement, Talcott Parsons (1951) assumed the existence of a sexual division of labor in this society whereby men largely do the work of the public sphere (the economy) and women perform the socio-emotional work of the private sphere (the family). Parsons fastened on the fact that the economy demands that action be based upon deliberative, calculated premises which are as free as possible from "contaminating" personal or emotional considerations. Simultaneously, in Parsons's theory, the family—women's specialized domain—serves as respite and haven from the harsh coldness of the economy. For Parsons, learning experiences that shape men into inexpressive ways of relating to others, while reserving for women nurturant and expressive modes of relating, serve nicely to reproduce and perpetuate American institutions.

Only relatively recently, spurred by the insights of the women's and gay people's movements for change in American institutions, have sociologists begun to rethink the neat link Parsons postulated between what men (and

*This is a revision of "The Inexpressive Male: Tragedy or Sexual Politics?" in *Social Problems*, 1976, 23, 469–77.

women) are and do in this society. Unfortunately, much of the analysis thus far has focused so narrowly on inexpressiveness as a personality trait of men that one is left with the impression that the problem's solution lies in merely re-educating individual adult men toward their (human) capacity to feel deeply or authentically. In this essay I want to criticize such analyses as fundamentally shallow—the problem, I want to argue, lies not in men's inexpressiveness per se, but in the power and investment men hold *as a group* in the existing institutional and social framework. I am not denying the fact of male inexpressiveness; neither would I deny the destructive consequences inexpressiveness has for individual men and for the tenor of their social relationships (Balswick & Peek, 1971; Jourard, 1971; Farrell, 1974). However, I would deny or certainly argue against an interpretation that fails to connect inexpressiveness to the social and sexual division of labor.

A 1971 article, "The Inexpressive Male: A Tragedy of American Society," typifies a line of argument which has become widespread. The authors, Balswick and Peek, conceptualize male inexpressiveness as a culturally produced personality trait which is simply learned by boys as the major characteristic of their anticipated adult masculinity. Such inexpressiveness is evidenced in two ways: first, in adult male behavior that does not indicate affection, tenderness, or emotion, and second, in men's tendency to not support the affective expectations of others, especially their wives. Balswick and Peek imply that both boys and men *devalue* expressive behavior in others as non-masculine; the taunts and "put-downs" of expressive or sensitive adolescents are a ready example of how such devaluation enforces a masculine style among men. For Balswick and Peek, the "tragedy" of inexpressiveness lies in the inability of the American male to relate effectively to women in the context of the increasingly intimate American style of marriage; that is, the victim of this tragedy is the American male and the traditional American family.

I think this conceptualization of inexpressiveness has two important weaknesses. First, Balswick and Peek assume that inexpressiveness originates in, and is the simple result of, two parallel and basically equal sex-role stereotypes into which male and female children are differentially socialized:

> Children, from the time they are born both explicitly and implicitly are taught how to be a man or how to be a woman. While the girl is taught to act "feminine", . . . the boy is taught to be a man. In learning to be a man, the boy in American society comes to value expressions of masculinity . . . [such as] toughness, competitiveness, and aggressiveness. (1971, 353–54)

Such an attempt to ground inexpressiveness in socialization overlooks the fact that masculinity is not the opposite of femininity. The starting point for understanding masculinity lies, not in its contrast with femininity, but in the asymmetrical dominance and prestige which accrue to males in this society. Male dominance takes shape in the positions of formal and informal *power* men hold in the social division of labor; greater male prestige includes, and is evidenced by, the greater *reward* which attaches to male than to female activities, as well as the codification of differential prestige in our language and customs (cf. Henley, 1977). What our culture embodies, in other words, is not simply two stereotypes—one masculine, one feminine—but a set of power and prestige arrangements attached to gender. That is what is meant when we talk of this society as being "sexist."

My argument is that one reason little boys become inexpressive is not simply because our culture expects boys to be that way—but because our culture expects little boys to grow up to hold positions of power and prestige. What better way is there to exercise power than *to make it appear* that *all* one's behavior seems to be the result of unemotional rationality. Being impersonal and inexpressive lends to one's decisions and position an apparent autonomy and "rightness." This is a style we quickly recognize in the recent history of American politics: Nixon guarded the assault to his position by "stonewalling" it; Gerald Ford asked us to "hang tough and bite the bullet"; while Edmund Muskie was perceived as unfit for the Presidency because he cried in public.[1]

Keeping cool, keeping distant as others challenge you or make demands upon you, is a strategy for keeping the upper hand. This same norm of political office—an image of strength and fitness to rule conveyed through inexpressiveness—is not limited to the public sphere; all men in this culture have recourse to this style by virtue of their gender. The structural link usually overlooked in discussions of male inexpressiveness is between gender and *power,* rather than gender and inexpressiveness.

There is a second problem with the way Balswick and Peek conceptualize male inexpressiveness. They regard inexpressiveness as the source of communicative barriers between men and women. Balswick has particularly focused on this as *the* problem in contemporary marriages: "men who care, often very deeply, for their wives . . . cannot communicate what is really going on in their hearts" (Balswick, 1979: 110). Perhaps, but one of the repeated insights of my students—particularly older women students—is that male inexpressiveness in interpersonal situations has been *used against women* in a fashion Balswick's description fails to capture. Let me share a page of dialogue from Erica Jong's sketch of upper-middle-class sexual etiquette, *Fear of Flying,* to suggest the use of male inexpressiveness to control a situation. The scene is the couple's honeymoon, just after they have returned from a movie:

SHE: "Why do you always have to do this to me? You make me feel so
         lonely."
  HE: "That comes from you."
         "What do you mean it comes from me? Tonight I wanted to be happy.
       It's Christmas Eve. Why do you turn on me? What did I do?"
         Silence.
         "What did I do?"
         He looks at her as if her not knowing were another injury.
         "Look, let's just go to sleep now. Let's just forget it."
         "Forget what?"

He says nothing.

"Forget the fact that you turned on me? Forget the fact that you're punishing me for nothing? Forget the fact that I'm lonely and cold, that it's Christmas Eve and again you've ruined it for me? Is that what you want me to forget?"

"I won't discuss it."

"Discuss what? What won't you discuss?"

"Shut up! I won't have you screaming in the hotel."

"I don't give a fuck what you won't have me do. I'd like to be treated civilly. I'd like you to at least do me the courtesy of telling my why you're in such a funk. And don't look at me that way. . . ."

"What way?"

"As if my not being able to read your mind were my greatest sin. I *can't* read your mind. I *don't* know why you're so mad. I *can't* intuit your every wish. If that's what you want in a wife you don't have it in me."

"I certainly don't."

"Then what is it? Please tell me."

"I shouldn't have to."

"Good God! Do you mean to tell me I'm expected to be a mind reader? Is that the kind of mothering you want?"

"If you had any empathy for me. . . ."

"But I *do.* My God, you don't give me a chance."

"You tune me out. You don't listen."

"It was something in the movie, wasn't it?"

"What, in the movie?"

"The quiz again. Do you have to quiz me like some kind of criminal? Do you have to cross-examine me? . . . It was the funeral scene. . . . The little boy looking at his dead mother. Something got you there. That was when you got depressed."

Silence.

"Well, *wasn't* it?"

Silence.

"Oh, come on, Bennett, you're making me *furious.* Please tell me. Please."

(He gives the words singly like little gifts. Like hard little turds.) "What was it about that scene that got me?"

"Don't quiz me. Tell me!" (She puts her arms around him. He pulls away—she falls to the floor holding onto his pajama leg. It looks less like an embrace than a rescue scene, she's sinking, he reluctantly allowing her to cling to his leg for support.)

"Get up!"

(Crying.) "Only if you tell me."

(He jerks his leg away.) "I'm going to bed."

(1973: 108–9)

The dialogue clearly indicates that inexpressiveness on the part of the male is *not* just a matter of inarticulateness nor even a deeply socialized inability to respond to the needs of others—the male here is *using* inexpression to guard his own position. To not say anything in this situation is to say something very important indeed: that the battle we are engaged in is to be *fought* by my rules and when I choose to fight. Inexpressiveness signals the limits of the discussion and the tactical alignments of the participants.[2] In general, male inexpressiveness emerges as an intentional manipulation of a situation when threats to the male position occur.

I would extend this point to include the expressive quality of men's interaction with other men. In a perceptive article, "Why Men Aren't Talking," Fasteau (in Pleck & Sawyer, 1974) observes that when men talk, they almost inevitably talk of "large" problems—politics or art; cars or fishing—but never of anything personal. Even among equal-status peers, men seldom make themselves vulnerable to each other, for to do so may be interpreted as a sign of weakness, an opportunity for the other to secure advantage. As Fasteau puts it: men talk, but they always need a reason—and that reason often amounts to another effort at establishing who *really* is best, stronger, smarter, or, ultimately, more powerful.

Those priorities run deep and are established early. In Pleck and Sawyer's (1974) collection on masculinity, there is a section dealing with men and sports. Sport activity is important because it is often held out as one area of both authentic and expressive interaction among men. I wonder. Here is an adult male reminiscing about his fourteenth year:

> I take off at full speed not knowing whether I would reach it but knowing very clearly that this is my chance. My cap flies off my head . . . and a second later I one-hand it as cool as can be . . . I hear the applause . . . I hear voices congratulating my mother for having such a good athlete for a son . . . Everybody on the team pounds my back as they come in from the field, letting me know that I've MADE IT. (Peter Candell in Pleck & Sawyer, 1974: 16)

This is a good picture of boys being drawn together in sport, of sharing almost total experience. But is it? The same person continues in the next paragraph:

> But I know enough not to blow my cool so all I do is mumble thanks under a slightly trembling upper lip which is fighting the rest of my face, the rest of being, from exploding with laughter and tears of joy. (Ibid.)

Why this silence? Again, I don't think it is just because our culture demands inexpression; silence and inexpression are the ways men learn to consolidate power, to make the effort appear as effortless, to guard against showing the real limits on one's potential and power by making it all seem easy. Even among males, one maintains control over a situation by revealing only strategic proportions of oneself.

Much of what is called "men's liberation" takes as its task the "rescuing" of expressive capacity for men, restoring to men their emotional wholeness and authenticity. To the extent such changes do not simultaneously confront the issue of power and inexpressiveness, I see such changes as a continuation rather than a repudiation of sexism. Again, let me offer a literary example. In Alan Lelchuk's (1974) novel about academic life in Cambridge, *American Mischief*, there is a male character who has gleaned something from the women's movement. The "John Wayne" equivalent of the academic male may be passé, but if one is still concerned with "scoring" sexually with as many women as possible—which this character is—male expressiveness is a good way of coming on. Lelchuk's character, in fact, tells women fifteen minutes after he meets them that he is sexually impotent, but with the clear insinuation that "maybe with you it would be different. . . ." In this situation the man's skill at dissembling has less to do with handing a woman a "line" than in displaying his weakness or confidences as signs of authentic, nonexploitative male interest. Again, in a society as thoroughly sexist as ours, men may use expressiveness to continue to control a situation and to maintain their position of dominance.

I've tried to raise these points in my discussion thus far: that inexpressiveness is related to men's position of dominance; that inexpressiveness works as a method for achieving control both in male-female and in male-male interaction; and, that male *expressiveness* in the context of this society might also be used as a strategy to maintain power rather than to move toward non-sexist equality. I think my last point is most important. In 1979 Balswick wrote an article based on the conceptualization of inexpressiveness which I've criticized here. Entitled "How to get your husband to say, 'I love you,' " the article was published in *Family Circle,* a mass distribution women's magazine. Predictably, the article suggests *to the wife* some techniques she might develop for drawing her husband out of his inexpressive shell. I think that kind of article—at this point in the struggle of women to define themselves—is facile and wrong-headed. Such advice burdens the wife with additional "emotional work" while simultaneously creating a new arena in which she can—and most likely will—fail.

Sexism is not significantly challenged by simply changing men's capacity to feel or express themselves. Gender relationships in this society are constructed in terms of social power, and to forget that fact, as Andrew Tolson's book, *The Limits of Masculinity* (1977), so nicely points out, is to assume that men can somehow unproblematically experience "men's liberation"—as if there existed for men some directly analogous experience to the politics created by feminist and gay struggles. Men are not oppressed *as men,* and hence are not in a position to be liberated *as men.* This dilemma has prevented—thus far—the creation of a theory (and a language of liberation) which speaks specifically to men. Everyday language, with its false dichotomies of masculinity-femininity/male-female, obscures the bonds of dominance of men over women; feminist theory illuminates those bonds and the experience of women within patriarchy but has little need to comprehend the experience of being male. In the absence of such formulations, masculinity seems often to be a mere negative quality, oppressive in its exercise to both women and men, indistinguishable from oppression per se. What would a theory look like which accounts for the many forms being a man can take? An answer to that question poses not a "tragedy" but an opportunity.

NOTES

1. This link is reflected in the peculiarly asymmetrical rules of socialization in our society which make it more "dangerous" for a boy than for a girl to be incompletely socialized to gender expectations (compare the greater stigma which attaches to the label "sissy" than to "tomboy"). The connection of gender to power is also apparent in data that suggest parents, as well as other adults in the child's world, exert greater social control over boys to "grow-up-male" than girls to "grow-up-female" (Parsons & Bales, 1955).

2. It would be beside the point to argue that women sometimes will also use inexpressiveness in this manner; when they do so, they are by definition acting "unwomanly." A man acting in this fashion is *within* the culturally acceptable framework.

REFERENCES

Balswick, Jack. 1979. How to get your husband to say "I love you". *Family Circle,* 92, 110.

Balswick, Jack & Christine Avertt. 1977. Differences in expressiveness: Gender, interpersonal orientation, and perceived parental expressiveness as contributing factors. *Journal of Marriage and the Family,* 38, 121–27.

Balswick, Jack & Charles Peek. 1971. The inexpressive male: A tragedy of American society. *The Family Coordinator,* 20, 363–68.

Farrell, Warren. 1974. *The liberated man.* New York: Random House.

Henley, Nancy. 1977. *Body politics.* Englewood Cliffs, N.J.: Prentice-Hall.

Jong, Erica. 1973. *Fear of flying.* New York: New American Library.

Jourard, Sidney M. 1971. *Self-disclosure.* New York: Wiley-Interscience.

Lelchuk, Alan. 1974. *American mischief.* New York: New American Library.

Parsons, Talcott. 1951. *The social system* (Chap. VI and VII). Glencoe, Ill.: The Free Press.

Parsons, Talcott & Robert Bales. 1955. The American family: Its relation to personality and the social structure. In *Family socialization and interaction process.* Glencoe, Ill.: The Free Press.

Pleck, Joseph & Jack Sawyer. 1974. *Men and masculinity.* Englewood Cliffs, N.J.: Prentice-Hall.

Tolson, Andrew. 1977. *The limits of masculinity.* New York: Harper & Row.

CONSCIOUSNESS AS STYLE; STYLE AS AESTHETIC*

Julia Penelope (Stanley) and Susan J. Wolfe

Discussions of women's literature are apt to emphasize the fact that the "content" of women's literature is different from that written by men because women bring a "different sensibility" to literature. As Robinson (1976:1) has observed: "Women speak for women—for our experience and the viewpoint it shapes, if not necessarily in our common interest. No man, however sincerely our partisan, is able to speak with our authority about the lives, the feelings, or the consciousness of women." The unique perspective that women bring to the act of writing inheres in our social condition. Such discussions, emphasizing that the difference between the writing of women and the writing of men derives from a difference in life experience and perspective, may even contend that there is no such thing as "women's style"; that is, that although the realities perceived are interpreted differently, they are not represented differently. In this paper we argue that a distinctive style is evident in women's emergent writing, specifically that of self-identified feminists. We will show how such prose alters the English language to suit its unique expressive requirements.

"Women's style," as it has suddenly appeared in the 20th century, in a time when women in significant numbers have at last gained some degree of access to the benefits of mass media distribution, does in fact reveal that women's use of English has a long, if unfamiliar, development.[1] The consciousness of language, if not the public right to it, has been with us for some time. The women of the 20th century who write speak out of a tradition of silence, a tradition of the closely guarded, personal, revelatory language of diaries and journals. Our style, therefore, does not conform to the traditional patriarchal style we have been taught to regard as "literary" and "correct." Perhaps the autonomy of the written word frees women from the constraints of conversational and situational contexts, which serve patriarchal social structures and thought patterns; and the relatively informal context of the diaries frees them from the limitations of "formal" prose.

---

*This is a continuation of analysis begun in "Toward a Feminist Aesthetic" in *Chrysalis*, Winter 1978, no. 6, 57–71.

In fact, many feminist authors argue that the liberation of women presupposes a liberation from patriarchal language. Mary Daly, in *Beyond God the Father,* points out "that it would be unrealistic to dismiss the fact that the symbolic and linguistic instruments for communication—which include essentially the whole theological tradition in world religions—have been formulated by males under the conditions of patriarchy. It is therefore inherent in these symbolic and linguistic structures that they serve the purposes of patriarchal social arrangements" (1973:22). Another feminist, Peggy Allegro, contrasting women's relationship to language within the patriarchy and in our changing lives, defines the possibilities for women: "Our goal as I see it might be to constantly be open to new language, new ways of making the strange familiar, new ego images, and new ways of synthesizing our private languages with each other" (1975:184). Susan Griffin, speaking of the interconnectedness of feminists' writing and their lives, described how new images create new space:

> Why we write, as feminists, is not separable from our lives. We have woven together a kind of textured echo chamber, a flexible moving acoustical system, the new sounds we utter changing the space even before we hear each syllable. Our writing, our talking, our living, our images have created another world than the man-made one we were born to, and continuously in this weaving we move, at one and the same time, toward each other, and outward, expanding the limits of the possible. (1976:7)

Clearly there is an increasing acknowledgement among feminist writers that the expanding consciousness of women as autonomous beings demands a language adequate to reflecting the growth of meanings within ourselves and "in" the world. Only recently, as we have begun to think in ways alien to our culture (and its traditions and conventions), have we become engaged in the arduous processes of consciously remaking language for our own purposes.

Patriarchal expressive modes reflect an epistemology that perceives the world in terms of categories, dichotomies, roles, stasis, and causation, while female expressive modes reflect an epistemology that perceives the world in terms of ambiguities, pluralities, processes, continuities, and complex relationships. In certain contemporary feminist writers this consciousness has emerged as "women's style," a system of use rules that grows out of a frequently articulated set of conscious aesthetic principles. Mary Daly, Kate Millett, and Bertha Harris, for instance, employ women's style quite consciously, stating within their works the principles which underlie their attempts to extend the limits of English to encompass women's sensibilities and perceptions. Susan Griffin, seeking to explain in the Preface to *Women and Nature* the connection between the "unconventional" style and the content of her book, discusses her use of the "embodied" and "impassioned" voices from women and nature:

> In the process of writing I found that I could best discover my insights about the logic of civilized man by going underneath logic, that is by writing associatively, and thus enlisting my intuition, or uncivilized self. . . . One of the loudest complaints which this book makes about patriarchal thought (or the thought of civilized man) is that it claims to be objective, and separated from emotion, and so it is appropriate that the style of this book does not make that separation. (1978: xv)

In their efforts to break through the old patterns of English, many women are developing new uses and forms of language. The most obvious and striking evidence of women's concern for language and its role as a naming process is the frequency with which women are choosing new names for ourselves. In a short story by Maud Haimson, "Hands," the characters lack names—as labels. Instead, the naming of the women is itself a process, and the references to them change as their situations alter with respect to their environment, their relation to each other, and their understanding of these relationships.

> She waited a moment until this *little woman* came in. She wasn't regular little, smaller than that even. At first, the *little woman* didn't pay attention to the *other woman,* instead she *moved her looks* toward the rocks as though they were a matter of now importance. The *new-to-the-cave woman* nodded and waited. The *cave woman* picked up a small rock, touched it all around, and brought it to the *older woman.* The *older outside woman* took it, touched it and holding it asked the *inside woman* if she'd been outside. The *stone woman* shook her head and taking a look at her stove picked up some rocks and put them in her *many pocketed cloth-like thing going to the ground,* pockets in the back too with bulges from stones. She followed the *other woman* out.
>
> The *new-to-the-outside woman* stood at the entrance and looked out. . . . The *moving woman* would not leave the entrance of the cave.
>
> The *sea, sky and air woman* took the *new-to-the-outside woman*'s hand and led her out toward the sea. . . .
>
> "You like it here?" the *experienced woman* asked. . . . But they had to go, the *taller now standing-up woman* decided, taking her hand once more. . . . The *driving woman* asked the other if she could make the rocks stop their light and the woman stopped the light, "except one." (1975:60)

In addition to the shifting labeling process, which changes as the women shift identity in relation to each other, certain of the prenominal modifiers provide us with new information about the women. For example, the cave/stone woman becomes the new-to-the-outside woman with respect to her shift in position in her environment, while we learn that the outside/sea, sky, and air woman is both older and taller than she. The outside woman doesn't "look" at the rocks, she "moves her looks toward" them; the cave woman doesn't simply "touch" a rock, she "touched it all around"; and the stone woman doesn't put her rocks in a "coat." What she wears is more than a product, or material object, or categorized, fixed label. It is a "many pocketed cloth-like thing going to the ground." It has characteristics, but it too is engaged in the processes connected with its being and functions. Other phrases in the passage seem to have been adopted from patriarchal language, where they have sexist readings. "The little woman," for example, is a phrase which men use to refer jocularly to their wives, a phrase by which they indicate paternal amusement for the women they believe they possess. Haimson, however, has shown that the term merely denotes the relative size of one of the women: she "wasn't regular little, smaller than that even." The term "experienced woman" is frequently used by men as a pejorative to designate a woman who has had sexual experience and who, as a consequence, is no longer "chaste." "The other woman" is a phrase which has come to mean "an adulteress," a woman who shatters a happy (i.e., married) home. In wrenching such phrases from their patriarchal meaning and contexts, Haimson has created a new language without creating new words.

That the processes involved in reworking language are neither singular nor absolute may seem obvious to some, but it is nevertheless necessary to point out that no single approach to language is capable, in and of itself, of the kind of remaking we must undertake in order to get beyond the confines of masculinist expressive structures. We are, thus, engaged in a complex intermingling of processes that must go on simultaneously. In her Introduction to *Gyn/Ecology,* Mary Daly describes several of these cognitive/linguistic explorations and their relationship to radical feminist consciousness.

> Gynocentric writing means risking. Since the language and style of patriarchal writing simply cannot contain or carry the energy of women's exorcism and ecstasy, in this book I invent, dis-cover, re-member. At times I make up words (such as *gynaesthesia* for women's synaesthesia). Often I unmask deceptive words by dividing them and employing alternate meanings for prefixes (for example, *re-cover* actually says "cover again"). I also unmask their hidden reversals, often by using less known or "obsolete" meanings (for example, *glamour* as used to name a witch's power). Sometimes I simply invite the reader to listen to words in a different way (for example, *de-light*). When I play with words I do this attentively, deeply, paying attention to etymology, to varied dimensions of meaning, to deep Background meanings and subliminal associations. There are some woman-made words which I choose not to use for various reasons. Sometimes I reject words that I think are inauthentic, obscuring women's existence and masking the conditions of our oppression (for example, *chairperson*). In other cases my choice is a matter of intuitive judgment (for example, my decision not to use *herstory*). (1978:24)

In *Woman on the Edge of Time,* Marge Piercy projects the English into a nonsexist future. Some of her changes in the language are the sort one might expect (e.g., clipping, elision), but there are other changes that reflect different conceptual structures.

> 'Luciente and Bolivar have not been communing. Meshing badly. Sparks and bumps. Tonight we try to comprend that hostility and see if we can defuse it.'
> 'Aren't people allowed to dislike each other?'
> 'Not good when they're in the same core. Jackrabbit is close to both. Such bumping strains per. They compete for Jackrabbit's attent. They are picky toward each other's ways. We have critted them for it before, but matters lift only briefly. When they crit each other, it does not hold up under scrutiny as honest—but self-serving.' Parra smiled wryly.
> 'Suppose after worming they still can't stand each other?' (1976:199)

In this excerpted passage the language used to speak of the qualities of human relationships has become more concrete, less abstract. When two people cannot "get along" with each other they are said to "mesh badly." Their relating is characterized by the "sparks" of friction and the "bumps" of roughness. The "core," a group of self-defined people, friends, hand-mates, mems, has replaced the nuclear family. The unpleasantly descriptive term *worming* refers to a group session similar to, but more evolved than, either consciousness-raising or group therapy.

Although Piercy's use of concrete language rather than abstract nouns and verbs suggests that language, perception, and expression are all interrelated, her characters do not explore these relationships. Forty years earlier, however, observing the relationships which exist between the categories of English and the genres of prose and poetry, Gertrude Stein explained how the functions of nouns as permanent "names" gave rise to her syntactic style.

> One of the things that is a very interesting thing to know is how you are feeling inside you to the words that are coming out to be outside of you.
>
> Do you always have the same kind of feeling in relation to the sounds as the words come out of you or do you not. All this has so much to do with grammar and with poetry and with prose.
>
> Words have to do with everything in poetry and prose and some writers write more in articles and prepositions and some say you should write in nouns, and of course one has to think of everything.
>
> A noun is a name of anything, why after a thing is named write about it. A name is adequate or it is not. If it is adequate then why go on calling it, if it is not then calling it by its name does no good.
>
> . . . but generally speaking, things once they are named the name does not go on doing anything to them and so why write in nouns.
>
> . . . But nouns still have to be mentioned because in coming to avoid nouns a great deal happens and has happened.
>
> In The Making of Americans a long a very long prose book made up of sentences and paragraphs and the new thing that was something neither the sentences nor the paragraph each one alone or in combination had ever done, I said I had gotten rid of nouns and adjectives as much as possible by the method of living in adverbs in verbs in pronouns, in adverbial clauses written or implied and in conjunctions. ("Poetry and Grammar," in Stein, 1957, 209–28)

For Stein then, nouns as labels did not serve to point to reality. Instead, as she insisted, the writer had to live within the words, to remain aware of the feelings of the words as they were coming out, and in the feeling and sounds of the words one comes to possess oneself. In such a view of language and art there can be no easy separation of the artist from her language or the perceptions that her language must learn to body forth. Robinson has observed, with respect to trying to deal with art as "product," ". . . according to the prevailing view of the process, one is still supposed to act as if it is an *it*. . . . The expression cannot be arbitrarily divided from the feelings that give rise to it, nor either of these from the lived reality at the base" (1976:7). This refusal to split oneself from one's creating is perhaps one of the reasons so many readers have trouble reading Gertrude Stein: she is always PRESENT in her language, THERE before the reader as creator, as the controlling consciousness. Her writing reveals the processes of the act of writing, not an art object or a "product," but the *process* of creation itself, with its ambiguities and backtrackings.

In the early 1970s Jill Johnston took up the implications of Stein's approach to language in her prefatory "Remarks" to *Lesbian Nation:*

> All repetitions of thoughts ideas material projections plans reflections reveries fantasies in the same or varied phrases in different contexts constitute my way of working circles within circles. . . . Every departure from a point of origin carries within it a renewed approach to it. Each return to the point of origin completes the cycle of one existence and begins another. The style and the object are the same: the return to the harmony of statehood and biology through the remembered majesties of women. ("Remarks," in Johnston, 1973:12)

Johnston's debt to Gertrude Stein is apparent in the following quotation, in which she refers to the relationship between her syntax and her involvement with reality:

> I meant to lie so I could present the confusing nonsequitur of two such unhappy products in shock over ghastly disclosures blundering beautifully on to destruction by filling themselves inside as well as up against as spherical bodies all parts orientating themselves in an infinite number of positions in a rectangular space like sentences not too abruptly rotating their angular facets as cut stones or the multicolored ball we lost to the tide in the harbor waiting for the ferry playing volley catch . . . (1974:130)

For Johnston, like Stein, the sentence must capture the processes of reality as the writer perceives it; each returning of the sentence is another view of the interpretive creative process: "Every phrase and every sentence is an end and a beginning . . . And any action is a step to the block, to the fire, down the sea's throat . . . I awoke to my newborn day. Naturally we do not know how it happened until it is well over beginning happening" (1974: 60–61).

The intimate awareness and self-consciousness of the woman struggling with her impulse to create bleeds through the syntax of her prose, the struggle to live becoming the struggle to create becoming the struggle in language. One's living as "documentary," one's life as art, becomes the transformational substance of Kate Millet's *Flying*. Like the other writers we have quoted, her life overflows the narrow, restrictive syntactic boundaries of the conventional sentence that is "a complete thought," because there are no "complete thoughts" as our moments touch moments in other lives, as the places of touching are not "places" but interfaces from which other possibilities come into being with their own touchings beyond our own. The interfacings between fact/fiction and language/knowing become indeterminant, meshing, infinitely spreading.

> No apology justifies what I have done. But let this be brought forward by way of explanation: *it had occurred to me to treat my own existence as documentary.* [Italics in original.] . . . It had never before occurred to me to regard myself as subject matter. Though I like to imagine this is my first book, I seemed, at thirty-six, to be past the age of the obligatory autobiographical novel. Sensible friends recommended research topics: pollution, erudition, etc. The confessional should wait upon one's ripe old age. But it was apparent to me that I might have no ripe old age, was sure not to have one, if I did not take some steps toward recovering my being. (1974:81–83)

In *Flying*, a newly self-conscious Millett writes consciously of her self. Like the essays of Johnston, *Flying* is an ongoing book "with its own revision" (Johnston, 1974:127, 131); quick changes, instant revisions, force themselves into a new syntax.

> One morning I read manuscript in bed, the thing on Smith and Vassar, my first piece trying to write a new way. Celia favored regular sentences. (Ibid.:73)

Where the event as memory and the living of it as remembrance fuse in the immediate consciousness of the writer, the dichotomies of past/present, here/there, fact/fiction fall away, all move together in cascades of words where images break and flow. For Johnston, leaving herself "behind for a fiction,"

Words are very very heavy magic. So everything you say is true. The necessities of style distort both fact and fiction. . . . In the universal unstable compound of fable and fact that passes for our lives. (Ibid.:127–29)

In the act of creation, living in creation, where the language may make fable of fact and truth of fiction, in which the only belief is in the living of events, that living itself necessitates a language in which all are simultaneously possible. If language calls truth into question, then self-consciousness remakes language and presses it beyond its prescribed limitations.

The writer is her audience is her critic. The risk lies in the possibility that she may be talking only to herself, as many women have been doing all their lives for centuries. The "talking-to-oneself" of the diaries and journals becomes the prose of revelation and revolution, the turning around in consciousness, vulnerability, a rambling, associative style that characterizes reverie, interior monologue, and even third person narrations that capture internal ruminations. The following monologue of the "lady in yellow" in Ntozake Shange's *For Colored Girls Who Have Considered Suicide When the Rainbow is Enuf* illustrates the way in which consciousness and vulnerability merge to produce the talking-to-oneself quality.

> lady in yellow
> i've lost it
> touch wit reality/i dont know who's doin it
> i thot i waz but i waz so stupid i waz able to be hurt
> & that's not real/not anymore/i shd be immune/if i'm
> still alive & that's what i waz discussin/how i am still
> alive & my dependency on other living beins for love
> i survive on intimacy & tomorrow/that's all i've got going
> & the music waz like smack & you knew abt that
> & still refused my dance waz not enuf/& it waz all i had
> but being alive & being a woman & being colored is a metaphysical
> dilemma/i havent conquered yet/do you see the point
> my spirit is too ancient to understand the separation of
> soul & gender/my love is too delicate to have thrown
> back on my face   (1977:45)

The almost distant tone so common to reveries (or flash-back passages) derives at least in part from the repetitiveness and circularity of sentences that seem to tumble over each other, *and, and, and.* The following passage, from "O Yes" by Tillie Olsen, in which Alva recalls a religious experience, illustrates how the syntax creates the effect:

When I was carrying Parry and her father left me, and I fifteen years old, one thousand miles away from home, sin-sick and never really believing, as still I don't believe all, scorning, for what have it done to help, waiting there in the clinic and maybe sleeping, a voice called: Alva, Alva. So mournful and so sweet: Alva. Fear not, I have loved you from the foundation of the universe. And a small child tugged on my dress. He was carrying a parade stick, on the end of it a star that outshined the sun. Follow me, he said. And the real sun went down and he hidden his stick. How dark it was, how dark. I could feel the darkness with my hands. And when I could see, I screamed. Dump trucks run, never ceasing with souls, weary ones having to stamp and shove them along, and the air like fire. Oh I never want to hear such screaming. Then the little child jumped on a motorbike making a path no bigger than my little finger. But first he greased my feet with the hands of my momma when I was a knee baby. They shined like the sun was on them. Eyes he placed all around my head, and as I journeyed upward after him, it seemed I heard a mourning: 'Mama Mama you must help carry the world.' The rise and fall of nations I saw. And the voice called again Alva Alva, and I flew into a world of light, multitudes singing, Free, free, I am so glad. (1961:61)

Even in reported situations, in which an omniscient narrator describes for us the internal workings of a character's mind, this rambling, associative syntax recreates for us the intimate abstractedness of talking to oneself. In Toni Morrison's *Sula* the narrator describes the following shift in perception in Nel's consciousness:

On her knees, her hand on the cold rim of the bathtub, she waited for something to happen . . . inside. There was a stirring, a movement of mud and dead leaves. She thought of the women at Chicken Little's funeral. The women who shrieked over the bier and at the lip of the open grave. What she had regarded since as unbecoming behavior seemed fitting to her now; . . . But it seemed to her now that it was not a fist-shaking grief they were keening but rather a simple obligation to say something, do something, feel something about the dead. They could not let that heart-smashing event pass unrecorded, unidentified. It was poisonous, unnatural to let the dead go with a mere whimpering, a slight murmur, a rose bouquet of good taste. . . . And there must be much rage and saliva in its presence. The body must move and throw itself about, the eyes must roll, the hands should have no peace, and the throat should release all the yearning, despair and outrage that accompany the stupidity of loss. (1975:92)

Jill Johnston's prose in *Lesbian Nation* (1973) speaks directly to her reader as it works through the process of her shift in consciousness as she moves toward lesbian feminism; it is "an interlocking web of personal experience and history and events of the world forming a picture of an evolving political revolutionary consciousness of one who was female who emerged from straight middle unconscious postwar amerika." She repeats her observations in slightly altered forms, rephrasing them, shifting their meanings, "working circles within circles" such that "every departure from a point of origin carries with it a renewed approach to it." Her sentences run on unmarked by conventional punctuation; her puns restore the naming function of language, reclaiming the phrases and the literary conventions of patriarchal language and turning them to feminist phrases.

. . . the 350 years of Abraham intersample Abraham lived for 350 years because the bible ages are only a succession of sons and fathers and grandfathers intensely identifying with their ancestors their son so identified naturely with the father that he believed he was the father and of course he was as was Abraham and Isaac and Jacob and Esau and Reuben and Simeon and Levi and Judah and Joseph each one lived for 350 years, but who are the daughters of Rachel and Ruth and Sarah and Rebekah the rest we do not know the daughters never had any daughters they had only sons who begat more sons and sons so we have very little sense, from that peculiar book, of the lineage and ligaments and legacies and identities of mothers and daughters and their mothers and mothers and daughters and sisters who were naturally not lesbians if they had nothing of each other save sons so now we must say Verily Verily, I say unto thee, except a woman be born again she cannot see the Kingdom of Goddess a woman must be born again to be herself her own eminence and grace the queen queen-self whose mother has pressed upon her mouth innumerable passionate kisses so sigh us. . . .

... the beginning of the unifirst is rite now if all tinks are at this momentum being cremated and the end of the unihearse is right now for all thinks are at this momentus passing away ... (1973:266–70)

Johnston's style of ever-widening circles manifests her changing perspectives as her consciousness evolves, returning to themes as her narrative moves forward in historical time.

The syntactic structure and the punctuation found in the novels of Bertha Harris appear to be more "conventional" than Johnston's. There are no page-long run-on sentences, and most of the conventions of punctuation are observed. She violates the rules of traditional grammar only by her sentence fragments, which accentuate the humorous content of the paragraphs which contain them. When we examine whole paragraphs, however, we discover the parallel structures, short simple sentences, frequent repetitions, conjoined phrases and clauses characteristic of cumulative style.

> Like all painters in this women's group of women painters, she is engrossed in the preparation and eating of food. Mushes of lentils and Spanish onion. *Haute* Chinese. Arcane Hungarian. Elaborate; cheap. It always tastes wonderful; and Flynn, when they invite her to their long weekly dinner parties, eats the most. In her thirties, she is filling out. She has buttocks. Her breasts are wonderful. (1976:88)

> Some call the woman I love silver, and some call her gold. Before I got to be her lover, she painted a painting and presented it to me. It is entitled "One Hundred and Forty-Seven Cunts." Much of it she painted with her fingers. It is still rolled up, the three panels of it, and wrapped in plastic at the bottom of a cardboard box. I still don't have a wall of my own. The painter's frequent headaches intimidate me—I believe them a superior manifestation of cognizance of all that is horrible; they are a function of mighty brain power. Her wondrous hair sprouts from those headaches. It is like those flowers whose petals grow backwards, yearning towards the stem. Like chrysanthemums, I remember now. Except when she takes up the scissors and cuts it all off; and then none of it is any longer than a clipped fingernail all over her skull; and then there is nothing that will hide the machinery of the headache: it shows. I use the word 'love' when I speak to her, and she uses my name. . . . (Ibid.:137–38)

Even these brief excerpts illustrate that Harris's prose style reflects the content of her novel. She has written what might be called a "simultaneous novel." All events—different pasts, present, and future—tend to be narrated in the "historic present" or simple present tense, and Harris even includes her random thoughts during the creative process as part of the narrative ("Like chrysanthemums, I remember now"), addressing the reader, making herself and her reader part of the narrative as she addresses her in an offhand, conversational manner.

> Meanwhile, listen to this: Bertha is a still, yellow moon reflected by troubled lake water. Bertha is the one with the duelling scar across her cheekbone, who lifts absinthe with two fingers, who sits still, as unmoved as God, while the lustful riff-raff blunders by. She is that stark dark outline high above the Cliffs of Whatever poised to leap—but too pleasured by the claptrap of her swirling cape yet to make a move. You remember her—she's the one who assassinated the Princess Royal of Transylvania and caused World War Four. Meanwhile, she dresses in white trousers and gallops her stallion through the Bois every morning and does not answer letters. . . . She comes by everything naturally. (Ibid.: 138–39)

The past tense is used, however, to recount actual historical events. Each section of the novel begins with a short italicized passage describing one such event; these are frequently tales of the torture and martyrdom of women, and are occasionally related ironically:

> Cyrica and Julitta were daughter and mother. When, for some unknown reason, the Governor Alexander took Cyrica at the age of five from her mother, Cyrica would not be comforted but howled, struggled, and kicked; and, at last, scratched the Governor's face. Alexander, understandably enraged, threw the child down the stone steps of the Tribune, killing her outright. Far from being downcast, Julitta rejoiced in her daughter's escape and went cheerfully to torture and death. (Ibid.:139)

Millett, like Johnston and Harris, requires the run-on, infinite syntax in which words explode, collide, brush, and fuse; she has broken through the boundaries of linear time in *Flying*. Utilizing words as though they were the frames of an autobiographical film, flashing back and forward in her paragraphs, Millett is able to capture events at different points in time, fusing them in her consciousness. She creates portraits through the use of sentence fragments which lack verbs, freezing events as if in a camera, uses the simple present and the progressive aspect to lend immediacy to past events and convey a sense of movement in and between time; it is the syntax of woman's consciousness, the rush of perception, the speech that tells all as it emerges.

> I look across the pond now as my mind's eye drinks that moment in color—and matches it against the black and white a Pentax saw, saw and held last summer at Brookfield as the sun fell in scatters through sycamore leaves. Celia, her hair uncombed after breakfast, played the lute for us in the open air. Now only these portraits remain: my mind's version in motion and sound, and the still shot upon paper. Celia bending then upon her lute, playing it in sunlight one fine morning our summer of delight, her straight hair merely braided, not dressed as now in five choirs upon her head for concert . . . Examining again her tomboy succulence that Connecticut June day, the extravagant delicacy of her face, something even of her eyes' fine beauty captured one forever time ago to pierce me now as they did that muddled September night I scrawled on yellow paper, cursing her good-bye. Eyes light a light through the tunnel of loss. And now the music rises, sound in air expanding as the lyrics come crisp and Elizabethan. . . . superior art of song defeating mere prose in its finer medium. Time, and again in time recurring. Sound once lost in space, now miraculously reassembled here within the same stones' echoes as it echoes in the mind while I sit again, this moment erasing the bird's chatter about the pond a hundred miles upriver from where the sound now echoes to their miracle performed. (1974:114–17)

Millett's command of the conjunctive style is evident when she describes her love-making in sentences which are at once fragmented and fused. Questions and imperatives flow into statements, unmarked by standard terminal punctuation. Phrases and clauses are juxtaposed and stacked upon one another, and frequently run together without conjunction. There are fragments which lack subjects and which contain progressives without auxiliary verbs, fragments and sentences in the simple present and future. Millett also shifts her point of view, addressing her lover and herself in the second person, addressing her lover in both second and third person.

> . . . I must doubt it, even this, her hand on my breast will she touch the nipple with exquisite care, feels like it connects to the clitoris begins the heat between my legs. . . What sick thought is

this, or is it that final safety with her, bewildered at the joy in her hand searching me, opening to her fingers upon the lips of my other mouth set making little noises, silence to be filled with her tongue while she sifts me, reams, files, selects, and plays upon the nerve like a button pressed all heat flooding out I open wider to receive her will split myself take her whole up to the elbow, straining in hope. I love the way you move as I move dancing under your hand's power deep in me shaking when you press hard fast against the wall deep like a storm in me. I must stop breathing, so fierce you are. So powerful. (Ibid.:481)

For centuries, women have written in a style which has been termed "confessional," using it for describing our own lives in private; now we are bringing it forth as our art, as a dynamic affirmation of our newly acquired identities as whole women. That this spirit owes much to our foremothers has been noted by Moffat and Painter: "we believe the women writers of the future will stand on the remarkably strong shoulders of women diarists who wrote to please no audience but themselves" (1975:12). Our style, which consciously reflects its heritage, is outside the literary world, "on the periphery," in Daly's terms. From this boundary, new visions are evolving, a "new species which redefines sexuality and reproduction; the production and exchange of use values; and all the languages of the conscious and subconscious" (Desmoines, 1976:70). Patriarchal language, as we have pointed out, is inadequate for describing our new ways of conceptualizing about ourselves in relation to each other and to the world. For this reason, women are challenging and shifting the boundaries of English in ways most often associated with poetic consciousness.

Our tradition, which has its sources in the unspoken lives of women, emerged as a recognizable style when Gertrude Stein and Virginia Woolf began to publish and gain recognition as "literary" writers.

This style continues to evolve, mirroring the new women's consciousness and the aesthetics that this style calls forth. This approach contrasts sharply with the patriarchal aesthetic, what Robinson has called the "bourgeois aesthetic."

> It is a fundamental precept—indeed, an axiom—of bourgeois aesthetics that good art, although probably adhering and contributing to a tradition, is art that celebrates what is unique and even eccentric in human experience or human personality. Achievement, from this perspective, reflects individual heroism. Isolation is an individual condition. This is the norm, whether the achievement and the isolation be that of the artist or the character. It seems to me that this is a far from universal way for people to be or to be perceived, but one that is intimately connected to relationships and values perpetuated by capitalism. For this reason, I would seriously question any aesthetic that not only fails to call that individualism into question, but that does so intentionally, in the name of feminism. (1976:3)

Robinson later asks "whether the best role for the arts or for criticism is to celebrate that which is basic or that which is marginal, what is common or what is exceptional" (Ibid.:6). With her, we would assert that the "best" criticism is that which draws on the shared experiences, the common life experiences of women, rather than the unique, or individual, experience.[2]

There can be little doubt that the women writing in the 20th century are intensely conscious of the many ways in which we must wrestle with English in our efforts to remake it as a language adequate to our conceptual processes. The previously separated strands of this remaking finally begin to weave themselves into a discernible whole with the large-scale publishing and distribution of women's writing that has begun. From Virginia Woolf and Gertrude Stein to Kate Millett and Susan Griffin, the relationship between consciousness and linguistic choice is confronted, played with, and articulated as the self expressing itself in and through a language remade, reordered: the feminist aesthetic. Virginia Woolf, in her diary, reflected on the connections between her consciousness and "random" style.

> . . . I got out this diary and read, as one always does read one's own writing, with a kind of guilty intensity. I confess that the rough and random style of it, often so ungrammatical, and crying for a word altered, afflicted me somewhat. I am trying to tell whichever self it is that reads this hereafter that I can write very much better; and take no time over this; and forbid her to let the eye of man behold it. And now I may add my little compliment to the effect that it has a slapdash and vigour and sometimes hits an unexpected bull's eye. But what is more to the point is my belief that the habit of writing thus for my own eye is good practice. It loosens the ligaments. Never mind the misses and the stumbles. Going at such a pace as I do I must make the most direct and instant shots at my object, and thus have to lay hands on words, choose them and shoot them with no more pause than is needed to put my pen in the ink. . . . Moreover there looms ahead of me the shadow of some kind of form which a diary might attain to. I might in the course of time learn what it is that one can make of this loose, drifting material of life; finding another use for it than the use I put it to, so much more consciously and scrupulously in fiction. What sort of diary should I like mine to be? Something loose knit and yet not slovenly, so elastic that it will embrace anything, solemn, slight or beautiful that comes into my mind. I should like it to resemble some deep old desk, or capacious hold-all, in which one flings a mass of odds and ends without looking them through. I should like to come back, after a year or two, and find that the collection had sorted itself and refined itself and coalesced, as such deposits so mysteriously do, into a mould, transparent enough to reflect the light of our life, and yet steady, tranquil compounds with the aloofness of a work of art. The main requisite, I think on rereading my old volumes, is not to play the part of censor, but to write as the mood comes or of anything whatever; since I was curious to find how I went for things put in haphazard, and found the significance to lie where I never saw it at the time. . . . *Easter Sunday, April 20th [1919]* (Virginia Woolf, in Moffat & Painter, 1975:226–27)

Woolf goes on to comment that the "looseness" of diary writing may quickly become "slovenly," and we see here, as we do in her concern for its lack of grammatical "correctness," that she held always before her mind's eye the established values of male writers in the language. Yet her consciousness of the expressive possibilities for diary-writing, her ruminations on its potential as a literary form, and her concept of its style as a mold capable of accommodating a random assortment of ideas, impressions, "odds and ends," a catch-all, within which such a mass might sort itself into patterns and meanings previously unimagined, all these possibilities are being realized in the writing of contemporary women.

A feminist aesthetic, as it emerges out of women's evolution, grounds itself in a woman's consciousness and in the unrelenting language of process and change. A feminist aesthetic encompasses the cultural and social attempts to cripple women, to bind us, to strip us of our self-awareness, and it also traces the unwinding of the patriarchal bonds that have limited our perceptions and descriptions of our experience. Such an aesthetic may well incorporate the "truth criterion" suggested by Marcia Holly (Donovan, 1975:38–47), the requirement that literature represent the realities of women's lives and that criticism demand such authenticity. But more importantly, it records the progressive development of a female culture, as Donovan has pointed out. Out of the consciousness of women unidentified by the other will come the aesthetic of women's knowledge, the perspective of women's experiences that has not been filtered through patriarchal definitions of the world, that has not been diluted or distorted in order to pacify the frightened others in the world. As Donovan has correctly observed, ". . . aesthetic judgments are rooted in epistemology: one cannot understand why someone thinks something is beautiful or significant until one understands the way s/he *sees,* knows the world" (1975:78). Walls fall away; what had been perceived as boundaries melt; categories become shape-changers; sentences are never "complete" because the perceiving is the movement itself.

As women strain to break through the limits of English, certain patterns begin to emerge, recurrences of similar syntactic ways of ordering perception that is always moving and often contradictory. What is said in one breath may be negated by the succeeding observation. The natural imagery of growth, proliferation, and evolution replaces nature as object and product. Flux is the only experience; stasis is impossible. Labels and abstract nouns as viable perceptive categories give way to active, process verbs and concrete nouns, the language of touch; verbs of specific action replace the abstract, more general verbs. On the discourse level, we find a discursive, conjunctive style instead of the complex, subordinating, linear style of classification and distinction. It is not that there is no classifying taking place, rather that the syntactic structure must accommodate itself to the shifting perspectives of the writer's observing mind. In contrast to a subordinate syntax (in which the complexity of experience is embedded in dependent clauses, reflecting experience already categorized, qualified, detached from its happening), the writer attempts to order her perceptions through a kind of cumulative syntax, using juxtaposed clauses to express the relationships as they suggest themselves. It is the syntax of woman's consciousness, the rush of perception, the speech that tells all as it emerges. It is the syntax that charges through time/space, taking into itself the urgency of speed; the trick is not to get "caught in time."

'It was a risk I had to take. Life itself is a risk, but it gets riskier somehow when it's canned. Preserved. You get caught in time.'

Suddenly terrified I might be caught in time. . . . Will I be caught here? I wonder. Trapped in this book forever? (Millett, p. 535)

When the book is finished I must die. It is myself stopping, held in time there, not going on. (Millett, 1974:540)

Finally there comes the terror of the sentence written even as it is lived, the risk of confronting one's experience *as* meaning, the fear that such knowledge itself must be lived with. In such risk, control sustains.

NOTES

1. Before proceeding further with an analysis, which may to some women appear to blur essential differences in our experiences, such as class and race, we would like to address what we perceive to be one of the most crippling effects of male control of education and the print medium. Most, but not all, of the writers we examine in this article have had access to the privileges and benefits of their relationships with white males. Most of them have had at least some education beyond the high school level. Johnston is only one such example. She has had the time to experiment with English; she knows the so-called "rules" of standard English (a male creation) because she has had the opportunity to learn them. Because she does know those "rules," she not only knows *how* to break them in ways that will work for her, but she also, to some extent, is thereby freed from the constraint of having to demonstrate to the masculinist arbiters of literary taste that she does know them. Women who are not so economically or educationally advantaged, on the other hand, either steadfastly adhere to the dialect of their class, race, or region, or they endeavor to imitate the language of power, i.e., standard English, in order to prove their competence to those who have economic power. In the past, in contrast to women like Johnston, Woolf, and Stein, such women have not felt they could "afford" to experiment with a language which might have been a second dialect. We see no way to avoid these issues. As long as there is a "prestige dialect" that everyone aspiring to status is expected to acquire, and as long as publishers, editors, and reviewers sanction only those works written in the prestige dialect, there will be no way to resolve this conflict in possibilities. To argue, however, that the conflict results only from racial or class differences is oversimplification. The present class structure in our society defines only white male class and access to power within that hierarchical structure. In most cases, women belong to a specific class only through their fathers or husbands, not through their own economic status as individuals within the system.

2. More recently, however, women such as Ntozake Shange and Sharon Isabell *(Yesterday's Lessons)* have managed to publish their work without sacrificing the integrity of their vision to the distortions of white male English. Black women especially have been willing to fight for their language by using it; by saying, in effect, "If you are to understand me, you must understand me *as I am, as I speak to you.*" In the past, the voices of Black women could not be found in the male media, because, as Barbara Smith has observed, "the form and language of these works is . . . nothing like what white patriarchal culture requires or expects" (1977:33). Their voices, now raised, have helped us to articulate better the common features of our experience.

2. In speaking of distinguishing between those experiences that are "basic" and those that are "marginal," Robinson explains that she is "not proposing a crude quantitative game," that, although most women are "heterosexual," lesbianism is a basic experience "because it puts women in direct touch with the social forces that define a sexist society."

REFERENCES

Allegro, Peggy, 1975. The strange and the familiar: The evolutionary potential of lesbianism. In Gina Covina & Laurel Galana (eds.), *The lesbian reader.* Oakland, Calif.: Amazon Press, 167–84.

Covina, Gina & Laurel Galana, eds. 1975. *The lesbian reader.* Oakland, Calif.: Amazon Press.

Crouch, Isabel M. & Betty Lou Dubois. 1976. Features of female/male undergraduates' language behavior. Manuscript, Dept. of Speech., New Mexico State Univ. 1973.

Daly, Mary. 1973. *Beyond God the father.* Boston: Beacon Press.

——— 1978. *Gyn/ecology: The metaethics of radical feminism.* Boston: Beacon Press.

Desmoines, Harriet. 1976. Go Tell Aunt Rhody. . . . *Sinister Wisdom,* I (1), 69–70.

Donovan, Josephine, ed. 1975. *Feminist literary criticism.* Louisville, Ky.: Univ. of Kentucky Press.

Dubois, Betty Lou & Isabel M. Crouch. 1975. The question of tag questions in women's speech: They don't really use more of them, do they? *Language in Society,* 4, 289–94.

Griffin, Susan. 1976. Transformations. *Sinister Wisdom,* I (2), 6–10.

——— 1978. *Woman and nature: The roaring inside her.* New York: Harper & Row.

Haimson, Maud. 1975. Hands. In Gina Covina & Laurel Galana (eds.), *The lesbian reader.* Oakland, Calif.: Amazon Press, 59–76.

Harris, Bertha. 1976. *lover.* Plainfield, Vt.: Daughters.

Isabell, Sharon. 1974. *Yesterday's lessons.* Oakland, Calif.: Diana Press.

Jespersen, Otto. 1922, 1964. *Language: Its nature, development and origin.* New York: W. W. Norton.

Johnston, Jill. 1973. *Lesbian nation: The feminist solution.* New York: Simon & Schuster.

——— 1974. *Gullible's travels.* New York: Links Books.

Lakoff, Robin. 1975. *Language and woman's place.* New York: Harper & Row.

Millett, Kate. 1974. *Flying.* New York: Alfred A. Knopf.

Moffat, Mary Jane & Charlotte Painter. 1975. *Revelations: Diaries of women.* New York: Random House.

Morrison, Toni. 1975. *Sula.* New York: Bantam.

Olsen, Tillie. 1961. *Tell me a riddle.* New York: Dell.

Piercy, Marge. 1976. *Woman on the edge of time.* New York: Alfred A. Knopf.

Robinson, Lillian. 1976. Who speaks for women—And is it poetry? Paper delivered at Modern Language Association, New York, December. Revised version, "Working/Women/Writing," published in *Sex, class, and culture.* (Bloomington: Indiana University Press, 1978), 223–53. The quote is from the original version.

Shange, Ntozake. 1977. *For colored girls who have considered suicide when the rainbow is enuf.* New York: Macmillan.

Smith, Barbara. 1977. Toward a Black feminist criticism. *Conditions,* 2, 25–44.

Smith, Barbara & Beverly Smith. 1979. "I am not meant to be alone and without you who understand": Letters from Black feminists, 1972–1978. *Conditions,* 4, 62–77.

Stein, Gertrude. 1957. *Lectures in America.* Boston: Beacon Press.

Thorne, Barrie & Nancy Henley, eds. 1975. *Language and sex: Difference and dominance.* Rowley, Mass.: Newbury House.

MEN'S SPEECH TO YOUNG CHILDREN*

Jean Berko Gleason and Esther Blank Greif

This paper will discuss the impact that fathers have on their children's language development, as well as how fathers may be using language to socialize their children in sex-typed ways. Only recently have linguists and developmental psychologists become interested in the effect that fathers have on their children. Within linguistics the interest in fathers' speech is tied to a larger movement that considers parent input an important factor in children's linguistic and social development. This new focus contrasts with earlier views, which assumed that young children acquire language from the complex adult speech around them without any real help from adults (Chomsky, 1967; McNeill, 1970). The earlier theory explained the fact that children become expert speakers in only three or four years by suggesting that children are biologically programmed to learn language. According to this view, children had only to be exposed to language, even language not directed to them, in order for their innate powers to begin to extract and formulate the rules of the language.

Researchers in child language began to challenge this view when they turned their attention to mothers' speech to children learning language (Broen, 1972; Farwell, 1973; Gleason, 1973; Snow, 1972). These studies of mothers' speech revealed that mothers make many special accommodations to their children when they talk to them; mothers' speech appears to be an ideal teaching language, one that is often quite grammatical, simple, and repetitious, typically delivered in a slow, clear voice. As children grow older, mothers gradually increase the complexity of what they say to them, so that it now seems clear that mothers are in some sense "tuned" to their children, and language acquisition can now be seen from an interactive perspective, one that involves both the child and a sensitive adult.

Once it was known that mothers' speech to young children has special input features, it became important to determine if these features are limited to

*Some of the material presented here appeared in "Fathers and Other Strangers: Men's Speech to Young Children" in Daniel P. Dato, ed., *Developmental Psycholinguistics: Theory and Application.* Washington, D.C.: Georgetown Univ. Press, 1975, pp. 289–97. The research was supported in part by Grant BNS 75–21909A01 from the National Science Foundation.

mothers' speech or if they are in a more general sense characteristic of adult language to young children. There are obvious practical consequences: with family roles changing and the advent of day-care, the question of whether or not non-mothers are able to provide the kind of linguistic environment that may be crucial to the interactive development of language becomes increasingly significant. Catherine Snow (1972) answered part of the question when she showed that women who were not mothers and who had little contact with children nonetheless had in their speech to children the same modifications as mothers. But men's language has remained a mystery; only recently have researchers begun to look at men's speech to children.

In this paper we will look at men's speech to children in a variety of situations, including the home, the laboratory, and the day-care center. Where data are available, we will compare fathers' and mothers' speech in similar situations. We will also look at some conversational features common in the speech of fathers. Finally, we will discuss the implications of fathers' speech for the socialization of their sons and daughters.

Our method, in general, has been to tape-record parent-child conversations, whether in the laboratory or at home. In the laboratory we have also made videotapes of these same interactions. Once we have recorded a session, research assistants who have been trained to attend to speech features make written transcriptions of the tape recordings. The written transcriptions are then subjected to a series of analyses. While many of the features we will be discussing are widely understood (e.g., calling a child by name), others are of a more technical nature. In the interest of clarity, we will describe them here:

- Sentence type - a syntactic description which refers to whether a sentence is in the form of a question, an imperative, a declarative, a fragment, etc.
- Imperative - a sentence type that expresses an order or command, usually without expressing the subject (e.g., "Shut the door").
- Question or interrogative - a sentence type that occurs in two basic forms: the *Wh*-question (e.g., "Where is the dog?") and the *yes/no* form (e.g., "Did you shut the door?").
- Declarative - a sentence type that is used for statements or descriptions (e.g., "The door is shut").
- Directive - any utterance whose intent is to cause the hearer to do something. Directives can take varying syntactic forms (e.g., "Shut the door"; "Would you shut the door?"; and "The door needs to be shut" can all be directives even though their form is imperative, interrogative, and declarative, respectively).
- MLU - the mean length of utterance, which is computed by counting all of a speaker's words over a period of time and dividing that total by the number of separate sentences (or utterances) that the speaker has made. This yields something like an average length of sentence, except that it is a more general term, since speakers frequently do not speak in complete sentences.

- Complexity - a measure of grammatical difficulty. The simplest or least complex sentences take the form of the subject-verb-object in the present tense (e.g., Mary hits the ball). The addition of prepositional phrases, subordinate clauses, etc., all make sentences more complex.
- Repetition rate - the frequency with which speakers repeat either their own just prior utterances or the utterances of those around them (see Snow, 1972).
- "Baby talk features" - some specific ways that adults modify their usual way of talking in order to talk to very young children. These include some special vocabulary (e.g., "bunny"), adding "ie" to words (e.g., "horsie", "doggie"), as well as a number of features that serve to simplify and clarify usual adult speech (e.g., repetition; easy vocabulary; the use of short and simple sentences; slow, clear pronunciation).

HOME AND DAY-CARE

Our first study of men's speech to children was based on observations of two male and two female teachers in a small day-care center and of three traditional white, middle-class families at home with their children, mostly at the dinner hour. By "traditional" we mean a family in which there is a division of labor by sex: a mother at home who does the bulk of child care, and a father employed outside the home. Each family had two preschool-aged children. The home and day-care samples cover various nonexperimental, loosely structured activities, like eating dinner or having juice and crackers and playing in the playground. We compared the fathers' and mothers' speech at home along a number of dimensions, and we compared the female with the male day-care teachers.

The mothers and fathers at home all simplified their speech when addressing their children. The mean length of utterance (MLU) of mothers and fathers within each family was almost identical (5.28 and 5.25 respectively), although the fathers' MLU was less closely tied to that of the child than was the mothers': mothers used less complex speech with their younger children and produced longer, more complex utterances when addressing the older of their two children. In one family, where the younger child by two years was a girl, the father nonetheless directed longer utterances to her than to his son, who was five. This is perhaps a reflection of the fact that there were large differences between fathers and mothers in the types of sentences they produced. For example, fathers' language was filled with direct imperatives, especially to their sons. Since imperative sentences lack subjects, they are typically short, and this contributes to the shorter average length of father-son utterances.

In the home samples, fathers produced a much higher percentage of imperatives than mothers (38.3% to 19.0%). Fathers also produced more threats and more jocular names, names that had a pejorative undertone, like *dingaling,* especially to their sons. One additional difference between fathers and mothers was that fathers seemed to use some fairly rare vocabulary, like telling a two-year-old that he is being *aggravating*. Like the mothers', the fathers' speech was essentially limited to the here and now, and was clearly a style of speech, or register, especially marked for talking to children. However, because of the imperatives, threats, and affectionately insulting names, the fathers' language seemed to be qualitatively different from the mothers' language. Finally, the fathers' language clearly demarked their role within the family. For example, one father, playing with his small son, broke off the game to send the child to his mother to have his diaper changed.[1]

While the mothers and fathers had a number of differentiating features in their language, male and female day-care teachers produced language that was very similar. The mean length of utterance of the five longest utterances for each was computed; the females averaged 14.9 and the males averaged 14.8. Repetition rates for the males were higher than for the females: males averaged 31% repetitions, while females' speech contained 24% repetitions. Again, we noted some unexpected vocabulary used by males: for example, one teacher asked a child if she found something *intimidating*. The child was in a class of three-year-olds. But both females and males used types of discourse which were very much in the present, and were concerned with the child's immediate needs, as is evidenced by the following excerpt from the transcript:

> Male teacher: (to Jenny) Does Jenny want to go to the toilet? Do you want to go to the toilet? (to Michael) Did you go to potty after nap?

Here the language of this male teacher is filled with baby-talk features, and the concern is one that in many homes is the exclusive province of mothers, but within the day-care center male and female teachers accepted responsibility for attending to the children's immediate needs, and their language reflected this.

There are two main features that distinguish between the language of the male and female day-care teachers. The first is in the use of the child's name. In a sample of 100 utterances, males called the child by name an average of thirty-two times. Women did so only one-fourth as often.

The second difference between the language of female and male teachers was in sentence type. As in the families, males used more imperatives than females, but that has to be seen in light of the fact that the women teachers' speech was singularly devoid of direct imperative constructions: they averaged 2%. Males averaged only 11%, which is a smaller proportion of imperatives than mothers use at home, and in a different universe from the fathers. (See Table 1.)

Table 1.   Percentage of Utterance Types

	Imperatives	Declaratives	Questions
Fathers	38	33	29
Mothers	19	52	29
Male teachers	11	47	42
Female teachers	2	48	50

In discussing differences between teachers and parents, it is important to note that the teachers were dealing with someone else's children. Parents are also aware that they cannot speak as strongly to their children's friends as to their own. As one nine-year-old girl we know said about visiting a friend's house, "My friend's mother is always much nicer to me than she is to her own child." Thus, one of the variables to be taken into account in studying language addressed to children is that adults have separate ways of talking to their own children and to other people's children.

The male and female day-care teachers were not as different from one another as were fathers and mothers at home. The differences that did exist, however, were in the same direction—males used a greater number of imperatives, for instance. But at the same time, day-care males, like mothers and female teachers, expressed many of their requests in question form and tended to state social rules in an impersonal and nonthreatening way. The following excerpt from a transcript indicates how one male day-care teacher handled a child transgressor:

> Mr. B: Mickey, do you know what the rule is? When someone screams and says they want to get up, you don't hold them down. Mickey, we don't hold people down when they say they want to get up. You were holding Sarah down and she kept saying she wanted to get up. Okay. So the next time someone says, "Excuse me, I want to get up," you let them up.

By contrast, a father at home, faced with a much less serious situation, expressed himself as follows:

> Mr. X: Anthony, stay out of here before I break your head. Don't go in there again or I'll break your head.

Both men's utterances are clearly marked as adult-child register: the child is called by name frequently and there are numerous repetitions, but the father is threatening and imperative, while the day-care attendant speaks in an understated, very explicit and rather preachy way that is perhaps itself an example of schoolteacher register. This is especially true of the "we don'ts" where "we" really means "you." Finally, it would appear that while the traditional father at home may not be attuned to the immediate needs of his child and may speak to that child in a gruff, imperious way, this is not at all the case where the male shares the nurturant role, as in the day-care center and, possibly by extension, in those families where fathers share child-care duties. The male day-care teachers' speech is singularly devoid of the kinds of threats used by the traditional fathers at home. In the use of the imperative constructions there is no overlap between home and school samples. In fact, mothers at home produce more imperatives to their children than do males in the day-care setting.

While the language of the fathers at home has the same basic syntactic features as the language of mothers, it is distinguished from mothers' speech to children along the lines that are connected with the father's traditional role, both as authority figure and as one who is not called upon to be completely sensitive to the needs and intentions of the child. Traditional fathers are not primary providers of nurturance, nor are they called upon to be sensitive to the signals that indicate nurturance is called for.

In the day-care center female and male teachers occupy the same role, and many of the differences that have been noted between mothers and fathers disappear. Male day-care teachers' speech to young children is more like the language of female day-care teachers than it is like that of fathers at home, even though it contains some markers characteristic of male speech in general. While the greater use of imperatives might indicate that males are more controlling, it is difficult to explain why men call children by name so much more frequently than women do. The use of the child's name at the beginning of an utterance may be an attention-getting or controlling device, but utterances frequently terminated with the child's name as well. One possibility is that the use of the child's name is a marker employed by males more frequently than females to indicate that they are speaking in adult-child register; females rely upon other devices, such as varied or exaggerated intonation patterns, to accomplish the same end.

It is probably possible to find other differences in the language of male and female day-care attendants, but the similarities in their language are striking. If the small day-care sample we have seen is in any way typical, we can take assurance from the fact that day-care teachers' speech is very like mothers' speech: both female and male day-care teachers appear to provide children with the kind of linguistic input that may be considered necessary for the development of language. Men, as well as women, modify their speech when addressing young children, and where the men occupy a nurturant role they become increasingly sensitive to the needs and intentions of the children.

LABORATORY STUDIES

Some differences between men's and women's speech to children have been supported by observations in varied natural situations. We will now turn to a brief discussion of several studies that were done in a laboratory setting by members of our research team.[2]

The laboratory studies were set up in order to investigate under controlled conditions some of the speech patterns that we and other observers had noted in natural settings. We brought preschool children and their parents into a laboratory playroom for a thirty-minute play session. Each child visited the lab twice, once with each parent, and was videotaped. The play sessions centered around three activities: playing with a toy car which could be taken apart, playing store with a toy cash register and a number of other store items, and reading a book which had no words. These activities were chosen because they called for different types of speech. For example, the book situation elicited a narrative style, playing store is characterized by more social and interactive language, and taking the car apart calls for directive and instructional speech. At the end of the laboratory session, we gave a gift to the child. This gave us the opportunity to study children's and parents' use of politeness routines in a gift-giving situation. A number of separate studies have emerged from this research project on parent-child language during play.

One recent study looked at the speech of parents to their preschool children during play with a toy car that came apart (see Masur & Gleason, 1980, for a full description of methods and statistical analyses). The car came with some tools, like a screwdriver and wrench, for removing such components as the wheels, engine, and steering wheel. Fourteen fathers and fourteen mothers, along with their children, participated in the study. An analysis of the parents' language to their children showed that fathers were significantly more likely than mothers to use the actual names of the car parts. For example, a father might ask his child to get the "screwdriver," while the mother would instead ask for the "thing you use to loosen screws." Fathers were also more likely than mothers to ask their children to provide the names for the car parts and to tell what their functions were. Interestingly, differences between mothers and fathers were greater with daughters than with sons. Mothers were least likely to ask daughters for information about car parts. This study showed that, at least in this type of play situation with a traditionally masculine toy, fathers provided more sophisticated information to their children and required more information in return than mothers did; in doing so, they treated girls and boys in essentially the same way. Mothers, on the other hand, were less demanding of information from their daughters than from their sons. In general, fathers were more likely to encourage children to display their knowledge, and were more cognitively and linguistically demanding of their children. Of course, in a play situation with a neutral toy, these differences might not be observed.

In a related study (again, we refer the reader to Bellinger and Gleason, 1982) we focused on the use of directives in parents' speech in the situation just described. A directive is a general term that refers to an utterance made by a speaker in order to get a hearer to perform some action. Our language offers many ways of expressing directive intentions. The home and day-care studies described earlier showed that men tend to use more direct imperatives or orders than women. However, there are other ways to request action besides simply giving a command. This study outlined three types of directives: (1) imperatives —these are in the form of orders (e.g., "Give me the screwdriver"); (2) indirect directives—these take the form of questions (e.g., "Would you give me the screwdriver?"); and (3) implied directives—these take the form of statements, and the hearer must infer what action is required (e.g., "I could really use the screwdriver"). Fathers used more directives altogether than mothers. In addition, there were also some differences in the types of directives used by parents. Fathers were more likely than mothers to use either imperatives or implied directives. That is, fathers used the most direct and the most subtle forms. Mothers, on the other hand, were more likely to express their requests in the form of questions. These indirect requests tend to be more polite. This study shows that fathers and mothers provide different models for their children, a factor in children's linguistic socialization. Fathers are in general more directive than mothers. Mothers' directives tend to be in polite question form, while fathers use more imperative and indirect statements to get their children to perform actions.

Another study (see Greif, 1980) focused on parents' tendency to interrupt their children's speech during the thirty-minute play session involving playing store, reading the book, and playing with the toy car. Typically, interrupting another speaker is an impolite thing to do, and it shows some insensitivity to the person interrupted. Additionally, the person who interrupts gains some control over the conversation by getting a chance to speak when it is not his or her turn. We examined speech of sixteen mothers and sixteen fathers and found that fathers overall were more likely to interrupt their children than mothers were. In addition, there were differences in the treatment of girls and boys. Mothers and fathers were in general more likely to interrupt the speech of girls than boys. The difference in behavior of parents suggests that fathers and mothers provide different speech models for their children. Fathers are somewhat more impolite or insensitive to their children during conversation, and at the same time exhibit more control over the conversations with their children.

Finally, we looked at politeness in the speech of parents and children, as measured in the situation where the children were given a gift (see Greif & Gleason, 1980). Typically, at the end of our laboratory play session an assistant entered the room with a gift for the child. As part of the study, the assistant had been instructed to follow a script in this gift-giving. The script was designed to get the child to produce three politeness routines: *hi, thanks,* and *goodbye.* It went as follows: after entering the playroom the assistant turned to the child and said, "Hi, I'm _____ . Hi, (*child's name*)." The assistant then paused to wait or allow time for a response. Next, the assistant said: Here's a gift for you for today's visit." (Pause). Then, after unstructured conversation, the assistant said to the child, "Goodbye, (*child's name*)."

A total of twenty-two children were seen twice in this situation, once with each parent. The forty-four episodes gave us the opportunity to look at such things as differences in the routines produced by boys and girls, as well as fathers' and mothers' tendency to say polite phrases themselves or to prompt their children or insist that they produce politeness routines.

Children produced very little on their own, but parents did tend to prompt them. Both mothers and fathers told their children to say "thank you," "goodbye," and "hi." While boys and girls were not treated differently, there were significant differences in the linguistic behavior of mothers and fathers; when the child received the gift, some parents (fifteen of them) said "thank you" themselves. The great majority of these were mothers: eleven of the fifteen. When the assistant left, parents could also say "goodbye" and eighteen of them did: thirteen of the eighteen were mothers. Thus, once again we observed that mothers and fathers provide different models for their children, and here we found that the models provided by fathers were less polite than the models provided by mothers.

DISCUSSION

Most early studies of input language to children were studies of mothers' speech. Until we began to study men's speech to children there was speculation that child language register was limited to females and that males were unlikely to produce appropriate speech when addressing young children. Our data, as well as the work of other researchers who have studied fathers (Engle, 1980; Rondal, 1978; Stein, 1976), indicate that the important features of adult-child speech are found in the language of both fathers and other men when addressing young children. This is not to say that men and women, fathers and mothers, all talk alike when dealing with young children, but rather that the important features of simplicity, well-formedness, repetition, and immediacy are present in the language of all of them.

At home with their own children, fathers frequently are cast into, or assume, the role of disciplinarian. Their language contains more direct imperatives, while the mothers tend to couch their directive intent in question form. Avoidance of direct imperatives appears to be a general feature of women's language in our society (Lakoff, 1973). The fathers also use more imperatives when speaking with their sons than with their daughters, and they use more gruff, affectionate terms toward the little boys. The heavy use of imperatives to the boys gives the impression that in our society males become accustomed early on to taking orders and, if their fathers provide role models, to giving them. Fathers are not as well-tuned-in to their children as mothers are in the traditional family situation. In reading books together, fathers sometimes misunderstand what the children say (see Stein, 1976, for additional evidence). They also concentrate on telling an interesting story, while mothers spend more time interacting with the child, asking questions, making sure he or she understands. The children have to exert themselves more for the fathers and try harder to make themselves both heard and understood.

When parents are brought into the laboratory, much of the role differentiation we see at home disappears, or at least becomes diminished. Few parents would threaten their children while being videotaped in the psychology laboratory of a university, for instance. But a number of differences in fathers' and mothers' speech could still be detected. These differences can be conceptualized along two dimensions: one has to do with the model of the father as a speaker who is a more direct, controlling, and relatively impolite person than the mother; the other shows the father to be cognitively and linguistically more challenging than the mother, at least in these situations.

Fathers interrupt their children more than mothers do; they issue more direct orders, and they are less likely to say polite things like "thank you" and "goodbye" when the opportunity arises. At the same time, fathers' style demands more of the child: fathers are more likely to use difficult words and to request relatively sophisticated information from their children. They spend more time testing the child's knowledge and encouraging the child to display that knowlege. By sometimes embedding their requests in indirect forms (e.g., "The wheel needs tightening"), they require children both to guess at their intentions and to figure out on their own what is called for.

These studies suggest that mothers and fathers are not providing the same sorts of cognitive and linguistic input to their children. While fathers are less polite and more insensitive than mothers, their interaction style can be seen to have a positive effect on children as well. Mothers appear to be exceptionally well tuned in to their children. In traditional families, where mothers are the primary caregivers, they know so well what the child has in mind that the child really does not have to say much at all. But children must learn to communicate with people who are not their mothers. They have to learn to talk to their fathers and other people who are not tuned in to them in the warm, sensitive ways their mothers are, and who are not satisfied with relatively imperfect linguistic performance. In this way fathers can be seen as a bridge to the outside world, leading children to change their language in order to communicate. We have long suspected that fathers speak in a style that differs from mothers, one that provides a distinct model for their children. These studies have shown this to be the case. They have also shown that in addition to this kind of sex role socialization, fathers' speech, while sometimes impolite and authoritarian, may serve special functions in their children's cognitive and linguistic development.

NOTES

1. Similar findings were reported by Stein (1976) and Engle (1980). Stein used a book-reading task and found that fathers concentrated on telling a good story and as a result interacted with their children less than mothers did. Engle, studying parents playing with their children, found that fathers' speech was less closely attuned to their children than was mothers' speech.

2. Our colleagues in this research include David Alderton, David Bellinger, Janet Fardella, Elise Frank Masur, Lise Menn, Rivka Y. Perlmann, and Sandra Weintraub.

REFERENCES

Bellinger, David C. & Jean Berko Gleason. 1982. Sex differences in parental directives to young children. *Sex Roles*, 8.1123–39.

Broen, Patricia. 1972. The verbal environment of the language learning child. *American Speech and Hearing Association Monograph 17*. Washington, D.C.

Chomsky, Noam A. 1967. The formal nature of language. Appendix A, to Eric H. Lenneberg, *Biological foundations of language*. New York: Wiley.

Engle, Marianne. 1980. Family influences on the language development of young children. *Women's Studies International Quarterly*, 3, 259–66.

Farwell, Carol, 1973. The language spoken to children. *Stanford University Papers and Reports on Child Language Development*, 5 and 6.

Gleason, Jean Berko. 1973. Code switching in children's language. In Timothy E. Moore (ed.), *Cognitive development and the acquisition of language*. New York: Academic Press.

Greif, Esther B. 1980. Sex differences in parent-child conversations. *Women's Studies International Quarterly*, 3, 253–59.

Greif, Esther B. & Jean Berko Gleason. 1980. Hi, thanks, and goodbye: More routine information. *Language in Society*, 9, 159–66.

Lakoff, Robin. 1973. Language and woman's place. *Language in Society*, 2, 45–79.

Masur, Elise F. & Jean Berko Gleason. 1980. Parent-child interaction and the acquisition of lexical information during play. *Developmental Psychology*, 16, 404–9.

McNeill, David. 1970. *The acquisition of language: The study of developmental psycholinguistics*. New York: Harper & Row.

Rondal, Jean A. 1978. Fathers' speech and mothers: Speech in early language development. Paper given at the 1st International Congress for the Study of Child Language, Tokyo.

Snow, Catherine. 1972. Mothers' speech to children learning language. *Child Development*, 43, 549–65.

Stein, Audrey R. 1976. A comparison of mothers' and fathers' language to normal and language deficient children. Doctoral dissertation, Boston Univ.

SEX SIMILARITIES
AND DIFFERENCES
IN LANGUAGE, SPEECH, AND
NONVERBAL COMMUNICATION:
AN ANNOTATED BIBLIOGRAPHY

Compiled by
Cheris Kramarae, Barrie Thorne, and Nancy Henley

CONTENTS

INTRODUCTION TO THE BIBLIOGRAPHY

A comparison of the bibliography in *Language and Sex: Difference and Dominance* (1975) with this updated version provides a condensed look at the development of the field. The rapid expansion of interest in language and the sexes is evident in the dramatic increase in the number of annotated items. Further, in organizing the bibliography—and thus helping to cast this field of inquiry—we have made changes from that 1975 edition which reflect shifts in research and action in the last decade.

Section I ("Comprehensive Sources") documents the array of books and review essays now available. The growing interest of scholars and activists working on and in languages other than English is evident in the "Other Languages" subsections which conclude most large sections of the bibliography. Many of these items were recommended by researchers from other countries; these references are suggestive and not comprehensive.

Reflecting intense interest in sexism in language structure and content, Section II has expanded to include many subtopics. We have added a section (III) on "Stereotypes and Perceptions of Language Use" which documents growing awareness that stereotypes and perceptions are heavily involved in the creation and maintenance of gender markings. Sections IV and V focus on different traditions of research on sex-related differences in language use: The title of Section IV now couples "similarities" with "differences" and includes studies which draw on traditional linguistic divisions. Section VI ("Genre and Style") includes material both on oral genres, such as gossip and humor, and on written language, and suggests the contribution of folklorists, literary critics, poets, and other writers. A subsection of Section VI, "Seizing the Language," recognizes the radically feminist questions raised by writers and theorists who explore women's experiences within and outside of patriarchal discourse. Sections VII ("Children and Language") and VIII ("Language Varieties in American English") explore the relation of gender to other sources of variation and inequality: age, race, ethnicity, sexualities, and social class. Section IX succinctly leads to a closely related subject: the sexual differentiation of nonverbal communication. Sections VI, IX, and the subsections on "Other Languages" are deliberatively selective. This subject area is ever more plentiful, connecting many closely related strands of research, and we have had to develop strategies for keeping the bibliography of manageable size.

We have gathered items from many sources; however, the rapid and continuing growth of this research makes it inevitable that we missed some citations. In addition, because of limited space, we omitted items we felt were basically duplicated in other annotated entries, or items that are difficult to obtain. We have, for example, included unpublished manuscripts only when we thought that the papers, even when represented only by our short annotations, might provide others with new ways of thinking about language, sex, and gender. Many items are relevant to more than one section. However, to save space, most items are annotated only once; most sections conclude with a list of relevant items annotated elsewhere in the bibliography. In the few cases where there is more than one annotation for the same item, we have included cross-references. In a few cases, with the context made clear, citations are listed without annotations.

We urge readers to consult the original sources rather than relying on the annotations, which convey scope and flavor but not full substance. An index to authors cited in the bibliography is included at the end.

I. COMPREHENSIVE SOURCES

A. American English

ADAMS, KAREN L. AND NORMA C. WARE.

Sexism and the English language: The linguistic implications of being a woman. In Jo Freeman, ed., *Women: A feminist perspective.* Palo Alto, Calif.: Mayfield, 1979, pp. 487–504.

Included in an anthology widely used in women's studies courses, this is a readable discussion of sexism in language content, sex differences in language use, and strategies for change.

ADLER, MAX K.

Sex differences in human speech. Hamburg: Buske, 1978.

A review of research from 1879 to 1975, with attention to different languages and including chapters on sex differences in the use of words, conversation, names, addresses and titles, and language development. Much of the text consists of quotations, and the author is not in touch with many of the conceptual and theoretical issues raised by scholars in the last decade of research on language and gender.

BERRYMAN, CYNTHIA L. AND VIRGINIA A. EMAN, EDS.

Communication, language and sex. Rowley, Mass.: Newbury House, 1980.

A collection of 16 papers given at the First Annual Conference on Communication, Language and Sex in 1978. Topics include stereotypes and attitudes, sex differences in language use, lesbian humor, and teaching of courses on male/female communication. [Some of the papers are separately annotated.]

BORKER, RUTH.

Anthropology: Social and cultural perspectives. In Sally McConnell-Ginet, Ruth Borker, and Nelly Furman, eds., *Women and language in literature and society.* New York: Praeger, 1980, pp. 26–44.

Borker discusses ways in which the positions of women and men in particular communities affect speech strategies (e.g., choice of language in multilingual situations; use of gossip), and the ways cultural ideas about language, gender, and power shape and give meaning to language use. [*Also see:* VI-A-4.]

BUTTURFF, DOUGLAS AND EDMUND L. EPSTEIN, EDS.

Women's language and style. Akron, Ohio: L & S Books, 1978.

A collection of papers, most of them originally given at a Conference on Language and Style at the Graduate Center, City Univ. of New York, April, 1977. Written by linguists, sociolinguists, and literary critics, the papers (some of them separately annotated in this bibliography) focus on both oral and written language.

CONKLIN, NANCY FAIRES.

The language of the majority: Women and American English. In Margaret A. Lourie and Nancy Faires Conklin, eds., *A pluralistic nation: The language issue in the United States.* Rowley, Mass.: Newbury House, 1978, pp. 222–37.

A review of research on sex-linked language differences in vocabulary, pronunciation, grammar, intonation and pitch, discourse styles, nonverbal language, and attitudes toward language. Conklin relates men's and women's varieties of English to roles they assume in American society.

CONKLIN, NANCY FAIRES.

Toward a feminist analysis of linguistic behavior. *University of Michigan Papers in Women's Studies,* 1, no. 1 (1974), 51–73.

Conklin briefly discusses linguistic issues introduced by supporters of the women's movement in the late '60s and early '70s. She argues that women should "recognize, legitimize, and creatively develop" our own speech genres.

DESTEFANO, JOHANNA S.

Women and language: By and about. In Reza Ordoubadian and Walburga von Raffler-Engel, eds., *Views on language.* Murfreesboro, Tenn.: Inter-University Publishers, 1975, pp. 66–77.

A review of research on sex differences in phonology, syntax, lexicon, language use, and attitudes toward women's language. DeStefano stresses the need for more empirical research and strengthened theoretical frameworks for sociolinguistics.

DUBOIS, BETTY LOU AND ISABEL CROUCH, EDS.

The sociology of the languages of American women. San Antonio, Texas: Trinity Univ., 1976.

Papers from a 1976 special conference at New Mexico State Univ., including several theoretical overviews, and empirical studies of sex-differentiated patterns in phonology, pitch, conversation, and bilingual code-switching. Seven of the 17 papers, plus two additional ones—most of them focusing on Black and bilingual Chicana speech—are reprinted in the *International Journal of the Sociology of Language*, 17 (1978). [Most of the papers are separately annotated.]

EAKINS, BARBARA W. AND R. GENE EAKINS.
Sex differences in human communication. Boston: Houghton Mifflin, 1978.

This textbook includes useful suggestions for classroom activities. Chapters review research on different ways the sexes use words, verbal interaction among the sexes, sex differences in nonverbal communication, and gender and sexism in language content.

FARB, PETER.
Word play: What happens when people talk. New York: Alfred A. Knopf, 1973, pp. 47–50.

Writing for a general audience, Farb reviews early literature on male/female differences in pronunciation, vocabulary, grammar, and the use of language among speakers in several cultures. Farb suggests that sex differences in English were probably more marked in the past, when the social lives of the sexes were more separate (and women, in particular, were more insulated than they are now).

FRANK, FRANCINE WATTMAN.
Women's language in America: Myth and reality. In Douglas Butturff and Edmund L. Epstein, eds., *Women's language and style.* Akron, Ohio: L & S Books, 1978, pp. 47–61.

A review of research on sex and intonation, pronunciation, syntax, vocabulary, and conversational interaction. Frank emphasizes the importance of sifting myth and stereotypes from fact, and argues that learned behavior is more extensive than often thought (e.g., in shaping voice pitch).

HAAS, ADELAIDE.
Male and female spoken language differences: Stereotypes and evidence. *Psychological Bulletin,* 86 (1979), 616–26.

A review essay which discusses traditional stereotypes of the form, topics, content, and use of male and female language, in relation to empirical studies, with attention to the speech of both children and adults. Haas urges researchers to be sensitive to context, and cautious in generalizing about sex-associated speech. [*Also see:* Haas, Sec. IV-B.]

HENLEY, NANCY AND BARRIE THORNE.
Womanspeak and manspeak. In Alice Sargent, ed., *Beyond sex roles.* New York: West Publishing, 1976, pp. 201–18.

An examination of the sexist bias of English and sex differences in speech and nonverbal communication. Each section concludes with suggestions for altering the current situation.

JENKINS, MERCILEE M. AND CHERIS KRAMARAE.
A thief in the house: Women and language. In Dale Spender, ed., *Men's studies modified.* Oxford: Pergamon Press, 1981, pp. 11–22.

Covers diverse perspectives in research on social interaction and gender. Studies which attend as much as possible to the culture of women reveal the deficiencies of most of previous communication research. The authors argue that it is important to avoid separating academic and movement concerns about language.

JESPERSEN, OTTO.

The woman. Chapter XIII of *Language: Its nature, development and origins*. London: Allen & Unwin, 1922, pp. 237–54.

The only traditional book on language to extensively discuss the sexual differentiation of language, including cross-cultural information on male vs. female dialects, and sex differences in phonetic choice, attitudes to language change, word choice, and syntax. [The discussion includes many stereotyped and unsupported claims.]

KEY, MARY RITCHIE.

Linguistic behavior of male and female. *Linguistics,* 88 (1972), 15–31.

An early, path-breaking paper on phonological differences in women's and men's speech, intonation patterns, and sex differences in syntax, semantics, and pronominal and nominal referents. [*Also see:* Sec. IV-D-3.]

KEY, MARY RITCHIE.

Male/female language. Metuchen, N.J.: The Scarecrow Press, 1975.

One of the first books on the gender differentiation of language, by a linguist who pioneered the subject. Topics include sex differences in social dialects, labels, and descriptors; names and greetings; sex differences in language learning, phonology, intonation, syntax, semantics, language change, bilingualism, and language planning. A lengthy bibliography is included.

KRAMARAE, CHERIS, ED.

The voices and words of women and men. Oxford: Pergamon Press, 1980. Also *Women's Studies International Quarterly*, 3, no. 2/3 (1980).

An entire journal issue, also published as a book, with papers on the social meaning of language structure, the evaluation of women's voices and words, methodology in language and sex research, and the sexual differentiation of language at home and in classrooms. [Some of the essays are separately annotated.]

KRAMARAE, CHERIS.

Women and men speaking. Rowley, Mass.: Newbury House, 1981.

The author reviews research on sexism in language, and the uses (and evaluation) of language by women and men, in the context of gender-sensitive theoretical frameworks: women as a muted group, reconstructed psychoanalysis, speech styles, and language strategies. [*Also see:* Sec. V-G; Sec. VI-A-2.]

KRAMER, CHERIS.

Women's speech: Separate but unequal? *Quarterly Journal of Speech,* 60 (Feb. 1974), 14–24. Reprinted in Barrie Thorne and Nancy Henley, eds., *Language and sex: Difference and dominance.* Rowley, Mass.: Newbury House, 1975, pp. 43–56.

A discussion of pre-1970s language and sex literature on word choice and syntax, including both empirical studies and criticism of the bias of some linguists when they describe women's speech.

KRAMER, CHERIS, BARRIE THORNE, AND NANCY HENLEY.
Review essay: Perspectives on language and communication. *Signs*, 3 (1978), 638–51.

A review which focuses on sex similarities and differences in language use, emphasizing problems with that line of work and the need to examine social context; sexism in language and relations between language structure and language use; and efforts and prospects for change.

LAKOFF, ROBIN.
Language and woman's place. New York: Harper & Row, 1975.

An influential book with two parts: (1) "Language and Woman's Place" (originally published in *Language in Society*, 2 [1973], 45–79, and a shorter version, "You Are What You Say," in *Ms.,* 3 [July 1974], 63–67); and (2) "Why Women Are Ladies." Lakoff discusses sexism patterns in language about women, and, drawing on introspection and anecdotal observation, argues that women use more "empty adjectives," tag questions, questioning intonation, and compound request forms, and that these patterns convey uncertainty and politeness. [Lakoff's speculations have been pursued by many researchers, with very mixed results; *see* items in Sec. IV.]

LARMER, LARRY E. AND MARY BADAMI, EDS.
Proceedings of the 2nd and 3rd conferences on communication, language and gender. Madison: Univ. of Wisconsin—Extension, 1982.

The 25 papers include examinations of measurements of androgyny, language change, stereotyping, patterns of interaction, and research approaches for gender and language studies. [Some of the papers are separately annotated.]

The Lonesome Node. (Suzette Haden Elgin, ed.)
The Ozark Center for Language Studies, Route 4, Box 192-E, Huntsville, AR 72740.

Bimonthly newsletter devoted to women and language, and five other areas of language research.

McCONNELL-GINET, SALLY.
Our father tongue: Essays in linguistic politics. *Diacritics,* 5 (1975), 44–50. (Review of Robin Lakoff's *Language and woman's place.*)

A satisfactory theory of sex-based linguistic variation considers language "as constitutive of the context in which it occurs rather than encoding an independently existing socio-psychological reality." To speak of a "woman's language" and women's *hypercorrect* speech diverts attention from questions about the significance of linguistic choices in different situations and from questions about the context of male domination.

McCONNELL-GINET, SALLY, RUTH BORKER, AND NELLY FURMAN, EDS.
Women and language in literature and society. New York: Praeger, 1980.

An anthology of original articles with sections on "Views from and to the Disciplines" (linguistics, anthropology, literary criticism), "Men's Power, Women's Language," "Language in Women's Lives," and "Reading Women's Writing." [Most of the papers are separately annotated.] This excellent volume is innovative in connecting sociolinguistic and literary issues and ideas.

MILLER, CASEY AND KATE SWIFT.

Words and women: New language in new times. Garden City, N.Y.: Doubleday, Anchor Press, 1976.

A well-documented and engaging discussion of sexism in language—naming customs, masculine generics, linguistic gender, semantic polarization, the language of religion, dictionaries, and the media—and issues of change.

MORAGA, CHERRIÉ AND GLORIA ANZALDÚA, EDS.

This bridge called my back: Writings by radical women of color. Watertown, Mass.: Persephone Press, 1981.

Essays on racism, prejudice, elitism, homophobia, misogyny, revolution, and the language that is available or that can be constructed to talk about them. The essays reflect diverse perspectives and language styles and the book contains an extensive bibliography of writings of and about Third World women in the U.S.

ORASANU, JUDITH, MARIAM K. SLATER, AND LEONORE LOEB ADLER, EDS.

Language, sex and gender: Does 'la différence' make a difference? New York: The New York Academy of Sciences, 1979.

While several of the seven articles in this volume of interdisciplinary work reveal ignorance of feminist scholarship, the collection includes careful studies of the acquisition of genderlects, interruptions, and theories concerning "generic" *he*. [Some of the papers are separately annotated.]

PARSONS, ELSIE CLEWS.

Sex dialects. In Elsie Clews Parsons, *The old-fashioned woman: Primitive fancies about the sex.* New York: G.P. Putnam's Sons, 1913.

The chapter "Sex Dialects" includes a wide-ranging discussion of the habits and assumptions of Americans and people of many other cultures. Parsons argues that sex-linked language differences in the U.S. are "taboos"—as seemingly illogical as the taboos of other cultures. Her work points out the similarity of the arguments used through the years to criticize women who seek linguistic and other social changes. [*Also see:* Sec. III-B.]

PATTON, BOBBY R. AND BONNIE RITTER PATTON.

Living together . . . Female/male communication. Columbus, Ohio: Charles E. Merrill, 1976.

This readable, interdisciplinary text designed for college interpersonal communication classes includes material on socialization, relational patterns, and ways of evaluating and improving verbal and nonverbal communication.

PHILIPS, SUSAN U.

Sex differences and language. *Annual Review of Anthropology,* 9 (1980), 523–44.

In this useful review Philips discusses contextual variation in the occurrence of specific forms, such as tag questions and hedges; the applicability of the notion of "style" to gender-differentiated speech; and potential contributions of cross-cultural research.

SILBERSTEIN, SANDRA.

Bibliography: Women and language. Michigan Occasional Papers in Women's Studies, no. XII (Winter 1980). (Women's Studies, Univ. of Michigan, Ann Arbor, MI 48104.)

A comprehensive U.S. bibliography finished in 1979, with an addendum of recent books.

SMITH, PHILIP M.

Sex markers in speech. In Klaus R. Scherer and Howard Giles, eds., *Social markers in speech.* Cambridge: Cambridge Univ. Press, 1979, pp. 109–46.

A review of research on sex differences in pronunciation, grammar, vocabulary, speech style, code and dialect choice. Smith observes that many features that do not in fact differentiate the sexes are nevertheless typically associated with one sex or the other. He examines processes which affect the recognition and interpretation of sex-associated speech.

SPENDER, DALE.

Man made language. London: Routledge & Kegan Paul, 1980.

A wide-ranging discussion which emphasizes women's experiences with language in the context of patriarchal order. Topics include the construction of women's silence, the sexes as dominant and muted groups, the politics of "woman talk," sexism in language and meaning, the politics of naming, and women and writing. [*Also see:* Spender, Sec. V-A; Sec. VI-C.]

THORNE, BARRIE AND NANCY HENLEY.

Difference and dominance: An overview of language, gender, and society. In Barrie Thorne and Nancy Henley, eds., *Language and sex: Difference and dominance.* Rowley, Mass.: Newbury House, 1975, pp. 5–42.

The authors trace the development of research on the sexual differentiation of language, assess the relevance of sociolinguistic frameworks and issues of methodology, examine language in the context of the sexual division of labor and male dominance, and discuss issues of social change.

THORNE, BARRIE AND NANCY HENLEY, EDS.

Language and sex: Difference and dominance. Rowley, Mass.: Newbury House, 1975.

A collection of 12 articles from various fields (sociology, psychology, lexicography, linguistics, speech communication, English, anthropology), with a comprehensive annotated bibliography, forerunner to this one. [The articles are annotated separately.]

VETTERLING-BRAGGIN, MARY, ED.

Sexist language: A modern philosophical analysis. Totowa, N.J.: Littlefield, Adams, 1981.

A collection of essays, mostly by philosophers, on the nature of sexist language, why it should (or should not) be changed, and parallels with racist language. [Some of the papers are separately annotated.]

Women and Language News. (Cheris Kramarae and Paula Treichler, eds.)

244 Lincoln Hall, Univ. of Illinois, 702 S. Wright, Urbana, IL 61801.

An interdisciplinary newsletter carrying information about publications, conferences, research projects, and news coverage of language and gender work.

Women's Studies in Communication. (Karen Foss, ed.)
Dept. of Speech Communication, Humboldt State Univ., Arcata, CA 95521.

A forum for short essays, published by the Organization for Research on Women and Communication of the Western Speech Communication Association.

B.   Other Languages

AUTORINNENGRUPPE (A GROUP OF WOMEN WRITERS) UNI WIEN.
Das Ewige Klischee: Zum Rollenbild und Selbstverständnis bei Männern und Frauen. (The eternal cliché: Toward role-model and self-understanding of men and women). Wien: Hermann Böhlaus, 1981.

This collection includes essays on the political discourse of women, women's writing, and male speech behavior.

BLAKAR, ROLV MIKKEL.
How sex roles are represented, reflected and conserved in the Norwegian language. *Acta Sociologica,* 18 (1975), 162–73.

The social inequality between women and men is represented in and perpetuated by the Norwegian language. The subtle (but strong) interaction between social reality and language means that many people are unaware of influential sexism in language.

BROUWER, DÉDÉ.
Taal en sekse in feministisch-wetenschappelijk perspektief. (A critical feminist survey of studies on language and sex). In P. Van de Craen and R. Willemyns, eds., *Sociolinguistiek en ideologie.* (Autumn, 1981).

This survey by a Dutch researcher relates studies of language and sex to the aim and methods of the social sciences.

BROUWER, DÉDÉ, MARINEL GERRITSEN, DORIAN DE HAAN, ANNETTE VAN DER POST, AND EVELINE DE JONG.
Vrouwentaal en mannenpraat: Verschillen in taalgebruik en taalgedrag in relatie tot de maatschappelijke rolverdeling. (The language of women and men in relation to role specialization in society). Amsterdam: Van Gennep, 1978.

The four chapters of this book deal with sex differentiation research in anthropological linguistics, dialectology, language development, and sociolinguistics. Topics include: speakers' attitudes about sex-dependent speech differences; the role of women in language change; the differential treatment of girls and boys in school; and the influence of linguists' attitudes on the study of women as a social group.

FROITZHEIM, CLAUDIA.
Sprache und Geschlecht: Bibliographie, April, 1980. (Univ. of Trier, D-5500 Trier, West Germany.)

An extensive bibliography of North American and European sources, organized both alphabetically and according to topic.

GERRITSEN, MARINEL AND DÉDÉ BROUWER.
Sociolinguïstiek en de tweede sekse (Sociolinguistics and the second sex). In G. Geerts and A. Hagen, eds., *Sociolinguistische studies i, bijdragen uit het nederlandse tallgebied (Sociolinguistic studies I: Dutch language contributions).* Groningen: Wolters-Noordhoff, 1980, pp. 50–65.

This is a survey of the problems, use, and necessity of sex as a variable in sociolinguistics.

HANSSEN, ESKIL.
Some notes on language and sex research in Norway. In Verena Aebischer, Helga Andresen, Helmut Glück, and Theodossia Pavlidon, eds., *Osnabrücker Beiträge zur Sprachtheorie* (Sprache und Geschlecht Bd. III), 1979, 99–112. (Essays from March 1979 symposium).

The research questions of recent Scandinavian studies are similar to those found in other European countries and the U.S., including professional names and titles, gender pronouns, sexism in mass media, and phonological and morphological features of speech. Hanssen argues that a purely linguistic approach to the study of language is certain to result in a dead end. [*See also:* Hanssen, Sec. IV-G.] (See also the essays in Else Ryen, *Språk og kjønn, Oslo, 1976; Tor Hultman, Sak och person, in Kerstin Nordin and M. Thelander, eds., Könsroller i språk*, FUMS report no. 49, 1977, Uppsala Univ., Uppsala, Sweden.)

Könsroller i språk (Sex roles in language).
FUMS report no. 49, 1977. Uppsala universitët, Forskningskommittén i Uppsala, för modern svenska (FUMS), Thunbergsvägen 7I, 752 38. Uppsala, Sweden.

Symposium papers and a lengthy bibliography whose sources include Barrie Thorne and Nancy Henley, eds., *Language and sex: Difference and dominance;* Else Ryen, *Språk og kjønn;* Mary Ritchie Key, *Male/female language;* Educational Resources Information Center (ERIC); FUMS; and *Psychological Abstracts.*

Könsroller i språk 1, 2, 3 (1977, 1978, 1979). (Sex roles in language).
FUMS, Thunbergsvägen 7I, 752 38. Uppsala Univ., Uppsala, Sweden.

Essays in Swedish on European and North American languages and gender.

MESEGUER, ALVARO GARCÍA.
Lenguaje y discriminación sexual. Madrid: Editorial Cuadernos Para El Dialogo, 1977.

A pioneering work which analyzes linguistic sexism in Spanish dictionaries.

NICHOLS, PATRICIA.
Overview: Language and social stratification. Paper given at the Language and Power Conference, Bellagio, Italy, April, 1980.

Nichols argues that current social classification methodologies often do not adequately describe the interaction of language use and speakers' places in society. Further, researchers in various countries and times make quite different assumptions about how and by whom social status is described. [Thus, we need to be cautious about comparing studies of women's and men's speech across time or cultural boundaries.]

Osnabrücker Beiträge zur Sprachtheorie. 8, 9, 1979. (Sprache und Geschlecht I, II).

These two issues include language and gender research from Germany, other European countries, and the U.S. (OBST, Fachbereich 7 der Univ. Osnabrück, Postfach 4469, D 4500, Osnabrück, West Germany).

PENG, FRED C. C., ET AL.

Male and female differences in Japanese. Special issue of *Language Sciences,* 3, no. 1 (April 1981).

Topics of the essays include personal pronouns, nonverbal communication, hesitations, honorifics, language acquisition, speech impairment, and cross-cultural communications.

TRÖMEL-PLÖTZ, SENTA.

Frauensprache in unserer Welt der Männer. (Monograph) Konstanzer Universitätsreden. Universitätsverlag, Konstanz, 1979.

Linguistic and sociological research demonstrates the pervasive nature of discrimination against women. The author argues that sensitivity to sexist linguistic practices will bring about language changes, and, along with them, new linguistic behavior. (See also Ruth Wodak's useful review of this book in *Journal of Pragmatics,* 4 [1980], 543–45.)

TRÖMEL-PLÖTZ, SENTA.

Linguistik und Frauensprache. *Linguistische Berichte,* 57 (1978), 49–68.

This overview includes discussions of German "generic" nouns, and the linguistic devices women use to assure being heard—devices not necessary for those with greater power.

TYLER, MARY.

Men's use of language: Data and implications. In Verena Aebischer, Helga Andresen, Helmut Glück, and Theodossia Pavlidon, eds., *Osnabrücker Beiträge zur Sprachtheorie* (Sprache und Geschlecht Bd. III), 1979, pp. 48–63. (Essays from March 1979 symposium).

A cross-cultural review of language and sex research found that men talk less formally than women; men tend to focus on objects and concepts rather than on emotions or interpersonal relationships; and men talk and interrupt more than women talk or interrupt.

WEST, CANDACE AND DON H. ZIMMERMAN

Gender, language and discourse. In Teun A. van Dijk (ed.), *Handbook of discourse analysis.* London: Academic Press (in press).

A review of research on language, speech, and gender, emphasizing conversation: women's interaction work and patterns of male dominance in cross-sex talk; and competition, cooperation, and conflict in talk among children.

YAGUELLO, MARINA.

Les mots et les femmes: Essay d'approache socio-linguistique de la condition féminine. Paris: Payot, 1979.

A review of sociolinguistic work on language and gender in the U.S. and an attempt to relate it to French and to French feminism.

II. GENDER MARKING AND SEX BIAS IN LANGUAGE STRUCTURE AND CONTENT

A.   General and Comprehensive

Ås, Berit.

On female culture: An attempt to formulate a theory of women's solidarity and action. *Acta Sociologica,* 18 (1975), 142–61.

Language is considered as one part of the master culture which makes female culture invisible.

Beatty, John.

Sex, role and sex role. In Judith Orasanu et al., *Language, sex and gender.* New York: New York Academy of Sciences, 1979, pp. 43–49.

Beatty examines interrelationships among concepts of sexual status, biological sex, social role, and sexuality, and argues for cross-cultural analysis, similar to that for kinship terms, of systems of terms regarding "sex role."

Bosmajian, Haig A.

The language of sexism. *Etc.,* 29 (1972), 305–13.

Bosmajian's basic premise is that language is often used to "define and dehumanize individuals or groups ... into submission." He provides examples of "male supremist language" that dehumanizes women, and argues that the liberation of women will have to include an effort by women to no longer allow men to define them. (See also Bosmajian, *The language of oppression.* Washington, D.C.: Public Affairs Press, 1974.)

Falco, Kristine L.

Word consciousness: A look at sexist language and attitudes. In Jean R. Leppaluoto, ed., *Women on the move: A feminist perspective.* Pittsburgh: KNOW, 1973, pp. 289–95. Also in Martin Hoyles, ed., *The policy of literacy.* London: Writers and Readers Publishing Cooperative, 1977, pp. 114–24.

Research indicates that attitudes will change to conform to behavior rather than vice versa, so we had best change sexist actions. We need to become aware of the effects of words that define women in terms other than human (as animal, vegetable, fruit); in terms of sexuality (*flirt, hussy*); in terms of childishness and weakness (*girl*); and in terms which emphasize differentness (*businesswoman, actress, suffragette, woman lawyer*).

Farwell, Marilyn.

Women and language. In Jean R. Leppaluoto, ed., *Women on the move: A feminist perspective.* Pittsburgh: KNOW, 1973, pp. 165–72.

The English language emphasizes the either/or pattern of masculine and feminine and rigidifies the secondary social status of women. Farwell suggests introducing non-masculine generic terms and using the creative language of writers like Plath and Rich.

FORTUNATA, JACQUELINE.

Lakoff on language and women. In Mary Vetterling-Braggin, ed., *Sexist language: A modern philosophical analysis.* Totowa, N.J.: Littlefield, Adams, 1981, pp. 81–91.

Fortunata argues that Lakoff's real thesis is that certain linguistic usages always demean women as a whole, regardless of the speaker's intent or the awareness of women. This may be a self-fulfilling hypothesis, leading once neutral terms to be interpreted as demeaning.

GREGERSEN, EDGAR A.

Sexual linguistics. In Judith Orasanu, et al., eds., *Language, sex and gender.* New York: New York Academy of Sciences, 1979, pp. 3–19.

An anthropological linguist, Gregersen attempts to refute what he considers the unproved Whorfianism of feminists by the argument, with examples from various languages, that there is no correlation between the status of women in a society and the gender differentiation present in its language. A sampling from his own rich collection of verbal abuse of women (primarily mother insults) is included.

GRIM, PATRICK.

Sexist speech: Two basic questions. In Mary Vetterling-Braggin, ed., *Sexist language: A modern philosophical analysis.* Totowa, N.J.: Littlefield, Adams, 1981, pp. 34–51.

This paper explores two different yet complementary philosophical approaches (attitudinal and historical) to understanding sexist language in the context of two basic questions: "What does sexist mean as applied to things said?" and "Precisely what is it that is sexist?"

HENLEY, NANCY M.

This new species that seeks a new language: On sexism in language and language change. Paper given at Conference of the Assoc. for Women in Psychology, Pittsburgh, 1978; revised, at Conference on Language and Gender, Santa Cruz, Calif., 1979.

This paper describes and illustrates sexism in language, examines some historical origins, gives reasons why change is needed, and tells of neutral alternatives which have been proposed or used, with particular attention to science fiction examples. Prospects for individual and societal change are discussed, and arguments against change are examined and countered.

HOLE, JUDITH AND ELLEN LEVINE.

Feminist social critique: The politics of language, Chapter 4 of *The rebirth of feminism.* New York: Quadrangle Books, 1971, pp. 222–25.

This history of the new wave of feminism includes "The politics of language," which describes language as one of the institutions feminists are questioning and seeking to change. The authors also note that the feminist movement has developed its own special language and set of symbols (e.g., *sexism, male chauvinist).*

KRAMARAE, CHERIS.

False truisms: Androcentrism and language study. Paper given at meeting of Modern Language Assoc., New York, Dec. 1978.

This paper challenges four "Truisms in Trouble": (1) Linguistics is objective, apolitical, benevolent; (2) English "arises from and serves the needs of its speakers in their particular environment"; (3) The relationship between language and sex may be understood by adding sex to other variables in quantitative sociolinguistic studies; (4) "Sexism in language is basically a matter of a few 'generics' and some derogatory words for women."

McDOWELL, MARGARET B.

The new rhetoric of woman power. *Midwest Quarterly,* 12 (1971), 187–98.

McDowell raises general questions, such as what types of rhetoric can be found in the women's liberation movement and how this rhetoric compares with that of other protest movements, such as the New Left, Black power, and 19th-century feminism.

Media Report to Women. (Martha Leslie Allen, ed.).

Women's Institute for Freedom of the Press, 3306 Ross Place, N.W., Washington, D.C. 20008.

This periodical provides monthly international reports on language usage in the media, including notices of, and commentary on, guidelines for nonsexist language usage.

MERRIAM, EVE.

Sex and semantics. Part IV of *After Nora slammed the door.* Cleveland: World Publishing, 1958. Also published as Sex and semantics: Some notes on BOMFOG. *New York University Education Quarterly*, 5, no. 4 (1974), 22–24.

This brief essay deftly covers the origin of BOMFOG, the masculine generic, issues of naming, male as norm and feminine markers, diminuzation of the female, the *girl/woman* distinction, occupational designations, first-naming of women, and sexist news reporting. Alternatives are offered to the Brotherhood-Of-Man-under-the-Fatherhood-Of-God style.

MILLER, CASEY, AND KATE SWIFT.

One small step for genkind. *New York Times Magazine,* (April 16, 1972), 36. Reprinted as Is language sexist? *Cosmopolitan*, (Sept. 1972), 89–92.

The authors examine sexist language, claiming that words associated with males often imply positive traits while words associated with females define fewer attributes. Miller and Swift discuss sexism in the media in their presentation and treatment of women.

MORTON, NELLE.

The rising woman's consciousness in a male language structure. *Andover Newton Quarterly*, 12 (1972), 177–90.

An analysis of "notes, diaries, evaluations, findings, minutes, tapes, correspondence, and interviews" from six workshop-retreats around the country, this paper describes stages of consciousness-raising among women and the language they use to voice it. "It was the male pronouns and nouns used generically that stirred the women first as they moved about their community."

MURRAY, JESSICA.

Male perspective in language. *Women: A Journal of Liberation*, 3, no. 2 (1973), 46–50.

Language reflects the assumption that "all people are male until proven female." Murray offers examples from art, literature, and textbooks. A conspicuous example of woman-as-special-case is the sexualization of *women*.

NILSEN, ALLEEN PACE.

Sexism in English: A feminist view. In Nancy Hoffman, Cynthia Secor, and Adrian Tinsley, eds., *Female Studies VI.* Old Westbury, N.Y.: Feminist Press, 1972, pp. 102–9.

Analyzing a standard desk dictionary, Nilsen found three patterns of sexism: (1) women's bodies are emphasized while men's minds and activities are valued; (2) women are expected to play a passive role and men, an active one; and (3) masculine-marked words have more positive connotations than feminine words (e.g., *chef* vs. *cook*).

NILSEN, ALLEEN PACE, HAIG BOSMAJIAN, H. LEE GERSHUNY, AND JULIA P. STANLEY, EDS.

Sexism and language. Urbana, Ill.: National Council of Teachers of English, 1977.

A collection of eight articles by the four authors [annotated individually], plus guidelines and a bibliography.

ORDOUBADIAN, REZA.

Sexism and language structure. In Adam Behes and Valerie Mahhai, eds., *5th LACUS Forum.* Columbia, S.C.: Hornbeam Press, 1978, pp. 415–21.

Comparing English, Persian, Azarbayjan, Yoruban, and Ibo, the author proposes that "lexical sexism" does not accurately reflect a society's sexism, whereas "metaphorical sexism" (having sex-linked connotations), which is more widespread, is a better reflection of it.

PATEMAN, TREVOR.

Language, truth, and politics: Towards a radical theory for communication (2nd edition). Sussex, England: Jean Stroud, 1980.

Pateman challenges words and actions which we "take for granted," exploring the impact of individual, conscious, and sustained changes in daily language. He believes we have responsibility for words in daily life which depersonalize people.

SAPORTA, SOL.

Language in a sexist society. Paper given at Modern Language Assoc. meeting, Dec. 1974.

Saporta presents issues, with examples, "which have to be accounted for by any general statements regarding the nature and function of sexist language in this society": masculine as the unmarked form; syntactic asymmetries; lexical asymmetries (metaphors, euphemisms, and epithets for women and their activities). He concludes that probably language is sexist, people are sexist, and society is sexist.

SCHNEIDER, MICHAEL J. AND KAREN A. FOSS.

Thought, sex, and language: The Sapir-Whorf hypothesis in the American women's movement. *Bulletin: Women's Studies in Communication*, 1, no. 1 (1977), 1–7.

This brief paper argues that feminists writing on sexism in language adopt a (strong) Whorfian position (that language determines thought) that is misguided and will cost them credibility. However, the focus on language bias is useful for discovering cultural bias and for raising consciousness, and the changes achieved enhance morale. [*See* Shimanoff, this section, for a response.]

SCOTT, PATRICIA BELL.

The English language and Black womanhood: A low blow at self-esteem. *Journal of Afro-American Issues,* 2 (1974), 218–24. (Special issue on Black women in America). Reprinted in

Willa Johnson and Thomas Greene, eds., *Perspectives on the Afro-American woman.* Washington, D.C.: ECCA Publications, 1975.

The English language carries both racism and sexism. In dictionaries of Black English, women are defined by names of animals (*fox, mink, butterfly, chick, filly, fine fryer*), by physical attractiveness (*hammer, stone fox, little mama*), and color of complexion (*redbone, spotlight, banana high yaller, pinky*). Change will come from the growing wealth of Black revolutionary literature and from the refusal of Black women to use or be addressed by such labels. The racism and sexism which permeate the language used in films and in scholarly literature must also be combatted.

SHIMANOFF, SUSAN B.

Man = human: Empirical support for the Whorfian hypothesis. *Bulletin: Women's Studies in Communication*, 1, no. 2 (1977), 21–27.

This brief critique of Schneider and Foss [this section] argues that those authors failed to distinguish the "deterministic" (strong) and "tendency" (weak) versions of the Whorfian hypothesis; feminist arguments have been of the latter, more acceptable, form. Shimanoff cites research showing masculine-biased interpretation of masculine generics, including her own study, which elicited paragraphs more often about a male following a masculine generic than following either of two neutral generic forms.

SHUTE, SARA.

Sexist language and sexism. In Mary Vetterling-Braggin, ed., *Sexist language: A modern philosophical analysis.* Totowa, N.J.: Littlefield, Adams, 1981, pp. 23–33

Shute theorizes that the elimination of sexist language is fundamental to societal equality; sexist language limits and/or controls the actions of one sex over the other.

SMITH, DOROTHY E.

Using the oppressor's language. In Mary K. Shirley and Rachel Vigler, eds., *In search of the feminist: The changing potency of women.* Toronto: Resources for Feminist Research, 1979, pp. 10–18.

Smith, a Marxist sociologist, presents the issue of language and oppression, specifically language and domination in a capitalist system, and the problem for women using the oppressor's language.

STANLEY, JULIA P.

Usage and formal descriptions of language. Paper given at the 9th World Congress of Sociology, Uppsala, Sweden, August 1978.

Stanley explores relationships between language usage and the formal descriptions constructed by linguists, an exploration shown necessary by research on the influence of sexist attitudes on the structure of English. The problems posed cannot be solved without examining usage that calls into question existing formal descriptions of linguistic phenomena.

STRAINCHAMPS, ETHEL.

Our sexist language. In Vivian Gornick and Barbara K. Moran, eds., *Woman in sexist society.* New York: Basic Books, 1971, pp. 240–50.

An article with a philological bent, tracing the historical origins, use, and censorship of *fuck, cunt, twot, condom, diaphragm*. Strainchamps cites evidence of male dominance in English: *man* and *he* as generics; words which were non-emotive when they referred to either gender have become contemptuous after being applied to women alone, and some that were pejorative lost that sense when they acquired an exclusively male reference.

TOTH, EMILY.

How can a woman "man" the barricades? Or linguistic sexism up against the wall. *Women: A Journal of Liberation,* 2, no. 1 (1970), 57.

An early feminist analysis of linguistic sexism.

VARDA ONE.

"Manglish." Reprint available from KNOW, Inc., P.O. Box 86031, Pittsburgh, Penn. 15221. Reprinted from *Everywoman.*

The author suggests "Manglish" is the degradation of women in language. It includes the myth of lexicographic objectivity; women as appendage, an afterthought to men; relating function to gender vocationally; married names, patronymics, historical omissions; woman as "the Other"; slang expressions for sexual organs; sexist expressions.

B.　Historical

KELLY, EDWARD HANFORD.

A "bitch" by any other name is less poetic. *Word Study,* 45, no. 1 (1969), 1–4.

In a historical analysis of change in meanings of the word *bitch,* the author claims "it would be incorrect to think that the many modifications evident in the history of 'bitch' point toward linguistic degeneration ending in mere vulgarism" (p. 1).

MEREDITH, MAMIE.

"Doctoresses," "authoresses," and others. *American Speech,* 5 (1930), 476–81.

This letter documents numerous examples of the feminine suffix *-ess* in American English historically, including *beastess, rebeless,* even *nabobess.* An early tendency to stigmatize women workers outside the home with the *-ess* designation declined as their novelty wore off. There is also discussion of the term *female* as a pejorative.

MUSACCHIO, GEORGE L.

Milton's feminine pronouns with newer antecedents. *Journal of English Linguistics,* 2 (1968), 23–28.

"In early seventeenth-century England, when gender in the purely grammatical sense had disappeared from the language and when the neuter pronoun *its* was a neologism unacceptable in formal writing . . . decorous writers usually used the Old English masculine-neuter *his* or occasionally *it* . . . . But one finds Milton, Shakespeare, and other thoughtful authors of the period using *her* in such places." Musacchio reviews Milton's pronoun usages (and personification), and several proposed explanations for this usage.

NILSEN, ALLEEN PACE.

Linguistic sexism as a social issue. In Alleen Pace Nilsen et al., eds., *Sexism and language.* Urbana, Ill.: National Council of Teachers of English, 1977.

A chronology of events in media pertinent to sexism in language from spring 1974 until June 1976, including articles, books, and people that have catalyzed public and academic interest in fields of study relating to sexism in language.

STANLEY, JULIA P.

Sexist grammar. *College English,* 39 (March 1978), 800–11.

This paper illustrates the history of grammar as a male-dominated field. Since the 1700s grammarians and others have been developing and reinforcing male-oriented word usage. Many selections of past and contemporary linguists and grammarians reveal sexist bias, especially in pronoun and noun usage. Transformational grammarians reflect this tradition. Stanley emphasizes the need to change texts and language.

STANLEY, JULIA AND SUSAN ROBBINS.

Going through the changes: The pronoun "she" in Middle English. *Papers in Linguistics,* 11 (1978), 71–88.

Linguistic explanations of the emergence of the *sh* forms of the feminine nominative pronoun and their gradual spread throughout the dialects of Middle English have been inadequate. The authors argue that male bias influenced this development of labels that made maleness coextensive with humanity and isolated femaleness as inferior.

STANNARD, UNA.

Mrs. man. San Francisco: Germain Books, 1977.

A history of naming conventions which have submerged married women's identities, and women's struggles to keep their own names from the 19th century to today. Stannard traces the history of the Lucy Stone League, challenges to and changes in laws regulating names, and varied naming patterns (e.g., keeping one's birth name, different public and private names, hyphenated surnames, and "liberation names").

STOPES, CHARLOTTE CARMICHAEL.

The sphere of "man": In relation to that of "woman" in the Constitution. London: T. Fisher Unwin, 1908.

This 64-page history of the uses of *man* and *woman* in British charges and statutes, and of women's participation in the old social and trade guilds, argues that, while 19th century lawyers "have decided for us that the word 'man' always includes 'woman' when there is a penalty to be incurred and never includes 'woman' when there is a privilege to be conferred," this was not the case in earlier centuries.

WESCOTT, ROGER W.

Women, wife-men, and sexist bias. *Verbatim: The Language Quarterly,* 1, no. 2 (1974), 1.

This brief note, tracing women to Old English *wifman* ("wife-man"), presents seven possible roots for pre-Germanic terms for *wife* (from *wey-*) and three for *man* (from *men-, man-,* and *mon-*).

WOLFE, SUSAN J. AND JULIA PENELOPE STANLEY.

Linguistic problems with patriarchal reconstructions of Indo-European culture: A little more than kin, a little less than kind. In Cheris Kramarae, ed., *The voices and words of women and men.* Oxford: Pergamon Press, 1980, pp. 227–37. Also *Women's Studies International Quarterly,* 3 (1980).

The authors challenge traditional linguistic reconstructions of Indo-European which suggest an early patriarchal culture, especially in the light of recent archeological discoveries of major female deities in the areas of those languages. Earlier analyses of kinship and religious terminology overlooked or dismissed evidence of a matrilineal, matriarchal substratum in Europe and India.

Also see: Sec. VI-C: "Seizing the Language," which focuses on feminist critiques of patriarchal language which are more sweeping than those emphasizing masculine generics or specific practices of labeling. *Also see:* II-C for entries which treat grammatical gender historically.

C. Linguistic Gender

BARON, NAOMI S.
A reanalysis of English grammatical gender. *Lingua,* 27 (1971), 113–40.

This historical account finds that Modern English gender developed from a grammatical to a natural gender system not gradually but in a series of discrete stages.

ERADES, P. A.
Contributions to modern English syntax: A note on gender. *Moderna Sprak,* 50 (1956), 2–11.

In English, the use of a tripartite system of pronominal references, *he, she,* and *it,* is not based on nouns but rather on subjective ideas and psychological attitude of the speaker. Erades establishes his observation through literary examples and comparisons to the pronominal references in French and German.

ERVIN, SUSAN.
The connotations of gender. *Word,* 18 (1962), 249–61.

Ervin raises the question of whether gender carries meaning, reviews previous evidence, and suggests means of investigating the question. She reports a study of words artificially constructed with phonetic features connoting feminine and masculine, presented to Italian bilinguals who rated them on four semantic differential scales. Her conclusion: "... there is a tendency to ascribe different connotations to masculine and feminine words in Italian ..." The differences are related to male/female stereotypes.

FODOR, ISTVAN.
The origin of grammatical gender, Parts I and II. *Lingua,* 8 (1959), 1–41, 186–214.

In Indo-European languages, gender appears to result from the interplay of syntactic and morphological causes. The development of congruence in a language is held to be the key to the problem of the origin of gender. There is no need for gender to evolve in any language; but if it does, it may hold several important functions.

FRANK, FRANCINE WATTMAN.
Sexism, grammatical gender, and social change. Paper presented at the 9th World Congress of Sociology, Uppsala, Sweden, August 1978. (ERIC document ED 168 368, 1979).

A survey of linguistic gender in several Indo-European languages finds it has frequently been subject to extralinguistic pressures as well as ones internal to the language. The potential for change to less sex-marking appears to be limited by the structure of languages with formal gender concord, but certain accommodating tendencies exist in the spoken language which can be expanded.

FRAZER, J. G.

A suggestion as to the origin of gender in language. *Fortnightly Review,* 67 (1900), 79–90.

Frazer proposes that the origin of grammatical gender lies in historical roots of sex-differentiated speech. He reviews instances of sex differentiation in various cultures (tracing the first-known report to the mid-seventeenth century) and points to the frequency of exogamic, even exodialectic, marriage and of marriage by conquest (in which women are captured for wives and men are driven out). His thesis is that the languages of wife and husband would undergo mixing over time to the point that only one of any single form would remain, and this form would have the "gender" of its original speaker.

HALL, ROBERT A.

Sex references and grammatical gender in English. *American Speech,* 38 (1951), 170–72.

In the romance languages sex reference follows and is subordinate to grammatical gender. English has no grammatical gender—overt or covert—and apparent instances of gender agreement (e.g., substitution of *she* for *Jane*) are actually examples of sex reference as an aspect of nominal and pronominal meaning.

NICHOLS, PATRICIA C.

Gender in English: Syntactic and semantic functions. Paper given at meetings of the Modern Language Association, 1971.

Nichols reviews the ideas of Fodor (and Meillet, Martinet, and Baron), and gives evidence that the evolution in English from grammatical to natural gender is not yet complete, in the "generic" usage. She suggests this use is in transition and that the transition may be actively encouraged; she also offers rules for gender as a grammatical category and for its emotional and expressive uses.

D.   Generics

A note on proposed alternative third person singular pronouns: over the years various proposals have been made for a genderless pronoun. Miller and Swift [*see* sec. II-H-1] and Baron [this section] give good accounts of the various proposals.

BARON, DENNIS E.

The epicene pronoun: The word that failed. *American Speech,* 56 (1981), 83–97.

A discussion and glossary of 35 proposals (gathered from a variety of 19th- and 20th-century sources) for the third person, singular, common gender pronoun. Lack of knowledge of earlier neologisms means some are invented several times. The chances of general adaptation of any of the coinages seem slight given the widespread use of both singular *they* and of *he.*

BATE, BARBARA.

Generic man, invisible woman: Language, thought, and social change. *University of Michigan Papers in Women's Studies,* 2, no. 1 (1975), 83–95.

A thorough examination of the problems of the masculine used as generic, including both ambiguities and detrimental effects on females. Alternative solutions of "reversal" (generic *she*) and "visibility for all" are proposed.

BENDIX, EDWARD H.

Linguistic models as political symbols: Gender and the generic "he" in English. In Judith Orasanu, et al., eds., *Language, sex and gender. Annals* of the New York Academy of Sciences, 1979, vol. 327, pp. 23–39.

This article examines the (often implicit) linguistic theories underlying arguments for or against masculine generic forms, to evaluate the theories' relative strength in serving as political symbols. Arguments for "language as a system of symbols for communicating information" are less strong than those for "language as a sociopolitical system in its own right"; the former may be more valid for children, the latter for adults.

BODINE, ANN.

Androcentrism in prescriptive grammar. *Language in Society,* 4 (1975), 129–46.

Despite prescriptive grammarians' claim that there is no sex-indefinite pronoun for third person singular and their preference for *he,* English "has always had other linguistic devices for referring to sex-indefinite referents, notably the use of *they (their, them)."* Prior to the 18th century, singular *they* was widely used in written and presumably in spoken English. It is significant that grammarians sought to eradicate it by focusing on agreement with the antecedent in number but not in gender.

CALDIE, ROBERT W.

Dominance and language: A new perspective on sexism. Washington, D.C.: University Press of America, 1981.

This is a report of an experiment in which six groups of participants were given descriptions (that used either male pronouns, neutral pronouns, or none) of an honorary position for which they were to rank candidates and give them an evaluation using the Bem Sex Role Inventory. Caldie concludes that language style, while having enormous social significance, does not control short-term sex stereotyping as measured by the rankings and BSRI scores.

CONVERSE, CHARLES CROZAT.

A new pronoun. *The Critic and Good Literature,* 4 (1884), 55; 5 (1884), 79–80.

Converse proposes *thon* (that + one) as a "third personal demonstrative." (See also "That desired impersonal pronoun," *The Writer,* 3, no. 3 [1889], 24, for further comments on the wide support the term received in academia and from the public.)

DeSTEFANO, JOHANNA, MARY KUHNER, AND HAROLD PEPINSKY.

An investigation of referents of selected sex-indefinite terms in English. Paper given at 9th World Congress of Sociology, Uppsala, Sweden, 1978.

Children and adults responded to sentences containing masculine (e.g., *man*) or sex-neutral (e.g., *person*) terms for people, and chose from a chart illustrating stick figures for female and male, plural and singular, mixed or single sex or neutral. Masculine terms tended to influence choices of masculine figures, more so by males than by females.

DOWNEY, PEG.

The invisible woman—where is he? *The Graduate Woman,* 73, no. 2 (1979), 8–13.

Downey discusses the "generic" *he* in education, literature, linguistics, etc. and its effect on females. Citing feminist research, she examines the exclusionary properties of *he* and suggests language alternatives.

DURAN, JANE.

Gender-neutral terms. In Mary Vetterling-Braggin, ed., *Sexist language: A modern philosophical analysis.* Totowa, N.J.: Littlefield, Adams, 1981, pp. 147–54.

Duran argues that neither Moulton nor Korsmeyer [this section] is entirely correct; rather, "that there is gender-neutral usage of masculine terms, and that such usage may not always function in marked contrast to that of designated feminine terms where such terms exist" (p. 147).

EBERHART, OZELIA MAE YOWELL.

Elementary students' understanding of certain masculine and neutral generic nouns. Unpublished Ph.D. dissertation, Kansas State University, 1976. *Dissertation Abstracts, 37* (1976), 4113A–4114A.

A test was constructed with pictures and statements either using masculine generic nouns or neutral generic nouns. 126 first, third and sixth grade students included pictures of females significantly more often when neutral generic nouns were used than when masculine generic nouns were used. Grade level and sex of subjects did not affect this pattern of understanding.

GREEN, WILLIAM.

Singular pronouns and sexual politics. *College Composition and Communication, 28* (1977), 150–53.

Green had 184 college students match pronouns with antecedents in 30 sentences. Many students selected pronouns according to gender rather than number; *they, them,* and *their* were especially prevalent, used more often with singular common nouns ("a teacher") than with singular specific nouns ("a good teacher"). Given the sexual politics of recent decades, the singular function of *they* is likely to expand.

HACKER, SALLY L.

Man and humanism: An essay on language, gender and power. *Humanity and Society, 2* (1978), 273–82.

In this personal essay, sociologist Hacker reviews her own research and experiences with the use of the masculine form as generic. She suggests that "a masculine focus in humanism—stemming from and reflected in its language—limits our range of imagination to far fewer alternatives than would a more inclusive orientation" (p. 277).

HARRISON, LINDA.

Cro-Magnon woman—In eclipse. *Science Teacher, 42,* no. 4 (1975), 9–11.

Junior high school students (N = 503) in science courses were given a survey asking their knowledge of early humans. One form of the survey used the terms *man, men,* etc. (I); another used *humans, people* (II); and a third used *men and women* (III). Both female and male students more often drew only male figures in response to I than to either of the other two forms, and more often to II than to III. More male than female students drew only male figures overall.

HARRISON, LINDA AND RICHARD N. PASSERO.

Sexism in the language of elementary school textbooks. *Science and Children, 12,* no. 4 (1975), 22–25.

Eight statements about human activities were presented to 85 third-graders in either a neutral or masculine generic form, and the pupils were asked to choose an illustrative picture from portrayals of women, children, and men. Masculine statements elicited exclusively male-oriented responses from between 49 and 85% of the students, compared with only 3 to 31% who gave male responses to neutral statements.

KIDD, VIRGINIA.

A study of the images produced through the use of the male pronoun as the generic. *Moments in Contemporary Rhetoric and Communication*, 1, no. 2 (1971), 25–30.

Eighteen sentences using the masculine pronoun in the generic sense were presented to 68 college students, who were asked to give for the antecedent either: (a) the sex, social status, race, and financial position; or (b) labels of rich/poor, black/white, female/male, strong/weak, successful/unsuccessful. The masculine pronoun was overwhelmingly understood as referencing male: in the first set of questions, male was given 407 times, female 31 times (there were 174 other responses); in the second set, male was chosen 526 times to female, 53.

KORSMEYER, CAROLYN.

The hidden joke: Generic uses of masculine terminology. In Mary Vetterling-Braggin, ed., *Sexist language: A modern philosophical analysis*. Totowa, N.J.: Littlefield, Adams, 1981, pp. 116–31.

He and *man* may be gender-neutral, but *she* used in the same contexts would always be gender-specific; therefore the *he/man* usage is sexist. Using humor as a medium, Korsmeyer explores language to reveal sexist practices and distinctions. (*See* Duran, this section.)

LANGENDOEN, D. TERENCE.

Essentials of English grammar. New York: Holt, Rinehart & Winston, 1970.

Langendoen asked 46 English teachers to respond to statements with generic nouns by generating tag questions; *they* was often used as a singular pronoun for the nouns (pp. 10–28). [*See* Marcoux, Sec. II-E.]

MACKAY, DONALD G.

Language, thought and social attitudes. In Howard Giles, W. Peter Robinson, and Philip M. Smith, eds., *Language: Social psychological perspectives*. Oxford: Pergamon Press, 1980, pp. 89–96.

An experiment is reported in which students read paragraphs containing either plural *they* or prescriptive *he* (i.e., *he* used generically), with results of lower comprehension and less personal relevance with the prescriptive *he* paragraph for females, the opposite for males (not replicated with presumably less feminist subjects). MacKay suggests that prescriptive *he* influences attitudes, but its effects depend on the perceiver's evaluative framework.

MACKAY, DONALD G.

On the goals, principles, and procedures for prescriptive grammar. *Language in Society*, 9 (1980), 349–67.

This paper presents a cost-benefit analysis of singular *they* as an alternative to prescriptive *he*. Benefits of neutrality and naturalness were found in substituting *they* for *he*, but costs were found in ambiguity, questionable conceptual availability, distancing connotations, and other such problems.

MacKay, Donald G.

Prescriptive grammar and the pronoun problem. In this volume.

MacKay makes explicit 14 assumptions which have been used (explicitly or implicitly) to bolster the prescriptive use of *he,* under the five categories: Production, Comprehension, Learning, Language and Cognition, and Language Change assumptions. Examining research evidence relevant to each, he finds them untenable. He proposes two research programs, one to establish which of the already available alternatives to prescriptive *he* works best in which contexts, and another to establish a simpler prescription, possibly a search for a best neologism.

MacKay, Donald G.

Psychology, prescriptive grammar and the pronoun problem. *American Psychologist,* 35 (1980), 444–49.

Three untested assumptions made by those who advocate the masculine pronoun as generic are examined: that the pronoun is a neutral surrogate for the noun, that it will mean what one says it will, and that context can determine pronoun meaning without ambiguity. Generic *he* led to exclusion of females 50% of the time; neologisms *E, e* or *tey* did so less often. MacKay discusses ways to determine the best possible neologism for a sex-indefinite pronoun.

MacKay, Donald G. and Fulkerson, D. C.

On the comprehension and production of pronouns. *Journal of Verbal Learning and Verbal Behavior,* 18 (1979), 661–73.

This study examines the linguistic claim of "neutralization" of the pronoun *he* when used generically. In a reaction-time experiment, subjects responded excluding females 87% of the time when they heard *he* in a generic frame; when generic nouns were used, the exclusion rate was 43%. The authors offer a two-stage model of pronoun comprehension.

Martyna, Wendy.

Beyond the he/man approach: The case for nonsexist language. In this volume. Revised from *Signs,* 5 (1980), 482–93.

This paper, a good source of examples of backlash to language change proposals in recent years, explores arguments and prospects for change away from the masculine generic usage.

Martyna, Wendy.

The psychology of the generic masculine. In Sally McConnell-Ginet, Ruth Borker, and Nelly Furman, eds., *Women and language in literature and society.* New York: Praeger, 1980, pp. 69–78.

Martyna's research examines how individuals choose pronouns to respond to the generic meaning of sentence fragments. Responses were determined by mental imagery and gender, and empirically show how generic masculine language influences how and what we think.

Martyna, Wendy.

Using and understanding the generic masculine: A social-psychological approach. Paper given at the 9th World Congress of Sociology, Uppsala, Sweden, 1978.

Martyna used a social-psychological approach to examine the use, comprehension, and implications of the generic masculine. She argues that the inherent meaning of the generic masculine and its relationship to the psychology of the sexes is politically and socially detrimental.

MARTYNA, WENDY.

What does "he" mean? Use of the generic masculine. *Journal of Communication,* 28, (1978), 131–38.

Female and male students (N = 40) were given sentence fragments with male-related subjects, half in written and half in oral form, and asked to complete them in the same mode. Female-related subjects tended to elicit feminine pronouns and masculine-related subjects to elicit masculine pronouns; alternatives were found most often in response to neutral subjects. Women used *he* less often generically than did men, and were more likely to use alternatives. With neutral subjects, 60% of the males had imagery, but only 10% of the females; imagery for both was overwhelmingly male.

McCONNELL-GINET, SALLY.

Prototypes, pronouns and persons. In Madeleine Mathiot, ed., *Ethnolinguistics: Boas, Sapir and Whorf revisited.* The Hague: Mouton, 1979, pp. 63–84.

An analysis of patterns of usage of *she, he or she,* and *they,* including discussion of ways in which *she* functions generically, contexts in which *they* seems more or less satisfactory as a sex-indefinite pronoun, and implications of the sexualization of fictive prototypes.

MILLER, CASEY, AND KATE SWIFT.

De-sexing the English langauge. *Ms.,* 1 (1972), 7.

The authors suggest the generic personal pronoun *he* has a negative effect on female personality development, whereas it bolsters male ego. Their alternative: nominative case, *tey* (for *he or she*); objective case, *tem* (for *him or her*); possessive case, *ter(s)* (for *his or her(s)*).

MOULTON, JANICE.

The myth of the neutral "man." In Mary Vetterling-Braggin, ed., *Sexist language: A modern philosophical analysis.* Totowa, N.J.: Littlefield, Adams, 1981.

Moulton asserts that indirect and unconscious meanings associated with supposedly neutral gender terms *he* and *man* cause such terms actually to be gender specific. Language is not neutral. [*See* Duran, this section.]

MOULTON, JANICE, GEORGE M. ROBINSON, AND CHERIN ELIAS.

Sex bias in language use: "Neutral" pronouns that aren't. *American Psychologist,* 33 (1978), 1032–36.

Nearly 500 college students were asked to make up a story on a given theme, which was presented using a sex-neutral noun and one of three pronouns. When *his* was the pronoun, 35% of the story characters were female; with *their,* 46% were; with *his or her,* 56% were.

MURPHY-BERMAN, VIRGINIA AND PAULA J. JEAN.

The factors affecting the gender connotations of language for the deaf child. *American Annals of the Deaf,* 126 (1981), 57–63.

In a study of how supposedly generic terms such as *man* are understood by hearing-impaired individuals, students in a school for the deaf tended to consider their own sex more than the other sex only when the word was accompanied by concrete visual options. For the deaf child making a word like *someone* more relevant than *he* may require including visual materials.

The Peacemaker.

Minutes, Letters in issues of Jan., Feb., March, 1979 (vol. 32, nos. 1, 2, 3).

A report of a December meeting described the difficulty members had in discussing a nongendered pronoun; *co* is used in the report. A long letter about the issue of sexist language stimulated other letters in subsequent issues.

SALTER, MARTY M., DEBORAH WEIDER-HATFIELD, AND DONALD B. YARBROUGH.

The effects of the generic use of *she, he,* and *they,* sex of speaker, and sex of listener on speaker credibility. Paper given at meeting of National Women's Studies Assoc., Bloomington, Ind., May 1980.

Subjects heard a speech on engineering or nursing recorded by a female or male speaker, in one of three versions varying generic pronoun (*she, he,* or *they*). They rated the speaker on semantic differential scales relating to credibility. Both speakers using *she* were perceived as more dynamic than when using *he* or *they*.

SCHNEIDER, JOSEPH AND SALLY HACKER.

Sex role imagery and the use of the generic "man" in introductory texts. *American Sociologist,* 8 (1973), 12–18.

Students in introductory sociology classes were asked to submit pictures to represent the major sections of an introductory text. When the terms used the word *man* generically (e.g., social man, political man), 64% of the pictures showed male only. When the generic label *man* was removed (e.g., social behavior, political behavior), 50% of the students illustrated the concepts with pictures of males only.

SCHULZ, MURIEL.

Man (embracing woman): The generic in sociological writing. Paper given at 9th World Congress of Sociology, Uppsala, Sweden, 1978.

Schulz examines sociological writing from the 18th to the 20th century, analyzing use of masculine pronouns and nouns as generic terms. Early writers considered human behavior from a masculine point of view; some contemporary sociologists still do.

SHEPELAK, NORMA J.

Does "he" mean "she" too? The case of the generic anomaly. Paper given at annual meeting of Assoc. for Women in Psychology, St. Louis, Mo., Feb. 1977.

Shepelak reviews current linguistic and social-psychological research and contends that the masculine generic does not represent both women and men; she discusses its detrimental effects and proposes alternative language forms.

SILVEIRA, JEANETTE.

Generic masculine words and thinking. In Cheris Kramarae, ed., *The voices and words of women and men.* Oxford: Pergamon Press, 1980, pp. 165–78. Also *Women's Studies International Quarterly,* 3, no. 2/3 (1980).

This paper separates the people = male bias in our thought and culture from the generic = specific bias in language, and asks what are the causal relations among masculine generic word forms, the people = male bias, and the sexist environment. Reviewing her own and others' research,

Silveira provisionally concludes that a reduction in the use of the masculine generic would result in a long-term reduction in sexist thinking, and that women experience more alienation from the masculine generic usage than do men.

STERICKER, ANNE.

Does this "he or she" business really make a difference? The effect of masculine pronouns as generics on job attitudes. *Sex Roles*, 7 (1981), 637–41.

Undergraduates (66 female, 66 male) read six job descriptions referring to the jobholder (s) either as *he, he or she,* or *they.* Following each description subjects indicated their interest both in the job and a related category, and estimated how difficult the job would be to get for categories of people varied by race, ethnicity, sex, age, and handicap. Several significant sex-of-subject-by-pronoun-interactions generally support the notion that generic use of masculine pronouns narrows the reader's attitudes.

STRAUMANIS, JOAN.

Generic "man" and mortal woman. In Beth Reed, ed., *The structure of knowledge: A feminist perspective.* Proceedings of the 4th Annual GLCA Women's Studies Conference, Nov. 1978, pp. 25–32.

An examination of problems of the masculine generic usage, illustrating many contradictions, answering defenses of the usage, and looking at changing patterns. The author differentiates between the sexism of language and the sexism expressed in language.

TIMM, LENORA.

Not mere tongue-in-cheek: The case for a common gender pronoun in English. *International Journal of Women's Studies,* 1 (1978), 555–65.

Timm proposes as a common gender pronoun: *heesh* (possessive: *hiser(s)*, objective: *herm*, and reflexive: *hermself*). She compares this with other proposals (*co, she, tey, E, ho, hesh*).

TODD-MANCILLAS, WILLIAM R.

Masculine generics = sexist language: A review of literature and implications for speech communication professionals. *Communication Quarterly,* 29 (Spring 1981), 107–15.

This review of studies which demonstrate gender-based perceptions resulting from use of generics concludes with alternative suggestions.

VEACH, SHARON.

Sexism in usage: Intentional, conveyed, or all in the mind? Paper given at Conference on Language and Gender, University of California, Santa Cruz, April 1979.

In the *Stanford* (University) *Daily* newspaper over three months' time, female student heads of committees were always called *chairpersons;* female faculty and administrators, *chairwomen* or *spokeswomen* (except the highest-ranking women who were *chairmen*). Male students were referred to both as *chairmen/spokesmen* and *chairpersons/spokespersons,* and male faculty and administrators were always *chairmen* or *spokesmen.* Thus *man* was the highest, and *person* the lowest, prestige ending.

WILSON, LAVISA CAM.

Teachers' inclusion of males and females in generic nouns. *Research in the Teaching of English,* 12 (1978), 155–61.

Elementary and secondary teachers (N = 104) were tested for their inclusion of females and males in understanding "generic" nouns, given in either masculine or sex-neutral form (using Eberhart's instrument). The masculine form significantly influenced the teachers' responses, though women interpreted the terms more generically than men did.

WISE ERICA, AND JANET RAFFERTY.

Sex bias and language. *Sex Roles,* 8:12 (1982), 1189–96.

Stricker (1977) has proposed that even explicitly generic terms such as "adult" and "person" may not be gender neutral. The conclusions of the highly controversial and influential Broverman, Vogel, Broverman, Clarkson, and Rosenkrantz (1970) study were based directly on the assumption that "adult" is a gender-neutral term. The present study consisted of a modified replication of the Broverman et al. study followed by an addendum that asked subjects in the "gender-neutral" condition to indicate whether they had thought of a neutral, male, or female stimulus person. As predicted, subjects did not tend to think of a neutral stimulus person. The implications of this finding for sex-role stereotype research as well as for "guidelines for nonsexist language" are discussed. (From author's abstract.)

E.   Gender Marking, Naming (Labels, Slang)

ACKERMAN, LOUISE M.

Lady as a synonym for *woman. American Speech,* 37 (1962), 284–85.

This brief note purports to give evidence that *lady* and *woman* are synonymous. [*See* the more substantial reply by Hancock, this section.]

ANDERSON, LYNN R., MARTHA FINN, AND SANDRA LEIDER.

Leadership style and leader title. *Psychology of Women Quarterly,* 5 (1981), 661–69.

College students (183 female and 191 male) gave reactions to case studies of leadership in a committee, with variation in form of address for the leader (*Mr., Ms., Miss, Mrs.*) and in leadership style (democratic or authoritarian). Leader style affected the ratings (on semantic differentials of subordination and friendship), but leader title produced no significant main effects, although authoritarian leaders using *Ms.* evoked higher subordination reactions than other authoritarian leaders.

ATWOOD, E. BAGBY.

The pronunciation of "Mrs." *American Speech,* 25 (1950), 10–18.

This study examines local and regional differences in the pronunciation of address terms in the northeast and southwest U.S. At one time in the Charleston area "Mis" developed as the pronunciation of *Mrs.* and it became "impossible to distinguish the title of a married woman from a spinster."

BAKER, ROBERT.

"Pricks" and "chicks": A plea for "persons." In Mary Vetterling-Braggin, ed., *Sexist language: A modern philosophical analysis.* Totowa, N.J.: Littlefield, Adams, 1981, pp. 161–82.

In this revision of a well-known paper, Baker points to metaphorical identification as a conceptual structure of our sexual identity. Our language is male chauvinist because our concepts of women (demeaning and hurtful) permeate the language.[*Also see* Ross, this section.]

BAUCHNER, JOYCE ELLYN.

The cognitive development and social learning interaction in the acquisition of sex role semantics. Paper given at the 9th World Congress of Sociology, Uppsala, Sweden, 1978.

Bauchner posits an underlying sex-role semantic dimension in language and discusses this dimension in English, presenting a chronological curve of the impact of the sex-role semantic dimension over the life span.

BEARDSLEY, ELIZABETH.

Referential genderization. *Philosphical Forum*, 5 (Fall/Winter 1973–1974), 511–12.

Referential genderization occurs when a speaker must, in referring to human beings, make a distinction based on sex. It substitutes a dichotomy—male and female persons—for a unitary category—persons—and has negative ethical implications bearing on concepts of personhood and selfhood.

BEARDSLEY, ELIZABETH JANE.

Degenderization. In Mary Vetterling-Braggin, ed., *Sexist language: A modern philosophical analysis.* Totowa, N.J.: Littlefield, Adams, 1981, pp. 155–60.

Beardsley examines nouns ending in -*man*. Is the suffix a suffix of agency or does it denote sex? Contextual degenderization (". . . increasing the frequency of explicit application of *chairman* to females . . .") should be tried where genderization is present.

BEM, SANDRA L. AND DARYL J. BEM.

Does sex-biased job advertising "aid and abet" sex discrimination? *Journal of Applied Social Psychology*, 3 (1973), 6–18.

High school students responded preferentially to jobs cued to their own sex.

BERRYMAN-FINK, CYNTHIA AND KATHLEEN VERDERBER.

Attributions of the term "feminist": A factor analytic development of a measuring instrument. *Psychology of Women Quarterly,* in press.

Undergraduates (761, male and female) completed a 91-item semantic differential test relevant to the label "feminist." Factor analysis gave factors of general evaluation, behavioral characteristics, political orientation, sexual preference, and gender classification. A 54-item scale was produced to measure attributions associated with the term "feminist."

BOONE, LALIA PHIPPS.

Vernacular of menstruation. *American Speech*, 29 (1954), 297–98.

A brief addition to the work of Joffe [this section], adding some 40 items to her collection.

BORDEN, GEORGE.

The perceived sexuality of passages written in predominantly masculine or feminine language. Paper presented at annual meeting of Speech Communication Assoc., Chicago, 1974.

Fifty female and male university students rated the sexuality of the most frequently used American English words. The 147 words perceived by both sexes as feminine were more likely to depict emotion, domesticity, goodness, weakness, passivity, smallness, aesthetics, and religion than were the 291 words perceived as masculine, which were more likely to depict violence, professionalism, politics, badness, activity, strength, wealth, endurance, and control.

BRANNON, ROBERT.

The consequences of sexist language. Paper presented at American Psychological Assoc. convention, Toronto, 1978.

College students (N=462) read a story describing a female's application for a high-level executive position, in which she is referred to either as *girl* or *woman*. Students' ratings of personality traits described the "woman" as more tough, mature, dignified, and brilliant than the "girl," more qualified to be hired, and deserving of a salary of about $6000 per year more.

CARSON, JULIE.

The Rumpelstiltskin syndrome: Sexism in American naming traditions. In Dana V. Hiller and Robin Ann Sheets, eds., *Women and men: The consequences of power*. Cincinnati: Office of Women's Studies, Univ. of Cincinnati, 1973, pp. 64–73.

Exploring Jespersen's association of consonant word endings with masculinity and vowel endings with femininity, Carson examines women's and men's names for their endings as well as for other features. American vowel-final names and nicknames are primarily reserved for women and children, and conjure associations of a trivializing nature; males tend to have consonant-final names and nicknames.

COYNE, JAMES, KAREN O'BRIEN, AND RICHARD SHERMAN.

Expletives and woman's place. *Sex Roles,* 4 (1978), 826–35.

This paper investigates the usage and implications of the terms *bastard* and *bitch*. Empirical study by the authors reveals that *bitch* acts as an expletive to enforce adherence to the female sex role. Male and female interpretations of these two words are analyzed.

ERNSTER, VIRGINIA L.

American menstrual expressions. *Sex Roles.* 1 (1975), 3–13.

An examination of 128 terms collected from 70 females and 24 males, from Folklore Archives at the Univ. of California at Berkeley. Ernster finds nine categories of reference: (1) female visitor; (2) male (visitor); (3) time/cycle; (4) negative; (5) red/blood; (6) material used; (7) nature; (8) literal behavior; (9) combinations of these. The most frequent terms supplied by females were of class (4), followed by (1) and (6). Some terms were nearly exclusive to males or females. The transmission of menstrual euphemisms involves learning not only the terms but also menstrual stereotypes that accompany them.

FALK, JOAN AND REESA M. VAUGHTER.

The effects of sexist language upon the evaluative behavior of persons making sex and gender attributions. Paper given at meetings of the American Psychological Assoc., New York, Sept. 1979.

In two studies, undergraduates read job descriptions written in masculine, feminine, or sex-inclusive (*he or she*) language, then rated photos of applicants on their suitability for the job. In the first study, which varied both nouns (e.g., *spokesman/spokeswoman)* and pronouns, males were preferred for male-described jobs and females for female-described jobs. When the descriptions were sex-inclusive, neither sex was given preference. In the second study, conducted a year later, using only sex-typed pronouns and not nouns, sex-biased evaluations were not obtained.

FRANZWA, HELEN.

Woman's place in semantic space. Paper presented at Speech Communication Assoc. convention, 1974.

Data from four research studies are presented to provide support for the hypothesis that there are semantic spaces for females and for males which are well-defined—here as $E+P-$ (good, weak) and $E+P+$ (good, strong) respectively. Further research is projected to test the hypothesis that the evaluative dimension of meaning operates to constrain "strong" behavior on the part of females and "weak" behavior on the part of males by negative labeling attached to such behavior.

FRIED, BARBARA.

Boys will be boys will be boys: The language of sex and gender. In Ruth Hubbard, Barbara Henifine, and Barbara Fried, eds., *Women look at biology looking at women.* Cambridge, Mass.: Schenkman, 1979, pp. 37–59.

Fried criticizes the methodology of John Money's and Anka Ehrhardt's *Man and woman, boy and girl*, and criticizes their conclusions, for example, regarding "female behavior" of girls/women with androgen insensitivity. Fried points out that the language of "objective" science shapes our perceptions and descriptions of reality.

FRIEDMAN, HOWARD S.

The scientific error of sexist research: A case study. *Sex Roles,* 6 (1980), 747–50.

In an application of the APA Guidelines for Nonsexist Language [*see* Sec. II-H. 1: Cofer et al.], Friedman criticizes an article examining the reactions of male and female hospital patients to touching by female nurses. That article did not specify the nurses' sex (nor use nurses of both sexes), thus conceptually (as well as experimentally) confounding gender expectations and the social role of nurse.

GILL, WAYNE S. AND CHARLES A. HOGAN.

The effect of language upon gender shaping. *International Journal of Symbology,* 2 (1970), 9–12.

A study similar to that of Ludwig and Moore [this section] of bilingual Spanish-English subjects and an English-speaking control group; no significant differences were found in the attributions of gender to either masculine or feminine words.

GLAZER-WALDMAN, CATHY AND L. W. WENDLER.

Identifying sex biased and sex fair language. Paper given at the American Educational Research Assoc. convention, San Francisco, April 1979.

Female and male college students (N = 175) rated 33 sex-biased and sex-fair statements according to degree of sex bias. Bias was less recognized when contained in terms in common use; females showed greater sensitivity to both sex-biased and sex-fair statements; and subjects over 35 tended to perceive less sex bias in the statements.

GOTTFREDSON, GARY D.

A note on sexist wording in interest measurement. *Measurement and Evaluation in Guidance*, 8 (1974), 221–23.

Girls in a college preparatory school (N = 94) responded to a vocational interest inventory with four items worded in either a masculine or sex-neutral way. No preference for either form over another was found with this population.

GREER, GERMAINE,

Abuse. In *The female eunuch*. New York: McGraw-Hill, 1971, pp. 259–69.

In the chapter on "Abuse" Greer discusses terms which originally applied to both sexes and become pejorative when applied to women. The most offensive words reveal male disgust for illicit or casual sex (e.g., *tramp, pig, pussy*).

GRIM, PATRICK.

A note on the ethics of theories of truth. In Mary Vetterling-Braggin, ed., *Sexist language: A modern philosophical analysis.* Totowa, N.J.: Littlefield, Adams, 1981, pp. 34–51.

Grim proposes that statements framed in sexist/racist ways are neither true nor false, and argues a choice between theories of truth on ethical grounds. [*Also see* Stenner, Taylor, this section.]

HANCOCK, CICELY RAYSON.

"Lady" and "woman." *American Speech*, 38 (1963), 234–35.

This brief note challenges Ackerman's [this section] assertion that *lady* and *woman* are synonymous, and identifies three distinct groups which are different in their usage of the terms. Hancock claims that those who prefer to use *lady* for contemporaries nevertheless refer to historical women as *woman*; that those who prefer *woman* are more apt to use it for women better known and identified, applying *lady* "politely" to social subordinates and strangers.

HAYES, JOSEPH J.

Lesbians, gay men, and their "languages." In James W. Chesebro, ed., *Gayspeak: Gay male and lesbian communication*. New York: Pilgrim Press, 1981, pp. 28–42.

A section on "Labels" discusses the history and connotations of various terms for lesbians and gay men. A section on "Language that separates and oppresses" reviews terms for lesbians and gay men and slang associated with them.

HEILMAN, MADELINE.
> Miss, Mrs., or none of the above. *American Psychologist*, 30 (1975), 516–18.

In two studies, male high school and college students rated two courses of which they had read descriptions, and whose instructors were listed as *Miss, Mrs., Ms., Mr.*, or without title. In both studies the less technical course was rated as potentially less enjoyable and intellectually stimulating when it was to be taught by a *Miss* or *Mrs.* than when it was to be taught by *Ms., Mr.*, or someone without a title.

JACOBSON, MARSHA B.
> A rose by any other name: Attitudes toward feminism as a function of its label. *Sex Roles,* 5, (1979), 365–71.

Subjects rated various labels for feminism on a variety of evaluative dimensions. "Equal rights for women" was most positively evaluated, and "women's liberation" was the least so; females' ratings on some dimensions were more favorable than males'.

JACOBSON, MARSHA B.
> You say potato and I say potahto: Attitudes toward feminism as a function of its subject-selected label. *Sex Roles*, 7 (1981), 349–54.

Male and female subjects were asked which of four labels they were likely to use for a given definition of feminism (unlabeled): equal rights for women (ERW), feminism (FEM), women's liberation (WLN), and women's lib (WLB); and rated the concept on a variety of evaluative dimensions. FEM and WLN were rated more positively, and WLB more negatively, in this study than in Jacobson (1979). ERW and WLB were used more frequently than FEM and WLN.

JESPERSEN, OTTO.
> Gender (XVIII-6, pp. 346–48). In *Language: Its nature, development, and origin.* New York: Holt, 1924.

This section has a discussion both of grammatical gender and of gender distinctions in the pronoun system. Jespersen observes that most English pronouns make no distinction of sex and that many other languages do not have separate forms for *he and she.* He gives examples of the difficulty arising from not having a sex-neutral pronoun, and of alternatives used. [*Also see* Sec. I-A.] A related reference: Jespersen, "Sex and gender," in *The philosophy of grammar.* New York: W. W. Norton, 1965 (orig. 1924).

JOFFE, NATALIE F.
> Vernacular of menstruation. *Word,* 4 (1948), 181–86.

Joffe gives over 90 menstrual terms, telling whether they are used by females or males and categorizing them by reference to periodicity or time, color, visitors, male or female personification, disability, material used, or sexual unavailability. [*Also see* Boone, this section.]

LANGENFELT, GOSTA.
> *She* and *her* instead of *it* and *its. Anglia,* 70 (1951), 90–101.

This article expands on Svartengren's 1927 paper [this section], suggesting other possible sources of the American tendency to personification than those Svartengren suggests.

LARSEN, VIRGINIA L.

Psychological study of colloquial menstrual expressions. *Northwest Medicine,* 62 (1963), 874–77.

Terms referring to cyclicity were found to be most commonly used by all age groups; in other categories there was some variation by group.

LAWRENCE, BARBARA.

Dirty words can harm you. *Redbook,* 143 (1974), 33.

Lawrence examines the systematic derogation of women through obscenity; e.g., tabooed sexual verbs *(fuck, screw)* suggest negative implications for the object, the female. Lawrence notes that racial or ethnic obscenities shock the same people who do not question obscenities which derogate women.

LEGMAN, GERSHON.

Rationale of the dirty joke: An analysis of sexual humor. New York: Grove Press, 1968.

This study analyzes over 2000 erotic jokes and folklore collected in the U.S. and abroad; examples include jokes about mothers-in-law and pubic hair. Legman claims that most "dirty jokes" are originated by men, with women as the butt of humor, and that speech is a form of sexual display for males, akin to bodily ornamentation for females.

LERNER, HARRIET.

And what do little girls have? . . . some thoughts on female sexuality. *Behold the Women,* 4, no. 8 (Sept. 1975), 5–6.

This article focuses on one determinant of women's sexual difficulties: "Parental failure to acknowledge and adequately label the female child's genitals," causing daughters' inabilities to "achieve pride and comfort with sexual functions."

LERNER, HARRIET.

Girls, ladies, or women? The unconscious dynamics of language choice. *Comprehensive Psychiatry,* 17 (1976), 295–99.

Lerner suggests that the use of *girl* or *lady* reflects the anxiety and unconscious attitudes of mental health professionals toward females; *women* traditionally implies aggression, sexuality, or "destruction," and provokes anxiety. Therapists then reinforce intrapsychic pressure to be a *girl/lady* and avoid *woman.* When anxiety about these qualities changes, language will change.

LESHER, MARGY.

Choose four: Lesbian/feminist, woman, dyke, gay, chick, homosexual, lesbian, amazon, girl. *Lesbian Connection,* 1 (Feb. 12, 1974), East Lansing, Mich.

An analysis of stereotypes in the words lesbians use, often without reflection, to describe themselves. *Chick* and *girl* suggest pre-adolescence; *homosexual* implies neurosis and masculinity; lesbians are invisible in *gay,* a male term; the most accurate labels are *amazon, dyke, woman,* and *lesbian,* which give self-identity, a sense of history, community, and militancy.

LEVIN, MICHAEL.

Vs. Ms. In Mary Vetterling-Braggin, ed., *Sexist language: A modern philosophical analysis.* Totowa, N.J.: Littlefield, Adams, 1981, pp. 217–22.

Levin believes unconscious word choices are allied to human reality, nature, evolution, and physiological needs. Thus, "desexing language is pernicious." Language which denotes power, status, or physiological reality is not sexist but linked to fundamental biological/physiological "facts," e.g., the "Miss/Mrs." designation is a sexual signal for males. [*Also see* Purdy, Soble, this section.]

LUDWIG, DAVID AND MICHAEL MOORE.

Language and gender shaping. *International Journal of Symbology,* 1 (1969), 25–27.

A group of English-speaking students who had studied German and a control group speaking only English were asked to attribute gender to a list of 50 English words. There were significant, positive differences in 28 out of 50 words. [*Also see* Gill and Hogan, this section.]

MACDOUGALD, DUNCAN, JR.

Language and sex. In Albert Ellis and Albert Abarbanel, eds., *The Encyclopedia of sexual behavior,* vol. 2. New York: Hawthorn Books, 1961, pp. 585–98.

This encyclopedia entry is a mixed bag, but has etymologies and historical comments for a number of words referring to female and male body parts and for sexual activities, and has a useful reference list.

MACKAY, DONALD AND TOSHI KONISHI.

Personification and the pronoun problem. In Cheris Kramarae, ed., *The voices and words of women and men.* Oxford: Pergamon Press, 1980, pp. 140–63. Also *Women's Studies International Quarterly,* 3, no. 2/3 (1980).

This paper argues that the rule that pronouns are chosen to agree with their antecedents in number, gender, and person is not the primary basis for pronoun selection for nonhuman antecedents, rather that they "are selected on the basis of psychologically deep attitudes toward the antecedent." Two studies are reported: one, of personification in children's literature, and another, of pronoun switching by adults.

MAINARDI, PATRICIA.

Quilts: The great american art. *Radical America,* 7, no. 1 (1973), 36–68.

Mainardi shows the sexism implicit in writing about quiltmaking. For example, Jonathan Holstein appraised pieced quilts at a museum exhibit as "strong," "bold," etc. However, he dismisses appliqué quilts (which current male artists have not chosen to imitate) as "pretty," "elegant," "beautiful but decorative." Phallic criticism of women's art is inaccurate since women made both types of quilts.

MAMOLA, CLAIRE.

Are robots roboys? Paper given at meetings of the National Women's Studies Assoc., Bloomington, Ind., May 1980.

An examination of media and popular tendencies to personify robots as male, despite manufacturers' precautions not to personify. Of 156 seventh grade students who wrote robot stories for a class assignment, 69% personified them as male, 12% as female, and 19% did neither.

MARCOUX, DELL R.

> Deviation in English gender. *American Speech,* 48 (19973), 98–107.

This study of personification partially replicates previous research of Langendoen [Sec. II-D] and others in presenting statements for which respondents were to add tag questions, forcing a pronoun choice for antecedents which were countries, ships, animals, or humans. Respondents did not consistently choose pronouns according to natural gender or prescribed grammatical gender, but were influenced by overt syntactic markers or certain semantic markers in the statements.

MATHIOT, MADELEINE (assisted by Marjorie Roberts).

> Sex roles as revealed through referential gender in American English. In Madeleine Mathiot, ed., *Ethnolinguistics: Boas, Sapir and Whorf revisited.* The Hague: Mouton, 1979, pp. 1–48.

Drawing upon naturally occurring instances, Mathiot analyzes uses of pronominal forms in American English. She relates patterns of usage to conceptions of humanness; to four contrasts men imply in distinguishing maleness and femaleness (e.g., using *she* vs. *he* to allude to incompetence vs. competence); and to one contrast women use (infantile vs. mature corresponds to *he* vs. *she*).

MILLER, D. GARY.

> English vs. Woman. Available from Academics Plus, Inc., P.O. Box 254, Micanopy FL 32667.

The English pattern of feminines derived from basic masculines is examined for its sociocultural and linguistic implications. Sex(ism), like number, is a Linguistic Postulate in the Indo-European languages; non-sexist languages like Aymara do not exhibit anything like English's symbolic attachment and subordination of females to males in the culture. Ample documentation is provided for the recent productivity of these suffixes, revealing that English is in serious danger of developing *obligatory* feminine markers that are simultaneously diminutive derogatives. (From author's abstract.)

MOE, ALBERT F.

> "Lady" and "woman": The terms used in the 1880's. *American Speech,* 38 (1963), 295.

An amusing discussion of an era when some regarded it an insult to be called a "woman."

MOELY, BARBARA E. AND KIMBERLY KREICKER.

> Ladies and gentlemen, women and men: A study of the connotations of words indicating gender. *Psychology of Women Quarterly*, in press.

College students rated *gentleman* as implying greater competence and warmth than *man* while *lady* suggests less competence and warmth than *woman*. The differentiation of the feminine but not the masculine words was predictable on the basis of personal characteristics of the raters.

MONTEMAYOR, RAYMOND.

> Children's performance in a game and their attraction to it as a function of sex-typed labels. *Child Development*, 45 (1974), 152–56.

A study of 60 girls and 60 boys, ages six-eight, playing in an unfamiliar game found that both sexes performed highest when the game was labeled sex-appropriate, intermediate when no sex label was affixed, and lowest when the game was labeled sex-inappropriate.

MOULTON, JANICE.

Sex and reference. In Mary Vetterling-Braggin, ed., *Sexist language: A modern philosophical analysis.* Totowa, N.J.: Littlefield, Adams, 1981, pp. 100–15.

Language reflects sexual activity as male-dominated and male-defined (e.g., the dictionary definition of *coitus* as an "act conveying male semen to the female reproductive tract").

NEY, JAMES W.

Sexism in the English vocabulary: A biased view in a biased society. *Etc.* 33 (March 1976), 67–76.

Ney continues Nilsen's [this section] analysis of sexist vocabulary and offers criticism and new evidence, touching on differences between female and male, ameliorative, pejorative, and neutral terms.

NILSEN, ALLEEN PACE.

Sexism as shown through the English vocabulary. In Alleen Pace Nilsen et al., eds., *Sexism and language.* Urbana, Ill.: National Council of Teachers of English, 1977, pp. 27–41.

Nilsen found 517 dictionary items visibly marked for +Masculine (e.g., *fellow, son*) or +Feminine (e.g., *daughter, frau*), and analyzed and compared certain of their semantic features. There were 385 masculine terms and 132 feminine, but negative feminine words outnumbered masculine ones 25 to 20; of those marked for +Prestige, masculine outnumbered feminine ones six to one.

NILSEN, ALLEEN PACE.

Sexism in the language of marriage. In Alleen Pace Nilsen et al., eds., *Sexism and language.* Urbana, Ill.: National Council of Teachers of English, 1977, pp. 131–40.

This brief article explores differing sex-related expectations and roles in the wedding celebration, marriage, surname customs, and self-identity within the language of marriage.

NUESSEL, FRANK H., JR.

The language of ageism. *The Gerontologist*, 22 (1982), 273–76.

Many ageist terms are also sexist, for example, *biddy, crone, granny, grimalkin, hag, witch, maid, lady.* While there are derogatory terms for old men (*codger, coot, gaffer*), ageist terms for women are more derisive and usually present them as thoroughly disgusting.

PURDY, L. M.

Against "Vs. Ms." In Mary Vetterling-Braggin, ed., *Sexist language: A modern philosophical analysis.* Totowa, N.J.: Littlefield, Adams, 1981, pp. 223–28.

Purdy claims Levin's analysis in "Vs. Ms." [this section] is naive and committed to a subjective world view of male sexual aggression as the human sexual behavior pattern, underpinned by "false statements and morally unacceptable ones." The Miss/Mrs. distinction still conveys inaccurate and unnecessary stereotyped information which can cause discriminatory action.

RICHARDS, GRAHAM.

Sea without a shore: 1,706 proverbs on women and marriage. Unpublished paper, 1979. Northeast London Polytechnic, Three Mills, Abby Lane, Stratford, E15, 2RP England.

A collection of proverbs about women as wives, daughters, old women, whores, and maidens. The proverb is understood to be a formative and often oppressive linguistic force conveying sexist attitudes toward women.

ROSS, STEPHANIE.

How words hurt: Attitudes, metaphor and oppression. In Mary Vetterling-Braggin, ed., *Sexist language: A modern philosophical analysis.* Totowa, N.J.: Littlefield, Adams, 1981, pp. 194–216.

Building on Baker's "Pricks and chicks" [this section], Ross claims that "metaphors express attitudes of contempt and disdain towards women." Words do hurt, demean, oppress, and control.

RUBIN, JOAN.

How does the way women are referred to and described affect their participation in development and democracy? Paper given at Women, Language, and Development Conference, Mysore, India, 1981.

Rubin discusses the assumption that, given the close relationship among labels, attitudes, and behavior in language, "one can predict that if we change the labels used . . . changes in attitude and behavior toward women will follow." She discusses language "labels" inhibiting females and males in political and economic spheres (occupational designations, marketing research).

RUDES, BLAIR A. AND BERNARD HEALY.

Is she for real? The concepts of femaleness and maleness in the gay world. In Madeleine Mathiot, ed., *Ethnolinguistics: Boas, Sapir and Whorf revisited.* The Hague: Mouton, 1979, pp. 49–61.

An analysis of concepts of maleness and femaleness revealed by usages of *she* and *he* to refer to men in the gay male world in Buffalo, New York. When used in a positive way, *she* alludes to physical beauty; negatively, *she* indicates lower social status, inferior intelligence, lack of control, verbosity, "bitchiness" (hence evoking derogatory stereotypes of women). The concept of maleness is defined only in opposition to the concept of femaleness.

SCHULZ, MURIEL.

The semantic derogation of women. In Barrie Thorne and Nancy Henley, eds., *Language and sex: Difference and dominance.* Rowley, Mass.: Newbury House, 1975, pp. 64–73.

This is a study of the tendency for terms designating women in English to acquire debased or obscene reference; equivalent terms for men have almost totally escaped such pejoration. Schulz largely rejects association with a contaminating concept and euphemism as explanations, seeing prejudice as the most likely cause.

SOBLE, ALAN.

Beyond the miserable vision of "Vs. Ms." In Mary Vetterling-Braggin, ed., *Sexist language: A modern philosophical analysis.* Totowa, N.J.: Littlefield, Adams, 1981, pp. 229–48.

Soble criticizes Levin's "Vs. Ms." [this section] as simplistic, distorted by flawed logic on the nature of human sexual patterns and behavior, and judgmental of moral and social precepts and "norms." Spontaneity of word choice does not always indicate accuracy of attitude or intent, nor is word choice always made in good judgment.

STANLEY, JULIA P.

Gender-marking in American English: Usage and reference. In Alleen Pace Nilsen et al., eds., *Sexism and language*. Urbana, Ill.: National Council of Teachers of English, 1977, pp. 43–74.

Stanley suggests using explicit gender markings rather than gender-neutral terms because gender-neutral terms continue to make women "invisible" outside of traditionally defined female roles in our sexist society and language.

STANLEY JULIA P.

Paradigmatic woman: The prostitute. In David L. Shores and Carole P. Hines, eds., *Papers in language variation*. University, Ala.: Univ. of Alabama Press, 1977, pp. 303–21.

Stanley found 220 terms for sexually promiscuous women, 22 for promiscuous men. These words "reveal the underlying metaphors by which men conceive of their relationships with women, and through which women learn to perceive and define themselves." The semantic features which define the categories of this set are: A. Denotative (cost, method of payment, type of activity) and Connotative; B. Dysphemistic or euphemistic; C. Metonymic; D. Metaphoric.

STANLEY, JULIA P.

When we say "Out of the closets!" *College English*, 36 (1974), 385–91.

Gay slang, which is used more by men than women, is racist, sexist, patriarchal, and preoccupied with sexual objectification. Gays oppress each other with dichotomies like *femme/butch* and *trade/piss-elegant;* as gays become militant, they either stop using gay slang or give terms new, political meanings (e.g., *dyke* and *faggot,* indicating level of political awareness).

STENNER, A.J.

A note on logical truth and non-sexist semantics. In Mary Vetterling-Braggin, ed., *Sexist language: A modern philosophical analysis*. Totowa, N.J.: Littlefield, Adams, 1981, pp. 299–306.

Stenner poses an alternative to Grim's [this section] rejection of a theory of truth for sexist and racist utterances.

STRAINCHAMPS, ETHEL.

The story of *o* and *oo* (hidden gender in the English language). Unpublished paper.

In this exploration of phonetic symbolism, Strainchamps proposes that "The gender system that the English began to develop in the twelfth century was phono-semantic," i.e., the English altered the pronunciation or meaning of their words "to conform to the relative size, status or importance of things the words referred to . . ." The author suggests this development explains the Great Vowel Shift of the 14th–16th centuries.

SVARTENGREN, T. HILDING.

The use of the personal gender for inanimate things. *Dialect Notes*, 6 (1928–39), 7–56.

This is a discussion of grammarians' views of personification, followed by over 200 examples of present-day usage and a discussion of inconsistency in gender assignment in personification. The author concludes that *she* "does not so much mark the gender . . . as denote the object of an emotion." (See other papers by this author: The feminine gender for inanimate things in Anglo-American, *American Speech*, 3 (1927), 83–113; The use of feminine gender for inanimate things in American colloquial speech, *Moderna Sprak*, 48 (1954), 261–92.)

SWATOS, WILLIAM H., AND JUDITH A. KLINE.

The lady is not a whore: Labeling the promiscuous woman. *International Journal of Women's Studies*, 1 (1978), 159–66.

The different connotations of *prostitute* and *whore* were examined through intensive interviews with 250 subjects. *Prostitute* was found to include payment of money in its meaning, and to carry some respect for its referent businesswoman, whereas *whore* does neither but rather implies a lustful woman with numerous and uncommitted sexual relationships. The authors suggest a Marxist-Weberian interpretation of the distinction.

TAYLOR, KRISTE.

Reference and truth: The case of sexist and racist utterances. In Mary Vetterling-Braggin, ed., *Sexist language: A modern philosophical analysis*. Totowa, N.J.: Littlefield, Adams, pp. 307–17.

Taylor proposes, following Grim [this section], that sexist or racist utterances lack truth value not on ethical grounds but because the sexist/racist terms have no valid referents.

TEGLASI, HEDWIG.

First and third person pronouns in sex role questionnaires. *Psychology of Women Quarterly*, 5 (1981), 785–89.

No correlation was found between women's scores on two versions of an attitude questionnaire, one worded in the first person and one worded in third person, suggesting that, despite similar content, the items are not equivalent. Third person scores of women were much higher than first person scores, and were similar to third person scores of men. This was interpreted as indicating that normative expectations regarding women were far more traditional than were stated preferences of college women in this sample.

WHITE, JULIE BELLE.

Sacred and profane metaphors about women. Paper given at the Central States Speech Assoc. convention, Chicago, April 1980.

An analysis of the social reality created about women through the process of naming. First names, terms of endearment, proper nouns, and profanities for women are symbols which cluster around inanimate, animate, and supernatural topics, and each cluster of names forms a major metaphor about women (e.g., women as jewels) which is quite different from the metaphors about men.

WIEST, WILLIAM M.

Semantic differential profiles of orgasm and other experiences among men and women. *Sex Roles*, 3 (1977), 399–403.

Semantic differential profiles for Orgasm, Tickle, Pain, Ache, and The Way I Feel Right Now were obtained from 44 female and 38 male college students. Subjective descriptions of Orgasm, sometimes assumed to be qualitatively different for the two sexes, were indistinguishable. (From author's abstract.)

WITHINGTON, ROBERT.

"Lady," "woman" and "person." *American Speech*, 12, no. 2 (1937), 117–21.

Periodically, the connotations of *lady, woman,* and *person* undergo change. In the U.S., democracy is responsible for the changes from the British usage, where courtesy is the reason the terms *lady* and *gentlemen* have been extended to all human beings. In England it is not safe to assume all women are ladies, the author claims. He also observes the "growing dignity" of women in the U.S. (See also Robert Withington, "Woman-lady," *American Speech*, 12 (1937), 235, for responses to this paper.)

WOBST, SUSAN.

Male and female reference in semantic space in Russian. *Russian Language Journal*, 35:121–122 (1981), 35–44.

Russian dictionaries served as the basic sources for this analysis of six male and female root pairs, supplemented by information from other studies and the author's observations on current usage.

Also see: IV-B: Hopper, Knapp and Scott; Johnson and Fine.

F. Terms of Address

BARON, NAOMI S.

Professor Smith, Miss Jones: Terms of address in academe. Paper given at annual meeting of Modern Language Assoc., New York, Dec. 1978.

In a hypothetical situation students called male faculty *Professor* almost 10% more often than female faculty. Male faculty preferred *Mr.* to *Professor* or first name. More female faculty preferred being addressed by first name than by *Professor* or *Miss/Mrs./Ms*.

FISKE, SHIRLEY.

Rules of address: Navajo women in Los Angeles. *Journal of Anthropological Research*, 34 (1978), 72–91.

Three billingual Navajo women (ages 29 to 33) reported terms of address they used in 152 everyday interactions. The women used more formal address (title and last name) with Anglos, especially if the Anglos had higher occupational status, and with older Indians. Thus information about ethnicity and recognition of both traditional Navajo and English address systems entered their language use. No comparison is made with language use by Navajo men.

HOOK, DONALD D.

Sexism in English pronouns and forms of address. *General Linguistics*, 14, no. 2 (1974), 86–96.

Hook examines existing pronouns, titles, and forms of address used for both genders and considers feminist arguments for changing sexist address terms *(Miss, Mrs., headmistress, authoress).*

KRAMER, CHERIS.

Sex-related differences in address systems. *Anthropological Linguistics*, 17 (1975), 198–210.

Women and men have different repertoires of address, with women more restricted in their possible choices. Asymmetry in address forms is one way that asymmetry in social rights is reflected and maintained.

McCONNELL-GINET, SALLY.

Address forms in sexual politics. In Douglas Butturff and Edmund L. Epstein, eds., *Women's language and style*. Akron, Ohio: L & S Books, 1978, pp. 23–35.

Most address forms—first names, kin and titles—are marked for sex of the person addressed. Females receive more endearments than do males and perhaps use more. The use of last name address among females seems to be relatively slight and associated with typically "masculine" contexts (e.g., team activities). Female first names can be used to ridicule boys or to identify a male as homosexual.

RUBIN, REBECCA.

Ideal traits and terms of address for male and female college professors. *Journal of Personality and Social Psychology*, 41 (1981), 966–74.

Female professors, especially those 26 to 33, were addressed by first name more often than were their male colleagues. Possibly students perceive more equal status with female professors than with male professors. (From author's abstract.)

WOLFSON, NESSA AND JOAN MANES.

Don't "dear" me! In Sally McConnell-Ginet, Ruth Borker, and Nelly Furman, eds., *Women and language in literature and society*. New York: Praeger, 1980, pp. 79–92.

Analysis of observational and other data on service encounters revealed that men customers are routinely addressed by a respect form, *sir*, while women customers receive such forms as *hon, honey*, or *dear*, which imply that no sign of respect is needed. While suggesting intimacy, this supposed friendliness is nonreciprocal.

G. Institutional Support

This section documents support for sexism in the language of dictionaries, literature, children's books, textbooks, religion, law, and media.

BOSMAJIAN, HAIG.

Sexism in the language of legislatures and courts. In Alleen Pace Nilsen et al., eds., *Sexism and language*. Urbana, Ill.: National Council of Teachers of English, 1977, pp. 77–104.

Language in courts and legislatures stereotypes women as: (1) mother/wife; (2) infantile/incompetent; (3) seductive/immoral; and (4) nonpersons/entities. Since law reflects and determines important perceptions of females in society, female self-identity is hindered by legislative and institutionalized sexism.

BURR, ELIZABETH, SUSAN DUNN, AND NORMA FARQUHAR.

Women and the language of inequality. *Social Education*, 36 (1972), 841–45.

This article examines sexist writing customs particular to textbooks; for example, hypothetical persons are usually male, and girls and women are usually referred to as nameless wives, daughters, and mothers of named males.

COLLINS, RONALD K.

Language, history and the legal process: A profile of the "reasonable man." *Rutgers-Camden Law Journal*, 8, no. 2 (Winter 1977).

A contribution to the understanding of female/male grammatical-semantic categories. Other essays pointing out the legal ramifications of genderized language include: Marguerite E. Ritchie, W.C., "Alice through the statutes," *McGill Law Journal*, 21 (Winter 1975); E. A. Driedger, Q.C., "Are statutes written for men only?," *McGill Law Journal*, 22 (Winter 1976); Carol Amyx, "Sex discrimination: The textbook case," *California Law Review*, 62 (July–Sept. 1974); Beverly J. Hodgson, "Sex, texts and the first amendment," *Journal of Law and Education*, 5, no. 2 (April 1976). [Collected by Wendy Martyna.]

GERSHUNY, H. LEE.

Public doublespeak: The dictionary. *College English*, 36, no. 8 (1975), 938–42.

Gershuny investigates word definitions in the *Random House Dictionary of the English Language* (1966). Sex role stereotypes and cultural clichés about men and women are reinforced and perpetuated by this supposedly objective, neutral resource.

GERSHUNY, H. LEE.

Sexism in dictionaries and texts: Omissions and commissions. In Alleen Pace Nilsen et al., eds., *Sexism and language*. Urbana, Ill.: National Council of Teachers of English, 1977, pp. 143–59.

Dictionaries and texts stereotype both sexes into static definitions. In an informal survey, Gershuny found greater male-influenced patterns in "naming" people.

GERSHUNY H. LEE.

Sexism in the language of literature. In Alleen Pace Nilsen et al., eds., *Sexism and language*. Urbana, Ill.: National Council of Teachers of English, 1977, pp. 107–29.

Gershuny points out that the ". . . idea of poetic creation as both masculine and divine has been a consistent part of our literary heritage." Writers and poets are not immune to sexism. Women and women's words as readers and writers are identified and defined by males.

GERSHUNY, H. LEE.

Sexist semantics in the dictionary. *Etc.*, 31, no. 2 (1974), 159–69.

Results of empirical study and analysis of illustrative sentences in the *Random House Dictionary* show feminine gender contexts and feminine words are less represented than masculine (1:3 and 1:2, respectively). Use of gender words as subjects, objects, or possessives was about equal for the two sexes, but males and females were significantly stereotyped.

GONZALEZ, IRIS.

Words and women: Sexism in the language of the church. Paper given at the 9th World Congress of Sociology, Uppsala, Sweden, 1978.

Gonzalez examines ways in which sexist language (verbal and nonverbal) dominates written and oral communication in the church and leads to both female invisibility and negative attitudes toward women. She provides examples in English and Spanish to illustrate modifications for more inclusive usage.

GRAHAM, ALMA.

The making of a nonsexist dictionary. *Ms.*, 2 (1973), 12–16. Reprinted in Barrie Thorne and Nancy Henley, eds., *Language and sex: Difference and dominance.* Rowley, Mass.: Newbury House, 1975, pp. 57–63.

A computer analysis of 5,000,000 words in American school books showed that boys and girls were being taught separate values, expectations, and goals (masculine activity, strength; feminine inactivity, beauty). To counter stereotypes, lexicographers in this project developed new illustrative usages.

KAHN, LYNDA.

Sexism in everyday speech. *Social Work*, 20 (1975), 65–67.

This brief article considers examples of sexist language and inferences in *Webster's Dictionary, Roget's Thesaurus,* and slang in general. Kahn discusses the ways social workers participate in supporting sexist attitudes of their clients by usage of sexist referents and language attitudes.

KINGSTON, ALBERT J. AND TERRY LOVELACE.

Sexism and reading: A critical review of the literature. *Reading Research Quarterly*, 13 (1978), 133–61.

In this review of 78 articles (most of them from 1970–1975) analyzing sexism in writing for children, the authors note that most articles present frequency tallies of various kinds of female and male representation, but fail to demonstrate the impact of biased representation on children. A convenient table shows which articles have investigated certain features of language.

NILSEN, ALLEEN PACE.

Sexism in children's books and elementary teaching materials. In Alleen Pace Nilsen et al., eds., *Sexism and language.* Urbana, Ill.: National Council of Teachers of English, 1977, pp. 161–79.

In most children's books girls are not shown as independent or as leaders. Rather they are shown as "supportive and appreciative" of boys, with boys being illustrated as physically larger than girls. In addition, boy-oriented books are seen as better sellers than books for girls. Such bias can be harmful to education, i.e., "reading seen as sissy recreation . . . can prevent learning to read or write . . ."

O'DONNELL, HOLLY SMITH.

Sexism in language. *Elementary English*, 50 (1973), 1067–72.

A review of various issues and findings in this area, directed at elementary school teachers, with a brief annotated bibliography on the topic.

RUSSELL, LETTY M.

Changing language and the church. In Letty M. Russell, ed., *The liberating word: A guide to nonsexist interpretation of the Bible.* Philadelphia: Westminster Press, 1976.

This book chapter discusses the context in which churchpeople are examining masculine-biased language in religious writing and services, and offers suggestions for alternative usage.

SALE, MARILYN.

Some opinions on sexist language. *Scholarly Publishing*, 10, no. 1 (Oct. 1978), 84–89.

Sale examines the policies of publishing houses toward authors' use of sexist language. Publishing houses have different policies, ranging from believing sexist language is not an important issue, to staff training to recognize stereotyping and sexist language, to the encouragement of authors to use nonsexist language (but not forcing compliance).

SCHULZ, MURIEL.

How sexist is *Webster's Third? Vis à Vis,* 2, no. 3 (1974), 7–15.

Schulz says feminists are generally misguided to criticize dictionaries, which are sexist for many reasons inherent in the language but not attributable to them. However, in definitions and citations dictionaries often carry stereotypes. The *Third* is culpable in ascribing different qualities to women and men, and in frequently belittling women.

SPEARS, JOANNA S.

Sexism in religious education. *Friends General Conference Quarterly*, 2 (1978), 5.

An analysis and critique of sexist language, especially pronouns, used in religious education curriculum materials. The author emphasizes the importance of conscious decisions regarding the use of pronouns in religious education.

STIMPSON, CATHARINE R.

The power to name. In Julia Sherman and Evelyn T. Beck, eds., *The prism of sex: Essays in the sociology of knowledge.* Madison: Univ. of Wisconsin Press, 1979, pp. 55–78.

Stimpson examines literature and literary circles (the Modern Language Association, its publication *PMLA,* and the *Partisan Review*) and their attitudes toward women and women writers. The role of avant-garde art and literature in changing values and attitudes, and the sex-biased treatment of women writers, are also carefully considered.

SUTTON, WILLIAM A.

Linguistic sexism in *Time* magazine. Paper given at 9th World Congress of Sociology, Uppsala, Sweden, 1978.

Updating a previous study, Sutton examines sexist language practices of *Time* and suggests revisions.

TITTLE, CAROL KEHR, MCCARTHY, KAREN, AND JANE FAGGEN STECKLER.

Women and educational testing. In *Women and educational testing: A selective review of the research literature and testing practices.* Princeton, N.J.: Educational Testing Service, 1974. Also in Janice Pottker and Andrew Fishel, eds., *Sex bias in the schools.* Teaneck, N.J.: Fairleigh Dickinson Univ. Press, 1976.

Analysis reveals educational achievement tests and college achievement tests are biased against women in language usage and gender role stereotyping.

WARREN, DENISE.

Commercial liberation. *Journal of Communication,* 28 (Winter 1978), 169–73.

The words and feminist discourse associated with social change have been used by the ad industry to promote its products. "The texts of advertising are emblematic of the discourse of power which women must examine to comprehend their relationship to the culture by which they are dominated and to which they are inextricably bound."

WORBY, DIANA ZACHARIA.

In search of a common language: Women and educational texts. *College English,* 41 (1979), 101–15.

Worby discusses sexism in the third edition (1979) of Strunk and White's *The Elements of Style.* Women are still portrayed as timid, foolish housewives in the language examples.

H. Critiques and Proposals

ALTER, LANCE AND MILLICENT RUTHERFORD.

Do the NCTE guidelines on non-sexist use of language serve a positive purpose? *English Journal,* 65, no. 9 (1976), 10–13.

In this debate, Alter argues that the guidelines do not serve a useful purpose. "At best, they are mischievous and unnecessary. At worst, they introduce ideology and partisan activism into the language arts. The authors of the guidelines are creating problems which only exist in the minds of certain ideologues." Arguing for the importance of the NCTE official action, Rutherford lists five reasons the guidelines are needed by English teachers and suggests additional action to eliminate sexism from booklists and teaching units.

ASSOCIATION FOR WOMEN IN PSYCHOLOGY AD HOC COMMITTEE ON SEXIST LANGUAGE.

Help stamp out sexism: Change the language. *APA Monitor,* 6, no. 11 (1975), 16.

A discussion of reasons and ways to change sexist language, directed primarily toward psychologists.

BATE, BARBARA.

Sex bias in language: An issue worth talking about. *Thresholds in Education,* 4 (1978), 27–31.

This article directed to teachers urges them to provide information to students so they may make informed choices concerning sex equity in language; reports on the author's own study of changing patterns in language [*see* Sec. II-I]; and provides guidelines for alternatives to sexist language.

CROWLEY, SHARON.

The semantics of sexism. *Etc.,* 30 (1973), 407–11.

A brief discussion applying general semantic concepts and terminology to issues of women's liberation.

DENSMORE, DANA.

Speech is the form of thought. In *The Female State: A Journal of Female Liberation,* 4 (April 1970), 9–15.

Densmore proposes a new glossary of personal pronouns: nominative case, *she* (includes both *he* and *she* in one word); objective case, *herm* (includes *her* and *him*); possessive case, *heris (her* or *his)*; and emphasizes the use of alternatives to the generic *man*. See also: Densmore, "On communication," *No More Fun and Games: A Journal of Female Liberation,* 5 (July 1971).

ETHEL.

Ethel in genderland: Some concrete proposals. *Ethel,* 5 (1980), 21–23.

This essay on sexism in the English language suggests ways in which teachers can handle language in the classroom; it is one of many other "Ethel strategies" in this magazine for teachers of English abroad.

FAUST, JEAN.

Words that oppress. In *Women Speaking,* April, 1970. Reprint available from KNOW, Inc., P.O. Box 10197, Pittsburgh, PA 15232.

Language forms imply that the female is an extension of the male: titles, occupations, etc., are traditionally masculine; language emphasizes differences between the sexes; women are often defined by their sexuality. Faust examines the increase of sexual insults and claims men's fear of women and of sexual inadequacy motivates this derogatory language.

FEMINIST WRITERS WORKSHOP.

An intelligent woman's guide to dirty words. Vol. 1 of *The feminist English dictionary.* Chicago: Chicago Loop YWCA, 1973.

This first and only volume to date of a projected series reviews language as a prime force in the deprecation of women, sees lexicographers as prejudicial, and suggests alternative definitions to those derived from male-dominated culture. Words and definitions from established dictionaries are arranged in categories such as "Woman as Whore," "Woman as Body."

FOLSOM, JACK.

Teaching about sexism and language in a traditional setting: Surmounting the obstacles. *Women's Studies Quarterly,* 11:1 (1983), 12–15.

Folsom reports on the approach and materials he uses to introduce discussions about sexism and language issues in his course for prospective teachers.

FULLER, MARY.

In business the generic pronoun "he" is non-job related and discriminatory. *Training and Development Journal,* 27, no. 5 (1973), 8–11.

Fuller examines the use of "generic" *he* in work environments and suggests specific language alternatives to job-related sexism.

FURTH, CHARLOTTE.

The language of inequality: An editorial. *Journal of Asian Studies,* 34 (1974), 5–6.

Furth argues that male-oriented language damages in two ways: (1) "through its subliminal psychological message that females are inferior"; (2) through its tendency "to foster misleading or unproven assumptions of fact . . . the impression of female irrelevance is commonly conveyed more by the form of language than by results of research."

HENION, REEVE, ELAINE LEVINE, SUSAN MILLER, WILLIAMS RIVERS, JOE RUSSIN, DEWITT SCOTT, AND IRIS YOUNG.

Kissing 'the girls' goodbye: A discussion of guidelines for journalists. *Columbia Journalism Review,* 14 (May/June 1975), 28–33.

Discussion among seven representatives of the media with different points of view about "Guidelines for Newswriting About Women," developed by the Women's News Service at Stanford University. Policies and practices of newspapers are also examined.

HORTON, PAUL B.

A sexless vocabulary for a sexist society. *Intellect,* 105 (Dec. 1976), 159–60.

An informal consideration of the need to change and problems in changing sexist language. Alternatives to sexist grammar are considered.

JOHNSON, CAROLE SCHULTE AND INGA KROMANN KELLY.

"He" and "She": Changing language to fit a changing world. *Educational Leadership,* 32 (1975), 527–30.

The authors argue for "inclusionary" rather than "exclusionary" language use in the classroom, using analogies of medical prescription and preventive measures in general; they include both anecdotes and evidence from research.

NILSEN, ALLEEN PACE.

Changing words in a changing world. Newton, Mass.: WEEA Publishing Center, 1981. (C/o Education Development Center, 55 Chapel St., Newton, MA 02160)

This instructional program for secondary and post–secondary levels analyzes sex-role stereotyping, ways language shapes cultural values and reflects viewpoints of powerful groups, and issues of possible language change.

PICKENS, JUDY.

Without bias: A guidebook for nondiscriminatory communication. New York: Wiley, 1982 (2nd ed.).

This second edition from the International Association of Business Communicators expands the number of examples and anecdotes to discriminatory practices in written and visual communication. It includes guidelines to deal with sexism in media, guides toward communication free of racial and ethnic bias, and a new chapter on age discrimination.

SAFILIOS-ROTHSCHILD, CONSTANTINA.

Social policy to liberate the society from sexism: Social policy to liberate language. Chapter 5 in *Women and social policy.* Englewood Cliffs, N.J.: Prentice-Hall, 1974, pp. 122–25.

Safilios-Rothschild delineates strategies, social action, policies and laws necessary "to uncover, publicize and eradicate sexism." The author discusses the effect of sexist language and gender stereotypes on the expression and formulation of ideas.

1. Guidelines and Guidebooks

BEASLEY, MAURINE AND SHELIA SILVER.

Guidelines for equal linguistic treatment of sexes and races: A bibliography. In Maurine Beasley and Shelia Silver, eds., *Women in media: A documentary source book.* Women's Institute for Freedom of the Press, 3306 Ross Place, N.W., Washington, D.C. 20008.

COFER, CHARLES N., ROBERT S. DANIELS, FRANCES Y. DUNHAM, AND WALTER HEIMER.

Guidelines for nonsexist language in APA journals. *American Psychologist,* 32 (1977), 486–94.

An update of the American Psychological Assoc. manual, this change sheet provides policy on sexist language in journal articles. It offers basic principles for authors, suggests ways to avoid sexist language, and examines problems of designation and of evaluation (ambiguity of referent, stereotyping).

MATTHEWS, MARY W.

A teacher's guide to sexist words. *Social Education,* (May 1977), 389–97.

Matthews categorizes sexist words and suggests educational strategies for developing awareness of sexist language. Categories for both male and female include: no parallel job titles; comparisons to animals, plants, and mythological beings; words of approval/disapproval; words and phrases derived from names.

MILLER, CASEY AND KATE SWIFT.

The handbook of nonsexist writing: For writers, editors and speakers. New York: Lippincott and Crowell, 1980.

Citing studies, and using quotations, etymology, and illustrations from many sources, Miller and Swift succinctly detail ideas of sexism in language and practical ways to avoid exclusive, distorting, ambiguous, and injurious words and phrases.

PERSING, BOBBYE SORRELS.

The nonsexist communicator. East Elmhurst, N.Y.: Communication Dynamics Press, 1978.

This is a manual primarily directed toward business and organizational use, providing informative background, detailed guidelines, and numerous exercises for letters, memoranda, reports, and other organizational writing, as well as for oral and nonverbal communication.

The following is a sampling of other guidelines to the recognition and correction of sexist language (on ordering, inquire about prices):

AMERICAN SOCIETY FOR PUBLIC ADMINISTRATION.

The right word: Guidelines for avoiding sex-biased language. ASPA National Committee On Women, 1225 Connecticut Ave., N.W., Washington, D.C. 20036.

APA TASK FORCE ON ISSUES OF SEXUAL BIAS IN GRADUATE EDUCATION.

Guidelines for nonsexist use of language. *JSAS Catalog of Selected Documents in Psychology,* 4, no. 107 (1974), ms. no. 733. *American Psychologist,* 30 (June 1975), 628–84. *The School Counselor,* 23 (1976), 271–74.

BURR, ELIZABETH, SUSAN DUNN, AND NORMA FARQUHAR.

Guidelines for equal treatment of the sexes in social studies textbooks. Los Angeles: Westside Women's Committee, 1973. (P.O. Box 24 D 20, Los Angeles, CA 90024.)

CHICAGO WOMEN IN PUBLISHING.

Equality in print: A guide for editors and publishers. (Box 11837, Chicago, IL 60611.)

INTERNATIONAL ASSOCIATION OF BUSINESS COMMUNICATORS.

Without bias: A guidebook for nondiscriminatory communication. (870 Market St., Suite 928, San Francisco, CA 94102.)

MARSHALL, JOAN K.

On equal terms: A thesaurus for nonsexist indexing and cataloging. New York: Neal-Schuman, 1977.

McGRAW-HILL BOOK COMPANY.

Guidelines for equal treatment of the sexes. New York: McGraw-Hill, 1975.

NATIONAL COMMISSION ON THE OBSERVANCE OF INTERNATIONAL WOMEN'S YEAR.

Media guidelines. (President's Advisory Committee for Women, Room N-3437, 200 Constitution Ave., N.W., Washington, D.C., 20210.)

NCTE PUBLICATIONS.

Guidelines for nonsexist use of language. In Alleen Pace Nilsen et al., eds., *Sexism in language.* Urbana, Ill.: National Council of Teachers of English, 1977, pp. 181–91.

OROVAN, MARY.

Humanizing English. Available from author, 130 E. 18th St., New York, NY 10003.

RACISM/SEXISM RESOURCE CENTER.

Racism in the English language. (Guide on nonsexist language) (1841 Broadway, Room 300, New York, NY 10023.)

SCOTT, FORESMAN AND COMPANY.

Guidelines for improving the image of women in textbooks. Glenview, Ill.: Scott, Foresman, 1972.

SUTTON, WILLIAM A.

Sexual fairness in language. (English Dept., Ball State Univ.)

TIEDT, IRIS M.

Sexism in language, an editor's plague. *Elementary English,* 50 (1973), 1073–74.

UNITED PRESBYTERIAN CHURCH IN THE U.S.A.

The power of language among the people of God: A resource document. (The Advisory Council on Discipleship and Worship, 475 Riverside Drive, Rm. 1020, New York, NY 10115.)

I. Change

ADAMSKY, CATHRYN.

Changes in pronominal usage in a classroom situation. *Psychology of Women Quarterly,* 5 (1981), 773–79.

Adamsky used *she* as the generic singular in teaching an undergraduate class. Both men and women students reduced their use of *he* as the generic singular, and used *she* more frequently, in their written work over the course of the term.

BATE, BARABARA.

Nonsexist language use in transition. *Journal of Communication,* 28 (1978), 139–49.

Bate interviewed ten female and ten male faculty members on their use of sexist/nonsexist language, and reports on their use of professional terms for women, male/female labels, pronoun choices, and "generic male" forms and alternatives, by respondents' sex and closeness to the women's movement. Encouragement from a woman, the presence of sensitive listeners, pronounce-ability of an alternative, and knowledge of alternatives were factors contributing to change.

BLAUBERGS, MAIJA S.

An analysis of classic arguments against changing sexist language. In Cheris Kramarae, ed., *The voices and words of women and men.* Oxford: Pergamon Press, 1980, pp. 135–47. Also *Women's Studies International Quarterly,* 3, no. 2/3 (1980).

Blaubergs reviews the following arguments: (1) "cross-cultural"; (2) "language is a trivial concern"; (3) "freedom of speech/unjustified coercion"; (4) "sexist language is not sexist"; (5) "word etymology"; (6) "appeal to authority"; (7) "change is too difficult, inconvenient, impractical or whatever"; (8) "it would destroy historical authenticity and literary works."

BLAUBERGS, MAIJA S.

Changing the sexist language: The theory behind the practice. *Psychology of Women Quarterly,* 2 (1978), 244–61.

Implementation of suggestions for change has been difficult because of differing or contradictory proposals, misunderstanding of them, and ridicule. Blaubergs identifies three types of suggestions; (1) indirect change (through social change); (2) change via circumvention (eliminating gender-specific terms); (3) change via emphasis on feminine terms.

DARSEY, JAMES.

From "commies" and "queers" to "gay is good." In James W. Chesebro, ed., *Gayspeak: Gay male and lesbian communication.* New York: Pilgrim Press, 1981, pp. 224–47.

An analysis of the development of the gay (male) movement through analysis of its rhetorical stages.

DUBOIS, BETTY LOU AND ISABEL CROUCH.

Man and its compounds in recent prefeminist American English. *Papers in Linguistics,* 12 (1979), 261–69.

These authors examine generics, including pronouns, nouns of indefinite reference, and agent nouns, in the Brown Univ. Standard Corpus to discover patterns of use in the near prefeminist period. Examples of generics found in the 1970s suggest that a significant language change may be in progress.

EBLE, CONNIE.

How to name a revolution. Paper given at Southeastern Conference on Linguistics, 1973.

Eble examines issues of rhetoric, suggesting that the "working vocabulary" of the women's liberation movement can be divided into four subject areas: the vocabularies of male supremacy, female unity, action-reform-revolution, and shock.

FLANAGAN, ANNA M. AND WILLIAM R. TODD-MANCILLAS.

Teaching inclusive generic pronoun usage: The effectiveness of an authority innovation-decision approach versus an optional innovation-decision approach. *Communication Education*, 31 (October 1982), 277-374.

College students were given instructions (in either an authority or optional mode) on inclusive pronoun usage. Examinations of their papers (written both before and after instruction) found that both modes were effective in producing change, with the authority mode resulting in a total adoption of non-sexist usage; in the optional decision group, 30% of the students who had initially used exclusive language continued to use it in post-instruction essays.

HOFSTADTER, DOUGLAS R.

"Default assumptions" and their effects on writing and thinking. *Scientific American*, 247 (November 1982), 18, 22, 26, 30, 36.

An account of one man's thoughts and actions as he tries to "demasculinize" his prose. He mentions some problems with other languages he has studied--French, German, and Chinese.

MORAHAN, SHIRLEY.

A woman's place: Rhetoric and readings for composing yourself and your prose. Albany: State Univ. of New York Press, 1981.

Recognizing the sexism of most composition texts and readers, Morahan approaches writing as self-definition and deals with the relationship between gender and writing. The topics of the readings and the inventive writing suggestions include: power, language and culture, and nurturance of creativity.

NICHOLS, PATRICIA.

Planning for language change. *San Jose Studies*, 6, no. 2 (1980), 18–25.

Nichols reviews the history of gender problems in language and calls for planning and experimentation in directing future language changes.

NOGLE, VICKI.

Lesbianfeminist rhetoric as a social movement. In James W. Chesebro, ed., *Gayspeak: Gay male and lesbian communication*. New York: Pilgrim Press, 1981, pp. 260–71.

An overview of stages of the lesbian feminist movement through its rhetoric, with discussion of labels and terms (particularly, *dyke*) and of the relation between language and power in the movement.

PEI, MARIO.

> The paeon of the liberated woman. Chapter 6 of *Double-speak in America.* New York: Hawthorn books, 1973.

Writing in a chatty and critical vein about newly minted phrases in the American public language scene, Pei catalogues various terms resulting from the women's movement (e.g., *sexism, male chauvinist pig, sex object, chairperson*) and mentions satiric responses to feminist proposals for language change.

PENELOPE, JULIA.

> John Simon and the "Dragons of Eden." *College English*, in press.

Using as illustration several recent articles by John Simon (a columnist who has attacked feminist suggestions for linguistic change), Penelope analyzes arguments used by linguistic authoritarians to support ideas about "correctness."

PENELOPE, JULIA.

> Power and the opposition to feminist proposals for language change; or, What can we learn from this? *College English*, in press.

An analysis of six classes of arguments which critics use against proposals to eradicate sexist usage in English. Reviewing grammarians' contributions to sexism in English. Penelope states that instead of arguing about whether attitude change must precede language change, we need to ascertain whose changes will become a part of the grammar.

RICHMOND, VIRGINIA P. AND PAULA DYBA.

> The roots of sexual stereotyping: The teacher as model. *Communication Education,* 31 (October 1982), 265-73.

Secondary and elementary teachers, taking a graduate speech communication course, made major reductions in the amount of sexist language they used in essays after 15 minutes of instruction on "appropriate use of gender-related language."

SHEPELAK, NORMA.

> The socio-political nature of language: Understanding the resistance to language change. Paper given at National Women's Studies Assoc. convention, Bloomington, Ind., 1980.

Gender roles are reinforced specifically by the generic masculine, and in general, by sexist language. Shepelak analyzes the resistance to language change by academics and linguists and contends that the basis for resistance is the continuation of socio-political control by men.

J.   Other Languages and Cultures

AWBERY, GWEN.

> Men and women in the Welsh language. Unpublished manuscript, Cardiff, Wales, 1975.

Welsh nouns are of either feminine or masculine gender. Some adjectives have different forms for the two genders in the singular but not the plural. Some job titles have distinct forms for the male and female: e.g., *athro* (male teacher) and *athrawes* (female teacher). Derivative feminines seem to be increasing; these forms (e.g., *awdures*) do not have the patronizing overtones of equivalents in

English (e.g., *authoress*). Groups of mixed sex are referred to by the masculine plural even if there is a feminine plural.

BLAKAR, ROLV MIKKEL.
    Kan mannssamfunnet sprengast utan språkrevolusjon? (Can we do away with our male dominated society without a language revolution?) *Syn Og Segn*, 77 (1977), 550–61.

Language often resists change and is used to transmit sex roles to succeeding generations. Blakar suggests ways language can be used for social change, e.g., through the women's movement.

BLAKAR, ROLV M.
    Språk er makt. (Language as a means of social power). In Jacob L. Mey, ed., *Pragmalinguistics: Theory and practice*. The Hague: Mouton, 1979.

Blakar analyzes control and power issues and male and female conceptualization of reality in language use in Norway.

BLAKAR, ROLV M.
    Språk og kvinneundertrykkingeit managesedig problem. (Language and the oppression of women: A complex issue). *Ventil*, no. 4 (1974), 3–10.

Blakar argues that language must be studied in social context.

BLAKAR, ROLV M.
    Språk som makt og kvinneundertrykking: Språksosiologi som motefag. (Language and the oppression of women: Sociolinguistics and the zeitgeist) In J. Kleiven, ed., *Språk og samfunn*. Oslo: Pax, 1979.

Blakar argues that many studies of sexism and language have questionable scientific quality and are confused because of composite, unclear questions. He identifies fundamental questions in research on sexism in language.

BLAKAR, ROLV M.
    Stakkars store, sterke mann undertrykkingas tragiske dialektikk. (Poor strong man: The dialects of oppression). *Sinnets Helse*, 54, no. 1 (1974), 3–7; reprinted in R. M. Blakar, ed., *Kontakt Og Konflict*. (Contact and conflict). Oslo: Pax, 1978, p. 257.

In this analysis of the male role in the Norwegian language, Blakar suggests that despite male control of the language (at the cost of females), men are not the content oppressors of women, but rather are equally oppressed by definition of their own roles.

BROOKS, MARIA Z. AND KENNETH L. NALIBOW.
    The gender of referentials in Polish. *International Journal of Slavic Linguistics and Poetics*, 13 (1970), 136-42.

The rather complex Polish gender system (four genders in singular, two in plural) is presented, followed by a discussion of requirements for the gender of referentials. Contrary to previous claims, a referential does not have to agree with its referend in gender, and often will not, for semantic rather than grammatical reasons. Masculine gender may be used to convey respect or esteem for feminine gender referends; feminine gender may convey derogatory meaning to non-feminine referends.

Brouwer, Dédé.

De vorming van vrouwelijke persoonsnamen: Is seksedifferentiatie noodzakelijk? Manuscript, 1981. Institute for General Linguistics, University of Amsterdam, Spuistraat 210, Amsterdam.

Because of the presence of grammatical gender in their languages, feminists in Holland, Germany, and France have debated whether the distinction between female and male personal nouns is necessary or desirable. Brouwer argues that the female suffixes in Dutch are becoming obsolete while the unmarked (male) forms are increasingly used as sex neutral terms.

Colaclides, Peter.

The pattern of gender in modern Greek. *Linguistics*, 5 (1964), 65-68.

Where grammatical gender is motivated semantically, the tripartite gender system--feminine, masculine, neuter--features two-termed marked-unmarked oppositions. There are three kinds of semantic marking: for diminution (1), the neuter is the marked form; for augmentation (2), either feminine or masculine may be marked; for sex (3), the feminine is marked.

Comrie, Bernard and Gerald Stone.

The Russian language since the revolution. Oxford: Oxford Univ. Press, 1978.

A review of Western and Soviet sociolinguistic research with a chapter on "Sex, gender, and the status of women."

Connors, Kathleen.

Studies in feminine agentives in selected European languages. *Romance Philology,* 24 (1971), 573–98.

An analysis of the formation of feminine agentives, especially of occupational terms (e.g., *aviatrix*), in the major Romance languages, English and German. An increased number of women in occupations formerly closed to them does not necessarily result in spreading acceptance and use of feminine agentives. But in Russia and Israel where women have shared many jobs with men, feminine agentives are plentiful and do not appear to be used facetiously.

Cramer, Anne Quinn.

Frau or *Fräulein:* How to address a woman in German. *Die Unterrichtspraxis,* 9, no. 1 (1976), 28-29.

Frau is often translated as "Mrs." and *Fräulein* as "Miss"; however, *Frau* is the correct form of address not only for married women but also for unmarried women over about 30 (the age has been decreasing) and for women of social position, e.g., those with a doctorate ("Frau Doktor") of any age. It has also become unacceptable for a woman to be addressed with her husband's title.

Durand, Marguerite.

Le genre grammatical en français parlé à Paris et dans la région parisienne. Paris: Bibliothèque du "français moderne," 1936.

A comprehensive study of grammatical gender in spoken French in the period before World War II, including a dialect study of gender in Paris and the surrounding region. Among the topics discussed by Durand are the formation of agent nouns for professions, the morphology of gender in French, agreement, and pronoun usage. Numerous examples are cited of the use of masculine adjectives, nouns and pronouns with nouns designating women; among these are some cases of self-reference by women. Durand concludes that the grammatical category of gender is becoming less important for speakers of the language.

EL SAADAWI, NAWAL.
The hidden face of Eve: Women in the Muslim world. Boston: Beacon Press, 1982.

El Saadawi states that Muslim women 1400 years ago had the feminine form of the word *Muslim* added alongside the masculine form in the Koran.

FRIEDRICH, PAUL.
Social context and semantic feature: The Russian pronominal usage. In John J. Gumperz and Dell Hymes, eds., *Directions in sociolinguistics.* New York: Holt, Rinehart and Winston, 1972, pp. 270–300.

An examination through literature of the use of second person singular (address) terms in Russian. Women are said to use formal address *(vy)* more than men, "among the gentry because of their greater concern for propriety, among all classes because of their partially subordinate status."

GUENTHERODT, INGRID.
Behördliche Sprachregelungen gegen und für eine sprachliche Gleichbehandlung von Frauen und Männern. *Linguistische Berichte,* 69 (1980), 22–36.

Guentherodt describes semantic asymmetries and details governmental decrees issued between 1937 and 1972 regulating address forms for adult women in Germany. She also analyzes classifications of professions in governmental surveys and describes language planning measures which have introduced some changes in the direction of linguistic equality.

HAMPARES, KATHERINE J.
Sexism in Spanish lexicography? *Hispania, 59* (1976), 100–109.

The author examines the existence of feminine forms for 105 nouns referring to occupations and professions in Spanish dictionaries, all claiming to be descriptive. She finds inconsistencies between the dictionaries' rationales and practice, between their practice in different sections, and between the forms in the different dictionaries, which questions their true descriptiveness. Suggestions for lexicographers' descriptive research and systematization of method are given.

HAUGEN, EINAR.
Sexism and the Norwegian language. Paper given at Society for the Advancement of Scandinavian Study, Washington, D.C., May 1974.

Haugen traces the controversy Rolv Blakar created by calling attention to sexism in the Norwegian language, offering evidence from the use of titles of address, occupation descriptions, synonyms for *man* and *woman*, word association tests, etc. Haugen concludes that language reflects social reality, and when reality changes, the language will respond.

HELLINGER, MARLIS.
Effective social change through group action: The use of feminine occupational titles in transition. In Cheris Kramarae, Muriel Schulz, and William O'Barr, eds., *Language and power.* Beverly Hills, Calif.: Sage, in press.

Hellinger argues that women in Western countries have used two basic strategies to eliminate sexism in occupational terminology: The generic strategy (e.g., in U.S., Great Britain, and

Sweden), which insists on the use of morphologically unmarked occupational terms for females (e.g., salesperson) and the visibility strategy (e.g., in Italy and France) which makes women visible by explicit reference.

HELLINGER, MARLIS.

"For men must work, and women must weep": Sexism in English language textbooks used in German schools. In Cheris Kramarae, ed., *The voices and words of women and men.* Oxford: Pergamon Press, 1980, pp. 267–75. Also *Women's Studies International Quarterly,* 3, no. 2/3 (1980).

HELLINGER, MARLIS.

Zum Gebrauch weiblicher Berufsbezeichnungen im Deutschen—Variabilität als Ausdruck aussersprachlicher Machtstrukturen. *Linguistische Berichte,* 69 (Oktober 1980), 37–58.

The semantic differential technique was used to test the hypothesis that overtly feminine occupational titles are not semantic equivalents of the corresponding masculine terms. Variability in the use for female referent (Sie ist Lehrer/Lehrerin) is interpreted as a reflection of women's conflicting strategies: the wish to be integrated into the man's world (and semantic space) and the desire for visibility of the female identity.

HIDALGO, CESAR.

Towards a non-sexist language: A study of the code system of some Austronesian languages. Paper given at the 9th World Congress of Sociology, Uppsala, Sweden, 1978.

Hidalgo challenges the assumption that sex differentiation in language is universal, hypothesizing that ambiguity in sex specification leads to a nonsexist language. He examines kinship and authority terms and the pronoun system of Philippine languages. (There is no sex differentiation in the pronoun systems.) Hidalgo submits proposals toward a nonsexist language.

JANSSEN-JURREIT, MARIELOUISE.

Sexism: The male monopoly on history and thought. New York: Farrar, Straus & Giroux, 1982. (Trans. from German by Verne Moberg)

The chapter "The genitals of speech" contains grammarians' theories about the origins of, and reasons for, gender in many languages.

KITAIGORODSKAJA, M. V.

Variation in the expression of gender of noun to denote women by profession. In L. P. Krysin and D. N. Shmelev, eds., *Sociolinguistic investigations.* Moscow: Nauka, 1976, pp. 144–55.

The emergence of the construction of the type "Vrach prishla—the doctor came" is connected with the tendency to denote women's professions not only by adding suffixes to nouns of male gender (*udarnik,* m., *udarnitsa,* f., "advanced worker") but also by using nouns of male gender, which thus acquire wider meaning, as they begin to refer to both sexes. The tendency toward agreement according to the real gender is more evident in the speech of people with a secondary education than in that of the college educated. (Trans. and abstract by Irene Tatarnikova.)

KOPELIOVICH, A. B.

A contribution to the problem of determining the category of common gender in modern Russian linguistics. In *Proceedings of Vladimir State Pedagogical Institute named after P. I. Lebedev-*

Poljanskij. Series Russian Language, 2, no. 3. House of Vladimir State Pedagogical Institute Publishing, 1970, pp. 87–115.

LEE, MOTOKO Y.

The married women's status and role as reflected in Japanese: An exploratory sociolinguistic study. *Signs,* 1 (1976), 991–99.

The inventory of terms used for a married woman in Japanese reflects the husband's superordinate status. Some terms are always used only by one spouse, while other terms have no equivalent for reference to the other sex.

LEVICKIJ, VICTOR V.

Semantic word-structure and extralinguistic factors. In Jan Pruche, ed., *Soviet studies in language and language behavior.* Amsterdam: North-Holland, 1976, pp. 125–36.

The semantic center of a word is influenced by sex, a variable which is more important in this context than is profession.

MALINOWSKI, ARLENE.

Form and application of feminine agentives in French occupational terms. *Michigan Academician,* 13, no. 2 (Fall 1980), 207–17.

Malinowski looks at ways the French-speaking community in recent years has attempted to develop an adequate occupational terminology for women entering professions previously closed to them. Feminine agentives which could be formed are not; the masculine still prevails and leads to grammatical anomalies and inconsistencies. (See the references of this article for further sources on French agentives and gender distinctions.)

MESEGUER, ALVARO GARCIA.

Lenguaje y discriminacion sexual. Madrid: Editorial Cuadernos Para el Dialogo, 1977.

This book, in Spanish, investigates the social functions of the language of intellectualism, sexism, and sexuality; the human couple in language; religious language; and the degradation and occlusion of women in language. The second part of the book contains notes on the presentation of sex and gender in the dictionary of the Royal Spanish Academy of Language. Meseguer does not deal with the issue of Spanish grammatical gender.

MIRTOV, A. V.

Category of grammatical gender in the Russian langauge. Unpublished Ph.D. dissertation, Tashkent, 1943, Book 2.

The necessity for the wide development of feminine forms is disappearing. (Trans. and abstract by Irene Tatarnikova.)

MUCHNIK, I. P.

Category of gender and its development in the modern Russian literary language. In S. I. Ozhegov and M. V. Panov, eds., *Development of the modern Russian language.* Moscow: Publishing House of the Academy of Sciences of the USSR, 1963, pp. 39–82.

A study of the development of syntactic expressions of gender in nouns denoting profession or occupation. The constructions of the type "Vrach prishla—The doctor came," where the predicate is in the female gender and agrees with the subject denoting a woman, are innovations of the Soviet epoch and are currently widely used. (Trans. by Irene Tatarnikova.)

MUCHNIK, I. P.

Grammatical categories of verb and substantive in the modern Russian language. Moscow: Nauka, 1971.

Masculine gender is neutral and not marked and can be applied both to men and women, while the feminine correlate is marked. The author argues that complete equality of women doesn't mean the abolition of the complex differences between men and women; these differences are still active under any social order and are preserved in their linguistic reflection. (Trans. and abstract by Irene Tatarnikova.)

PANOV, M. V., ED.

Russian language and Soviet society: Sociolinguistic investigation. Book 3, *Morphology and syntax of the modern Russian language.* Moscow: Nauka, 1968.

A study of the development of new means of expressing the gender of nouns denoting professions and occupations, particularly in reference to women after the October, 1917 revolution. A questionnaire completed by more than 4,000 Russian informants showed a growing tendency to use words of masculine gender to denote women in the professions. (Trans. and abstract by Irene Tatarnikova.)

PUSAVAT, YOKO.

Address terms of married mates in contemporary Japan. Paper given at Conference of Asian Studies of the Pacific Coast, Honolulu, Hawaii, June 25, 1981.

Pusavat examines address terms used by Japanese couples. Power terms of address for men have no female equivalent. The social role of Japanese women is changing, but the inferior, submissive, domestic role remains.

PUSCH, LUISE, AND SENTA TRÖmel-PLÖTZ, EDS.

Sprache, Geschlecht und Macht I. (Language, sex and power I). Special issue of *Linguistische Berichte,* 69 (Oct. 1980).

Contains essays (by Ingrid Guentherodt, Marlis Hellinger, Luise F. Pusch, and Senta Trömel-Plötz) on sexism in the German langauge and guidelines for nonsexist use.

ROBBINS, SUSAN WOLFE.

Gender and agency in Indo-European languages. Paper given at 9th World Congress of Sociology, Uppsala, Sweden, 1978.

Several modern Indo-European languages use unmarked agentive nouns as both masculine and generic forms, corresponding feminine forms requiring a marker. Such languages assume that male agency is the cultural norm (this norm was extended to all nouns in the creation of the artificial language Esperanto, thus all semantic space is masculine). Explanations of historical linguists for this phenomenon are based on the untested assumption that earlier stages of the language must have reflected patriarchal values.

ROTHSTEIN, ROBERT A.

Sex, gender and the October revolution. In S. R. Anderson and P. Kiparsky, eds., *Festschrift for Morris Halle.* New York: Holt, Rinehart and Winston, 1973, pp. 460–66.

Rothstein explores the connections between the formation of new feminine agent nouns spurred by the "relative liberation of women after 1917" and the category of gender in Russian. The initial tendency was to create parallel terminology for the professions, but gradually many of the feminine terms were replaced by their masculine counterparts. He proposes some agreement rules for Russian nouns and notes a number of systematic violations of the rules, including the stylistic use of feminine gender nouns as "essentially hostile epithets, to apply to male human beings."

SAINT-JACQUES, BERNARD.

Sex, dependency and language. *La Linguistique,* 9, no. 1 (1973), 89–96.

In an examination of Japanese, the author demonstrates that differences based on sex are well integrated throughout its linguistic system through the concept of dependency. He cites examples from English (from Lakoff, 1973) and from French to argue that similar, though more subtle, sex distinctions exist in those languages and are also based on dependency. He suggests this pattern may be a language universal.

STEHLI, WALTER.

La formation du féminin en français moderne. *Orbis,* 2 (1953), 7–18.

Stehli examines the situation regarding the formation of feminine agent nouns in French following World War II. He finds that the wide variety of feminine endings in French, many of them pejorative, is a principal source of confusion. He also notes the disagreement among feminists of the time about the desirability of "feminine" or sex neutral terms.

STERN, RHODA H.

Sexism in foreign language textbooks. *Foreign Language Annals*, 9, no. 4 (Sept. 1976), 294–99.

This is an examination of the content and illustrations of twenty-five foreign language textbooks for all levels published between 1970-1974, for evidence of sexism. The author finds that all of the books perpetuate sexism. College textbooks tended to reflect more sexism than books for younger students, and in several cases, revised editions had more sexist content than earlier versions.

STONE, GERALD AND BERNARD COMRIE.

Sex, gender, and the status of women. Chapter 6 in *The Russian language after the revolution.* Oxford: Clarendon Press, 1978, pp. 159–71.

A discussion of post-Revolution occupational terms for women and men.

SUARDIAZ, DELIA E.

Sexism in the Spanish language. *University of Washington Studies in Linguistics and Language Learning*, XI, 1973. (M.A. thesis).

Drawing on a variety of spoken and written sources, Suardiaz documents sexism in professional names; false generics; language usage which treats women as passive sex objects, children, and as men's property; and sexist assumptions (reflected in language use) that everyone is heterosexual.

TSCHUDI, FINN.

Gender stereotypes reflected in asymmetric similarities in language. Paper given at meetings of the American Psychological Assoc., New York, Sept. 1979. Psykologisk Institutt, Universitetet i Oslo, Boks 1094, Blindern, Oslo, Norway.

Following Tversky's (1977) analysis of asymmetric similarity, Tschudi constructed in Norwegian (with supporting research in English) pairs of sentences presenting similarities stated in either of two directions (e.g., "men resemble women," "women resemble men") and had subjects rate their "naturalness." Pronounced asymmetry was found for sentences giving sex-stereotypic context, and a tendency to asymmetry for sentences with context unspecified. No differences for subject sex or "androgyny" were found.

WISE, C. M.

Chiefess—a Hawaiian word. *American Speech,* 26 (1951), 116–21.

In the letters and notes of New England missionaries, the term *ali'i* (Hawaiian for male and female royalty) was translated to mean Chief and Chiefess. However, female royalty was often described in these letters as "queen" or "honorable woman," indicative of an unease in the usage of *ali'i* to indicate both male and female royalty.

WITTIG, MONIQUE.

Paradigm. In George Sambolian and Elaine Marks, eds., *Homosexualities and French literature: Cultural contexts and critical texts.* Ithaca, N.Y.: Cornell Univ. Press, 1979.

In this simply written and powerful essay on sexualities and categories of individuals, Wittig states that "The concept of heterosexuality was created in the French language in 1911," part of the effort to normalize the dominant sexuality. Since "woman" designates a slave/dominated class and becomes reality only in opposition to "man" (particularly through marriage), lesbians are not "women." "The designation 'woman' will disappear no doubt just as the designation 'man' with the oppression/exploitation of women as a class by men as a class. Humankind must find another name for itself and another system of grammar that will do away with genders, the linguistic indicator of political oppositions" (p. 121). [*Also see* discussion of Wittig following Sec. VI-C.]

WOBST, SUSAN.

Dev-, zen-, mal-, muz: Speaking of the sexes in Russian. Paper given at the American Assoc. of Teachers of Slavic and East European Languages. New York, Dec. 1978.

In Russian, dealing with females emphasizes sexual or marital life, reticence, purity, tenderness and abuse toward women. Maleness is associated with physical and inner strength, valor, and the adroit and coarse.

III. STEREOTYPES AND PERCEPTIONS OF LANGUAGE USE

A. General and Theoretical Issues

BERRYMAN, CYNTHIA L. AND JAMES R. WILCOX.

Attitudes toward male and female speech: Experiments on the effects of sex-typed language. *Western Journal of Speech Communication,* 44 (1980), 50–59.

College undergraduates evaluated written messages with the same content, but one a "female sex-typed version" (more intensifiers, references to self, questions, tag questions, phrases implying feeling or emotion, and an unfinished sentence) and the other "male sex-typed" (with obscenity, slang, and incorrect grammar). The source of the first was more often judged female, less commanding, and more flexible; and the male-typed message, the reverse.

BORSTEIN, DIANE.

As meek as a maid: A historical perspective on language for women in courtesy books from the Middle Ages to Seventeen Magazine. In Douglas Butturff and Edmund L. Epstein, eds., *Women's language and style.* Akron, Ohio: L & S Books, 1978, pp. 132–38.

Women's personal identity is submerged by learned language use characterized by triviality and uncertainty. An historical review of courtesy books reveals that "a feminine ideal of meekness and politeness has been used to keep women in their place." Bornstein offers suggestions for changing the stereotypes.

BRADLEY, PATRICIA.

The folk-linguistics of women's speech: An empirical examination. *Communication Monographs,* 48 (1981), 73–90.

The use of qualifying phrases had an adverse effect (in the small decision-making groups studied) only when used by women. The findings suggest that linguistic devices used by women are devalued not because they are inherently weak but because of the lower status of the female speakers.

BRODERICK, DOROTHY M.

Image of the Black in children's fiction. New York: R. R. Bowker, 1973.

A study of the Black image in the recommended books in the *Children's Catalog,* 1909–1968. "For the whites within the books, the blacks exist to make [whites] more comfortable; for the white authors, the blacks exist as objects one can poke fun at, to make ridiculous, to draw a laugh from a bigoted reading audience" (p. 68). The review contains little specific discussion of the speech of the fictive females and males, but does include many passages of conversations from the books.

BUSBY, LINDA.

Sex-role research on the mass media. *Journal of Communication,* 25 (1975), 107–31.

An overview and summary of research on the portrayal of women and men in the mass media.

EBLE, CONNIE.

Girl talk: A bicentennial perspective. In Reza Ordoubadian and Walburga Van-Raffler Engel, eds., *Views on language.* Murfressboro, Tenn.: Interuniversity Publishing, 1975, pp. 77–86.

Guidebooks to female intellectual development and social behavior from the Middle Ages to the 1970s have set forth society's standards of appropriate talk, advising women "how to sound pretty."

Even now women seeking liberation are advised, through Assertiveness Training, to change their speech (once again) to express themselves better.

GOFFMAN, ERVING.

The arrangement between the sexes. *Theory & Society,* 4 (1977), 301–31.

Verbal and nonverbal interactions produce gender differences which many perceive as expressions of natural differences. For example, by giving bear hugs and dunkings, and by threatening with pushes and with snakes, a male can encourage a female "to provide a full-voiced rendition of the plight to which her sex is presumably prone." Every social setting provides materials and opportunities for the display of gender.

GRADY, KATHLEEN.

The belief in sex differences. Paper presented at the Eastern Psychological Assoc. Meetings, Boston, April 1977.

There is a recurring discrepancy between actual sex similarities and the belief in sex differences which Grady explored using a field study and a lab experiment. The results indicate that subjects think gender is extremely descriptive, attending to it not only when it is functionally useful, but also when it is either irrelevant or actually counterproductive to a concise description of a person.

HAYES, JOSEPH J.

Lesbians, gay men, and their "languages." In James W. Chesebro, eds., *Gayspeak: Gay male and lesbian communication.* New York: Pilgrim Press, 1981, pp. 28–42.

Hayes discusses the methodological and political problems—which parallel those in the study of other "out-groups" (e.g., women and Blacks)—confronted by those who study the speech of lesbian and gay male subcultures. The speech of white, hetersexual males has been assumed as the norm; because of oppression, gays have been forced into secrecy and their history has been erased. [*Also see* Sec. IX.]

KRAMARAE, CHERIS.

Gender: How she speaks. In Ellen Bouchard Ryan and Howard Giles, eds., *Attitudes toward language variation: Social and applied contexts.* London: Edward Arnold, 1982, pp. 84–98.

This overview discusses the impact of attitudes on social interaction, the linguistic features stereotypically associated with each sex, the connections of these stereotypes with other variables of social status, and suggestions for analyses to guide observations.

KRAMARAE, CHERIS.

Perceptions and politics in language and sex research. In Howard Giles, W. Peter Robinson, and Philip M. Smith, eds., *Language: Social psychological perspectives.* Oxford: Pergamon Press, 1980, pp. 83–88.

Kramarae argues that the evaluations of theoretical frameworks used by language and gender scholars are highly political, involving decisions about who has the right to know.

KRAMARAE, CHERIS.

Proprietors of language. In Sally McConnell-Ginet, Ruth Borker, and Nelly Furman, eds., *Women and language in literature and society.* New York: Praeger, 1980, pp. 58–68.

A study of the strategies employed by women concerned with language use and structure, and a look at the types of responses by their critics. Kramarae argues that the long tradition of male control of language, determining both the symbols developed and the norms for usage, means that women's speech will not be evaluated the same way as men's speech.

KRAMARAE, CHERIS.

Suggested questions for language and gender research. In Verena Aebischer, Helga Andresen, Helmut Glück, and Theodossia Pavlidon, eds., *Osnabrücker Beiträge zur Sprachtheorie, Oktober 1979*, Beihefte 3, Sprache and Geschlecht, 96–98. (Papers from the Sprache und Geschlecht symposium, March, 1979.) OBST, Fachbereich 7 der Univ. Osnabrück, Postfach 4469, D-4500 Osnabrück, West Germany.

Suggested research questions come from women's and men's perceptions about the limitations of the lexicon, the locus of control, and the evaluation of women's and men's speech.

LEGMAN, G.

Rationale of the dirty joke: An analysis of sexual humor. New York: Grove Press, 1968.

This extensive analysis of erotic folklore includes a section on "the voice as phallus" (pp. 336–37), which begins with a psychoanalytic argument that there is an unconscious identification of the voice as "the virile prerogative of the dominant sex."

McCONNELL-GINET, SALLY.

Making linguistic connections. *Human Ecology Forum,* 11, no. 1 (1980), 12–15.

Linguistic methods, in conjunction with sociocultural analyses and study of people's goals, can reveal attitudes and beliefs about the sexes.

MORRIS, JAN.

Conundrum. London: Faber and Faber, 1974.

While living "a double life," known as male by some people and as female by others, Morris found that people saw what they expected. If they knew Morris as a female, "if I had come down the street wearing flying boots and a crash helmet, woman they would have thought me still."

MORSE, BENJAMIN W. AND VIRGINIA EMAN.

The construct of androgyny: An overview and implications for research. In Cynthia L. Berryman and Virginia A. Eman, eds., *Communication, language & sex.* Rowley, Mass.: Newbury House, 1980, pp. 76–90.

Arguing that the "dichotomous biological" classification male/female tells us little about why people think and behave as they do, the authors suggest looking instead at the individual's psychological orientation, e.g., through the use of the Bem Sex-Role Inventory.

NEWCOMBE, NORA AND DIANE B. ARNKOFF.

Effects of speech style and sex of speaker on person perception. *Journal of Personality and Social Psychology,* 37 (1979), 1293–1303.

Undergraduates (females and males), and female secretaries rated the assertiveness, warmth, and politeness of two female and two male speakers who did or did not use tag questions, qualifiers, and compound requests. Use of each of these forms decreased the perceived assertiveness of speech. Use of qualifiers led to higher ratings of warmth. Sex of speaker had only small effects on ratings. The results suggest that changes in speech style might allow women and men to change the way they are perceived. However, the authors note that there are unanswered questions involving the interaction of speech patterns, social status, and listener expectations.

SAYERS, DOROTHY L.

Are women human? Grand Rapids, Mich.: Wm. B. Eerdmans, 1971.

Asked how, in her writings, she managed to make men's conversation so convincing, Sayers stated, "Indeed, it is my experience that both men and women are fundamentally human, and that there is very little mystery about either sex, except the exasperating mysteriousness of human beings in general." [Sayers is one of several authors who suggests that the categories of male/female are the constructs primarily of men. Men create, and continue to recreate the division, and then call the class of female an enigma.]

SHIELDS, STEPHANIE A.

Functionalism, Darwinism, and the psychology of women: A study in social myth. *American Psychologist,* 30 (1975), 739–54.

A review of the scientific literature on sex differences from the last half of the 19th century and first third of the 20th, demonstrates that "science played handmaiden to social values. . . ."

STEADMAN, J. M., JR.

Affected and effeminate words. *American Speech,* 13, no. 1 (1938), 13–18.

After analyzing lists (composed by women and men college students) of affected or effeminate words the author concludes that "the fear of appearing affected or effeminate (and the students make little distinction in their own minds between the two) is one of the strongest taboos I have found among college students."

THAKERAR, JITENDRA, HOWARD GILES, AND JENNY CHESHIRE.

Psychological and linguistic parameters of speech accommodation theory. In C. Fraser and K. Scherer, eds., *Social and psychological dimensions of language behaviour.* Cambridge: Cambridge Univ. Press, in press.

While not dealing with stereotypes of women's and men's speech in particular, this empirical study and reformulation of speech accommodation theory suggests the critical role of speech stereotypes in the interaction of speakers identified with different social groups.

TUCHMAN, GAYE.

Women's depiction by the mass media. *Signs,* 4 (1979), 528–42.

A perceptive review of research on the relationship between mass media images and women's social roles, reasons for the persistence of sexism in the media, and the effects of these patterns.

Also see: I-A: Kramarae; III-B: O'Barr and Atkins; III-D: Johnson and Goodchilds; IV-D-1: Aronovitch; Crystal; IV-D-3: Elyan; V-A: Leik.

B.   Actual/Perceived

CENTINEO, GIULIA.

Survey on children's attitudes toward women's and men's language. Unpublished paper, Dept. of Linguistics, Univ. of California, Berkeley, 1980.

Asking 18 middle-class children (ages 5–11) questions about whether a male or a female was likely to say certain sample sentences, the researchers found that boys were more likely than girls to assign an utterance decisively to either a male or a female, and were more emphatic about how women and men talk.

EDWARDS, JOHN.

Social class differences and the identification of sex in children's speech. *Journal of Child Language,* 6, (1979), 121–27.

Adults, listening to tapes of children's voices, guessed the sex of each child. Results showed more incorrect guesses of voices of working-class girls than boys, and more incorrect guesses of middle-class boys than girls.

GILES, HOWARD AND PATRICIA MARSH.

Perceived masculinity, androgyny and accented speech. *Language Sciences,* 1 (1978–79), 301–15.

The results of this matched-guise study suggest that (British) "prestige" speakers are heard by listeners as more competent, liberated, and masculine than speakers with a regional (South Welsh) accent. The findings are in conflict with Trudgill's (1975) suggestion that nonprestige speech is associated with masculinity, and previous matched-guise studies which found regional accented speakers rated higher than "prestige" speakers on social attractiveness traits. (In matched-guise studies the stimulus voices are taped by bidialectical or multidialectical speakers who read the same passage in several accents.)

HAWKINS, JAMES L., CAROL WEISBERG, AND DIXIE W. RAY.

Spouse differences in communication style: Preference, perception and behavior. *Journal of Marriage and the Family,* 43 (1980), 585–93.

An interview study in which 171 white couples were asked about preferences for and beliefs about patterns of communication in their marraiges. Wives perceived their husbands to be much more controlling than the men believed themselves to be. Analysis of the couples interacting for five minutes revealed no significant differences between wife and husband in the style used.

KRAMER, CHERIS.

Folklinguistics. *Psychology Today,* 8 (June 1974), 82–85.

Kramer discusses and compares stereotypes of female and male speech (as depicted in cartoons) with differences found in actual speech in an experimental study. She suggests that beliefs about sex-related language differences may be as important as the actual differences, and as long as women play a subordinate role their speech will be stereotyped as separate and unequal.

KRAMER, CHERIS.

Perceptions of female and male speech. *Language and Speech,* 20 (1977), 151–61.

An elicitation of stereotypes of speech behavior revealed that the speech of females and the speech of males, as perceived by women and by men, do not have the same subject matter, or the same manner of delivery. Participants rated 36 speech characteristics as differentiating between female and male speech.

KRAMER, CHERIS.

Stereotypes of women's speech: The word from cartoons. *Journal of Popular Culture,* 8 (1974), 624–30.

Working with cartoon captions, college students of both sexes characterized stereotyped women's speech as being stupid, vague, emotional, confused, and wordy; men's speech was stereotyped as logical, concise, and businesslike. Often when the woman talks, it is the way she talks that is commented on and joked about.

MONTGOMERY, BARBARA AND ROBERT W. NORTON.

Sex differences and similarities in communicator style. *Communication Monographs,* 48 (1981), 121-32.

This research investigates sex differences in self perceptions of communicator style. College students completed the Communicator Style Measure; the scores indicate that males see themselves as more precise than females see themselves. Females reported higher levels of animated style. Males and females reported more similarities than differences in styles.

O'BARR, WILLIAM M. AND BOWMAN K. ATKINS.

'Women's language' or 'Powerless language'? In Sally McConnell-Ginet, Ruth Borker, and Nelly Furman, eds., *Women and language in literature and society.* New York: Praeger, 1980, pp. 93–110.

Tapes of actual criminal court trials were examined for evidence of "women's language" features such as hedges, (super) polite forms, tag questions, and formal grammar. These features were not characteristic of all women or limited only to women. An additional study used four specially produced tapes. The "powerful" versions of testimony taped by a female and a male were similar. The male version of "powerless" speech contained fewer hesitations and intensifiers than the female "powerless" version. The "powerless" style of both the female and male "witness" produced less favorable reactions from listeners. "Women's language" features can be better understood as "powerless language."

RABE, MARY BRESLIN AND MARGARET W. MATLIN.

Sex role stereotypes in speech and language tests. *Language, Speech, and Hearing Services in Schools,* 9, no. 2 (1978), 70–77.

Eight language tests were examined to determined how males and females were represented. Females were underrepresented in pictures and in sentences; both sexes engaged in sex-stereotyped activities more frequently than they engaged in "neutral" activities or activities characteristic of the other sex; sex stereotyping was more marked for adults than for children.

REIK, THEODOR.

Men and women speak different languages. *Psychoanalysis,* 2, no. 4 (1954), 3–15.

This is a rambling, psychoanalytic article which notes in a number of "primitive" societies each sex has unique words and expressions which are tabooed for the other sex. In modern societies women form a speech community of their own, their talk, especially about sexual and bodily matters, being "elusive and allusive," "indirect," and "delicate."

SCOTT, KATHRYN P.

Perceptions of communication competence: What's good for the goose is not good for the gander. In Cheris Kramarae, ed., *The voices and words of women and men.* Oxford: Pergamon Press, 1980, pp. 199–208. Also *Women's Studies International Quarterly,* 3, no. 2/3, 199–208.

Characteristics stereotypically associated with women's speech were rated more socially desirable and better for affective communication than those associated with men's speech. Scott offers several possible explanations for these findings which run counter to discussions of women's speech as inferior to men's, including the possibility that power differentials may have a greater impact on interaction than the characteristics measured here.

SMITH, J. JEROME.

Male and female ways of speaking: Elaborately restricted codes in a CB speech community. *Papers in Linguistics*, 12, no. 1 and 2 (1979), 163–84.

In CBers' conversation, men and women express themselves in ways that do not conform to our stereotyped ideas about "masculine" and "feminine" behavior. Patterns of conversation are discussed in terms of Basil Bernstein's theory of elaborated and restricted codes, and Sandra Bem's theory of androgyny.

SPENDER, DALE.

Language and sex differences. *Osnabrücker Beiträge zur Sprach-theorie: Sprache und Geschlecht II*, (Feb. 1979), pp. 38–59.

Spender argues that differences in the way females and males talk has little to do with the sex of the speaker but a lot to do with the situations in which they find themselves. An asymmetry in speaking rights can explain the perceptions of participants of a sexism and education workshop in London who thought there were more female speakers than male speakers when actually there were 24 male and 13 female speakers.

STALEY, CONSTANCE.

Male-female use of expletives: A heck of a difference in expectations. *Anthropological Linguistics*, 20 (1978), 367–80.

Thirty men and 25 women college students indicated what expletives they and people of the other sex might use in response to various situations. Although women and men were about equal in the number of strong expletives they said they would use, men predicted women would use fewer expletives than they actually did, and women predicted men would use more strong expletives than they actually used.

THAKERAR, JITENDRA N. AND HOWARD GILES.

They are—so they spoke: Noncontent speech stereotypes. *Language and Communication*, 1, no. 2/3 (1981), 255–61.

The authors include a review of studies which indicate that the evaluative impact of different speech styles varies depending on additional information about speakers (e.g., sexual preference of a woman) available prior to, during or after listening to them.

TUCKER, SUSIE I.

Protean shape: A study in eighteenth-century vocabulary and usage. London: Athlone Press, 1967.

Tucker mentions 18th-century language practices greeted with disapproval by such critics as Dr. Johnson—e.g., foreign words, sailors' language, and "women's usage."

Also see: I-A: Parsons; Smith; V-F-2: Boersma, Gay, Jones, Morrison, and Remick; Karp and Yoels; Parker; VII-C: Meditch; IV-D-1: Sachs.

C.   Person Perception

ABRAHAMS, ROGER D.

The advantages of Black English. In Johanna S. DeStefano, ed., *Language, society, and education: A profile of Black English.* Worthington, Ohio: Charles A. Jones, 1973, pp. 97–106.

Black women's talk is associated with respectability and "the values of the home," while men's talk is a declaration of masculinity. Black men's talk is more troubling to whites than is the Black women's "sweet" talk, which is closer to standard English.

ADDINGTON, D. W.

The relationship of selected vocal characteristics to personality perception. *Speech Monographs,* 35 (1968), 492–503.

Addington used an experiment to explore whether male and female speakers using the same vocal characteristics elicit different personality perception and found that "changes in male voice affect personality perception differently than do similar changes in female voices." For example, increased throatiness in male speakers led to their being stereotyped as older, more realistic, mature, sophisticated, and well adjusted. Females with more throaty voices were seen as less intelligent, lazier, more boorish, ugly, sickly, careless.

BAIRD, JOHN E., JR. AND PATRICIA HAYES BRADLEY.

Styles of management and communication: A comparative study of men and women. *Communication Monographs,* 46 (1979), 101–11.

A questionnaire was given to 150 subjects from three organizations to study perceptions about men and women managers. In communication style, men were perceived as more dominant, quick to challenge others, and directing the course of conversation; women scored higher on showing concern and being attentive to others. The relation of specific aspects of communication style to employee morale was also studied.

BALSWICK, JACK O. AND CHARLES W. PEEK.

The inexpressive male: A tragedy of American society. In Deborah S. David and Robert Brannon, eds., *The forty-nine percent majority.* Reading, Mass.: Addison-Wesley, 1976 pp. 55–57.

This short essay dealing with a social problem and with solutions argues that the inexpressive male comes in two types: the inexpressive feeling man (the cowboy) and the inexpressive non-feeling man (the playboy). [*Also see:* Sattel, "Men, Inexpressiveness, and Power." In this volume.]

BENNETT, SUZANNE AND BERND WEINBERG.

Sexual characteristics of preadolescent children's voices. *Journal of the Acoustical Society of America,* 65 (1979), 179–89.

One hundred sixteen college-age women tried to identify sex of speaker from recordings of 73 girls and boys (ages six to eight) speaking a sentence normally, and in a monotone. The monotone sentences (with decreased fundamental frequency) were more often heard as male.

BERRYMAN, CYNTHIA L.

Attitudes toward male and female sex-appropriate and sex-inappropriate language. In Cynthia L. Berryman and Virginia A. Eman, eds., *Communication, language and sex.* Rowley, Mass.: Newbury House, 1980, pp. 195–216.

This study compared subjects' perceptions of male and female communicators who used "sex-appropriate" language features with perceptions of those who used "sex-inappropriate" features. Whether used by a female or male communicator, "female" features (e.g., pronunciation of *-ing* word endings; fewer interruptions) contributed to the communicator's credibility; users of "male" language features were rated as more extroverted.

BOSTROM, ROBERT AND ALAN KEMP.

Type of speech, sex of speaker, and sex of subject as factors influencing persuasion. *Central States Speech Journal*, 20 (1969), 245–51.

Undergraduates listening to tapes judged the female speaker more effective when she delivered the racist speech and they judged the male speaker more effective when he delivered the non-racist speech. The authors suggest that when the female violated expectations in this situation she gained credibility.

BRADAC, JAMES J., MICHAEL R. HEMPHILL, AND CHARLES H. TARDY.

Language style on trial: Effects of "powerful" and "powerless" speech upon judgments of victims and villains. *Western Journal of Speech Communication*, 45 (1981), 327–41.

In two experiments college undergraduates were asked to evaluate versions of hypothetical courtroom testimony, one in a "powerless" style (with hedges, intensifiers, polite and hesitation forms), and the other in a "powerful" style (without these forms and including short replies). In the first experiment, but not the second, subjects attributed greater fault to both plaintiffs and defendants who used the high power style. There were no relationships between power of style and judgments of masculinity or femininity of the message source.

CANTOR, JOANNE R.

What is funny to whom? *Journal of Communication*, 26 (Summer 1976), 164–72.

Several studies involving manipulation of a joke about a male (or female) dominating a male (or female) resulted in similar findings. Both women and men rate highest the joke version of the male dominating the female. The sex of the person ridiculed is an important determinant of the humor response.

CONDRY, JOHN AND SANDRA CONDRY.

Sex differences: A study of the eye of the beholder. *Child Development*, 47 (1976), 812–19.

Half the viewers of a videotape were told they were watching a boy; half were told they were watching a girl. Viewers were asked to rate the type and intensity of emotions the child displayed. Those who thought they were watching a boy thought the child displayed more pleasure and less fear than did those who were told they were watching a girl. Observing the same response the first group labeled it "anger" and the second group labeled it "fear."

EAGLY, ALICE H.

Sex differences in influenceability. *Psychological Bulletin,* 85 (1978), 86–116.

There is scant empirical support for sex difference in persuasion and conformity not involving group pressure. It is possible that various sex differences in social influence studies are a product of contextual features of experimental settings. The importance of the cultural context is suggested by the fact that findings reporting greater influenceability among females were more prevalent in studies published prior to 1970 than in those published in the 1970s.

EBLE, CONNIE C.

If ladies weren't present, I'd tell you what I really think. In David L. Shores and Carole P. Hines, eds., *Papers in language variation*. University, Ala.: Univ. of Alabama Press, 1977, pp. 295–301.

Eble writes that to determine "acceptable" and "prohibitive" language use it is important to consider the speaker's age, geographic region, socioeconomic class, ethnic identification, occupation, and the specific situation as well as gender. Eble speculates that in general the use of abusive terms is associated with blue-collar males on the job, and with parties and night clubs. Talk about sex is common to the conversations of men among all occupations and social classes. While women do talk about sex, their conversations are more likely to be concerned with questions of affection and love.

EDELSKY, CAROLE.

Subjective reactions to sex-linked language. *The Journal of Social Psychology*, 99 (June 1976), 97–104.

Adults were asked to associate sex-linked lexical forms with ten attributes represented by adjective scales, each scale having a "male" and a "female" pole. Results indicate that stereotyped male and female language evoked associations of other stereotyped male and female traits.

ELYAN, OLWEN, PHILIP SMITH, HOWARD GILES, AND RICHARD BOURHIS.

RP-accented female speech: The voice of perceived androgyny? In Peter Trudgill, ed., *Sociolinguistic patterns in British English*. London: Edward Arnold, 1978, pp. 122–31.

Female speakers of "standard" varieties of English are rated higher in competence and occupational prestige, while "non-standard"-sounding females are rated more likeable and sincere, and less aggressive and egotistical.

ERICKSON, BONNIE, E. ALLAN LIND, BRUCE C. JOHNSON, AND WILLIAM O'BARR.

Speech style and impression formation in a court setting: The effects of "power" and "powerless" speech. *Journal of Experimental and Social Psychology,* 14 (1978), 266–79.

In two experiments college students listened to testimony of a female or male witness who used either "powerless" speech (e.g., frequent use of intensifiers, hedges, questioning intonation) or "power" speech (few such features) to deliver the same basic evidence. In both experiments (one involving tape recordings, and the second, transcripts) and for witnesses of both sexes, listeners evaluated the witness using the "powerless" style more negatively.

FILLMER, H. THOMPSON AND LESLIE HASWELL.

Sex-role stereotyping in English usage. *Sex Roles,* 3, no. 3 (1977), 257–63.

First to fifth grade children from Southern, low-income city schools were asked to identify statements that would be said by a woman or by a man. (E.g., It is a nice day; It is such a nice day.) More than 50% of the children chose the answer that reflected sex-stereotyped language usage.

GALL, MEREDITH D., AMOS K. HOBBY, AND KENNETH H. CRAIK.

Non-linguistic factors in oral language productivity. *Perceptual and Motor Skills,* 29 (1969), 871–74.

Correlating word count scores with personality variables as assessed by the California Psychological Inventory, the authors found that, for women, verbal fluency had a negative correlation with "good impression"; but for men, the correlation was consistently positive.

GILES, HOWARD, PHILIP M. SMITH, CAROLINE BROWNE, SARAH WHITEMAN, AND JENNIFER WILLIAMS.

Women's speech: The voice of feminism. In Sally McConnell-Ginet, Ruth Borker, and Nelly Furman, eds., *Women and language in literature and society.* New York: Praeger, 1980, pp. 150–56.

Studies were conducted to determine whether listeners perceive differences in taped speech of feminist and nonfeminist women. Even with controls for content, feminists were rated more lucid, confident, intelligent, likeable and sincere, and less monotonous and superficial than nonfeminists. Subsequent analysis leads the authors to argue that listeners were distinguishing not only feminist and nonfeminist voices, but, more generally, the speech of politically active and nonactive people.

GROULAND, N. E. AND L. ANDERSON.

Personality characteristics of socially accepted, socially neglected, and socially rejected junior high school pupils. *Educational Administration and Supervision,* 43 (1957), 329–38.

Junior high school girls and boys agreed that popular girls were good-looking, tidy, friendly, cheerful, quiet, and interested in dating, while popular boys were known for being active in games, good-looking, tidy, friendly, cheerful, and able to tell a joke.

HAVILAND, JEANNETTE M.

Sex-related pragmatics in infants' nonverbal communication. *Journal of Communication,* 27, no. 2 (1977), 80–84.

Infants expressing "negative emotions" (fear, anger, and distress) are more likely to be judged boys; infants expressing "positive expressions" (e.g., joy), girls. For a second group of under-graduates who watched the segments of videotape, correct and incorrect designations of the sex of each infant were distributed (on the coding sheets) randomly across students and infants. Once labeled "girl" four of the five boys were seen as 12 to 16% more joyful.

HILPERT, FRED, CHERIS KRAMER, AND RUTH ANN CLARK.

Participants' perceptions of self and partner in mixed sex dyads. *Central States Speech Journal,* 26 (1975), 52–56.

In this study mixed-sex dyads discussed a specified problem. Then each participant completed a questionnaire. Overall, women had accurate perceptions of who spoke more in 78% of the dyads and men in 70%, but where women were incorrect, their errors tended to be systematic, designating the man as dominant speaker.

KRAMER, CHERIS.

Women's and men's ratings of their own and ideal speech. *Communication Quarterly,* 26, no. 2 (1978), 2–11.

A study comparing women's and men's ratings of their own and ideal speech showed that a greater number of speech characteristics of males differed from the speech characteristics of the ideal speaker. The results of the study combined with the writings of women who have made a conscious effort to change their language indicate that before women try to alter their speech by such means as assertiveness training they should consider the desirable characteristics associated with female speech.

KRAMER, ERNEST.

Personality stereotypes in voice: A reconsideration of the data. *The Journal of Social Psychology,* 62 (1964), 247–51.

This study suggests that relationships have not been demonstrated between judgments from voice and other criteria of personality. Two problem areas of current research are the use of monologues when the qualities being sought would more likely occur in interaction, and a neglect of individual differences among listeners.

LASS, NORMAN J., PAMELA J. MERTZ, AND KAREN L. KIMMEL.

The effect of temporal speech alterations on speaker race and sex identifications. *Language and Speech,* 21, part 3 (1978), 279–91.

Ten Black and ten white speakers recorded four sentences each. Listeners heard the tapes played forward, backward, or time-compressed. Temporal cues appeared to play a role in race identification but not in sex identification.

LAWSON, EDWIN D.

First names on the campus: A semantic differential analysis. *Names,* 28 (1980), 69–83.

The first names of all students at a university (2,215 men, with 304 different names; 2,419 women, with 514 different names) were rated by women and men judges, using a semantic differential technique. Both women's and men's names were rated closer to Good than Bad, and to Strong than Weak (though more so for men's names); women's names were rated closer to Passive, and men's to Active.

MULAC, ANTHONY AND TORBORG LOUISA LUNDELL.

Differences in perceptions created by syntactic-semantic production of male and female speakers. *Communication Monographs,* 47 (June 1980), 111–18.

Students judging the sex of the speaker from transcripts of topic-controlled monologues were unable to guess correctly at a better than chance level. However, students reading the transcripts and marking semantic differential scales rated the monologues of the female speakers substantially higher than those of the male monologues on aesthetic quality and male speeches higher on dynamism. Preliminary analysis did not locate possible causal links between the syntactic-semantic variables of the transcripts and the readers' differing evaluations of the female and male monologues.

MULAC, ANTHONY, AND TORBORG LOUISA LUNDELL.

Linguistic determinants of the gender-linked language effect in spoken discourse. Paper given at meeting of the International Communication Association, Boston, 1982.

As a follow-up to Mulac and Lundell (1980), a multiple regression approach was used to determine what linguistic variables raters used in the earlier study to rate aesthetic quality and dynamism of transcribed female and male monologues. While combinations of variables were predictive of the ratings in the earlier study, the involved nature of the findings suggests that "the gender-linked language" is a complex phenomenon.

NEWTON, ESTHER.

Mother camp: Female impersonators in America. Englewood Cliffs, N.J.: Prentice-Hall, 1972, pp. 72–3.

A female impersonator speaks and sings not in falsetto but at the top of his normal vocal range: "The impression of femininity is conveyed more by the intonation, stress, and punctuation than by the pitch itself. This intonation is parodying sweetness, rather mincing."

ROBYAK, JAMES.

Effects of gender on the counselor's preference for methods of influence. *Journal of Counseling Psychology,* 28 (1981), 7–12.

Male and female university counselors were asked to estimate the utility of responses to each of three methods of influence in facilitating behavioral change in either a male or female depressed client. Preferences for the legitimate response varied according to the gender of both the counselor and the client.

SATTEL, JACK W.

The inexpressive male: Tragedy or sexual politics? *Social Problems,* 23 (April 1976), 469–77.

Sattel argues that men use inexpressiveness to maintain positions of power. [*Also see* revised version, "Men, Inexpressiveness, and Power." In this volume.]

SCHWARTZ, E.

Sex roles and leadership dynamics: A study of attitudes toward the female sex role. Senior Honors Thesis, Univ. of Pennsylvania, 1970.

In an experiment with a mixed-sex group in which a female was encouraged to talk much more, increase her participation, and exhibit leadership, Schwartz found that the men disliked the overly loquacious female more than a similarly behaving male. Furthermore, they continued to dislike her even after she stopped behaving in a "sex-inappropriate manner."

SHEPPARD, ALICE.

Humor and sex-role stereotypes. Paper given at Pioneers for Century III, Conference on the Power of Women and Men, Cincinnati, April 1976.

Sheppard argues that because men are supposed to be strong and unemotional, their admission of weakness is perceived as inherently funnier than women's. Since much humor is aggressive, female comedians are more suspect than male comedians, and women's gender may be more distracting because in our culture women frequently serve [often unwillingly] as sex symbols.

SIEGLER, DAVID M. AND ROBERT S. SIEGLER.

Stereotypes of males' and females' speech. *Psychological Reports,* 39 (1976), 167–70.

The authors suggest that negative stereotypes toward females' speech may have remained constant, but the social desirability of overtly expressing such stereotypes may have diminished. Their studies found that (1) strongly assertive forms were attributed relatively more often to males and less assertive forms relatively more often to females and (2) syntactic forms associated with males were rated more intelligent than those associated with females.

SMITH, PHILIP M.

Judging masculine and feminine social identities from content-controlled speech. In Howard Giles, W. Peter Robinson, and Philip M. Smith, eds., *Language: Social Psychological Perspectives*. Oxford: Pergamon Press, 1980, pp. 121–26.

In this study listeners heard recordings of several speakers reading a short passage, and rated each speaker on M and F stereotype scales. Ratings of speakers' F and M corresponded closely to speakers' self-ratings, suggesting that, indeed, speech serves as one link between attributions of F and M, and actual gender identity. (From author's abstract)

TRENHOLM, SARAH AND WILLIAM R. TODD DE MANCILLAS.

Student perceptions of sexism. *The Quarterly Journal of Speech*, 64 (1978), 267–83.

College students were asked to list personal experiences and media portrayals they perceived as sexist. Women and men appeared equally sensitive to sexism, and both found it much easier to list examples of sexism directed to women. Women were more likely to be cited as targets of objectification and men as victims of inflexible role prescriptions.

WHEELESS, VIRGINIA EMAN AND LAWRENCE R. WHEELESS.

The relationships among self-reported gender orientation, other-reported gender orientation, and social desirability: Methodological and research issues. In Larry E. Larmer and Mary Kenny Badami, eds. *Proceedings of the 2nd and 3rd conferences on communication, language, and gender*. Madison: Univ. of Wisconsin—Extension, 1982, pp. 36–58.

For related discussions, see Diana Baumrind, "Are androgynous individuals more effective persons and parents?" (pp. 44–75), and Janet T. Spence, "Comments on Baumrind's 'Are androgynous individuals more effective persons and parents?' " (pp. 76–80), *Child Development*, 53 (1982).

WILLIAMS, JOHN E., HOWARD GILES, JOHN R. EDWARDS, DEBORAH L. BEST, AND JOHN T. DAWS.

Sex-trait stereotypes in England, Ireland and the United States. *British Journal of Social Clinical Psychology*, 16 (1977), 303–09.

University students in England, Ireland, and the U.S. gave similar ratings in a study of traits attributed to men and to women. The students indentified as "male adjectives" *dominant, forceful, inventive, logical, rude, stern,* and *unemotional;* and the "female adjectives" *appreciative, changeable, emotional, fussy, gentle, nagging, submissive,* and *talkative.*

ZILLMANN, DOLF AND S. HOLLY STOCKING.

Putdown humor. *Journal of Communication*, 26 (Summer 1976), 154–63.

Students rated the funniness of cartoons and stories involving self-disparagement. Women, more than did the men, enjoyed humorous self-disparagement of a female. Women rated the self-disparager, female or male, as more intelligent, provocative, and skillful, than the men did.

Also see: II-D: MacKay ("Language, thought and social attitudes"); MacKay and Fulkerson; Murphy-Berman and Jean; II-E: Anderson, Finn, and Leider; MacKay and Konishi; Stanley ("Paradigmatic woman"); III-A: Bradley; IV-D-1: Aronovitch; Batstone and Tuomi; Sachs; Sachs, Lieberman, and Erickson; IV-D-2: Austin; V-A: Nemeth, Endicott, and Wachtler; V-F-2: Macke and Richardson; VII-C: Edelsky; Garcia-Zamor.

D.   Behavioral Consequences

COSTRICH, NORMA, JOAN FEINSTEIN, AND LOUISE KIDDER.

When stereotypes hurt: Three studies of penalties for sex-role reversals. *Journal of Experimental Social Psychology,* 11 (1975), 520–30.

Experiments indicated men have no more leeway to deviate from gender stereotypes than do women.

HENNESSEE, JUDITH.

Some news is good news. *Ms.,* 3 (July 1974), 25–29.

Hennessee comments on the presumed relationship between a low-pitched voice and credibility for women TV news broadcasters. In American culture the norm for an authoritative voice is male; "higher-pitched voices are still associated with unpleasantness, evoking nagging mothers or wives, waspish schoolteachers, acerbic librarians." Yet a survey of attitudes toward television newswomen, done by researchers at the Univ. of Wisconsin [*See* Stone, this section] showed that only about one-fifth of those polled said they would be more likely to believe a news report by a man.

JOHNSON, FERN L.

Illusions of equity in language. Paper given at the Symposium on Power and Communication, Minneapolis, May 1981.

Reviewing common sentiments about Black and female speech, Johnson argues that our society continues to discourage language diversity, and concludes that teaching Blacks and women the skills of successful white men (e.g., through assertiveness training programs) may strengthen the affirmative action reports, but is far from a social reorganization based on diversity in communication style and relational orientation.

JOHNSON, PAULA B. AND JACQUELINE B. GOODCHILDS.

How women get their way. *Psychology Today,* Oct. 1976, pp. 69–70.

Asked how they would try to influence their dates to have sexual intercourse, college students evidently used stereotypes to guide their responses. The men said they would use direct arguments, stressing expertise. The women said they were likely to use more indirect and body language. Asked how they would avoid intercourse, women indicated they would be direct, stressing their right to refuse, while men said they would be more indirect.

MARACEK, JEANNE, JANE ALLYN PILIAVIN, ELLEN FITZSIMMONS, ELIZABETH C. KROGH, ELIZABETH LEADER, AND BONNIE TRUDELL.

Women as TV experts: The voice of authority? *Journal of Communication,* 28, no. 1 (Oct. 1978), 159–68.

While more TV commercials show women experts selling products now than at the beginning of the 1970s, the women are still usually backed up by the "authoritative" male voice-over.

O'DONNELL, WILLIAM J. AND KAREN O'DONNELL.

Update: Sex-role messages in TV commercials. *Journal of Communication,* 28, no. 1 (1978), 156–58.

Of the commercials which used voice-overs (254 in the sample), 93% were done by men. The percentage was slightly higher than that noted in studies published in 1972–1976. Women were three times more likely than men to advertise domestic products, a slight increase over earlier findings.

PHILIPSEN, GERRY.

Speaking like a man in Teamsterville: Culture patterns of role enactment in an urban neighborhood. *Quarterly Journal of Speech,* 61 (Feb. 1975), 13–22.

This article examines men's speech in a blue-collar, low-income white neighborhood of Chicago, especially the relationship of speech to the social identity "male." "In Teamsterville, speech [for males] is proper and functional in asserting male solidarity, but not in asserting power and influence in interpersonal situations." As a counter to threat or as an expression of status asymmetry, a show of physical power is considered to be more appropriate than speech.

QUINN, SALLY.

What is sexy, feminine, assertive? *New Woman,* 7, no. 3 (1977), 41–43.

Hired to co-anchor CBS Morning News, Quinn was critized by the media as being a blonde bombshell who had used her feminine wiles to get the job. Frightened of being thought "feminine" and "loose," she tried to look, act and talk "masculine." She asks, "Have you ever heard a man apologize for being masculine? Have you ever heard anyone say about a man, he's *too* masculine?"

RUBIN, LILLIAN BRESLOW.

Worlds of pain: Life in the working-class family. New York: Basic Books, 1976.

In this interview study, Rubin found that heterosexual, working-class couples believe that women are irrational, passive, verbal, emotional, tender, intuitive. These are considered naturally female and also bad, weak, and childlike traits. Men are associated with sane and strong adult traits such as tough, active, logical, nonverbal, unemotional. These expectations affected their conversations; the couples often talked at or past, rather than with, each other.

STONE, VERNON A.

Attitudes toward TV newswomen. *Journal of Broadcasting,* 18 (Winter 1973–74), 49–62.

Although most of the 130 TV news directors who responded to a questionnaire said they thought their viewers would prefer a male evening newscaster, the most frequent response in all audience groups surveyed (university students, professors, grade school children and their parents) was that it made no difference to them whether the newscaster was a woman or a man.

URIS, DOROTHY.

A woman's voice. New York: Barnes & Noble Books, 1978.

Uris offers a supportive program of speaking improvement for women, including discussion of voice, conversation, discussion, speech-making, mass media, and campaigning. The book is based on the premise that women have unique speech problems that result from a lack of experience and prejudicial attitudes toward their speech.

Also see: I-A: Kramer; III-C: Condry and Condry; Eagly; IV-D-1: Batstone and Tuomi; V-F-2: Elliott.

E.   Other Languages

AEBISCHER, VERENA.

> Chit-chat: Women in interaction. Paper given at the 9th World Congress of Sociology, Uppsala, Sweden, Aug. 1978.

Taped interviews of French women discussing chit-chat were analyzed. Aebischer considers women's informal talk as a creative *construction* by which they organize their experiences. Women's use and evaluation of chit-chat depend on their ideas of femininity.

BASHA, RUTH M.

> The image of women in verbal communication. Paper given at the International Seminar on Women, Language and Development, Mysore, India, 1981.

In a general essay on women, language and society, Basha points out that information on the restrictions and evaluations of women's speech can be found in many songs, proverbs, and religious writings.

BORKER, RUTH.

> Anthropology: Social and cultural perspectives. In Sally McConnell-Ginet, Ruth Borker, and Nelly Furman, eds., *Women and language in literature and society.* New York: Praeger, 1980, pp. 26–44.

Arguing that to understand gender-related differences in language use it is necessary to study cultural ideas about women and men, social life, and the nature of speech itself, Borker writes about varying cultural conceptions of gender, power, and language in more than a dozen countries. [*Also see* Borker, Sec. I-A.]

CHAMBERLAIN, ALEXANDER.

> Women's language. *American Anthropologist,* 14 (1912) 579–81.

Possible reasons for the existence of "women's language" among "primitive people" are discussed: speech forms handed down by female captives of foreign tribes; forms resulting from the differentiation of occupations; speech diversities from taboos of naming. "Religious and animistic concepts in woman's sphere of thought may also have had some influence . . . ; likewise the play-instinct, which often makes itself felt longer in woman."

SKUTNABB-KANGAS, TOVE AND ORVOKKI HEINÄMÄKI.

> When this very prestigious researcher met Mrs. Average Housewife, or: Where have all the women gone . . . *Journal of Pragmatics,* 3 (1979), 507–19.

During the lectures and discussions at a Nordic Summer Seminar in Psycholinguistics, linguists used exemplar sentences describing men as "active, independent, rational, strong, controlling agents" and describing women as silly persons with insignificant activities.

WISTRAND, BIRGITTA.

> *Swedish women on the move.* Stockholm: The Swedish Institute, 1981.

This book includes a brief discussion of recent Swedish Broadcasting Corporation and newspaper policies concerning women's participation and portrayal in radio and TV programs, newspapers and textbooks, pornography and advertising, and the use of Swedish words for *he* and *man*. (As in English, the pronoun for *he* is also the prescribed generic; the Swedish word *man* means both "man" and "one".)

Also see: I-B: Yaguello; IV-A: Trudgill; IV-G: Furfey; V-H: Brown; Werner.

IV. SEX DIFFERENCES AND SIMILARITIES IN LANGUAGE USE: LINGUISTIC COMPONENTS

A. Theoretical Issues

Citations concerning sex similarities and differences in writing are included in Section VI and have not been cross-listed in this section, which focuses on spoken language.

BECK, KAY.

Sex differentiated speech codes. *International Journal of Women's Studies,* 1, no. 6 (1978), 566–72.

Beck analyzed responses of 24 undergraduate students to TAT cards. She found women used less complex syntax and marked separate ideas with intonation; men used more subordinate clauses and an ordered selection of adverbs and adjectives. Beck [making a rather unjustified leap] concludes that women's speech is "disorganized and haphazard" and that women use a "restricted" and men an "elaborated" code. [She uses Basil Bernstein's framework, developed to discuss social class, taking it out of context.]

BORKER, RUTH.

Power in speech. Paper given at the 9th World Congress of Sociology, Uppsala, Sweden, August 1978.

Power can be located in the individual, in interaction between the speaker and hearer, and in the speech itself based on its value within a cultural frame and independent of the speaker. Specific speech forms may express particular ideological models of power which may structure interaction. For example, in our culture if power is thought to be located in the words as they are seen as expressing truth and reason, then slow, deliberate, intonationally flat speech will provide power to speakers skilled in these patterns. [*See also* Robert Hopper, "Powerful is as powerful speaks: Linguistic sex differences re-considered," pp. 162–70, and Linda Putnam, "Conversational power: What determines conversational control," pp. 171–83, in Larry E. Larmer and Mary Kenny Badami, eds., *Proceedings of the 2nd and 3rd conferences on communication, language, and gender.* Madison: Univ. of Wisconsin—Extension, 1982.]

BROWN, PENELOPE.

Women and politeness: A new perspective on language and society. *Reviews in Anthropology,* May/June (1976), 240–49.

In this review of Robin Lakoff's *Language and Women's Place,* Brown suggests that women's speech (and men's) is more usefully studied in terms of "social relationships and expectations about humans as interactants." Explanations of language usage should come from a theory of social forces and a consideration of social status, race, and individual goals.

BROWN, PENELOPE AND STEPHEN LEVINSON.

Social structure, groups and interaction. In Klaus R. Scherer and Howard Giles, eds., *Social markers in speech.* Cambridge: Cambridge Univ. Press, 1980, pp. 291–341.

In a theoretical essay, the authors argue that most linguistic markers of sex are the result of deference or power, or they stem from the speakers' different social networks or activities.

CARROCCI, NOREEN.

Clarifying gender differences or communication effectiveness: Which is our aim? In Larry E. Larmer and Mary Kenny Badami, eds., *Proceedings of the 2nd and 3rd conferences on communication, language, and gender.* Madison: Univ. of Wisconsin—Extension, 1982, pp. 329–37.

To avoid the production of isolated empirical generalizations about language and the sexes, Carrocci argues that researchers need to work within the context of communication theory.

EAGLY, ALICE H. AND LINDA L. CARLI.

Sex of researchers and sex-typed communications as determinants of sex differences in influenceability: A meta-analysis of social influence studies. *Psychological Bulletin,* 90 (1981), 1–20.

This is an analysis of the research which has found women to be more influenceable than men. Sex differences are generally small in magnitude; male researchers have been far more likely than female researchers to find sex differences in influenceability, and to obtain larger differences in the direction of greater persuasability and conformity among women.

EICHLER, MARGRIT.

The double standard: A feminist critique of feminist social science. New York: St. Martin's Press, 1980.

Eichler argues that feminist thought remains tied to what it criticizes, unintentionally reinforcing sex distinctions. For example, the concepts "sex roles" and "sex identity" are ambiguous and reified; our language is so tied to sex we are unable to describe the absence of sex differences when it occurs. Eichler also criticizes masculinity-femininity scales and the concept of androgyny.

EMAN, VIRGINIA A. AND BENJAMIN W. MORSE.

The construct of androgyny: An overview and implications for research. In Cynthia L. Berryman and Virginia A. Eman, eds., *Communication, language and sex.* Rowley, Mass.: Newbury House, 1980, pp. 76–90.

The authors argue against using "dichotomous biological classification" in research, suggesting that one's psychological orientation toward one's sex allows better understanding of such variables as relational control, interpersonal attraction, self-disclosure, interpersonal competency, and language. [For other research based on the Bem Sex Role Inventory, *see* Jose, Crosby, and Wong-McCarthy, Sec. V-A and Sandra Lipsitz Bem, "Gender schema theory and its implications for child development: Raising gender-aschematic children in a gender-schematic society," *Signs,* in press.]

ERVIN-TRIPP, SUSAN.

"What do women sociolinguists want?": Prospects for a research field. In Betty Lou Dubois and Isabel Crouch, eds., *The sociology of the languages of American women.* San Antonio, Texas: Trinity Univ., 1976, pp. 3–16.

Offering a rationale for research, Ervin-Tripp suggests that the sources, and implications, of differences in the talk of women and men will only become clear if we look at a variety of contexts and variables. Some situations may emphasize sex differences. In others, differences may be more directly explained by such factors as social networks, aspirations, task pressures, class, and age.

FAVREAU, OLGA EIZNER.

Sex bias in psychological research. *Canadian Psychological Review,* 18 (Jan. 1977), 56–65.

The assumption of male superiority often affects the kinds of research questions asked, the erroneous citations used to support arguments, the kinds of generalizations made in academic literature and in public statements, and the ways results are explained. For example, a recurrent theme is that whatever men are found better at is recurringly said to be finer than what women are proficient at. If women appear to have an advantage in linguistic skills, then these skills are said to require minimal cognitive involvement.

GOLD, ELLEN REID.

How to do historical research in communication, language, and gender. In Larry E. Larmer and Mary Kenney Badami, eds., *Proceedings of the 2nd and 3rd conferences on communication, language and gender.* Madison: Univ. of Wisconsin—Extension, 1982, pp. 338–54.

This essay and bibliography include information about theoretical perspectives, and location of primary and secondary materials for work on history, language, and gender topics.

HYMES, DELL.

On the origins and foundations of inequality among speakers. *Daedalus,* 102, no. 3 (1973), 59–85.

Hymes argues that many linguists consider language primarily as something to praise rather than to study as a product and problem of human life. A study of "ways of speaking" should attend to the meaning of speech for speakers and listeners. For a given speaker and setting a language "can do some things well, some clumsily, and others not intelligibly at all." Verbal skills considered necessary for males or females in one society may be unessential in another.

JACKLIN, CAROL NAGY.

Methodological issues in the study of sex-related differences. *Developmental Review,* 1 (1981), 266–73.

Jacklin discusses ten methodological problems, including the frequent heavy focus on group differences rather than individual differences, a bias toward publishing positive findings (which could be corrected in part by the acceptance of a label such as "sex-similarities" or "sex-unrelated characteristics"), the problem of generalization from a within-sex to a between-sex difference, lack of consideration of variables that are confounded with sex, and the assumption that all sex-related differences are genetic or innate.

KAPLAN, CORA.

Language and gender. In Papers on patriarchy (conference papers). Lewes, Sussex: Women's Publishing Collective, 1976.

A provocative theoretical essay, arguing that women have a "special relation to language which becomes theirs as a consequence of becoming human, and at the same time not theirs as a consequence of becoming female." At puberty, girls internalize a suppression of their public speech, a social silence.

KRAMER, CHERIS.

The problem of orientation in sex/language research. In Betty Lou Dubois and Isabel Crouch, eds., *The Sociology of the languages of American women.* San Antonio, Texas: Trinity Univ., 1976, pp. 17–29.

Summarizes and responds to arguments often used against attending to gender in communication research, observing that much social science research has taken the norm to be male speech.

KUYKENDALL, ELEANOR.

Breaking the double binds. *Language and Style,* 13 (Fall 1980), 81–93.

A critical analysis of Robin Lakoff's claims about gender and language, suggesting that she conflates properties of sentences, speakers' intentions, and speakers' social relationships—which, in fact, need careful separation.

LAKOFF, ROBIN TOLMACH.

Language and sexual identity. *Semiotica,* 19 (1977), 119–30. (Review of Mary Ritchie Key, *Male/female language.)*

"The special characteristics of women's language [not detailed] stem from denial of responsibility, itself arising from a lack of self-confidence . . . ." Lakoff believes that women's speech choices can be best explained by society's view of women's roles and nature and that linguists have special expertise which, in discussions of women's and men's language use, can "shed light where others produce only heat."

MACAULAY, RONALD K. S.

Sex differences in language use. Mellon Women's Studies Teaching Module, 1977, Pitzer College, Claremont, Calif.

In this review of research, Macaulay concludes that stereotypical statements about men's and women's speech are often contradicted by results of empirical studies. However, many of the empirical studies are limited by the coding methods used (e.g., the determination of the social status of adult females by consideration of only their husbands' social rankings) and by the speech studied (e.g., investigations of pronunciation in short speech samples). He states that we still know relatively little about differences in language use by men and women.

MCCONNELL-GINET, SALLY.

Feminism in linguistics. In Paula Treichler, Cheris Kramarae, and Beth Stafford, eds., *For alma mater.* Urbana, Ill.: Univ. of Illinois Press, in press.

By treating language as an autonomous structure, linguists have achieved theoretical rigor and descriptive precision. However, the author argues, one must consider speakers' and writers' aims and purposes, the effects of language on hearers, and the context of speech events in order to understand how language maintains and transmits male-centered values and social structure.

McCONNELL-GINET, SALLY.

Linguistics and the feminist challenge. In Sally McConnell-Ginet, Ruth Borker, and Nelly Furman, eds., *Women and language in literature and society*. New York: Praeger, 1980, pp. 3–25.

A reflective essay which notes both the useful tools linguistics provides for understanding language in society and literature, and the importance of understanding the context of use in the study of sexist language and sex-linked differences.

NICHOLS, PATRICIA C.

Linguistic options and choices for Black women in the rural South. In this volume.

Nichols used both participant-observation and quantitative sociolinguistic methods to study language patterns in two Black speech communities. She found that when occupational opportunities expand (along sex-segregated lines) men and women are encouraged to make different kinds of linguistic preparation to take advantage of them.

NICHOLS, PATRICIA C.

Women in their speech communities. In Sally McConnell-Ginet, Ruth Borker, and Nelly Furman, eds., *Women and language in literature and society*. New York: Praeger, 1980, pp. 140–49.

Drawing upon sociolinguistic studies of women in three cultures, Nichols aruges that, while in each community the women spoke differently than men did, the specific contrasts depend upon the roles, educational experiences, and activities of the women and men in their speech communities.

RAPP, RAYNA.

Review essay: Anthropology. *Signs*, 4 (1979), 497–513.

While not focusing on verbal interaction, Rapp's review of feminist research in anthropology mentions work done on the domestic strategies of women in several cultures, and discusses the interaction of gender and class stratification. Gender "status" is not expressed similarly among cultures anthropologists have grouped as similar.

ROSALDO, M. Z.

The use and abuse of anthropology: Reflections on feminism and cross-cultural understanding. *Signs*, 5 (1980), 389–417.

In this provocative article Rosaldo argues against the tendency of feminists, as well as traditionalists, to think of gender as a unitary, almost primordial fact; instead, gender should be understood as a product of social forms and modes of thought.

SILVERMAN, ELLEN-MARIE.

Women and men who stutter: Presentation of self. Paper prepared for the 9th World Congress of Sociology, Uppsala, Sweden, 1978.

Silverman found that teachers and parents usually consider stuttering in boys to be more of a problem than stuttering in girls; the concern of adults may exacerbate stuttering problems. Stereotypes and "sex-appropriate" expectations may help account for the sex ratio of approximately four males to each female who stutters, and for the greater stigma attached to stuttering for men than for women speakers.

THORNE, BARRIE.

Gender . . .How is it best conceptualized? Paper given at meeting of the American Sociological Association, San Francisco, 1978.

A critical assessment of two frameworks often used to study gender in face-to-face interaction: the search for individual sex differences (which neglects similarities, mistakes description for explanation, and ignores social context); and the notion of "role" (as in "sex roles") which leads to misconceptualization and obscures social relationships. Thorne encourages attention to group behavior, interactive processes, and a sense of context and situation.

TRUDGILL, PETER.

Sex, covert prestige, and linguistic changes in the urban British English of Norwich. *Language in Society*, 1 (1972), 179–95. Reprinted in Barrie Thorne and Nancy Henley, eds., *Language and sex: Difference and dominance.* Rowley, Mass.: Newbury House, 1975, pp. 88–104.

Among speakers of urban [British] English in Norwich, women, allowing for other variables such as age, education, and social class, use "standard" language more than do men. Trudgill speculates that because of their subordinate social position women need to signal their status linguistically. He suggests that men value non-standard speech as a signal of masculinity and group solidarity.

VALIAN, VIRGINIA.

Linguistics and feminism. In Mary Vetterling-Braggin, Frederick A. Elliston, and Jane English, eds., *Feminism and philosophy.* Totowa, N.J.: Littlefield, Adams 1977, pp. 154–66.

This critique of Robin Lakoff's essay on language and sex ("Language and Woman's Place") concludes that linguists do not have special political expertise to guide women in making decisions about oppression; that Lakoff's analysis of linguistic and social change is in error; and that the assumption that women's language usage is somehow inferior is based on sexist values.

WALKER, BARBARA A. AND SANDRA HERROD.

An empirical approach to the critique of sex bias in communication research. Paper for gender and language seminar, Speech Communication Assoc. convention, San Antonio, Texas, Nov. 1979.

Reviewing previous research the authors note that most studies in communication journals prior to 1977 did not report sex of participants. Of those that did, studies involving all males outnumbered those using all females by three to one. Of more than 2,000 articles in communication journals over a ten-year period, 74% were by males, 14% by females, 9% co-authored by males and females; the rest could not be clearly categorized by authors' names.

YERKOVICH, SALLY.

Gossiping as a way of speaking. *Journal of Communication,* 27, no. 1 (1977), 192–96.

An account of gossiping as a process, a form of sociable interaction built upon the strategic management of information and shared evaluative categories. "[T]he content of the talk is not as important as the interaction which the talking supports."

Also see: I-A: Smith; III-B: O'Barr and Atkins; III-D: Johnson and Goodchilds; VI-C: Halliday.

B.   Word Choice and Syntactic Usage

ANSHEN, FRANK.

Sex and obscenity at Stony Brook. Unpublished paper, State Univ. of New York at Stony Brook, 1974 [summarized in Frank, Sec. I-A].

College students recorded all obscenities they heard over a period of three weeks; men used 64.8% and women 35.2% of the obscenities recorded. Sex of hearer was more important than sex of speaker in determining choice of obscenity. Both sexes, but especially men, were more likely to swear in single-sex groups; men seemed to switch to weaker obscenities in mixed company, while women switched to stronger words.

BAILEY, LEE ANN AND LENORA A. TIMM.

More on women's—and men's—expletives. *Anthropological Linguistics*, 18 (1976), 438–49.

College students were asked to indicate which expletives they might use if faced with each of 20 briefly described situations. Women chose fewer strong expletives than men, and women ages 31 to 34 used more strong expletives than did women in their twenties.

BAUMANN, MARIE.

Two features of women's speech? In Betty Lou Dubois and Isabel Crouch, eds., *The sociology of the languages of American women*. San Antonio, Texas: Trinity Univ., 1976, pp. 33–40.

Analysis of tapes of conversations in three settings found 20 examples of tag questions and qualifying prefatory statements, 9 spoken by women, and 11 by men. Both features *can* be used to maintain the flow of conversation. Researchers need to study actual speech and to note the functions of speech features before making generalizations about "women's speech."

BENTZ, JANET MILLS.

Female jargon: Women's language in man's place. Paper given at the Western Social Science Assoc. convention, Albuquerque, N. M., April 1980.

Current literature on women in management provides a dictionary of male jargon. There is also a female vernacular—associated with childrearing, homemaking, and cooking—which men pick up in the home and speak in the male world of business and politics: e.g., "tied to his mother's apron strings"; "baby" (one's invention or project); "child's play"; "get the cobwebs out"; "hang your dirty linen in public"; "doormat"; "set one's house in order"; and "half-baked."

BRUNER, EDWARD M. AND JANE PAIGE KELSO.

Gender differences in graffiti: A semiotic perspective. In Cheris Kramarae, ed., *The voices and words of women and men*. Oxford: Pergamon Press, 1980, pp. 239–52. Also *Women's Studies International Quarterly*, 3, no. 2/3 (1980), 239–52.

Male and female restroom graffiti, analyzed from a semiotic point of view as structures of meaning, illuminate basic societal processes. There are fundamental gender differences in graffiti which can be understood as a political discourse about the distribution of power in our society.

CROSBY, FAYE, AND LINDA NYQUIST.

The female register: An empirical study of Lakoff's hypotheses. *Language in Society*, 6 (1977), 313–22.

Use of stereotypical "female register" speech characteristics (expressive, polite, and non-assertive) was studied in women's and men's speech in a lab setting, at a police station, and at an information booth. Women used more "female register" than men did in the first two settings but not in the third. The authors recommend that researchers use a role differentiation analysis to explore and explain characteristics of women's and men's speech in our culture.

CZAJKOWSKI, SUSAN M.

Role, gender and the feminine syntactic style. Unpublished M.A. thesis, Dept. of Psychology, Univ. of Maryland, College Park. 1981.

Subjects in same and mixed-sex dyads interacted in both an unstructured and a counseling situation, assigned to roles of counselor or client. The data were coded for frequency of intensifiers, tags, modal constructions, and imperatives in question form. Overall, there was only one significant sex difference: men used more declarative tag questions. When in the roles of counselor and client, subjects used more question tag questions, future modal constructions, and imperatives in question form than when in the unstructured situation.

DUBOIS, BETTY LOU AND ISABEL CROUCH.

The question of tag questions in women's speech: They don't really use more of them, do they? *Language in Society*, 4 (1975), 289–94.

Men but not women were heard to use tag questions in tape recordings of interactions at a small academic conference. The authors contrast the results of their study with Robin Lakoff's claim that women use more tag questions and that such use expresses insecurity.

EBLE, CONNIE C.

Etiquette books as linguistic authority. In Peter Reich, ed., *LACUS Forum II* (1975). Columbia, S.C.: Hornbeam Press, 1976, pp. 468–75.

Eble provides a study of the advice (which is addressed particularly to women) in courtesy/etiquette books in America from colonial times to World War I. Women should speak softly and infrequently.

FOLB, EDITH A.

Runnin' down some lines: The language and culture of Black teenagers. Cambridge, Mass.: Harvard Univ. Press, 1980.

Drawing on observations and interviews with more than 250 Black teenagers in South Central Los Angeles, Folb describes name terms, verbal strategies for social control, performances, and special vocabularies. Young men have far more derogatory than praising terms for women (e.g., describing them as dissected body parts and pieces of meat); women evaluate men with a wider range of desirable qualities. Males use more vernacular expressions, and use some terms almost exclusively (e.g., fight and gang expressions); some expressions (relating to giving birth, childrearing, female hygiene and appearance) are used almost exclusively by women. [*Also see* Folb, Sec. VI-A-1; VI-A-2.]

GALLAHORN, GEORGE E.

The use of taboo words by psychiatric ward personnel. *Psychiatry*, 34 (1970), 309–21.

Gallahorn recorded the use of taboo words in staff meetings on a psychiatric ward over six months. The average number of taboo words which ward personnel used was not related to their formal status. Only two genital words *(screw, whore)* were said by both sexes; the remaining 11 words were used exclusively either by men *(balls, hot pants, laid, piece of ass)* or by women *(broad, come, fuck, pimp, shack up, slut, wet dream)*. Curses and anal words were used similarly by both sexes.

GARCIA, GILBERT NARRO AND SUSAN F. FROSCH.

Sex, color and money: Who's perceiving what? Or, men and women: Where did all the differences go to? In Betty Lou Dubois and Isabel Crouch, eds., *The sociology of the languages of American women.* San Antonio, Texas: Trinity Univ., 1976, pp. 63–71.

The authors asked 40 Black, Anglo, and Spanish-speaking adults, ages 18 to 65, to describe magazine pictures of a "feminine" room and a "masculine" outdoor scene. There were no differences by ethnic group and no sex differences in choice of adjectives. Men used more spatial terms, and women more terms of pattern and color; each group provided more detail in describing the picture stereotyped for their sex.

GILLEY, HOYT MELVYN AND COLLIER STEPHEN SUMMERS.

Sex differences in the use of hostile verbs. *Journal of Psychology*, 76 (1970), 33–37.

Fifty males and 50 females were asked to make up sentences from a given pronoun and a given verb. Male subjects used hostile verbs at a greater average frequency than did female subjects.

GLESER, GOLDINE C., LOUIS A. GOTTSCHALK, AND JOHN WATKINS.

The relationship of sex and intelligence to choice of words: A normative study of verbal behavior. *Journal of Clinical Psychiatry*, 15 (1959), 182–91.

Plant employees were asked to talk for five minutes about an experience of theirs. Women used a higher percentage of words implying feeling, emotion, and motivation, made more references to self, and used more auxiliary words and negations. The men used a greater percentage of words implying time, space, or quantity and a greater percentage of words referring to destructive action.

HAAS, ADELAIDE.

Male and female spoken language differences: Stereotypes and evidence. *Psychological Bulletin,* 86 (1979). 616–26.

This review presents stereotypes of sex differences in usage and compares them with the then available empirical evidence. [*Also see:* Haas, Sec. I.]

HALABY, R. AND D. LONG.

Future shout: Name calling in the future. *Maledicta: The International Journal of Verbal Aggression,* 3 (1979), 61–68.

A survey of college students' attitudes toward use of dirty words in different contexts found that men used more profane words when with other men, and women used more when with other women.

HARTMAN, MARYANN.

A descriptive study of the language of men and women born in Maine around 1900 as it reflects the Lakoff hypotheses in *Language and woman's place.* In Betty Lou Dubois and Isabel Crouch, eds., *The sociology of the languages of American women.* San Antonio, Texas: Trinity Univ., 1976, pp. 81–90.

A descriptive case study method was used to test Robin Lakoff's hypotheses that there is a traditional language used by women, that language reflects women's place in society, and that language is changing. Transcripts of interviews with 28 men and women provide some support for the hypotheses.

HARTMAN, MARYANN.

Sex roles and language. Paper given at the 9th World Congress of Sociology, Uppsala, Sweden, 1978.

Interviewers asked women and men, aged 74–94 and 25–31, questions about their lives and opinions. The language used by the older women and the language used to talk about them indicated that only the younger women expected women to function in "serious" activities outside the home. The older women's language was more hesitant, tentative, flowery, and polite than that of any other group. The speech of the younger men was more hesitant and unsure than that of older men.

HAYES, JOSEPH J.

Gayspeak. *The Quarterly Journal of Speech,* 62 (1976), 256–66. Reprinted in James W. Chesebro, ed., *Gayspeak: Gay male and lesbian communication.* New York: Pilgrim Press, 1981, pp. 45–57, followed by James Darsey, Gayspeak: A response, pp. 58–67.

An analysis of lexicon, usages, imagery, and rhetoric of language used in gay male subcultures—in secret, social, and radical activist settings. In a response, James Darsey extends Hayes's analysis, emphasizing historical and cultural contexts of gay male speech.

HOPPER, ROBERT, MARK L. KNAPP, AND LOREL SCOTT.

Couples' personal idioms: Exploring intimate talk. *Journal of Communication,* 31 (1981), 23–33.

Married women and men were interviewed about personal idioms used with their partners. Men defined the nicknames they used for their wives as terms of endearment, but wives perceived them as insults or criticism. Both sexes credited men with originating the majority of idioms (or perhaps male creations "stuck").

JAY, TIMOTHY B.

Sex roles and dirty word usage: A review of the literature and a reply to Haas. *Psychological Bulletin,* 88 (1980), 614–21.

A review of empirical research on sex differences and similarities in the use of profanity and obscenity, including experiments exploring frequency of usage, types of words used, recognition time, and memory; the use of jokes, storytelling, insults; and word-rating studies. Jay argues for more attention to the characteristics of speakers and listeners, setting, and intent of message.

JOHNSON, FERN L. AND MARLENE G. FINE.

The "vision" of obscenity: Sex differences in victimizing and victimization. Paper given at the Speech Communication Assoc. convention, New York, Nov. 1980.

Self-report data indicate that women are much more likely than are men to be reticent about using obscenities that denote sexual acts or anatomy. The authors argue that women's use of obscenity is dangerous since it is a language that victimizes women. They quote Mary Daly (*Gyn/Ecology,* p. 323): "Exorcising this invasive presence [of obscenities] requires acknowledging its existence and refusing to shuffle . . . ."

KUTNER, N. G. AND D. BROGAN.

An investigation of sex-related slang vocabulary and sex-role orientation among male and female university students. *Journal of Marriage and the Family,* 36 (1974), 474–84.

When asked to list slang expressions for sex-related words, men listed more words than women did, and the men used more imagery involving sexual exploitation.

LAKOFF, ROBIN TOLMACH.

Women's language. In Douglas Butturff and Edmund L. Epstein, eds., *Women's language and style.* Akron, Ohio: L & S Books, 1978, pp. 139–58.

Women's speech style is discussed both as an illustration of how linguistic forms and behavior normally coincide and as an instance of conflict between an external set of expectations and internal coherency.

LAPADAT, JUDY AND MAUREEN SEESAHAI.

Male versus female codes in informal contexts. *Sociolinguistics Newsletter,* 8 (Fall 1978), 7–8.

In all-male and all-female group conversations in a university dorm women used five times more intensifiers, more indirect imperatives, and fewer tag questions than men.

MANBER, MICHELE R.

Sex differences in perceived status as reflected in linguistic style. Unpublished manuscript. San Francisco State Univ., 1976.

Conversations of mixed and same-sex pairs were taped in a lab and frequency counts were compiled for questions, *mm hmm's,* other types of agreements, hedges, and number of words. (Tag questions were not analyzed because only one was used.) The only significant differences found: in same-sex groups females were more unassertive in their politeness, using more *mm hmm's,* but fewer other types of agreements such as *That's right,* and *Okay.* Males, when politely supportive, were able to be more assertive as well (using *Yeah,* and *I think*).

MOREAU, NOËLLE BISSERET.

Power relationships at work in language: The hidden referent and class/sex identity. In Cheris Kramarae, Muriel Schulz and William O'Barr, eds., *Language and power.* Los Angeles, Calif.: Sage, in press.

Students of the humanities expressing their views on their occupational choice defined themselves according to whether they came from the dominated or the dominant class and whether they are men or women. Women, whatever their class, define themselves as part of a category, different from men (e.g., "I chose it because it's good pay for a woman"). Men do not speak of their masculine status.

NELSON, EDWARD A. AND EDWARD ROSENBAUM.

Language patterns within the youth subculture: Development of slang vocabularies. *Merrill-Palmer Quarterly,* 18 (1972), 273–85.

One thousand males and 916 females in grades 7 to 12 were asked to list slang terms for various topics. Males listed more terms for "money"; and "autos and motorbikes"; females, more terms for "clothes, styles and appearances"; "boys"; "a popular person"; and "an unpopular person". There was some variation by grade level and by school.

NICHOLS, PATRICIA C.

Black women in the rural south: Conservative and innovative. In Betty Lou Dubois and Isabel Crouch, eds., *The sociology of the languages of American women*. San Antonio, Texas: Trinity Univ., 1976, pp. 103–14. A revised version is included in this volume.

While some studies have shown women using more innovative linguistic forms than men use, others have shown women using more conservative (standard-prestige) forms than men use. The apparent paradox can be resolved by an examination of the methodology used in the studies. A study of the language varieties spoken by Black residents of a river island illustrates the importance of considering the life experiences of both women and men in each community.

O'BARR, WILLIAM.

Speech styles in the courtroom. Chapter 5 of *Linguistic evidence: Language, power, and strategy in the courtroom*. New York: Academic Press, 1982, pp. 61–91.

"Powerful" and "powerless" speech (based on Robin Lakoff's notions of "women's language") in the courtroom were found to be more closely associated with social class, educational background, and previous courtroom experience than with gender.

OLIVER, MARION M. AND JOAN RUBIN.

The use of expletives by some American women. *Anthropological Linguistics*, 17 (1975), 191–97.

On questionnaires filled out by white, upper-middle-class, college-educated women, ages 40–55, single women reported using expletives more often than did married women. Women "working on being liberated" reported frequent use of expletives.

ÖSTMAN, JAN-OLA.

You know: A discourse-functional approach. In the series *Pragmatics and beyond*. Amsterdam: John Benjamins, in press.

An initial study indicates that *you know* tends to be used more by women than by men. Women appear to use *you know* to qualify whole speech acts or information units, while men seem to use it more to modify phrases or words, i.e., to serve as a lexical hedge. Östman notes that in future studies it will be necessary to control for sex of both speaker and addressee.

POOLE, MILLICENT.

Social class, sex and linguistic coding. *Language and Speech* 22, part 1 (1979), 49–67.

Working with Bernstein's "elaborated" and "restricted" codes theory, Poole analyzed individual structured interviews with 96 16-year-olds, found sex differences with and between social classes, and points to the importance of considering both social class and sex dimensions simultaneously.

SANDERS, JANET S. AND WILLIAM L. ROBINSON.

Talking and not talking about sex: Male and female vocabularies. *Journal of Communication,* 29, no. 2 (1979), 22–30.

College students completing an anonymous questionnaire indicated they use gender-specific vocabularies in sexual communication. Females were more likely to use clinical and impersonal terms; males, more slang terms.

SAUSE, EDWIN F.

Computer content analysis of sex differences in the language of children. *Journal of Psycholinguistic Research,* 5 (1976), 311–24.

Kindergarten children were asked to talk about a block and a toy fire engine. A computer analysis of the words (out of context) leads Sause to conclude that boys were verbally more aggressive and showed a greater interest in space, quantity, and physical movement than did the girls, who were more likely than the boys to make references to females and to use female pronouns. The girls appeared to be shyer with the interviewer. [The sex of the interviewer (male) and the type of the toys chosen may have been (unmentioned) factors in the study results.]

SHAW, MARCIA.

Observed variations in language behavior in female and male interviewers and applicants. Unpublished manuscript, Oregon State Univ., Corvallis, n.d..

Tapes of students interviewing and being interviewed (a class assignment) were transcribed and put into machine-readable form. Measurements included total words, number of turns, self-referents, other referents, vocalized filler, questions, topic shifts. None of the measurements discriminated between talk of females and males, but women (and not men) were found to exhibit a different communication style in the roles of interviewer and interviewee. The specifics of a communication situation may have differential impact on women and men.

SHIMANOFF, SUSAN B.

Investigating politeness. In Elinor O. Keenan and Dina Bennet, eds., *Discourse across time and space.* Los Angeles: Univ. of Southern California, 1977, pp. 213–41.

The 165 conversational turns recorded at a receptionist's desk were coded for politeness, using a procedure proposed by Brown and Levinson. [*See* Sec. V-A.] Women and men were equally, although differentially, polite. For example, women were more likely to use positive features (which support the hearer) and men to use negative politeness features (which seek to minimize imposition).

STECKLER, NICOLE A. AND WILLIAM E. COOPER.

Sex differences in color naming of unisex apparel. *Anthropological Linguistics,* 22 (1980), 373–81.

To test Lakoff's hypothesis that women use more color terms than men, 18 men and 18 women college students were asked to write the names of colors of 20 different sweaters. Women used more specific color terms than men; men used significantly more saturation adjectives and more combinations of basic color terms.

SWACKER, MAJORIE.

The sex of the speaker as a sociolinguistic variable. In Barrie Thorne and Nancy Henley, eds., *Language and sex: Difference and dominance.* Rowley, Mass.: Newbury House, 1975, pp. 76–83.

Men and women were separately shown pictures and asked to describe what they saw, taking as much time as needed. The female mean time for all three descriptions was 3.17 minutes, and for males was 13.0 minutes; there were no significant sex differences in the speed of the discourse (words per minute). Women used more conjunctions, and men, more interjections to mark topic shifts.

WALSH, ROBERT AND WILBERT LEONARD.

Usage of terms for sexual intercourse by men and women. *Archives of Sexual Behavior,* 3 (1974), 373–76.

The male undergraduates listed more and somewhat different words than did the females when asked to name synonyms for sexual intercourse.

WARSHAY, DIANA WORTMAN, AND LEON H. WARSHAY.

The use of obscenity in the subordination of women. Paper given at Midwest Sociological Society, Omaha, Nebraska, April 1978.

Reviewing studies on terms which insult, the authors conclude that obscenity is most likely to occur when males (especially lower status, politically radical, and/or non-religious males under stress) gather in male-type physical activities. Men have a large obscene vocabulary which they use to control women—to exclude and to force compliance.

WOOD, MARION.

The influence of sex and knowledge of communication effectiveness on spontaneous speech. *Word,* 22, no. 1/2/3 (1966), 112–37.

An experimental study in which speakers described photographs to unseen listeners. Subjects were given different sets of "pseudofeedback" about success and failure. Men tended to use more words per utterance, and their length of verbal output (but not women's length) increased under conditions of "ineffective communication" and leveled off under conditions of "successful communication." Wood argues that men used an "empirical" and women a "creative" style of speech.

ZIMIN, SUSAN.

Sex and politeness: Factors in first- and second-language use. *International Journal of the Sociology of Language,* 27 (1981), 35–58.

Three groups of university students (foreign students in two levels of English courses, and native American English speakers) were required to respond to written role-play situations. Judges rated responses on a five-point scale with Extremely Deferent and Barely Deferent poles. Sex of addressee (but not sex of speaker) was a relevant variable with women addressees spoken to with more deference than were male addressees. The author stresses the importance of context for future studies of politeness.

Also see: I-A: Jespersen; Lakoff; II-E: Ernster; III-A: Bradley; III-B: Kramer ("Folklinguistics"); O'Barr and Atkins; IV-B: Baumann; V-A: Goodwin.

C. Phonetic Variants

ANSHEN, FRANK.

Speech variation among Negroes in a small southern community. Unpublished Ph.D. dissertation, New York Univ., 1969.

Anshen studied phonological variables (e.g., postvocalic *r;* pronunciation of *th* as in *this;* the suffix *-in* vs. *-ing*) in the Black population of Hillsboro, N.C. Among his findings: women use fewer stigmatized forms than men, and, compared with men, women are more sensitive to the prestige pattern.

CHESHIRE, JENNY.

Present tense verbs in Reading [England] English. In Peter Trudgill, ed., *Sociolinguistic patterns in British English*. London: Edward Arnold, 1978, pp. 52–68.

Adolescents (12 girls and 13 boys) were recorded in playgrounds, and in more formal settings. At the playgrounds the girls used non-standard verb forms with approximately the same frequency as the boys did. In the more formal situation, however, the girls modified their speech more sharply toward standard English usage than the boys did.

FASOLD, RALPH W.

A sociolinguistic study of the pronunciation of three vowels in Detroit speech. (mimeo) Washington, D.C.: Center for Applied Linguistics, 1968.

Using data from the Detroit Dialect Study, Fasold found that the fronting of three vowels, /æ/, /a/, and /ɔ/, was more characteristic of lower-middle-class speakers than of other speakers. He also found that, especially in the lower middle class, women outscored men in the fronting of all three vowels. Younger informants predominated in fronting these vowels.

FISCHER, JOHN L.

Social influences on the choice of a linguistic varient. *Word,* 14 (1958), 47–56. Reprinted in Dell Hymes, ed., *Language in culture and society.* New York: Harper & Row, 1964, pp. 483–88.

Analyzing recorded interviews with 24 children (half of each sex, ages 3–10) in a semi-rural New England village, Fischer found girls used *-ing* much more frequently, while more boys used *-in* as verb endings. There was a slight tendency for *-ing* to be associated with higher socioeconomic status. Personality was also a factor; a boy regarded as a "model" used the *-ing* ending almost exclusively.

HARTFORD, BEVERLY S.

Phonological differences in the English of adolescent Chicanas and Chicanos. In Betty Lou Dubois and Isabel Crouch, eds., *The sociology of the languages of American women.* San Antonio, Texas: Trinity Univ., 1976, pp. 73–80.

Hartford compares the English usage of female and male Chicano/a adolescents to determine which sex adapts prestige forms more readily. She found that even in a second language, girls are more likely than boys to use forms associated with middle-class native speakers. Those forms are also associated with upward mobility.

LABOV, WILLIAM.

Sociolinguistic patterns. Philadelphia: Univ. of Pennsylvania Press, 1972, pp. 243, 301–04.

In careful speech women use fewer stigmatized forms than men and are more sensitive than men to prestige patterns. There are implications for the role of women in furthering linguistic change. Some studies show that women use the most advanced forms in their casual speech and the most "correct" forms in their formal speech. Women do not, however, always lead in the course of linguistic change. [*See* Nichols, Sec. IV-B.]

LEVINE, LEWIS AND HARRY J. CROCKETT, JR.

Modal and modish pronunciation: Some sex differences in speech. In William C. McCormack and Stephen A. Wurm, eds., *Language and society: Anthropological issues.* The Hague: Mouton, 1979, pp. 207–20.

Thirty North Carolina speakers were asked to pronounce a set of words. The most frequent pronunciations were identified. Men, particularly those with relatively few years of formal education, were more consistent in pronunciation. The men appeared to be responding more to localized linguistic pressures, the women to more general, wider—and less clear—pressures.

LEVINE, LEWIS AND HARRY J. CROCKETT, JR.

Speech variation in a Piedmont Community: Postvocalic *r.* In Stanley Lieberson, ed., *Explorations in sociolinguistics.* The Hague: Mouton, 1966, pp. 76–98.

White females were more likely than white males to pronounce the postvocalic *r* (i.e., to use the more "correct" form), as were those of higher education, those in prestigeful occupations, newer community residents, and younger people. These groups may "spearhead" linguistic change, as the community shifts to the national norm.

MILROY, LESLIE.

Language and social networks. Baltimore: Univ. Park Press, 1980.

An empirical study of relationships between social networks, status, and linguistic variables among 46 (half women, half men) residents of three neighborhoods in working-class Belfast, Ireland. Sex differences in the use of a phonetic variant were greatest in neighborhoods with the densest networks. Some features of language appear to serve as sex markers, others as network markers for age groups.

SHUY, ROGER W., WALTER A. WOLFRAM, AND WILLIAM K. RILEY.

Linguistic correlates of social stratification in Detroit speech. Final Report, Project 6-2347. Washington, D.C.: U.S. Office of Education, 1967.

This study of the speech of 700 randomly selected Detroit residents correlated linguistic and social variables, including sex. With some variation by class, women showed greater sensitivity than men to multiple negation and pronominal apposition (as in "my brother *he* went to the park"). Males had a greater tendency to use nasalized vowels, e.g., /mæ̃/ for *man*, and to use -*in* rather than -*ing*.

Wolfram, WALTER A.

A sociolinguistic description of Detroit Negro speech. Washington, D.C.: Center for Applied Linguistics, 1969.

Wolfram found that within each social class, Black females approximated the standard English norm more than males. Females of all classes had fewer *f, t,* or Ø realizations of *th* (as in *tooth*); females more often pronounced final consonant clusters (as in *friend*) and the postvocalic *r* (as in *car*).

D.   Suprasegmentals

1.   General

ADDINGTON, DAVID W.

The effect of vocal variations on ratings of source credibility. *Speech Monographs,* 38 (1971), 242– 47.

In an empirical study utilizing tape-recorded messages of specially trained speakers, Addington found that vocal characteristics did not differentially affect the credibility of male and female speakers. These findings seemingly conflict with his earlier study [*see* Sec. III-C] which deals with perceived personality of speakers.

ARONOVITCH, CHARLES D.

The voice of personality: Stereotyped judgments and their relation to voice quality and sex of speaker. *Journal of Social Psychology,* 99 (1976), 207–20.

College raters used different cues to make judgments about the personality characteristics of female and male voices. While variation in rate was an important cue used to judge speakers of both sexes, the male speakers were assigned particular personality traits on the basis of the degree of variability of pitch and loudness while females were assigned particular personality traits on the basis of the average pitch and loudness. Aronovitch suggests that if men are assumed to be more stable, then it is the degree of men's variability that gives special information. Both women and men generally agreed in their perceptions of personalities based on voice cues.

BATSTONE, SUSAN AND SEPPO K. TUOMI.

Perceptual characteristics of female voices. *Language and Speech,* 24, part 2 (1981), 111–23.

Undergraduate students listened to the voices of 30 young adult females and rated vocal features using the semantic differential method. Listeners identified two groups of characteristics: (1) "passive" characteristics such as soft, gentle, sweet, and feminine; and (2) "active" characteristics such as lively, colorful, interesting, and sexy. The female listeners found the "active" characteristics more salient while the male listeners preferred the "passive" characteristics.

CRYSTAL, D.

Prosodic and paralinguistic correlates of social categories. In Edwin Ardener, ed., *Social anthropology and language.* London: Tavistock, 1971, pp. 185–206.

Crystal claims that non-segmental phonology (e.g., pitch, loudness, qualities of voices) variation is "one of the main ways of establishing the identity of social groups in speech"; non-segmental features have been found to correlate with sex, age, status, occupation, and speech genres. *Responses* to non-segmental vocal effects can be a valuable part of a description; for example, in Mohave the breaking of the male voice in adolescence is not considered an important or relevant indication of puberty, whereas in English it is.

LAVER, JOHN D. M.

Voice quality and indexical information. *British Journal of Disorders of Communication,* 33 (1968), 43–54.

Laver outlines a descriptive model of voice quality (which is determined by anatomy and voluntary muscular "setting," and includes variation in phonation type, pitch range, and loudness range of laryngeal setting, and supralaryngeal modifications, such as nasalization). Voice quality is described as an index to gender, psychological, and social characteristics of the speaker.

SACHS, JACQUELINE.

Cues to the identification of sex in children's speech. In Barrie Thorne and Nancy Henley, eds., *Language and sex: Difference and dominance.* Rowley, Mass.: Newbury House, 1975, pp. 152–71.

The research reported in this paper explores possible cues used by judges who can identify the sex of prepubertal boys and girls. Beyond the phonetic aspects of voices, normal sentences carry considerable information about the sex of the speaker.

SACHS, JACQUELINE, PHILIP LIEBERMAN, AND DONNA ERICKSON.

Anatomical and cultural determinants of male and female speech. In Roger W. Shuy and Ralph W. Fasold, eds., *Language attitudes: Current trends and prospects.* Washington, D.C.: Georgetown Univ. Press, 1973, pp. 74–84.

The authors studied pre-adolescent children (14 boys and 12 girls between ages 4 and 14) with no obvious anatomical basis for sex differences in formant frequencies; adult judges listened to tapes of their voices and were able reliably to identify the sex of the speakers. The paper suggests that pitch may not be totally determined by anatomical structure, but also by learned behavior. Adult men may tend to talk as though they are bigger, and women as though they are smaller, than they actually are.

Also see: III-C: Lass, Mertz, and Kimmel; IV-C: Fasold.

2. Pitch/Accent

AUSTIN, WILLIAM M.

Some social aspects of paralanguage. *Canadian Journal of Linguistics*, 11 (1965), 31–39.

In our culture little boys use nasal intonation. Since nasality is considered "tough" and "vulgar" it is somewhat discouraged by adults, and "gentlemanly" little boys tend to be oral. A little girl's voice is composed of high pitch and orality, which convey innocence, helplessness, and regression. Derogatory imitation, "one of the most infuriating acts of aggression," is stronger when a male or female imitates a male by using stereotypical female vocalization than vice versa.

LIEBERMAN, PHILIP.

Intonation, perception, and language. Cambridge, Mass.: MIT Press, 1967, pp. 44–45.

Lieberman cites a study of the vocalizations of a 10-month-old boy and a 13-month-old girl (recorded under different conditions). The average fundamental frequency of their babbling was lower when they were "talking" with their father than when they were "talking" with their mother, which suggests that intonation patterns may vary with the sex spoken to.

MATTINGLY, IGNATIUS G.

Speaker variation and vocal-tract size. Paper given at Acoustical Society of America, 1966. Abstract in *Journal of the Acoustical Society of America,* 39 (1966), 1219.

The separation between male and female distributions for some vowel formants was much sharper than variation in individual vocal-tract size could reasonably explain. The author concludes: "The variation must be stylistic, not physical; and the differences between male and female formant values, though doubtless related to typical male and female vocal-tract size, is probably a linguistic convention."

Also see: III-C: Elyan, Smith, Giles, and Bourhis; IV-D-1: Sachs; Sec. IV-E-1: Rousey and Moriarty.

3. Intonation

BREND, RUTH M.

Male-female intonation patterns in American English. *Proceedings of the 7th International Congress of Phonetic Sciences, 1971,* pp. 866–70. Reprinted in Barrie Thorne and Nancy Henley, eds., *Language and sex: Difference and dominance.* Rowley, Mass.: Newbury House, 1975, pp. 84–87.

Certain patterns are used predominantly by women: e.g., the "surprise" patterns of high-low down-glides ('Oh 'that's 'awful!); the "request confirmation" pattern (You 'do!); the hesitation pattern (Well, I 'studied . . .); and the "polite, cheerful" pattern (Are you 'coming?). Most men have only three contrastive levels of intonation, while many women have four. The methodology of the study is not discussed.

EDELSKY, CAROLE.

Question intonation and sex roles. *Language and Society,* 8 (1979), 15–32.

Male and female interviewers asked people a question to which they knew the answer. The most frequently used intonation pattern was the falling terminal contour. A rise-fall-rise contour was more often used when women were responding to a female interviewer. In this case, the speakers might be signaling a desire for a longer exchange.

ELYAN, OLWEN H.

Sex differences in speech style. Paper presented at 1st European Conference on sex role stereotyping. Cardiff, South Wales, July 1977.

Perceptions of sex-related differences are more central to the structure of social relationships than absolute differences. Therefore acoustic analyses which examine prosodic features in isolation rather than intonation patterns as a whole are not as valuable as linguistic analysis or evaluations by listeners. Analyzing taped monologues, Elyan found that males used a higher percentage of falls than did females, who used more equal proportions of rising and falling tones.

KEY, MARY RITCHIE.

Linguistic behavior of male and female. *Linguistics,* 88 (August 1972), 15–31.

One of Key's students, in an exploratory experiment, listened to children in the 3rd, 4th, and 5th grades retell a story. "The girls spoke with very expressive intonation, and the boys toned down the intonational features, even to the point of monotony, 'playing it cool'." [*Also see* in Sec. I-A.]

McCONNELL-GINET, SALLY.

Intonation in a man's world. *Signs,* 3 (1978), 541–59. A revised version is included in this volume.

A review and theoretical interpretation of research on gender and patterns of intonation noting the close link between intonation and gender attribution and display, speech strategies, issues of power and social control, and the androcentric nature of our hearing.

RICHARDS, DORIS M.

A comparative study of the intonation characteristics of young adult males and females. Unpublished dissertation, Case Western Reserve Univ., Cleveland, Ohio, Jan. 1975. (Available from Xerox Microfilms, Ann Arbor, MI. 48103.)

Females were more consistent in their inflection patterns from one sentence to another, and a greater percentage of them used rising inflection at the beginning; a greater percentage of males used falling inflection at the end. The inflection patterns described by linguists and others were not used consistently by the females and males studied.

Also see: I-A: Lakoff; IV-D-2: Lieberman.

4. Speech Intensity

COLEMAN, RALPH.

Male and female voice quality and its relationship to vowel formant frequencies. *Journal of Speech and Hearing Research,* 14 (1971), 565–77.

Speech samples, obtained from a group of adult males and females while they articulated the tone produced by a single-frequency electrolarynx, were played to a panel of listeners who were asked to determine the sex of each speaker. The judges were able to correctly identify the sex of the speakers 88% of the time. A distinct cue to speaker may be contained in the individual vocal tract resonances. [From author's abstract.]

MARKEL, NORMAN N., LAYNE D. PREBOR, AND JOHN F. BRANDT.

Bio-social factors in dyadic communication: Sex and speaking intensity. *Journal of Personality and Social Psychology,* 23 (1972), 11–13.

Male speakers spoke with greater intensity than females, and all subjects decreased intensity to the same-sex experimenter and increased intensity to the other-sex experimenter. These results are interpreted as participants showing greater affiliation to an experimenter of the same sex.

E.   Verbal Ability

1. General

DOWNING, JOHN.

Cultural expectations and sex differences in reading. In John R. Edwards, ed., *The social psychology of reading.* (Vol. 1 of *Language and literacy: An interdisciplinary monograph series for language professionals*), 1981, pp. 1–27.

In an extensive review of cross-cultural studies, Downing concludes: Differences in sex-related variations in reading attainments exist in many cultures, but the patterns of differences vary.

GARAI, JOSEF E. AND AMRAM SCHEINFELD.

Sex differences in mental and behavioral traits. *Genetic Psychology Monographs,* 77 (1968), 169–299.

Girls' earlier speech development, greater fluency (from 18 months on, girls surpass boys in sentence length and complexity), and greater language consciousness are related to earlier maturation of their speech organs, closer contact with mothers, greater interest in people, socialization to social responsiveness and compliance, and perhaps to genetic factors which produce more speech defects in boys (e.g., stuttering, poor articulation, and aphasia and dyslexia).

GUNDERSON, DORIS.

Sex differences in language and reading. *Language Arts,* 53, no. 3 (1976), 300–06.

This paper reviews research indicating a difference between girls and boys in the acquisition of language skills and in learning to read. Possible solutions and areas requiring further study are offered.

KLANN-DELIUS, GISELA.

Sex and language acquisition—Is there any influence? *Journal of Pragmatics*, 5 (1981), 1–25.

In this critical review of more than 150 studies, the author concludes that the stereotype of girls' verbal superiority can empirically neither be confirmed nor refuted and that the question may be wrongly put. Possible difference, not deficit, is the appropriate context for understanding the influence of sex on language acquisition. [*Also see* Klann-Delius, Sec. VII-C.]

LAMBERT, HELEN H.

Biology and equality: A perspective on sex differences. *Signs,* 4, no. 1 (1978), 97–117.

Biological sex differences are often a matter of degree rather than of absolute differences. Examining the scientific literature on observed differences between the sexes, including that of the differential lateralization of the cerebral hemispheres, Lambert concludes that we must be cautious about granting to biological differences "a special, [and] morally unjustified, value status." This special issue of *Signs* contains essays on the relationship of "natural" and "human" sciences and on the social values governing research questions and methodology. [*Also see* Vaid and Lambert, Sec. IV-F.]

LARMER, LARRY E. AND MARY KENNY BADAMI, eds.

Proceedings of the 2nd and 3rd conferences on communication, language, and gender [1979, 1980]. Madison, Wisc.: Univ. of Wisconsin—Extension, 1982.

The 25 papers include studies, either completed or proposed, of language and gender, critiques of theoretical and methodological approaches to studies, and sample pedagogical designs. Specific topics include critique of the Bem Sex-Role Inventory as tool for communication research, language and institutional change, stereotypes, conversational control, and ways to talk in the classroom about the label *homosexuality.* [Some of the essays are separately annotated.]

MACAULAY, RONALD K.

The myth of female superiority in language. *Journal of Child Language,* 5 (1978), 353–63.

After reviewing the literature on childhood sex differences in language, the author concludes that the findings are inconclusive and often self-contradictory; at present the only tenable position is that there are no significant differences between the sexes in linguistic ability.

MACCOBY, ELEANOR EMMONS AND CAROL NAGY JACKLIN.

The psychology of sex differences. Stanford, Calif.; Stanford Univ. Press, 1974.

In this informative and influential review of research (with an emphasis on young children), the authors conclude that firm sex-linked differences occur in only four areas: aggression (the only difference they believe is genetically governed), visual-spatial ability, mathematics, and verbal ability. They emphasize the mixed nature of findings on sex differences in verbal ability up to age 10 or 11, when girls begin to outscore boys in verbal performance.

NELSON, NICKOLA W.

Comprehension of spoken language by normal children as a function of speaking rate, sentence difficulty, and listener age and sex. *Child Development,* 47 (1976), 299–303.

The six-year-old females performed significantly better than did the six-year-old males, but differences between sexes at other age levels (7, 8, 9) were not significant.

PALMATIER, ROBERT A. AND GEORGE MCNINCH.

Source of gains in listening skill: Experimental or pre-test experience? *Journal of Communication,* 22 (March 1972), 70–76.

Eleventh grade students participated in a program of testing and training of note-taking skills and listening. Females made significantly greater gains than the males.

PLOMIN, R. AND T. T. FOCH.

Sex differences and individual differences. *Child Development,* 52 (1981), 383–85.

Measuring the size of group difference effects for published studies of verbal abilities, Plomin and Foch found that sex differences accounted for only 1% of the variance. They thus argue that knowing the sex of the child does not give us any information about the child's verbal ability.

ROSSITER, CHARLES M., Jr.

Sex of the speaker, sex of the listener, and listening comprehension. *The Journal of Communication,* 22 (March 1972), 64–69.

University students listened to, and then were tested on, 14 short, informative messages. There were no significant differences in listening comprehension between female and male listeners.

ROUSEY, CLYDE L. AND ALICE E. MORIARTY.

Diagnostic implications of speech sounds: The reflections of developmental conflict and trauma. Springfield, Ill.: Charles C Thomas, 1965.

Pitch which was "inappropriate for the sex of the child" was described as associated with a distorted sense of sexual identity. The authors recognize that the interpersonal factors involved in this speech task (an unusual speech event with an adult male examiner) may have influenced the evaluations.

STRAUCH, A. BARRY.

The development of sex differences in spatial and verbal abilities. Paper given at the American Psychological Assoc. meeting, Washington, D.C., Sept. 1976.

The visual and spatial ability test scores of males and females in three age groups from 6 to 16 were compared. The early female superiority in verbal ability disappeared by middle adolescence. The author suggests the results lend support to an argument of environmental differences to explain the decreasing female verbal ability scores.

THOMPSON, WAYNE N.

Quantitative research in public address and communication. New York: Random House, 1967.

This volume summarizes and evaluates early quantitative research on sex differences in public speaking, drawing mainly on research published in speech and communication journals. For each topic the author lists studies, with brief annotation, and then draws conclusions [which often claim more than the studies support].

Also see: VII-C: Harris; Klann-Delius; McCarthy.

2. Fluency

BROWNELL, WINIFRED AND DENNIS R. SMITH.

Communication patterns, sex, and length of verbalization in speech of four-year-old children. *Speech Monographs*, 40 (1973), 310–16.

Seventy-nine children in six Head Start centers were shown objects and asked to name them, to indicate which of the objects go together, and to tell why. Females produced significantly more speech across all conditions than did males.

CHERRY, LOUISE.

Teacher-child verbal interaction: An approach to the study of sex differences. In Barrie Thorne and Nancy Henley, eds., *Language and sex: Difference and dominance.* Rowley, Mass.: Newbury House, 1975, pp. 172–83.

Cherry recorded spontaneously occurrring conversations among four female preschool teachers and 38 children (16 girls, 22 boys) and looked at, among other factors, fluency as an interactive variable. She failed to find greater fluency (measured either by utterances or by turns per interaction) in teacher-girl interactions than in teacher-boy ones.

GILES, HOWARD AND JENNIFER A. GILES.

Comments on "Speech fluency fluctuations during the menstrual cycle." In Letters to the Editor, *Journal of Speech and Hearing Research*, 19 (1976), 187–88.

Answering Silverman and Silverman [*see* this section] who present evidence that the speech of women contains more disfluency at premenstruation than at ovulation, Giles and Giles argue that the findings are statistically insignificant, and lacking in interpretive justification.

MURDOCK, JOHNNY I. AND CATHERINE W. KONSKY.

An investigation of verbosity and sex-role expectations. *Women's Studies in Communication*, 5 (Fall 1982), 65-76.

College students listened to tape recordings of either a verbose female or a verbose male and evaluated the speakers. The study found no verbosity effects.

SILVERMAN, E. M. AND F. H. SILVERMAN.

Variability of stutterer speech disfluency: The menstrual cycle. *Perceptual and Motor Skills*, 38 (1974), 1037–38.
The findings of an empirical study "suggest that the speech disfluency of at least some stutterers may vary in a predictable manner during the menstrual cycle." [*Also see:* Giles and Giles, this section.]

SILVERMAN, ELLEN-MARIE AND CATHERINE H. ZIMMER.

> The fluency of women's speech. In Betty Lou Dubois and Isabel Crouch, eds., *The sociology of the languages of American women.* San Antonio, Texas: Trinity Univ., 1976, pp. 131–36.

Twenty female and male university students were compared on fluency levels, vocabularies and readiness of speech. Female subjects were found to be as fluent as male subjects, to wait longer before beginning to speak, and to use more silent pauses.

WARSHAY, DIANA W.

> Sex differences in language style. In Constantina Safilios-Rothschild, ed., *Toward a sociology of women.* Lexington, Mass.: Xerox College Pub., 1972, pp. 3–9.

Warshay analyzed samples of writing by 263 white, middle-class college students who described past events which were important to them. Compared with women, men wrote with less fluency, tended to refer to events in a verb (rather than a noun) phrase, and made more vague time references. Women referred more to others, and men to themselves.

WINITZ, HARRIS.

> Language skills of male and female kindergarten children. *Journal of Speech and Hearing Research,* 2 (1959), 377–86.

On most fluency measures and on measures of articulation and vocabulary there were no significant differences, girls and boys (about to enter kindergarten) showing superiority about equally. He takes up but dismisses the possibility that a reason for not obtaining significant differences was that the examiner was male.

Also see: III-C: Gall, Hobby, and Craik.

3.   Speech Disturbances

KIDD, KENNETH, JUDITH KIDD, AND MARY ANN RECORDS.

> The possible causes of the sex ratio in stuttering and its implications. *Journal of Fluency Disorders,* 3 (1978), 13–23.

Research consistently documents a higher incidence of stuttering in males than in females. Sampling biases, incomplete reporting, social role differences, and a combination of environmental and genetic elements are examined as possible causes. The authors suggest that gene/environmental interaction is the most useful hypothesis.

McCARTHY, DOROTHEA.

> Some possible explanations of sex differences in language development and disorders. *Journal of Psychology,* 35 (1953), 155–60.

McCarthy claims small but important differences favoring girls over boys in "practically all aspects of language" among white American children. Boys more frequently suffer language disorders, particularly stuttering and reading disabilities. The differences appear at such an early age that their roots must be in early infancy and there are enough environmental differences that genetic ones need not be postulated.

WITELSON, SANDRA F.

Sex differences in the neurology of cognition: Psychological, social, educational, and clinical implications. In E. Sullerot, ed., *The feminine situation*, in preparation.

In general, the verbal-spatial dichotomy between the left and right hemisphere is the same for both men and women. However, recent research indicates that females have less lateralization than males. The differences in neural organization between females and males may mean that different methods of teaching reading are differentially effective for girls and boys.

F. Bilingualism

DIEBOLD, A. RICHARD.

Incipient bilingualism. *Language,* 37 (1961), 97–112. Reprinted in Dell Hymes, ed., *Language in culture and society.* New York: Harper & Row, 1964, pp. 495–506.

In a peasant Indian village in Oaxaca, Mexico, the inhabitants speak Huave as a first language; Spanish is learned relatively late in life, if it is spoken at all (learning Spanish goes along with greater social contact with and participation in the national life). Diebold found that 80% of bilinguals were male; monolingual Huave speakers (proportionately more women) had less contact with the outside.

DWYER-SHICK, SUSAN.

Strategic performance in a language of concealment. Paper given at the 9th World Congress of Sociology, Uppsala, Sweden, August 1978.

The author describes 12 speech events in which the women of a well-to-do Turkish family selected English in order to exclude any participation by males present while including all of the females. The selection of English is an example of "anti-language" used, in these cases, to make comments upon taboo topics in the presence of males, without fear of retaliation.

GAL, SUSAN.

Peasant men can't get wives: Language change and sex roles in a bilingual community. *Language in Society*, 7 (1978), 1–16.

In the Austrian community Gal studied, a shift is underway from German-Hungarian bilingualism to the exclusive use of German. Young women have moved further in the direction of this change than older and younger men. Gal argues that women's speech choices must be explained within the context of their social position, life choices, and available linguistic alternatives.

HANNERZ, ULF.

Language variation and social relationships. *Studia Linguistica,* 24 (1970), 128–51.

Black ghetto women are often more skillful at speaking "Standard English" than are men, partly because women more often have "service roles" (domestic helper, waitress, salesperson) which encourage them to practice "Standard English." [*Also see* Nichols, Sec. IV-A.]

JOHN-STEINER, VERA AND PATRICIA IRVINE.

Women's verbal images and associations. In Betty Lou Dubois and Isabel Crouch, eds., *The sociology of the languages of American women.* San Antonio, Texas: Trinity Univ., 1976, pp. 91–102.

The authors investigate symbolic representations of women, as reflected in imagery and word associations of English-speaking Navajo women and men and other non-Indian college men and women. The largest differences emerged in the content of images, particularly those which touch on strong cultural themes such as "marriage" and "man."

LIEBERSON, STANLEY.

Bilingualism in Montreal: A demographic analysis. *American Journal of Sociology,* 71 (1965), 10–25. Reprinted in Joshua A. Fishman, ed., *Advances in the sociology of language II.* The Hague: Mouton, 1971, pp. 231–54.

Based on Canadian census data, this article analyzes trends in language usage in Montreal from the 1920s to the 1960s. Women have a consistently lower increase in bilingualism, and they also show a net decline in bilingualism at an earlier age than men. Lieberson attributes these gender differences to greater male participation in the labor force, contending that "the main supports of bilingualism are school and occupational systems."

PATELLA, VICTORIA AND WILLIAM P. KUVLESKY.

Situational variation in language patterns of Mexican American boys and girls. *Social Science Quarterly,* 37 (1979), 855–64.

The authors note that sex differences in patterns of bilingualism among Mexican-American children have received scant attention. They analyzed data gathered in 1967 from 669 Mexican-American boys and girls in South Texas and found that girls used Spanish less often, and English more often than boys at home, with friends in the neighborhood, and at school.

REDLINGER, WENDY.

Mother's speech to children in bilingual Mexican-American homes. In Betty Lou Dubois and Isabel Crouch, eds., *The sociology of the languages of American women.* San Antonio, Texas: Trinity Univ., 1976, pp. 119–30.

An investigation of how, when, and why respective languages are spoken by mothers to children in bilingual Mexican-American homes in Tucson, Arizona. The small sample limits the generalizability of the findings. Language choice of the mothers appears to be determined by the interplay of the given situation, the relative language ease of mother and children, how the mother perceives her role as teacher, and the degree of emotional involvement in the situation.

RUBIN, JOAN.

Bilingual usage in Paraguay. In Joshua A. Fishman, ed., *Readings in the sociology of language.* The Hague: Mouton, 1970, pp. 512–30.

More than half the population of Paraguay speak both Guarani (an Indian language) and Spanish, which has generally higher social status than Guarani. Men whose first language was either Spanish, or both Guarani and Spanish, tended to use more Guarani with other men, but to use Spanish with women intimates. Women, on the other hand, whose first language was either Spanish or both, tend to use Spanish to both male and female intimates. [*Also see* Gill and Hogan, Sec. II-E.]

SCHNEIDERMAN, ETA.

Sex differences in the development of children's ethnic and language attitudes. *International Journal of Social Languages*, 38 (1982), 37–44.

Bilingual children in Ontario 3 to 12 years old, were asked to assess character traits of French- and English-speaking puppets. Females preferred the French puppet at all age levels. Younger males were pro-English; males began to favor the French puppet from grade one on. Schneiderman compares these study results to those from other studies which found sex differences in language attitudes.

SOLE, YOLANDA RUSSINOVICH.

Sociocultural and sociopsychological factors in differential language retentiveness by sex. In Betty Lou Dubois and Isabel Crouch, eds., *The sociology of the languages of American women.* San Antonio, Texas: Trinity Univ., 1976, pp. 137–53.

A study of 164 college students found that intergenerational differences are far more potent in determining language usage within a Mexican-American population than are the sociocultural content of the speech situation or the topics. Females tend to favor mostly and only English more often than do the males, who favor code-switching, in Spanish and English, with equal frequency. Females were more open to language shift trends than were the males.

VAID, JYOTSNA AND WALLACE LAMBERT.

Differential cerebral involvement in the cognitive functioning of bilinguals. *Brain and Language,* 8 (1979), 92–110.

A general review of research in this area, including sex differences.

VALDÉS-FALLIS, GUADALUPE.

Code-switching among bilingual Mexican-American women: Towards an understanding of sex-related language alteration. *International Journal of the Sociology of Language,* 17 (1978), 65–72.

Four bilingual Mexican-American women, who taped themselves while conversing with other bilinguals, adapted more to the code-switching style of the men than of the women with whom they talked. The author explains the patterns in terms of women's lower status.

Also see: I-A: Borker; II-F: Fiske.

G.   Other Languages

ANIANSSON, EVA AND OLAUG REKDAL.

Language and sex reports. *Nordic Linguistic Bulletin,* 3, no. 2 (1979), 24–27.

A study of women's participation at the Scandinavian Conferences on Linguistics, 1974–79, shows that an increasing number of women are attending and reading papers. Most linguists who do interdisciplinary work on this topic make contacts with researchers in social sciences.

BEIT-HALLAHMI, BENJAMIN, J. C. CATFORD, RALPH E. COOLEY, CECELIA YODER DULL, ALEXANDER Z. GUIORA, AND MARIA RALUSZNY.

Grammatical gender and gender identity development: Cross cultural and cross lingual implications. *American Journal of Orthopsychiatry,* 44 (1974), 424–31.

The "gender loading" of language varies from zero in languages like Finnish and Hungarian, through very low in English, to very high in Hebrew. The Hebrew speaker in using present tense verbs marks her or his own sex when using the first person, and the sex of the addressee when using the second person.

BODINE, ANN.

Sex differentiation in language. In Barrie Thorne and Nancy Henley, eds., *Language and sex: Difference and dominance.* Rowley, Mass.: Newbury House, 1975, pp. 130–51.

Bodine's extensive review of the cross-cultural literature draws upon ethnographic studies of non-European societies, including Bengali, Carib, Cham, Chuckchee, Hebrew Semitic, Indo-

European, Japanese, and Thai. She notes that linguists often failed to classify gender with other forms of sex-based differentiation, overstated types of differentiation not occurring in their own languages, and made presumptions that the language used by males was the basic language, and that used by females a deviation (hence the prevalence of the term "women's language" over "men's language").

BROTHERTON, PATRICIA L. AND ROBYN A. PENMAN.

A comparison of some characteristics of male and female speech. *Journal of Social Psychology,* 103 (Oct. 1977), 161–62.

Thematic Apperception Test cards were used to elicit verbal material from male and female Australian university students, and the recorded conversations were analyzed to examine the stereotypic propositions that women speak more, speak faster, leave more sentences unfinished, and operate at a simpler conceptual level than do men. There were no significant sex differences on any of the speech variables.

BROUWER, DÉDÉ.

De invloed van de sekse van de aangesprokene op beleefdheid in taalgebruik. (The influence of the addressee's sex on politeness in language use.) In J. Matter, ed., *Toegepaste taalwetenschap in artikelen* (in press).

This sequel to the Central Station study reported in Brouwer, Gerritsen, and DeHaan [*see,* this section] concluded that the sex of the addressee determines the use of polite forms since both women and men were more polite when speaking to the male than the female ticker sellers.

BROUWER, DÉDÉ, MARINEL GERRITSEN, AND DORIAN deHAAN.

Speech differences between women and men: On the wrong track? *Language in Society,* 8 (1979), 33–50.

Requests for train tickets were tape-recorded at the Central Station in Amsterdam. No differences between men and women were found for the number of words used, use of diminutives or civilities. Women were more likely to hesitate and to request information. The sex of the person addressed played a prominent part in the travelers' choice of words.

CAPELL, A.

Studies in Socio-linguistics. The Hague: Mouton, 1966.

In Chapter 7, "Language and Social Groupings," Capell discusses "group or social dialects," which may be distinguished along the lines of sex, rank, profession, and occupation. He reviews cross-cultural literatures (from North and South America and Asia) showing sex differences in morphology, lexicon, and phonetic use.

EKKA, FRANCIS.

Men's and women's speech in Kurux. *Linguistics: An International Review,* 81 (April 1972), 25–31.

In Kurux [North India] the phonological and grammatical systems are the same for both men and women, except for a few morphological constructions. This difference, which begins in childhood, is maintained by different use of tense, gender, and number markers. The variation is determined by the sex of the hearer, sex of speaker, and sex of both the speaker and hearer. Ekka points out that the Kurux community is patriarchal; the men have higher social status.

FLANNERY, REGINA.

Men's and women's speech in Gros Ventre. *International Journal of American Linguistics,* 12 (1946), 133–35.

Studying the Gros Ventre of the Fort Belknap Reservation in Montana, Flannery noted differences in vocabulary and pronunciation in the speech of men and women. The Gros Ventre are aware that the sexes "talk differently," though no one could formulate the difference. When telling a story, the old people gave the interjections proper to the sex of the character quoted, but did not make the appropriate variation in pronunciation.

FURFEY, PAUL HANLY.

Men's and women's language. *The American Catholic Sociological Review,* 5 (1944), 218–23.

Furfey states that "there is no instance known to the writer in which the men and women of the same tribe speak entirely distinct tongues. The sex distinctions which have been discovered involve not the language as a whole, but certain specific features of the languages, such as phonetics, grammar, or vocabulary." He summarizes cross-cultural data on phonetic differences between men and women.

HAAS, MARY R.

Men's and women's speech in Koasati. *Language,* 20 (1944), 142–49. Reprinted in Dell Hymes, ed., *Language in culture and society.* New York: Harper & Row, 1964, pp. 228–32.

In Koasati, a Muskogean language spoken in southwestern Louisiana, there are well-defined differences in the speech of men and women. Haas lays out rules governing these differences by setting up the forms used by women as basic and the male forms as derived from these. At the present only middle-aged and elderly women use the women's forms; younger women have adopted men's speech. Haas summarizes other evidence of sex differences in speech from the Yana, the Eskimo, the Carib, the Chukchee, and the Thai.

HANSSEN, ESKIL.

Some notes on language and sex research in Norway. Paper given at the Sprache und Geschlecht conference, Univ. of Osnabrück, West Germany, March 1979.

In interviews conducted in homes (mostly by a university-educated male), men used more non-standard phonological and morphological forms than did women. Few syntactic and vocabulary differences were found. [*Also see:* Hanssen, Sec. I-B.]

HAUGEN, EINAR.

"Sexism" and the Norwegian language. Paper presented at the Society for the Advancement of Scandinavian Study meeting, Washington, D.C., May 1974.

Haugen summarizes various studies of language variation by sex in Scandinavian research—for example, studies of local dialects in Norway which found greater "carefulness" in the speech of women.

HERTZLER, JOYCE O.

A sociology of language. New York: Random House, 1965, pp. 318–21.

Hertzler briefly summarizes some of the studies of segregation of language by sex groups "among primitive people" (the Caribs; in Madagascar; among the Guaycurus of Brazil; in Surinam; in Micronesia; among American Indian tribes; in Japan). He concludes that "major differentiations of language between the sexes of a society are rare. Contact between the sexes is so continuous and so extensive that sharp differences cannot long be maintained."

IDE, SACHIKO.

Language of inferior and luxury: A sociolinguistic interpretation of Japanese women's language (I). *Studies in English and American literature,* 15 (1980), 215–25.

In speaking, Japanese women use more formal forms of the first person pronoun than do men. Since it is more important for women to be careful with linguistic forms, "the men are permitted more varied, wittier and relaxed speech." The essay contains an historical account of women's language as well as a discussion of children's acquisition of rules for personal pronoun choices.

KAHN, MARGARET.

Arabic emphatics: The evidence for cultural determinants of phonetic sex-typing. *Phonetica,* 31 (1975), 38–50.

The gender of teachers of Arabic to English-speaking students affected the learning of inflection. Students (of both sexes) of male teachers learned male-typed pitch and inflection; students of female teachers learned female-typed pitch and inflection.

LEOPOLD, WERNER F.

The decline of German dialects. *Word,* 15 (1959), 130–53. Reprinted in Joshua A. Fishman, ed., *Readings in the sociology of language.* The Hague: Mouton, 1970, pp. 340–64.

In postwar Germany many population movements contributed to the demise of local dialects and the strengthening of colloquial standard German. Leopold reports a study by Otto Steiner comparing south and north German dialects, and found that "boys use the local dialect far more commonly than girls, who prefer High German (standard German). In both regions, for both sexes, the share of High German is much larger in the cities than in the adjoining rural districts."

NOVITSKIJ, S. A.

Phonostylistic structures of oral formal business-like monologue in English (experimental phonetic investigation). Unpublished Ph.D. dissertation, Minsk Pedagogical Institute of Foreign Languages, 1977.

An acoustical analysis of female and male intonation patterns in formal business-like monologues in British English found differences mainly in the type of tone intervals, the fundamental frequency, the speed of the changes in terminal tones, intensity variability, and dynamic range (Trans. and abstract by Irene Tatarnikova.)

PINAEVA, Z. B.

About some intonational characteristics of reading English belles-lettres and science texts. Unpublished Ph.D. dissertation, Moscow Pedagogical Institute of Foreign Languages named after Moris Torez, 1975.

The author investigates intonation patterns of women and men reading belles-lettres and science texts in British English. (Trans. and abstract by Irene Tatarnikova.)

SAINT-JACQUES, BERNARD.

Sex, dependency and language. *La Linguistique,* 9 (1973), 89–96.

Examples from Japanese are used to explain the concept of *dependency* which creates differences between women's and men's linguistic forms and conversation topics. Included in this brief review of some of the early work on women's and men's speech is a summary of the reasons, given in a 1952 essay, why women supposedly make poor linguistic informants: They can't sit still for long, they have limited vocabulary and knowledge, and they would not want to answer delicate questions.

SCHENK-VAN WITSEN, R.

Sekseverschillen in het Franse taalgebruik: een exploratief onderzoek naar lexikale verschillen. (Sex differences in French language usage: An exploratory investigation for lexical differences.) In J. Matter, ed., *Toegepaste taalwetenschap in artikelen (Applied Phonology)*, 10, no. 2 (1981), 51–134. Les différences sexuelles dans le français parlé: Une étude pilote des différences lexicales entre hommes et femmes. *Langage et Société,* Sept. 1981, pp. 58–79.

A corpus of 51 interviews in French was analyzed with computer. Significant differences were found in the topics women and men talked about, and in their uses of abstract words and personal pronouns. (From author's abstract.)

STEPANOV, YU. S.

Fundamentals of general linguistics. Moscow: Prosveshchenije, 1975.

Since the social difference between men and women is preserved, so the peculiarities of female speech are preserved in practically all modern languages. Those peculiarities are more conspicuous in dialects than in literary language. In the Mongolian language, young people are prohibited from pronouncing names of older people, and women are prohibited from pronouncing the names of certain relatives. The existence of "female language" is supported not by biological, but by social causes. (Trans. and abstract by Irene Tatarnikova.)

STEPANOV, YU. S.

Fundamentals of linguistics. Moscow: Prosveshchenije, 1966.

Pronunciation in such languages as Russian, French, and English preserves conspicuous division into male and female variants; the proof is radio newscasters. These differences in pronunciation are still not well investigated. Russian old women, for instance, pronounce such words as "da—yes" not during the exhale, but during the inhale. (Trans. and abstract by Irene Tatarnikova.)

TABOURET-KELLER, ANDREE.

A contribution to the sociological study of language maintenance and language shift. In Joshua A. Fishman, ed., *Advances in the sociology of language II.* The Hague: Mouton, 1971, pp. 365–76.

The analysis stresses economic and migration patterns, but also mentions sex differences in use of the *patois* in Pays D'Oc, France. About the same percentage of girls and boys speak the *patois.* Children tend to speak it more with their fathers than with their mothers; use of *patois* with the father increases from the age of 12 onwards.

TAYLOR, ALLAN R.

"Male" and "female" speech in Gros Ventre. *Anthropological Linguistics*, 24 (1983), 301–07.

Two slightly different phonetic systems are used by speakers of the Montana Gros Ventre (Atsina) language. One form is used primarily by women, the other by men. The two systems were first reported by Flannery in 1946; the present paper looks at the phenomenon anew, and explores the question of why use of the two systems is not entirely predictable from the gender of the speaker.

VEILERT, A. A.

   About the dependence of quantitative indices of units on speaker sex. *Problems of Linguistics,* 5
   (1976), 138–43.

An analysis of speech samples of 30 men and 30 women speaking Middle German dialect in the
USSR indicates that the vocabulary of women is bigger than that of men, and women give more
colorful descriptions of objects and processes. [Translation and abstract by Irene Tatarnikova]

Also see: I-A: Jespersen; I-B: Hanssen.

V. CONVERSATIONAL INTERACTION

A.   General References

ABRAHAMS, ROGER D.

   Black talking in the streets. In Richard Bauman and Joel Sherzer, eds., *Explorations in the
   ethnography of speaking.* New York: Cambridge Univ. Press, 1974, pp. 240–62. Reprinted in
   Abrahams, *Talking Black.* Rowley, Mass.: Newbury House, 1976.

A description of the verbal performances Black men use in the world of the street, where they
establish reputations among peers; a taxonomy is included of terms (e.g., *running it down; talking
smart*) used to talk about talk.

ABRAHAMS, ROGER D.

   Negotiating respect: Patterns of presentation among Black women. *Journal of American
   Folklore,* 88 (Jan.-March 1975), 58–80. Reprinted as Claire R. Farrer, ed., *Women and
   folklore.* Austin: Univ. of Texas Press, 1975, pp. 58–80. Essay is also in Abrahams, *Talking
   Black.* Rowley, Mass.: Newbury House, 1976.

Black women's and men's speaking styles are related to divisions between home and street; in
their presentational strategies, women seek to maintain images of respectability, and men, to
maintain a reputation. Abrahams describes verbal styles by which women negotiate with children,
with men, and with each other. Women are expected to be more restrained, less loud, and less
abandoned than men are in their talk.

ADAMS, MISCHA B.

   Communication and gender stereotype: An anthropological perspective. Unpublished Ph.D.
   dissertation, Univ. of California, Santa Cruz, 1980.

Concerned with how individuals (especially women) become subjects, empowered to convey a
legitimate point of view, Adams analyzes specific incidents where women and men exercised choice
about being affected by gender stereotypes in interaction.

ALDOUS, JOAN.

   Family interaction patterns. In Alex Inkeles et al., eds., *Annual review of sociology,* vol. 3. Palo
   Alto, Calif.: *Annual Reviews,* 1977, pp. 105–35.

A critical review of research on interaction in nuclear families, noting that husband-wife
interaction has been studied more than that of parents and children or siblings, and discussing
conceptualizations of power, conflict, and love in research on family interaction.

ARGYLE, MICHAEL, MANSUR LALLJEE, AND MARK COOK.
   The effects of visibility on interaction in a dyad. *Human Relations,* 21 (1968), 3–17.

   In three experiments visibility was varied for both members of a dyad. In cross-sex pairs, men spoke more than women; when men were invisible, their amount of speech increased by an average of 40%, while women reduced their speech by a similar amount. Men dominated largely by interrupting and talking more.

ARIES, ELIZABETH.
   Interaction patterns and themes of male, female, and mixed groups. *Small Group Behavior,* 7 (1976), 7–18. Revised version: Male-female interpersonal styles in all male, all female and mixed groups. In Alice Sargent, ed., *Beyond sex roles.* St. Paul: West, 1977, pp. 292–98.

   An experimental study comparing interaction patterns of same and mixed-sex small groups of white college undergraduates. The male groups established a more stable dominance order, while the female groups were more flexible in rank order of speaking over time. All-female groups talked about feelings and relationships, and all-male groups about sports, competition and aggression, and things they had seen, read, or heard. In mixed-sex groups women initiated only 34% of total interaction and oriented themselves more to men than to women, while men talked more about feelings and were less competitive than in all-male groups.

ARIES, ELIZABETH.
   Verbal and nonverbal behavior in single-sex and mixed-sex groups: Are traditional sex roles changing? *Psychological Reports,* 51 (1982), 127–34.

   Seven all-female, and eight mixed-sex groups of career-oriented college students discussed an ethical dilemma. Women initiated more verbal acts than men, but interaction styles (men gave more opinions and information; women, more reactions) and nonverbal postures (males used more associated with dominance) were sex stereotypic. Group sex composition had little effect.

BAIRD, JOHN E., JR.
   Sex differences in group communication: A review of relevant research. *Quarterly Journal of Speech,* 62 (1976), 179–92.

   A review of sex differences (emphasized more than similarities) found in experimental studies of small groups. Topics include interaction patterns, task performance, conformity, bargaining and coalition formation, and leadership. The discussion is cast in the Bales framework, referring findings to "the male role" (aggressive, task-oriented) and "the female role" (empathetic, passive).

BERGER, JOSEPH, SUSAN J. ROSENHOLTZ, AND MORRIS ZELDITCH, JR.
   Status organizing processes. In Alex Inkeles et al., eds., *Annual review of sociology,* vol. 6. Palo Alto, Calif.: Annual Reviews, 1980, pp. 479–508.

   In this review of theory and research on status organizing processes in face-to-face social interaction, sex differences in opportunities to perform (e.g., greater male interruption in mixed-sex groups), performance output (e.g., findings that men talk more than women), more positive evaluations of male performance, and greater male influence are taken as evidence that sex functions as a status characteristic.

BERNARD, JESSIE.

Talk, conversation, listening, silence. Chapter 6 of *The sex game*. New York: Atheneum, 1972, pp. 135–64.

Drawing upon a range of research and anecdotes, Bernard generalizes about how the sexes talk and converse. In cross-sex talk women tend to draw men out, to provide emotional stroking, to talk less, and to concede dominance. Men's talk often involves a debating style, which may inhibit women, who tend to be less competitive than men.

BORGATTA, EDGAR F. AND JOHN STIMSON.

Sex differences in interaction characteristics. *The Journal of Social Psychology*, 60 (1963), 89–100.

An experimental study comparing same-sex groups, with interaction scored into the Bales categories. All-male groups showed more of the categories "draws attention" and "social acknowledgement," and less "disagrees" than female groups. In female groups there were more tension increases, awkward pauses, and withdrawal. Cautious interpretations are offered.

BROWN, PENELOPE AND STEPHEN LEVINSON.

Universals in language usage: Politeness phenomena. In Esther N. Goody, ed., *Questions and politeness: Strategies in social interaction*. Cambridge: Cambridge Univ. Press, 1978, pp. 56–289.

A ground-breaking essay which develops a theory of politeness strategies in interaction. Positive politeness strategies seek to affirm common ground (e.g., intensifying interest in the hearer through tag questions, use of in-group identity markers, avoiding disagreement). Negative politeness strategies, based on avoidance and respect, defer to the hearer's wish to maintain claims of territory and self-determination (e.g., using indirect forms of speech and deference forms). Dominated groups (including women) tend to have positive politeness subcultures among themselves, and dominating groups (including men) tend to have negative politeness subcultures.

CHESLER, PHYLLIS.

Women and madness. New York: Doubleday, 1972.

Dialogues between women sometimes seem "senseless" to men; the women seem to be reciting monologues at each other. But the women are approaching a kind of emotional resolution and comfort, telling parallel confessions and commenting upon one another's feelings by "reflecting them in a very sensitive matching process" (p. 268).

COSER, ROSE LAUB.

Laughter among colleagues. *Psychiatry*, 23 (1960), 81–95.

Coser recorded all conversations in which humor and laughter occurred at 20 staff meetings of a mental hospital. She found a hierarchy of joking: senior staff made witticisms more often than junior members, and men made 99 out of 103 witticisms, although women often laughed harder.

COURTRIGHT, JOHN A., FRANK E. MILLAR, AND L. EDNA ROGERS-MILLAR.

Domineeringness and dominance: Replication and expansion. *Communication Monographs*, 46 (1979), 179–92.

Tapes of 86 white married couples discussing their relationships were coded into categories such as assertion, question, and support. Among the complex findings: the more dominant the husband compared to his wife, the more questions asked by the wife, but the reverse did not hold; the more domineering a spouse, the more he or she interrupted the other.

DITTMAN, ALLEN T.

Developmental factors in conversational behavior. *The Journal of Communication*, 22 (1972), 404–23.

Videotapes were made of two groups—boys and girls ages 6 to 12, and males and females ages 14 to 35—talking in a laboratory setting. Older subjects gave significantly more listener responses (*yeah, uh-huh*, head nods) than did younger subjects, and females more than males. Analysis revealed minimal interaction between sex and age, no sex difference in responses related to content, and wide individual variation.

DUNCAN, STARKEY, JR., AND DONALD W. FISKE.

Face-to-face interaction. Hillsdale, N.J.: Lawrence Erlbaum Associates, 1977.

In developing a model for research on face-to-face interaction, the authors describe a study of 88 graduate students videotaped in same and cross-sex dyads. Among the relatively few sex differences: men took longer speaking turns, with a rate of filled pauses more than twice that of women. The length of speaking turns for men interacting with men was longer than for men with women or women with women. Women smiled and laughed longer and more often than men. The authors do not interpret these findings.

EAKINS, BARBARA AND GENE EAKINS.

Verbal turn-taking and exchanges in faculty dialogue. In Betty Lou Dubois and Isabel Crouch, eds., *The sociology of the languages of American women*. San Antonio, Texas: Trinity Univ., 1976, pp. 53–62.

Analysis of tapes of seven university faculty meetings revealed that compared with women, men took more turns at talk, spoke longer per turn, and initiated more interruptions. Comparing those of the same sex, individuals with higher rank talked and interrupted more than those of lower rank. Over half the turns of the two lowest-ranking women were interrupted. This study is also reported in Eakins and Eakins [Sec. I-A].

EDELSKY, CAROLE.

Who's got the floor? *Language in Society*, 10 (1981), 383–421.

In analyzing tapes of informal meetings of a mixed-sex university committee, Edelsky drew on her experience as a participant to distinguish "floor" from "turn." In addition to the usual one-at-a-time type of floor (F1)—in which men took longer speaking turns and did more joking, arguing, directing, and soliciting than women—there was a more informal and collaborative floor (F2). In F2's women talked, argued, directed, and solicited responses more, and men less than in F1's. Thus, when floors were more jointly constructed, the sexes interacted more as equals, whereas men dominated when floors were under single-party control.

EHRENREICH, BARBARA.

The politics of talking in couples. *Ms.*, 9 (May 1981), 46, 48.

Ehrenreich speculates that prior to the suburbanization of the 1950s there was not a "mass expectation that ordinary men and women should engage in conversation as a routine activity."

Raised expectations as well as men's greater power and fear of self-disclosure contribute to the "conversational mismatch between the sexes," evident, e.g., in research by Fishman, and West and Zimmerman.

ESPOSITO, ANITA.

Sex differences in children's conversation. *Language and Speech,* 22 (1979), 213–20.

Forty middle-class children, ages 3 and 4, were taped while playing in same and mixed-sex groups; the transcripts were analyzed for interruptions, overlaps, lapses, and number of initiated unit types. In mixed-sex groups all boys had higher scores for interruption; boys interrupted girls 2 to 1. There were no other sex differences.

EUBANKS, SHERYLE B.

Sex-based language differences: A cultural reflection. In Reza Ordoubadian and Walburga von-Raffler Engel, eds., *Views on language.* Murfreesboro, Tenn.: Inter-University Publishers, 1975, pp. 109–20.

In tapes of 15 mixed-sex pairs of students talking about pre-set topics, men talked more and more often signaled beginnings and ends; women more often apologized, asked questions seeking support, and used questioning intonation. [The analysis of data is not very carefully done.]

FASTEAU, MARK.

Why aren't we talking? *Ms.,* 1 (July 1972), 16.

Fasteau discusses obstacles to communication among men: "real men," males are taught, are never dependent and don't talk about or directly express feelings, especially ones that don't contribute to dominance. "There is nothing among men that resembles the personal communication that women have developed among themselves." See also Fasteau, *The male machine.* New York: McGraw-Hill, 1974.

FISHMAN, PAMELA M.

Conversational insecurity. In Howard Giles, W. Peter Robinson, and Philip M. Smith, eds., *Language: Social psychological perspectives.* New York: Pergamon Press, 1980, pp. 127–32.

Fishman provides a situational explanation for aspects of women's conversational style which others, such as Lakoff, have claimed are the result of female personality. In taped conversations of three couples at home, women asked two and one half times more questions than men, including three times more tag questions, and women more often said "you know." Both features of women's speech were efforts to get men to respond to topics the women introduced.

FISHMAN, PAMELA M.

Interaction: The work women do. *Social Problems,* 25 (1978), 397–406. A revised version is in this volume.

In tapes of three heterosexual couples conversing in their apartments, women made 62% of all attempts to introduce topics, but only 38% of their topics actually evolved into conversation. All but one of the men's topics succeeded, because of women's greater interaction work; women asked more questions and provided more active conversational support. A related paper: Fishman, "Interactional shitwork, "*Heresies,* no. 2 (1977), 99–101.

FISHMAN, PAMELA M.

What do couples talk about when they're alone? In Douglas Butturff and Edmund L. Epstein, eds., *Women's language and style.* Akron, Ohio: L & S Books, 1978, pp. 11–22.

In addition to findings also reported in "Interaction: The Work Women Do," this paper contains a list of topics raised and who raised them (the main sex difference was not in category of topics but in the fact that women raised so many more, whatever the category), and includes portions of transcripts to illustrate the development of success and failure of conversational topics.

GARDNER, CAROL BROOKS.

Passing by: Street remarks, address rights, and the urban female. *Sociological Inquiry,* 50 (1981), 328–56.

Men claim a license to direct comments to and about women as they pass by, as if public space were men's home territory. Women report answering back only when male retaliation seems unlikely or when the street remarks are especially offensive. Gardner argues that street remarks socialize men for rejection by women, while teaching women to passively accept criticism.

GOODWIN, MARJORIE HARNESS.

Directive-response speech sequences in girls' and boys' task activities. In Sally McConnell-Ginet, Ruth Borker, and Nelly Furman, eds., *Women and language in literature and society.* New York: Praeger, 1980, pp. 157–73.

Conversations were taped of same-sex groups of urban Black working class children, ages 8 to 13, in natural play situations. The girls' group had a fluid hierarchy; their directives were often proposals for future activity, such as *let's* and *we gotta* ("We gotta clean em first"). The boys' group was more hierarchical, with status enacted through giving direct commands, contradicting others, and usurping turn space. Boys bragged about achievements; girls talked about appearances and relationships. See also Goodwin, "Processes of dispute management among urban Black children," *American Ethnologist,* 9 (1982), 76–96; and Goodwin [Sec.VI-A-4].

GOODY, ESTHER N.

Towards a theory of questions. In Esther N. Goody, ed., *Questions and politeness: Strategies in social interaction.* Cambridge, England: Cambridge Univ. Press, 1978, pp. 17–43.

Goody examines forms and functions of question-asking, with cross-cultural data, and from the perspective of interaction strategies and speech acts. The discussion of the effect of hierarchy and position on the meaning assigned to a question may be applicable to communication between the sexes.

GREIF, ESTHER BLANK.

Sex differences in parent-child conversations. In Cheris Kramarae, ed., *The voices and words of women and men.* New York: Pergamon Press, 1980, pp. 253–58. Also *Women's Studies International Quarterly,* 3, no. 2/3 (1980). pp. 253–58.

In videotapes of 16 girls and boys, ages 2 to 5, separately playing with each parent, parents spoke more than children (there were no differences in amount of speech, by sex of speaker or spoken to). Fathers were more likely than mothers to interrupt and engage in simultaneous speech with their children, and both parents were more likely to interrupt and speak simultaneously with daughters than with sons. There were no differences between boys and girls in use of interruption or simultaneous speech.

HEISS, JEROLD S.

Degree of intimacy and male-female interaction. *Sociometry*, 25 (1962), 197–208.

Interactions of 54 dating, courting, and engaged heterosexual couples, each dyad discussing a topic on which they disagreed, were coded using the Bales system. Overall, men tended to dominate the task sections and women the positive reaction sections, but with increasing intimacy male and female scores were less differentiated.

HENLEY, NANCY.

Body politics: Power, sex and nonverbal communication. Englewood Cliffs, N.J.: Prentice-Hall, Spectrum, 1977.

Chapter 5, "Tinkling Symbols: Language," provides a framework for interpreting patterns found in conversations between the sexes: men's greater status and power and women's subordination are conveyed through asymmetric interruption, silence, self-disclosure, humor. [*Also see* Henley and Thorne, I-A.]

HERSHEY, SIBILLA AND EMMY WERNER.

Dominance in marital decision making in women's liberation and non-women's liberation families. *Family Process*, 14 (1975), 223–33.

Analysis of tapes of couples talking found that wives associated with the women's movement spoke longer than their husbands and were more likely to speak last. Wives who were not participants in the women's movement spoke less than their husbands and were less likely to speak last. There were no differences between the groups in husbands' total speaking time, number of joint decisions reached, patterns of talking first, or measures of conflict.

HIRSCHMAN, LYNETTE.

Analysis of supportive and assertive behavior in conversations. Paper given at meeting of the Linguistic Society of America, San Francisco, July 1974.

In an experimental study of four single-sex and eight mixed-sex pairs conversing about love, sexuality, and marriage, there were no sex differences in amount of speech, mean length of utterance, frequency of affirmative words and fillers, and ratio of completed to attempted clauses. The only striking sex difference: women outnumbered men 53 to 8 in the use of *mm hmm*; women used more *mm hmm's* in same-sex than in mixed-sex conversation. Men used almost twice as many *I think's* as women.

HIRSCHMAN, LYNETTE.

Female-male differences in conversational interaction. Paper given at meeting of Linguistic Society of America, San Diego, Calif., Dec. 1973.

Two male and two female white college students were taped in dyadic conversation, in all possible pairs of the four, with topic controlled. There were no sex differences in speaking time or proportion of qualifiers (e.g., *I think*). Women used more fillers (e.g., *uhm, you know*), more pronouns involving the other speaker, and more of the *mm hmm* response, especially with each other. The two women interrupted or overlapped each other more than any other pair; they tended to elaborate on each other's utterances, while the men tended to argue.

HOLMSTROM, LYNDA LYTLE AND ANN WOLBERT BURGESS.

Conversations between rapist and victim. Paper given at the 9th World Congress of Sociology, Uppsala, Sweden, Aug., 1978.

Analysis of linguistic strategies which recur in rape situations. To avoid being raped, victims try to talk their way out, reasoning with or threatening the assailant, and using joking and sarcasm. The rapist, seeking access to and power over the victim, threatens or "cons" her, orders her about, uses foul language, and taunts her.

HORNSTEIN, GAIL A.

Variations in conversational style as a function of the degree of intimacy between members of a dyad. Unpublished Ph.D. dissertation, Clark Univ., 1981.

A comparison of telephone conversations between women who were friends, acquaintances, or strangers. Friends used more implicit openings, raised more topics, were more responsive and self-disclosing, and used more complex forms of closing than did strangers. Acquaintances were generally similar to strangers, although in some ways (e.g., disclosure of personal feelings), they behaved like friends.

ICKES, WILLIAM AND RICHARD D. BARNES.

The role of sex and self-monitoring in unstructured dyadic interactions. *Journal of Personality and Social Psychology*, 35 (1977), 315–30.

An experimental study of initial interaction of same-sex dyads, with partners matched using scores on a test of their tendency to use impression management tactics. There was more involvement and affiliation in female than in male dyads: compared with men, women talked more frequently and for longer duration, looked at each other more frequently, and used more expressive gestures. Data on subjects' perceptions are included.

JENKINS, LEE AND CHERIS KRAMER.

Small group process: Learning from women. *Women's Studies International Quarterly,* 1 (1978), 67–84.

The authors trace the origin of consciousness-raising groups in the feminist movement, the valuing of collectivity, cooperation, emotionality, and personal testimony, and conflict over issues of hierarchy and structure. CR groups reveal the bias of small group research toward models based on competition and conflict; this research is critically discussed.

JENKINS, MERCILEE M.

Toward a model of human leadership. In Cynthia L. Berryman and Virginia A. Eman, eds., *Communication, language and sex.* Rowley, Mass.: Newbury House, 1980, pp. 149–58.

A critical discussion of research on female compared with male leadership, emphasizing the effects of men's higher external status on leadership processes within small groups, differential evaluations of women's and men's communication styles, and the effect of sex composition of groups. Jenkins argues that current models of leadership have been based primarily on men's experiences, and that studies of female groups may open new insights, e.g., into rotating leadership patterns.

JOHNSON, FERN L. AND ELIZABETH J. ARIES.

The talk of women friends. *Women's Studies International Forum,* in press.

The authors discuss the social contexts and distinctive nature of women's friendships, a topic neglected in past research. Depth interviews with 20 white women, ages 27–58, revealed the centrality of talk—a "mosaic" of noncritical listening and mutual support—in their close friendships with women.

JOHNSON, JANET L.

Questions and role responsibility in four professional meetings. *Anthropological Linguistics,* 22 (1980), 66–76.

In four mixed-sex meetings in an industrial corporation men and women asked proportionately the same number of questions. Engineers of both sexes used questions most frequently to request new information; computer graphics personnel used them more often as interactional strategies; and the leader (a man) asked disproportionately more questions (including over half of all tags), primarily to sustain interaction. Role, purpose, and intent—not gender—affected patterns of question-asking.

JOSE, P. E., F. CROSBY, AND W. J. WONG-MCCARTHY.

Androgyny, dyadic compatibility and conversational behaviour. In Howard Giles, W. Peter Robinson, and Philip M. Smith, eds., *Language: Social psychological perspectives.* New York: Pergamon Press, 1980, pp. 115–19.

The 96 undergraduates who filled out questionnaires like the Bem Sex Roles Inventory were paired into dyads to discuss an ethical dilemma. Sex-role self-concept did not predict patterns of interruption, number of turns, or number of back channels.

KALČIK, SUSAN.

". . . like Ann's gynecologist or the time I was almost raped": Personal narratives in women's rap groups. *Journal of American Folklore,* 88 (Jan.–March 1975), pp. 3–11. Reprinted as Claire R. Farrer, ed., *Women and folklore.* Austin: Univ. of Texas Press, 1975, pp. 3–11.

Kalčik discusses interaction strategies she found in women's consciousness-raising rap groups: politeness (careful attention to turn-taking, frequent use of apologies, avoidance of direct criticism); support (questions to show interest, sympathetic noises and gestures); and humor. The talk was collaborative, and personal narratives, including kernel stories, involved joint production.

KAPLAN, SUSAN L.

The assertion of power: Ideals, perceptions, and styles. Paper given at meetings of the American Psychological Assoc., Washington, D.C., Sept. 1976.

Sixty dating couples provided self-reports about their balance of power and were taped as they discussed hypothetical cases about dating relationships. Women viewed as powerful used more acts in Bales's categories of "request" (asking partner for information or opinion) and "oppose." Men viewed as powerful used a high proportion of the "propose" cluster (structuring the discussion, giving information and opinions).

KOCHMAN, THOMAS.

Communicating in Black and white: Styles in conflict. Chicago, Univ. of Chicago Press, 1981.

Kochman compares Black and white styles of negotiating heterosexual interest. Black cross-sex encounters acquire sexual meaning through direct verbal negotiation, through rapping and repartee.

In white cross-sex encounters sexual intent is conveyed circumstantially rather than verbally. Sources of cross-cultural conflict are analyzed, but the gender asymmetry in both styles is taken for granted rather than fully discussed.

KOMAROVSKY, MIRRA.
   Blue-collar marriage. New York: Random House, 1962; New York, Vintage, 1967.

In a study based on intensive interviews with 58 blue-collar couples Komarovsky found strong sex segregation of activities, interests, and talk. The husbands, who felt their wives talked about gossip and "silly" matters, talked to one another about cars, sports, work, motorcycles, carpentry, local politics. The women conversed about family and interpersonal matters; they complained that their husbands didn't listen, self-disclose, or talk enough in general. In several couples the dominant partner was the less talkative of the two.

LAKOFF, ROBIN.
   Stylistic strategies within a grammar of style. In Judith Orasanu, Mariam K. Slater, and Leonore Loeb Adler, eds., *Language, sex, and gender*. New York: The New York Academy of Sciences, 1979, pp. 53–78.

Lakoff proposes a scale of style based on degree of relatedness between speaker and hearer and argues that the stereotyped "male style" lies between *clarity* and *distance* and the stereotyped "female style" between *deference* and *camaraderie*.

LAMB, THEODORE A.
   Nonverbal and paraverbal control in dyads and triads: Sex or power differences? *Social Psychology Quarterly*, 44 (1981), 49–53.

Analysis of videotapes of 75 undergraduates in same-sex dyads and triads indicated that the sexes used the same methods of control: initial eye gaze dominance, initial speaking order, and consuming more time while speaking. The first few seconds of encounters are a dominance battle more for men than for women and the correlation between initial speaking order and talking the most was stronger for women than for men.

LEET-PELLEGRINI, HELENA M.
   Conversational dominance as a function of gender and expertise. In Howard Giles, W. Peter Robinson, and Philip M. Smith, eds., *Language: Social psychological perspectives*. New York: Pergamon Press, 1980, pp. 97–104.

Seventy same and mixed-sex pairs of college students discussed television programming, with some partners briefed with expert knowledge. Neither expertise nor sex alone accounted for the exercise of power; they interacted, with men experts using a style based on power, and women experts, a style based on solidarity and support. Men experts talked more than women experts; women experts assented more with men than with women partners. Participants perceived men experts as more dominant than women experts.

LEFFLER, ANN, DAIR GILLESPIE, AND JOSEPH C. CONATY.
   Top dogs and space hogs: The effects of status differentiation on nonverbal behavior. Unpublished paper, Dept. of Sociology, Univ. of Utah, 1980.

An experimental study varying gender and role as student or teacher. Overall, the same individuals talked, interrupted, touched, and pointed more, and took up more space, when they were the teacher than when they were the student. Gender, understood as a diffuse status characteristic, had a less dramatic overall effect than role of teacher or student.

LEIK, ROBERT K.

Instrumentality and emotionality in family interaction. *Sociometry,* 26 (1963), 131–45.

Nine families, each with a college-aged daughter, participated in different types of three-person discussions, with interaction coded using the Bales system. The fathers showed more instrumental, and the mothers more emotional behavior in groups of strangers than when interacting with their own family members. The findings, Leik argues, challenge the applicability of small group theory to interaction in families.

LEWIS, ROBERT A.

Emotional intimacy among men. *Journal of Social Issues,* 34 (1978), 108–21.

Although men report more same-sex friendships than women do, most of these are not intimate or self-disclosing; barriers to emotional intimacy among men include pressure to compete, homophobia, aversion to vulnerability, and lack of adequate role models.

LOCKHEED, MARLAINE E. AND KATHERINE PATTERSON HALL.

Conceptualizing sex as a status characteristic: Applications to leadership training strategies. *Journal of Social Issues,* 32 (1976), 111–24.

The authors review the research finding that in mixed-sex discussion groups males tend to be more verbally active, influential, and task-oriented than women. They argue that sex functions as a diffuse status characteristic; in the absence of other information, males will be deferred to in task-oriented group situations. Short-term interventions are suggested to lessen male dominance in mixed-sex groups.

MALTZ, DANIEL N. AND RUTH A. BORKER.

A cultural approach to male-female miscommunication. In John J. Gumperz, ed., *Language and social identity.* New York: Cambridge Univ. Press, 1983, pp. 196–216.

A theoretical essay arguing that children ages 5 to 15 learn rules for friendly conversation in same-sex peer groups. Boys' groups are overtly hierarchical, with speech used to assert dominance and to attract and maintain an audience—patterns linked to adult male verbal agression. Girls use speech cooperatively and to negotiate shifting alliances—patterns related to the support and signaling of attention in adult women's speech. These sex-differentiated rules of interpretation account for misunderstandings in adult cross-sex communication.

MARCH, JAMES G.

Husband-wife interaction over political issues. *Public Opinion Quarterly,* 17 (1953—54), 461–70.

Eight couples discussed problems of public policy, with interaction scored by the Bales system. Husbands initiated 55% of all acts in the categories "gives suggestions," "gives opinion," and "gives orientation." The difference in husband-wife contributions was greatest on labor affairs, least on local issues, and midway on foreign affairs.

MARKEL, NORMAN H., JOSEPH J. LONG, AND THOMAS J. SAINE.

Sex effects in conversational interaction: Another look at male dominance. *Human Communication Research*, 2 (1976), 356–64.

An experimental study of conversations of same and mixed-sex pairs of college students found women's speech acts were, on the average, longer than men's; communicators of both sexes talked more when the listener was a woman. In male dyads, far interpersonal distance was linked with significantly more simultaneous speech.

MCMILLAN, JULIE R., A. KAY CLIFTON, DIANE MCGRATH, AND WANDA S. GALE.

Women's language: Uncertainty or interpersonal sensitivity and emotionality? *Sex Roles*, 3 (1977), 545–59.

Results of this study of sex differences in speech in all-men, all-women, and mixed-sex problem-solving groups indicate support for the assertions that: (1) women use more linguistic forms connoting uncertainty; (2) these forms are used more often when men are present; and (3) men are more likely to interrupt women than vice versa.

MEEKER, B. F. AND P. A. WEITZEL-O'NEILL.

Sex roles and interpersonal behavior in task-oriented groups. *American Sociological Review*, 42 (1977); 91–105.

A useful review and recasting of the Bales tradition of research on "sex role differentiation" (task or instrumental vs. social or expressive) in task-oriented groups. The authors argue that sex differences in behavior are better understood in terms of status processes rather than role differentiation, and review a variety of empirical studies in support of understanding sex as a status characteristic.

MISHLER, ELLIOT G.

Studies in dialogue and discourse: II. Types of discourse initiated by and sustained through questioning. *Journal of Psycholinguistic Research*, 4 (1975), 99–121.

Three types of discourse initiated and sustained by questions were identified in taped conversations in four first-grade classrooms. Adults initiating conversations with children retained control through chaining, or successive questioning, a pattern more frequent when the respondent was a boy. Adult-initiated conversations were also longer with boys than girls (adults may exert more control over conversations with boys). Girl-initiated conversations with adults were longer than those initiated by boys and included more active efforts to control interaction with adults. Complex comparisons are made between the question forms used in same-sex and cross-sex conversations among children.

NEMETH, CHARLAN, JEFFREY ENDICOTT, AND JOEL WACHTLER.

From the '50s to the '70s: Women in jury deliberations. *Sociometry*, 39 (1976), 293–304.

A report of two studies of simulated jury deliberation, with interaction of mixed-sex juries of college students coded using the Bales system. In the first study, men were more likely than women to initiate communication and offer suggestions, opinions, and information; men were also the target of more communications. In the second study these sex differences were not found. Neither study found sex differences in socio-emotional categories, and in both, the sexes were perceived by participants in stereotypic ways.

OFSHE, RICHARD.

Gender-linked norms for speech regulation in discussion groups: An application of two-process theory. Unpublished paper, Dept. of Sociology, Univ. of California, Berkeley, 1981.

Gender-homogeneous and gender-heterogeneous discussion groups of undergraduates were taped as they engaged in both social and task activity. All-female groups generated much higher rates of simultaneous speech than did male groups, with the difference greater during social than task activity. In groups with skewed sex ratios (3 to 1) the group adhered to the pattern of the dominant (most verbally active) person's gender-homogeneous group. Majority dominance produced effects at the extremes of gender-linked behavior.

PAINTER, DOROTHY S.

Recognition among lesbians in straight settings. In James W. Chesebro, ed., *Gayspeak: Gay male and lesbian communication.* New York: Pilgrim Press, 1981, pp. 68–91.

In straight settings lesbians check out their intuitive recognition of one another by reading eye contact, listening for key words in conversation (e.g., names of gay bars or use of nonspecific gender terms, such as *person* or *friend* in references to evening activities), and noting the absence of verbal and nonverbal patterns women use to attract men. [*Also see* Sec. IX.]

PARLEE, MARY BROWN.

Conversational politics. *Psychology Today*, 12 (May 1979), 48–56.

A clear, popular discussion of conversational politics, the assertion of power through violation of turn-taking rules, control of topics, and speaking style. Parlee reviews research on cross-sex interaction and emphasizes cultural and situational variation in the nature of turn-taking rules.

PILIAVIN, JANE ALLYN AND RACHEL ROSEMANN MARTIN.

The effects of the sex composition of groups on style of social interaction. *Sex Roles*, 4 (1978), 281–96.

Tapes of mixed-sex and same-sex discussion groups were analyzed using the Bales categories. Regardless of group composition, women displayed more socio-emotional behavior (dramatizes, agrees, shows tension) and men, more task behavior (gives opinion, gives information, disagrees). However, both sexes showed less sex-role stereotypic behavior in mixed-sex than in same-sex groups.

PRIESTLY, J. B.

Journey down the rainbow. *Saturday Review*, Aug. 18, 1956, p. 35. Quoted in Carolyn G. Heilbrun, *Toward a recognition of androgyny*. New York: Alfred A. Knopf, 1973.

Priestly writes about life between the sexes in Dallas, Texas: "I am convinced that good talk cannot flourish where there is a wide gulf between the sexes, where the men are altogether too masculine, too hearty and bluff and booming, where the women are too feminine, at once both too arch and too anxious."

PUTNAM, LINDA L.

Conversational power: What determines conversational control? Paper given at 3rd annual conference on Communication, Language, and Gender, Lawrence, Kan., May–June, 1980.

Much past work on conversational dominance focuses on masculine patterns of power which include control of the floor and command by edict. "Feminine" patterns of power include obtaining the goodwill of those controlled and thus may involve more subtle submissive ploys. More flexible conversationalists may have the most control of the conversation.

RAUSH, HAROLD L., WILLIAM A. BARRY, RICHARD K. HERTEL, AND MARY ANN SWAIN.

Communication, conflict, and marriage. San Francisco: Jossey-Bass, 1974.

In the early 1960s the authors interviewed 46 white, middle-class, newly-wed couples, and later taped them as they each interacted in simulated conflict situations. Husbands and wives tended to respond the same way to each others' acts, and there was not an instrumental/expressive division. Husbands made more efforts to resolve conflict, and wives used more rejection, coercion, and personal attack. The authors suggest that men, who have external status, can offer support for those dependent on them, while women, with less power, resort to manipulative appeals and emotional coercion.

ROSENFELD, HOWARD M.

Approval-seeking and approval-inducing functions of verbal and nonverbal responses in the dyad. *Journal of Personality and Social Psychology,* 4 (1966), 597–605.

Rosenfeld secretly instructed one member of each of 34 same-sex and mixed-sex dyads either to gain or to avoid the approval of the other member. In general, women used shorter utterances than men, especially in the approval-avoiding condition, and more of their utterances were answers to questions. The ratio of speech disturbances to total words spoken was higher for men than for women; there were no sex differences in number of utterances.

SATTEL, JACK W.

Men, inexpressiveness, and power. In this volume; revision of The inexpressive male: Tragedy or sexual politics? *Social Problems,* 23 (1976): 469–77.

Sattel argues that male inexpressiveness is bound up with the power and investment men hold as a group in the social division of labor and in existing institutions. Inexpressiveness, as Sattel illustrates through empirical work and dialogue from fiction, is a strategy by which men keep the upper hand.

SCHAEF, ANNE WILSON.

Women's reality: An emerging female system in the white male society. Minneapolis: Winston Press, 1981.

Schaef argues that a "woman's talk" has evolved from women's perceptions about, for example, time as process, relationships as peer encounters, and the center of the universe as relationships rather than as self and work.

SHAW, MARVIN E. AND ORIN W. SADLER.

Interaction patterns in heterosexual dyads varying in degree of intimacy. *The Journal of Social Psychology,* 66 (1965), 345–51.

Heterosexual dyads of varying degrees of intimacy were asked to discuss two hypothetical problems in interpersonal relations (both male-centered). There were no sex differences in number of turns at talk, women interrupted their partners more frequently than did men, but men showed more initiative in breaking silences. The more intimate couples (especially married ones) were less likely to interrupt each other and more likely to remain silent.

Soskin, William F. and Vera P. John.

The study of spontaneous talk. In Roger Barker, ed., *The stream of behavior.* New York: Appleton-Century-Crofts, 1963.

Radio transmitters were used to record the talk of a wife and husband (Roz and Jock) during a 16-hour day at a summer resort. Jock's claim on available talking time varied from 29% when he was having golf lessons, to 79% when talking with Roz, his wife. Roz produced more affect-discharging messages; Jock, more directive and informational statements. Their talk was most similar in social settings calling for heavy reliance on informational language, and most different in more intimate contexts, where language was more relational.

Spender, Dale.

Man made language. London: Routledge & Kegan Paul, 1980.

In mixed-sex conversations women are queried and interrupted, and their conversations are devalued. Spender gives examples from conferences and describes the conflict that ensued when women challenged men's control of talk (pp. 46–47; 87–89). Consciousness-raising groups are a means to undermine male control and legitimate women's experience and talk. [*Also see* Spender, Sec. I-A.]

Stanback, Marsha Houston.

Language and Black woman's place: Toward a description of Black women's communication. Paper given at meeting of Speech Communication Assoc., Louisville, Kentucky, 1982.

An incisive review showing race, sex, and class biases in prior research on Black women's talk. Stanback explores Black women's experiences as an embedded minority, hidden within two more conspicuous social groups (Blacks and women) and argues that the registers Black women use are shaped by Black definitions of womanhood, Black peoples' ambivalent attitudes towards traditional prescriptions for women's roles, and the relative equality of expression (being outspoken and assertive) of Black men and women. She develops questions for future research.

Stein, Leonard I.

The doctor-nurse game. *American Journal of Nursing*, 68 (1968), 101–05.

A popularly written account of the rules by which doctors and nurses interact. The nurse must be responsible for making significant recommendations while appearing passive and as if the recommendations were initiated by the physician; open disagreement is to be avoided. The author relates the game to doctors' need to display omnipotence and the training of nurses for subservience; the game, he notes, reinforces "stereotyped roles of male dominance and female passivility."

Steinem, Gloria.

The politics of talking in groups. *Ms.*, 9, no. 11 (May 1981), 43, 45, 84, 86–89.

A popularly written article which draws upon findings that men talk and interrupt more than women, that groups of different gender composition have different patterns of talk, and that women's speech tends to be devalued. She offers useful practical suggestions for drawing groups into more symmetric patterns of conversation, for challenging paternalistic behavior, for changing one's own talk. Steinem concludes, "A feminist assault on the politics of talking—and listening—is a radical act."

STRODTBECK, FRED L. AND RICHARD D. MANN.

Sex role differentiation in jury deliberations. *Sociometry*, 19 (1956), 3–11.

Mock jury deliberations were recorded in a laboratory situation and analyzed with the Bales system. Almost twice as much of the women's talk consisted of agreeing, concurring, complying, understanding, and passively accepting; less than half as much of the women's talk showed antagonism or deflated the status of others. Men constituted about two-thirds of the juries, but contributed almost four-fifths of the talk.

SWACKER, MARJORIE.

Women's verbal behavior at learned and professional conferences. In Betty Lou Dubois and Isabel Crouch, eds., *The sociology of the languages of American women*. San Antonio, Texas: Trinity Univ., 1976, pp. 155–60.

In question-answer sessions of three linguistics conferences women's mean time in asking a question was less than half that of men; men were involved in five times more speaker-audience member dialogues; men used more background references in asking questions. Women more often introduced questions with personal reference ("I wonder if. . .") and used more past modal structures ("mightn't it be the case that . . .").

WHITEHEAD, ANN.

Sexual antagonism in Herefordshire. In Diana Leonard Barker and Sheila Allen, eds., *Dependence and exploitation in work and marriage*. New York: Longman, 1976, pp. 169–203.

An ethnographic account of the sex segregation and antagonism characterizing gender relations in a rural parish in England. Joking and teasing infused meetings between the sexes in undefined and informal situations: girls and boys at dances and older married women and men in the pub, where men used verbal dueling to demarcate status. Quarreling was frequent and publicly visible between husbands and wives.

WINTER, WILLIAM D., ANTONIO J. FERREIRA, AND NORMAN BOWERS.

Decision-making in married and unrelated couples. *Family Process*, 12 (1973), 83–94.

The decision-making process of 20 married and 20 unrelated cross-sex couples (all college students) was compared. The two types of couples took about the same time to reach decisions and had the same amount of silence. Married couples showed less politeness, more intrusive interruptions, and less exchange of explicit information.

Also see: I-A: Lakoff; IV-B: Shaw; Shimanoff; VII-B: Haas; Langlois, Gottfried, and Seay.

B. Amount of Speech

ASKINAS, BARRY E.

The impact of coeducational living on peer interaction. Unpublished Ph.D. dissertation, Stanford Univ., Stanford, Calif., 1971. *Diss. Abstracts International*, 1971, 32, 1634-A.

Twenty-four mixed-sex groups of undergraduates, homogeneous by type of residence (coeducational or single-sex) discussed university housing. Women talked more than men in groups from coed housing, but not in groups from single-sex housing. Askinas also studied participants' perceptions of amount of female and male talk. Whether differences were due to learning or to self-selction was unresolved.

COWAN, PHILIP A., J. WEBER, B. A. HODDINOTT, AND J. KLEIN.

Mean length of spoken response as a function of stimulus, experimenter, and subject. *Child Development*, 38 (1967), 191–203.

Ninety-six children, ages 5, 7, 9, and 11, were shown pictures and asked to talk about them. There were no main sex differences in average number of words per remark; sex differences within each age and SES group (divided into low and high SES) were not determined.

DOHERTY, EDMUND G.

Therapeutic community meetings: A study of communication patterns, sex, status, and staff attendance. *Small Group Behavior*, 5 (1974), 244–56.

A participant-observer coded rates of verbal interaction in therapeutic community meetings in a private psychiatric hospital. Male patients spoke most, then physicians (all men); nurses (all but one were women), social workers, occupational therapists, aides, and women patients had similar, lower rates of participation. Among both patients and staff men talked more.

HAMMEN, CONSTANCE L. AND LETITIA A. PEPLAU.

Brief encounters: Impact of gender, sex-role attitudes, and partner's gender on interaction and cognition. *Sex Roles*, 4 (1978), 75–90.

Hidden observers recorded patterns of proximity, looking, and amount of talking in same-sex and mixed-sex pairs of undergraduates who conversed for five minutes. Amount of talking correlated highly with amount of looking. Complex relations were found between amount of speech, gender, and sex-role attitudes (traditional or liberal—determined by a questionnaire).

KENKEL, WILLIAM F.

Observational studies of husband-wife interaction in family decision-making. In Marvin Sussman, ed., *Sourcebook in marriage and the family*. Boston: Houghton Mifflin, 1963, pp. 144–56.

Twenty-five married couples who were young, well-educated, had at least one child, and a homemaker wife were observed while deciding how to spend a sum of money; 52% of all husbands did most or more of the talking, and the remaining 48% were divided between equal-talking couples and those where wives talked more (exact figures aren't given). Only 17 of 50 participants accurately judged the distribution of talk in their own conversations.

MARLATT, G. A.

A comparison of vicarious and direct reinforcement control of verbal behavior in an interview setting. *Journal of Personality and Social Psychology*, 16 (1970), 695–703.

Ninety-six college students discussed personal problems in two separate interviews. In both interviews men talked longer than women, and subjects talked more with female then with male interviewers.

MOREAU, NOÊLLE BISSERET.

Power relationships at work in language: The hidden referent and class/sex identity. In Cheris Kramarae, Muriel Schulz, and William O'Barr, eds., *Language and Power*. Los Angeles: Sage, in press.

Analyzing relationships between language use and power relationships between dominant and dominated groups, Moreau writes: "Silence is often the language of the powerless, the only possible solution when the contradictions are insurmountable."

STRODTBECK, FRED L.

Husband-wife interaction over revealed differences. *American Sociological Review*, 16 (1975), 468–73.

Married couples filled out identical questionaires as individuals and then, together, arrived at common answers for questions on which their initial responses disagreed; the discussions were taped and analyzed. Husbands talked more in 19 of the cases, and wives in 15. For both wives and husbands, greater rate of talking was related to greater influence (winning more contested decisions).

STRODTBECK, FRED L., RITA M. JAMES, AND CHARLES HAWKINS.

Social status in jury deliberations. *American Sociological Review*, 22 (1956), 713–19.

Mock juries listened to a recorded trial, deliberated, and returned their verdict. Analysis of interaction showed that men, compared with women, and those of higher rather than lower status occupations participated more and had higher influence, satisfaction, and perceived competence. At all occupational levels, men talked more than women.

Also see: III-B: Kramer, "Folklinguistics"; Kramer, "Stereotypes of Women's Speech"; III-C: Hilpert, Kramer, and Clark; Schwartz; IV-B: Shaw; Swacker; Wood; IV-E-2: Brownell and Smith; IV-G: Brotherton and Penman; V-A: Argyle, Lalljee, and Cook; Aries; Bernard; Duncan and Fiske; Eakins and Eakins; Edelsky; Greif; Hershey and Werner; Hirschman ("Analysis of supportive . . ."); Hirschman ("Female-male differences . . ."); Ickes and Barnes; Jose, Crosby, and Wong-McCarthy; Komarovsky; Lamb; Leet-Pellegrini; Leffler, Gillespie, and Conaty; Lockheed and Hall; Markel, Long, and Saine; McMillan, Clifton, McGrath, and Gale; Mishler; Rosenfield; Shaw and Sadler; Soskin and John; Strodtbeck and Mann; Swacker; V-F-2: Nearly every item in this section ("Variation by Setting: Classrooms") contains information about sex similarities and differences in amount of speech, e. g., amount of interaction teachers have with girls compared with boys in their classrooms (to save space, these items are not separately cross-referenced here); VII-B: Langlois, Gottfried, and Seay; Langlois, Gottfried, Barnes, and Hendricks; Mueller; IX: Frances.

C. Interruption

ALEGUIRE, DAVID.

Conversational interruptions and male/female assertiveness. Paper given at the 9th World Congress of Sociology, Uppsala, Sweden, 1978.

Aleguire taped himself in separate, unstructured conversations with four men and one woman, all student friends; drawing on participants' recollections, he analyzed a sample of 69 instances of simultaneous speech. Only 7% of the interruption sequences were interpreted by participants as rude, intrusive, or inappropriate. He argues that until different types of interruption are specified, the equation of greater male interruption with domination is premature.

BEATTIE, GEOFFREY W.

Interruption in conversational interaction, and its relation to the sex and status of the interactants. *Linguistics*, 19 (1981), 15–35.

Analysis of videotapes of ten tutorial groups at a British university (each with three to six students and of varying gender composition; half the tutors were women, and half men) revealed that students interrupted tutors more than vice versa. There were no sex differences in either frequency or type of interruption used. The discussion of different types of interruption is especially useful.

HOFFMAN, SUSAN FREEMAN.

Interruptions: Structure and tactics in dyadic conversations. Paper given at the International Communication Assoc. convention, Acapulco, Mexico, 1980.

A study of interruptions in a dyadic situation indicated the sex of the person spoken to was more important than the sex of the speaker, and when interruptions occurred there was a strong tendency for that type of interruption to occur again in the following part of the conversation.

KENNEDY, CAROL W.

Patterns of verbal interruption among women and men in groups. Paper given at 3rd Annual Conference on Communication, Language, and Gender, Lawrence, Kan., 1980.

In meetings of six undergraduate academic work groups women were interrupted significantly more than men, and they did significantly more interrupting. Cross-sex interruptions occurred more often than same-sex interruptions. The frequency distribution of types of interruption was agreement (38%), subject change (23%), disagreement (19%), clarification (11%), and tangentialization (8%).

NATALE, MICHAEL, ELLIOT ENTIN, AND JOSEPH JAFFE.

Vocal interruptions in dyadic communication as a function of speech and social anxiety. *Journal of Personality and Social Psychology*, 37 (1979), 865–78.

Undergraduates conversed in 24 same-sex and 12 mixed-sex pairs. Men interrupted their partners more often than women. The more an individual talked, the greater his/her chance of being interrupted. A speaker's desire for social approval (measured by a personality test) was positively related to the amount of interruption; hence, some interruptions may express a positive state of excitement. Fear of negative evaluation was positively related to a speaker's propensity to give back-channel responses. The speaker's rather than partner's personality was the strongest predictor of interruptions.

OCTIGAN, MARY AND SHARON NIEDERMAN.

Male dominance in conversations. *Frontiers*, 4, no.1 (1979), 50–54.

In same-sex discussions among pairs of college students there were fewer interruptions, more evenly distributed among speakers; in mixed-sex pairs, regardless of stated attitudes of individuals toward sexual equality, men interrupted more, accounting for 68% of all interruptions and overlaps. After the observer said, "Did you know males tend to interrupt more than females?" both sexes interrupted and overlapped less often.

ROGERS, WILLIAM T. AND STANLEY E. JONES.

Effects of dominance tendencies on floor holding and interruption behavior in dyadic interaction. *Human Communication Research*, 1 (1975), 113–22.

A study of ten female and eight male dyads found that persons with more dominant personalities were able to hold the floor more often and attempted more interruptions than their less dominant counterparts. No significant sex differences were found, but the findings tended to be stronger among males.

WEST, CANDACE.

Against our will: Male interruptions of females in cross-sex conversations. In Judith Orsanu, Mariam K. Slater, and Leonore Loeb Adler, eds., *Language, sex and gender*. New York: New York Academy of Sciences, 1979, pp. 81–97.

In five unstructured male-female conversations between undergraduates in a laboratory setting, there were 28 instances of deep interruptions (disrupting a turn) of which 21 or 75% were initiated by men; in every conversation the male interrupted the female more often than the reverse. Both sexes tended to yield the floor to interrupting parties, a tendency less pronounced for women; hence, women did not "invite" interruption by seeming to tolerate such intrusions.

WEST, CANDACE.

"Ask me no questions . . .": An analysis of queries and replies in physician-patient dialogues. In Sue Fisher and Alexandria Todd, eds., *The social organization of doctor-patient communication*. Georgetown, Wash. D.C.: Center for Applied Linguistics, in press.

Analysis of 21 two-party exchanges between physicians and patients recorded in a family practice center in southern U.S. found that 91% of the questions were initiated by doctors. Neither sex nor race (of physician or patient) appeared to be a factor in the distribution of questions.

WEST, CANDACE.

When the doctor is a "lady": Power, status and gender in physician-patient dialogues. In Ann Stromberg, ed., *Women, health and medicine*. Palo Alto: Mayfield, in press.

Physician-patient talk was recorded in ten medical exams (with four women and six men physicians, all white; the six women and four men patients were of various ages and included Blacks as well as whites). Male physicians initiated 32% of interruptions relative to their patients' 68%. The most symmetric interchanges were between women doctors and women patients; in both cases the patients were Black.

WEST, CANDACE.

Why can't a woman be more like a man? An interactional note on organizational game-playing for managerial women. *Sociology of work and occupations* (forthcoming).

A review of the West and Zimmerman research on interruptions in relation to research on, and advice to, women in management. West argues that expensive "women in management" seminars which recommend changes in women's behaviors too often ignore the fact that "assertiveness" takes place in interactions *between* people.

WEST, CANDACE AND DON H. ZIMMERMAN.

Small insults: A study of interruptions in cross-sex conversations between unacquainted persons. In this volume.

The authors summarize findings from earlier research on interruptions between women and men conversing in natural settings and then describe a study of five cross-sex pairs of college students conversing in a laboratory setting. Of the 28 interruptions, 21 or 75% were initiated by men. Analysis of women's responses indicated that women did not "invite" interruption by somehow seeming to tolerate it, nor did men interrupt to "get a word in edgewise"; if anything, the reverse was true.

WEST, CANDACE AND DON H. ZIMMERMAN.

Women's place in everyday talk: Reflections on parent-child interaction. *Social Problems,* 24 (1977), 521–28.

In taped conversations between five different parents and their children in a pediatrician's office, 86% of the interruptions were by the adult. This asymmetric pattern of interruption resembles that between men and women in cross-sex conversations (Zimmerman and West, 1975). Both women and children have restricted rights to speak; men and adults use interruption to display dominant status.

WILLIS, FRANK N. AND SHARON J. WILLIAMS.

Simultaneous talking in conversation and sex of speakers. *Perceptual and Motor Skills,* 43 (1976), 1067–70.

Simultaneous talking was observed in a high school dicussion group, a university faculty office, and the cafeteria of a university student union. In general, listeners were more likely to talk simultaneously if the speaker was female, and men were much more likely to talk when a woman was speaking. Female listeners were more likely to express agreement with male speakers, while both sexes were more likely to disagree with female speakers.

ZIMMERMAN, DON H. AND CANDACE WEST.

Sex roles, interruptions and silences in conversation. In Barrie Thorne and Nancy Henley, eds., *Language and sex: Difference and dominance.* Rowley, Mass.: Newbury House, 1975, pp. 105–29.

The authors examined transcripts of 31 same-sex or mixed-sex, two-party conversations covertly recorded in public places. In same-sex conversations interruptions were distributed nearly equally between partners; in mixed-sex conversations men initiated 96% of all interruptions. Minimal responses (e.g., *um hmm*) and interruptions—both more prevalent in the speech of men in cross-sex conversations—function as mechanisms to control the topic.

Also see: IV-B: Wood; V-A: Argyle, Laljee, and Cook; Courtright, Millar, and Rogers-Millar; Eakins and Eakins; Edelsky; Esposito; Greif; Hirschman (both items); Jose, Crosby, and Wong-McCarthy; Leffler, Gillespie, and Conaty; McMillan, Clifton, McGrath, and Gale; Ofshe; Shaw and Sadler; Winter, Ferreira, and Bowers; V-F-2: Brooks.

D. Conversational Topics

ARIES, ELIZABETH AND FERN L. JOHNSON.

Close friendship in adulthood: Conversational content between same-sex friends. *Sex Roles,* in press.

Questionnaire data from adults (mostly middle-class, middle-aged, and white) indicate that female friends converse more frequently than male friends about intimate topics and daily, shared activities.

AYRES, JOE.

Relationship stages and sex as factors in topic dwell time. *Western Journal of Speech Communication,* 44 (1980), 253–60.

Two conversations between same and mixed-sex pairs of friends were taped a month apart. Male pairs talked longest about each topic, then female pairs, then mixed-sex pairs. In all three types most talk was about relationships with others and schools. Female pairs talked more about feelings, appearances, and home life, and males about entertainment events. Different topic change patterns were associated with each type of dyad.

BARRON, N. J. AND M. J. MARLIN.

Sex of the speaker and the grammatical case and gender of referenced persons. Technical Report No. C1 53, Center for Research in Social Behavior. Columbia: Univ. of Missouri, 1971.

Videotapes of teachers and students in sixth and eleventh grade classrooms were coded; both men and women teachers talked about males more than about females.

COZBY, PAUL C.

Self-disclosure: A literature review. *Psychological Bulletin,* 79 (1973), 73–91.

A number of studies (many by Jourard and his colleagues) found females more self-disclosing than males, but other studies found no sex differences. No study reported greater male disclosure.

HACKER, HELEN MAYER.

Blabbermouths and clams: Sex differences in self-disclosure in same-sex and cross-sex friendship dyads. *Psychology of Women Quarterly,* 5 (1981), 385–401.

Drawing on interviews with friendship pairs, Hacker found differences in self-disclosure only in mixed-sex dyads (men were more confiding but hid weaknesses; women concealed their strengths). Hacker suggests that men may be less willing to listen or feel less social distance toward women than women feel toward men.

JOHNSON, FERN L. AND ELIZABETH J. ARIES.

Conversational patterns among late-adolescent, close friends: A study of same-sex pairs. *Journal of Genetic Psychology,* in press.

Questionnaire data from 176 college students on conversations among same-sex close friends indicated that females conversed more often and in greater depth about themselves and their close relationships, and males about sports, reminiscences about the past, hobbies, and shared activities.

KLEIN, J.

The family in "traditional" working-class England. In Michael Anderson, ed., *Sociology of the family.* Baltimore, Md.: Penguin, 1971, pp. 70–77.

Within the culture of miners, woman's place is in the home, and man's place is with other men at work, at the club, the pub, the corner, the sports-ground. In some ways men form a secret society, deliberately excluding women, children, and strangers, partly through "pit-talk" or swear-words used familiarly within the group and offensively to those outside. Men in the clubs talk about work and sports, but never about their homes and families; women talk about *their* work, i.e., their homes and families. The men discourage transgressions across this division of interests.

LANDIS, CARNEY.

National differences in conversations. *Journal of Abnormal and Social Psychology,* 21 (1927), 354–75.

Landis collected 200 fragments of conversation overheard in London. As in the U.S. studies [Landis and Burtt, and Moore, separately annotated] the man-to-man conversations were about business and money, amusements or sports, and other men. Women talked to each other of other women and themselves. Men talked to women about women, clothes, and themselves, and women talked to men about other women and about themselves.

LANDIS, M. H. AND H. E. BURTT.

A study of conversations. *Journal of Comparative Psychology,* 4 (1924), 81–89.

The authors recorded 481 conversations overheard in Columbus, Ohio. Their findings were similar to those of Moore [this section].

LANGER, ELINOR.

The women of the telephone company. *New York Review of Books,* 14 (March 12, 1970, and March 26, 1970).

After three months working (and observing) as a Customer's Service Representative in the New York Telephone Co., Langer concluded that in her department, staffed mainly by women, religion and politics were avoided in conversation, whereas in the men's departments, political discussions were commonplace.

MOORE, H. T.

Further data concerning sex differences. *Journal of Abnormal and Social Psychology,* 4 (1922), 81–89.

Moore walked down Broadway in New York City, overhearing and recording 174 fragments of conversation. He found that men talked to men about money and business (48% of the fragments), amusements or sports (14%), and other men (13%). Women talked to women about men (44%), clothing or decoration (23%), and other women (16%). Men talked to women about amusements or sports (25%) and money and business (22%). Women talked to men about other men (22%) and other women (13%).

MULCHAHY, G. A.

Sex differences in patterns of self-disclosure among adolescents: A developmental perspective. *Journal of Youth and Adolescence,* 4 (1973), 343–56.

A self-disclosure questionnaire, administered to 97 adolescents, revealed that girls engaged in more same-sex disclosure than boys. For girls, there was high disclosure about tastes, interests, and personality; for boys, about tastes, interests, work (studies), and attitudes and opinions. For males, the lowest disclosure area was about the body; money was the lowest disclosure area for females.

MYERHOFF, BARBARA.

Number our days. New York: Simon & Schuster, 1980.

In this ethnography of a community of elderly Jews in Venice, California, Myerhoff describes sex-segregated seating and talk on the benches along the boardwalk. The men talked about "abstract, ideological concerns"—politics, religion, economics; the women talked about immediate, personal matters—children, food, health, neighbors, scandals, and "managing." Both sexes talked about Israel, about being Jews, and about the Senior Citizens' Center. Storytelling was an important activity for both sexes.

VIGIL, YVONNE TIXIER Y AND NAN ELSASSER.

The effects of the ethnicity of the interviewer on conversation: A study of Chicana women. In Betty Lou Dubois and Isabel Crouch, eds., *The sociology of the languages of American women.* San Antonio, Texas: Trinity Univ., 1976, pp. 161–69.

Fifteen Chicana respondents talked more about sex with an Anglo than with a Chicana interviewer who asked the same questions (both interviews were in English). There were complex patterns in talk about discrimination. The authors conclude that Chicanas operate in two distinct cultural systems which constrain topic and style.

Also see: III-C: Eble; V-A: Aries ("Interaction patterns . . ."); Fishman ("What do couples talk about . . ."); Goodwin; Komarovsky; March; VII-B: Haas.

E.   Control of Topics

The study of how topics are raised, dropped, developed, changed, and diverted in conversations may reveal sex differences; this is part of the general issue of control of conversations. Pamela Fishman [three papers in Sec. V-A] found that in cross-sex conversations the topics men raised were much more often developed than those women raised, largely because of women's greater "interaction work" (answering questions, providing active conversational support). Similarly, Don H. Zimmerman and Candace West [Sec. V-C] found that when a woman tried to develop a topic in her turns at talk, the man often gave minimal responses, which, along with more frequent male interruptions, became mechanisms by which men controlled the topic in mixed-sex conversations. Jessie Bernard [Sec. V-A] uses a tennis metaphor for this pattern of minimal response; one partner (more often the woman) supplies balls which are rarely returned.

In a study of talk of a couple in naturalistic settings, William F. Soskin and Vera P. John [Sec. V-A] found that the husband's conversation followed a single theme, while the wife tried to shift the conversation to other topics. Studying a sample of married couples, Harold Feldman (*Development of the Husband-Wife Relationship,* Ithaca, N.Y.: Cornell Univ. Press, 1965) found that the woman's initiative in starting conversations was less often rewarded. There was a negative relationship between initiation of discussion by the wife and the amount of time the couple spent talking with one another daily. Jack Sattel [Sec. V-A] analyzes a related phenomenon—male inexpressiveness, which he connects with men's defense of greater power.

F.   Variation By Setting

All speech takes place in a social context or setting. The context—with situation-specific rules for interaction and distinctive activities, size, and sex, race, and class composition—may influence the gender differentiation of talk. This section cross-references studies located in other sections to call attention to the importance of situation. Much research has been done in experimental laboratories; those studies are not cross-referenced here, but (as many researchers realize) it is important to understand laboratories as social situations. The section on classrooms [V-F-2], a relatively well-defined social situation, contains references not, for the most part, found elsewhere in the bibliography.

1.   Bars

See: V-A: Whitehead; VI-A-1: Mann; VI-A-2: Painter; VI-A-3: Leary.

2.   Classrooms

Interaction in classrooms has less often been studied at college than at earlier levels of schooling. The methods of research have typically involved observations with pre-set coding schemes which focus on only a few dimensions of talk, and questionnaires to tap attitudes and perceptions. This is an area where differentiation of talk according to sex of person spoken to (teacher speech to male vs. female students) has been extensively studied. This bibliography is selective, and further information can be found in review essays by Brophy and Good, and by Safilios-Rothschild, cited below. [Many of the items in this section are relevant to Sec. V-B ("Conversational Interaction: Amount of Speech") and to Sec. VII-A ("Children and Language: Language between Adults and Children") and, unless highly salient, are not separately cross-referenced to those sections.]

BIBER, HENRY, LOUISE B. MILLER, AND J. L. DYER.

Feminization in preschool. *Developmental Psychology,* 7 (1972), 86.

Analysis of videotaped segments of 14 preschool classes revealed that teachers had more instructional contact with girls than with boys. (A relatively unusual finding; there are far more studies finding that boys receive more contact with teachers.)

BOERSMA, P. DEE, DEBORA GAY, RUTH A. JONES, LYNN MORRISON, AND HELEN REMICK.

Sex differences in college student-teacher interactions: Fact or fantasy? *Sex Roles,* 7 (1981), 775–84.

Observations of 50 college classes found few sex differences in number and type of interaction between students and teachers, although in classes taught by women there were proportionately more student-teacher exchanges involving men than women students. Teachers apparently perceived this pattern; in a questionnaire 68% of women but only 23% of men teachers said men students participated proportionately more than women students in their classes.

BROOKS, VIRGINIA R.

Sex differences in student dominance behavior in female and male professors' classrooms. *Sex Roles,* 8 (1982), 683–90.

In six graduate classes in social work (half taught by women and half by men) men students were 24.5% of all students, but accounted for 40.7% of all student turns at talk, 39.8% of speech duration, and 50.3% of all interruptions. There were no significant sex differences in amount of talk in classes taught by men; in classes taught by women, men spoke significantly more often and longer than women students. More than three fourths of all interruptions occurred in classes of women professors, and there was twice as much student participation in classes taught by women than in classes taught by men.

BROPHY, JERE E. AND THOMAS L. GOOD.

Teacher-student relationships: Causes and consequences. New York: Holt, Rinehart and Winston, 1974.

Chapter 7, "The Influence of the Sex of the Teacher and Student on Classroom Behavior," reviews around 100 studies, some of them on verbal interaction, primarily in elementary schools. Brophy and Good summarize trends in the literature: compared with girls, boys are generally more salient and active, dominating interactions with teachers, making more contributions to discussions, and receiving both more criticism and more praise from teachers. In general, differences between male and female teachers seem to be less frequent and less intense than differences between male and female students. The authors argue that most of the sex differences in classroom data can be attributed to student sex differences in classroom behaviors (e.g., boys initiating more contact with teachers).

CHERRY, LOUISE.

The preschool teacher-child dyad: Sex differences in verbal interaction. *Child Development,* 46 (1975), 532–35.

In recorded conversations between four women preschool teachers and children in their classes teachers verbally interacted and initiated more, and used more attentional-marked utterances in speech with boys than with girls. There were no significant differences in reciprocity or length of verbal interactions of teachers with girls and with boys; girls received more verbal acknowledgement of their answers to teachers' questions.

CROUCH, ISABEL M. AND BETTY LOU DUBOIS.

Interpersonal communication in the classroom: Which sex's speech is inferior? *Journal of the Linguistics Association of the Southwest,* 2 (1977), 129–41.

Analysis of tapes of 12 lab sessions of a college speech communications class revealed no overall sex differences in turns at talk, number of questions, broken fluency, interjections, garbles, or semantically empty expressions. The authors note wide variation from session to session which bears further analysis.

ELLIOTT, JOHN.

Sex role constraints on freedom of discussion: A neglected reality of the classroom. *The New Era,* 55 (1978), 147–55.

In a mixed-sex discussion class which Elliott taught in a secondary school in Britain both girls and boys defined the discussion in terms of cross-sex competition, and same-sex solidarity often governed the participation of individuals. Boys participated more than girls, perhaps partly because the topic was war. The boys didn't worry about non-participating girls, although more talkative girls did.

GOOD, THOMAS L., J. NEVILLE SIKES, AND JERE E. BROPHY.

Effects of teacher sex and student sex on classroom interaction. *Journal of Educational Psychology,* 65 (1973), 74–87.

Observations of 16 junior high classrooms found boys interacted more with teachers than girls; boys initiated more in the classroom, and teachers provided them more response opportunities. Boys received more positive and more negative contacts from teachers, but proportionately more of the girls' contacts were positive. Female teachers' classes were more relaxed and discussion-oriented; male teachers' classes, more structured.

JACKSON, PHILIP W. AND HENRIETTE M. LAHADERNE.

Inequalities of teacher-pupil contacts. *Psychology in the Schools,* 4 (1976), 204–11.

An observational study of four sixth grade classrooms found that interaction patterns varied from room to room, but as a group, the boys received eight to ten times more messages from teachers than did the girls.

KAJANDER, CHERYL ANN.

The effects of instructor and student sex on verbal behaviors in college classrooms. Unpublished Ph.D. dissertation, Univ. of Texas at Austin, 1976. *Dissertation Abstracts,* 37 (5-A), 2743–44.

In English classes taught by 16 women and 16 men teaching assistants, female students answered more rote questions, while male students initiated more contact with teachers. Students with women teachers answered more questions, initiated more contact, and received more feedback. There were few sex differences, however, in coded teacher behaviors.

KARP, DAVID A. AND WILLIAM C. YOELS.

The college classroom: Some observations on the meanings of student participation. *Sociology and Social Research,* 60 (1976), 421–39.

In ten college classes with balanced sex ratios, men students participated more in all cases, but with women instructors the amount of participation by women students increased. Men teachers were more likely to directly question men than women students, a difference not present in classes taught by women. Students may not perceive these sex differences; in a questionnaire, both sexes said that the teacher's sex makes no difference in their likelihood of participating in class. The paper contains an interesting discussion of the organizational features of college classrooms.

KJERULFF, KRISTEN H. AND MILTON R. BLOOD.

A comparison of communication patterns in male and female graduate students. *Journal of Higher Education,* 44 (1973), 623–32.

Analysis of questionnaires administered to 27 women and 41 men graduate students in the same psychology department revealed that the men had proportionately more discussions with their research advisers, including more discussions concerning the adviser's problems or interests. Women students were more likely than men to discuss research interests with other graduate students.

MACKE, ANNE STATHAM AND LAUREL WALUM RICHARDSON, WITH JUDITH COOK.

Sex-typed teaching styles of university professors and student reactions. Columbus, Ohio: The Ohio State Univ. Research Foundation, 1980.

College classes were observed and interactions coded. There was more student input in women's than men's classes regardless of department, course level, or sex ratio or size of class. Women teachers overall, and men in fields where women predominate, were seen as more likable, but also as less competent in their subject matter, the more they generated student participation. Men teachers more often used direct, harsh, and ridiculing means of dealing with students.

MARTIN, ROY.

Student sex and behavior as determinants of the type and frequency of teacher-student contacts. *Journal of School Psychology,* 10 (1972), 339–47.

Second-grade boys whom teachers regarded as behavior problems interacted with teachers significantly more than boys who were not seen as behavior problems, and more than girls, regardless of their classroom behavior. Girls considered to be behavior problems may less often disrupt classroom routines, tending instead to be passive, dependent, and withdrawn.

MEYER, WILLIAM J. AND GEORGE O. THOMPSON.

Sex differences in the distributions of teacher approval and disapproval among sixth grade children. *The Journal of Educational Psychology,* 47 (1956), 385–96.

During observations of three sixth grade classes boys received both more teacher scolding and more praise than did girls. Both girls and boys perceived boys as receiving more teacher disapproval.

PARKER, ANGELE M.

Sex differences in classroom argumentation. Unpublished M.S. thesis, Pennsylvania State Univ., University Park, 1973.

Classroom observations were made of 200 college students, who were asked to rate discussion behavior from "highly masculine" to "highly feminine" on a 4-point scale. Men students participated significantly more often in discussions than women, yet a greater number of women made at least one statement. Students rated intellectual participation behaviors as "masculine."

RICHARDSON, LAUREL WALUM, JUDITH A. COOK, AND ANNE STATHAM.

Down the up staircase: Male and female university professors' classroom management strategies. In Laurel Richardson and Verta Taylor, eds., *Feminist frontiers.* Reading, Mass.: Addison-Wesley, 1983, pp. 280–86.

University teachers were interviewed about strategies for managing classrooms. At every rank, women's responses indicated they were less harsh, more accepting, and more likely than men teachers to engage in the give-and-take of classroom discussion, while men were more likely to publicly reprimand and directly correct students.

ROBERTSON, ANGELIKA.

The relationship of class sex composition, teacher sex, and selected attitudinal variables to the verbal class participation of female college students. Unpublished Ed.D. dissertation, Univ. of Massachusetts, Amherst, 1978.

Observation of four mixed-sex and four all-female small, discussion-oriented classes in the social sciences revealed no sex differences in overall amount of talk, although specific classes differed in notable ways. In mixed-sex classes conversation consisted mostly of comments rather than questions and answers, whereas in all-female classes participation was more often specifically invited and moderated by the teacher.

SAFILIOS-ROTHSCHILD, CONSTANTINA.

Sex role socialization and sex discrimination: A synthesis and critique of the literature. Washington, D.C.: National Institute of Education, 1979.

The author summarizes recurring findings in research published between 1960 and 1978: teachers both criticize and praise boys more frequently than girls, with low achieving boys receiving the most teacher criticism, and high achieving boys receiving the most praise and reward. She notes that concern about boys' poorer academic achievement motivated early extensive inquiry into possible sex differences in teacher behavior. Only recently has the "semi-ignored" status of girls in classrooms been considered a problem for research and action.

SERBIN, LISA, DANIEL O'LEARY, RONALD KENT, AND ILLENE TONICK.

A comparison of teacher response to the preacademic and problem behavior of boys and girls. *Child Development,* 44 (1973), 796–804.

Teachers in 15 preschool classrooms responded over three times as often to boys who hit or broke things as to girls, and boys received three times more loud reprimands. Teachers had longer conversations with boys, and gave them more praise and more brief and extended directions than girls. There were no sex differences in frequency of brief conversation. Girls, but not boys, got more teacher attention when they were physically close to the teacher.

SHYMANSKY, JAMES A. AND JOHN E. PENICK.

Do laboratory teaching assistants exhibit sex bias? *Journal of College Science Teaching,* 8 (1979), 223–25.

The behavior of 42 male and eight female teaching assistants in college science laboratory classes was coded into pre-set categories. Female TA's asked a higher proportion of short answer and extended-thought questions. Both male and female TA's spent less time interacting with cross-sex than with same-sex lab partners. In the rare times when TA's used sarcasm, it was invariably directed at students of the other sex.

SIKES, J. NEVILLE.

Differential behavior of male and female teachers. Unpublished doctoral dissertation, Univ. of Texas, Austin, 1971.

Sikes observed eight male and eight female teachers interacting with junior high school students. Boys were more active in the classrooms and received both more criticism and more positve contact with teachers. There was no significant difference in the behavior of women and men teachers, although in classes taught by women, students initiated more comments and questions, had more response opportunities, and initiated more private conversations with the teacher.

STERNGLANZ, SARAH HALL AND SHIRLEY LYBERGER-FICEK.

Sex differences in student-teacher interactions in the college classroom, *Sex Roles,* 3 (1977), 345–52.

Student-teacher interactions were observed and recorded in 60 college classes. In classes taught by men, male students engaged in proportionately more student-teacher interactions, largely because men students more often initiated interaction with the teacher. There was no sex difference in female-taught classes. Neither male nor female teachers appeared to respond differentially to male and female students.

THORNE, BARRIE.

Claiming verbal space: Women, speech, and language in college classrooms. Paper given at the Research Conference on Educational Environments and Undergraduate Women, Wellesley College, Wellesley, Mass., Sept. 1979.

This speculative paper suggests that women teachers and students may be at a verbal disadvantage because of the devaluation of women's talk (the male as the "voice of authority") and because of patterns of male verbal control. The cooperative forms of talk which have been found in all-female groups may suggest ways to transform the dominance and competition of much interaction in college classrooms.

TREICHLER, PAULA AND CHERIS KRAMARAE.

Women's talk in the ivory tower. *Communication Quarterly,* 31 (1983).

This review of the research on classroom interaction leads the authors to identify the structure of classroom talk itself as *one* reason many women find the classroom inhospitable. Norms of college classroom interaction are more closely aligned with typical male patterns of interaction than with typical female patterns.

Also see: II-I: Adamsky; Bate; IV-E-2: Cherry; V-A: Mishler; V-C: Beattie; V-H: Kuhn.

Guidelines for changing sexism in classroom interaction. Two guidelines have been developed to assist college teachers and students who may want to assess and change sexist patterns in classroom interaction: *The Classroom Climate: A Chilly One for Women?* Available from the Project on the Status and Education of Women, Assoc. of American Colleges, 1818 R St., N.W., Washington, D.C. 20009; and Mercilee M. Jenkins, major contributing author, *Guidelines for Student-Faculty Communication,* part of Judith M. Gappa and Janice Pearce, *Sex and Gender in the Social Sciences: Reassessing the Introductory Course.* Available from The Speech Communication Assoc., 5105 Backlick Rd. #E, Annandale, VA 22003, and available, bound with content guidelines for sociology, from the American Sociological Assoc. Teaching Resources Center, 1722 N St., N.W., Washington, D.C. 20036.

3. Intimate and Domestic Situations

See: I-A: Kramarae, Ch. IX, "Family—Ties that bind," in *Women and men speaking;* III-B: Hawkins, Weisberg, and Ray; III-D: Rubin; IV-B: Hopper, Knapp, and Scott; V-A: Aldous; Courtright, Millar, and Rogers-Millar; Fishman ("Conversational insecurity"); Fishman ("Interaction"); Fishman ("What do couples talk about . . ."); Greif; Heiss; Hershey and Werner; Kaplan; Komarovsky; Leik; Lewis; March; Raush, Barry, Hertel, and Swain; Shaw and Sadler; Soskin and John; Whitehead; Winter, Ferreira, and Bowers; V-B: Kenkel; Strodtbeck; V-D: Aries and Johnson; Ayres; Hacker, Johnson and Aries; Klein; V-E: Feldman; VII-A: Many of the references in this section, on language between adults and children, focus on parent-child interaction, and hence are pertinent to this section. They are not separately cross-referenced here.

4. Juries

See: III-B: O'Barr and Atkins; III-C: Bradac, Hemphill, and Tardy; Erickson, Lind, Johnson, and O'Barr; V-A: Nemeth, Endicott, and Wachtler; Strodtbeck and Mann; V-B: Strodtbeck, James, and Hawkins.

5. Meetings and Conferences

See: IV-B: Dubois and Crouch; V-A: Coser, Eakins and Eakins; Edelsky; Johnson; Spender; Swacker; V-B: Doherty; V-C: Kennedy.

6. Women's Consciousness-Raising Groups

See: V-A: Jenkins and Kramer; Kalčik; Spender; VI-A-3: Jenkins.

7. Work Settings

See: II-F: Wolfson and Manes; III-C: Baird and Bradley; IV-B: Bentz; V-A: Stein; V-C: West ("Ask me no questions. . . ."); West ("When the doctor is a 'lady' "); West ("Why can't a woman . . ."); V-D- Klein; Langer; V-F-1, 2, 5: Since bars, classrooms, meetings, and conferences are places of work, references in these sections may also be pertinent; VI-A-1: Mann; Sikes.

G. Changing the Way We Speak

Deliberate efforts to change the way people—especially women—talk and use nonverbal communication have emerged in the last decade, often in connection with the research reported in this bibliography. That there is a praxis to the study of women's and men's conversational interaction is evident, for example, in Nancy Henley's suggestions for "breaking the body-power barrier" and her discussion of "the limits of personal change" in *Body politics,* pp. 202–05 [Sec. IX]; in Gloria Steinem's "The politics of talking in groups" [Sec. V-A], which offers practical tips for making conversations more symmetric; and in analyses of ways in which feminist consciousness-raising groups have created new forms of naming and speech, making more visible and legitimate the cooperative styles of woman-woman talk [Sec. V-F-6].

Self-help books and programs have also emerged, e.g., Janet Stone and Jane Bachner, *Speaking up: A book for every woman who wants to speak effectively* (New York: McGraw-Hill, 1977) draws on research on women and communication to suggest ways to project self-confident body language and talk. Assertiveness training programs, with roots broader than the women's movement, have been directed more toward women than men, seeking to further women's equality in the public sphere. For a summary of basic tenets (e.g., a distinction between being assertive—speaking up, resisting interruption—and being aggressive—monopolizing conversation, interrupting others frequently), see Jean Withers, "Don't talk while I'm interrupting," *Ms.*, 3 (March 1975), pp. 106–09, and Patricia Jakubowski-Spector, "Facilitating the growth of women through assertive training," *The Counseling Psychologist*, 4 (1973), 75–86.

Some feminists have criticized the assumptions and practices of assertiveness training; e.g., Nancy Henley, "Assertiveness training: Making the political personal," paper given at meetings of the Society for the Study of Social Problems, August 1979; and Cheris Kramarae, Ch. X, "Women [and men] as rational speakers" in *Women and men speaking* [Sec. I-A]. They argue that the emphasis on individual power and on making it within the existing system neglects the political context, including the need for social change; and that emphasis on the "weaknesses" of women's speech tends to blame the victim, ignoring values in women's traditional ways of speaking, and taking men's speech as the norm, rather than regarding it as problematic. On this point, see Barrie Thorne, Cheris Kramarae, and Nancy Henley, "Language, gender and society," in this volume.

H.   Other Languages

ATTILI, GRAZIA.

Due Modeli di conversazione. *Studi di Grammatica Italiana*, 6 (1977), 191–206. (Instit Psicologia Consiglio Nazionale Richere, 00157, Rome, Italy).

Tapes were made of conversations of young, married men and women, divided into eight couples (matched for social class) of same and mixed sex. Conversations between females showed more cooperation and less competition among working class participants doing housework or manual work and among upper class participants doing housework, with more competition and less cooperation among upper class participants doing intellectual work. The female/female conversations were more horizontal and symmetrical than the female/male interchanges.

BLAKAR, ROLV MIKKEL AND TOVE BEATE PEDERSEN.

Control and self-confidence as reflected in sex-bound patterns in communication: An experimental approach. Unpublished manuscript, Institute of Psychology, Univ. of Oslo, Norway, 1979.

Two experimental communication situations were structured. In the first, male-explainer to female-follower dyads were the most efficient, and the female to male dyads were the most inefficient. In the second situation the male to female dyads were more inefficient than the female to male dyads or the same sex dyads. No generalizations about the communication efficiency of men versus women can be made without reference to the specific situation.

BROWN, PENELOPE.

How and why are woman more polite: Some evidence from a Mayan community. In Sally McConnell-Ginet, Ruth Borker, and Nelly Furman, eds., *Women and language in literature and society*. New York: Praeger, 1980, pp. 111–36.

Work on the speech of women and men needs to be analyzed in terms of social-structural pressures and constraints on their behavior; women in all cultures are rational and work toward achieving individual goals. Using data from Mayan Indians of Mexico, Brown indicates how women's expressions of politeness respect the feelings of others and show consciousness of women's place in the social structure. We must begin our work by recognizing the linguistic and social facts which have reality for the speakers.

KEENAN, ELINOR.

Norm-makers, norm-breakers: Uses of speech by men and women in a Malagasy community. In J. F. Sherzer and R. Baumann, eds., *Explorations in the ethnography of speaking*. New York: Cambridge Univ. Press, 1974, pp. 125–43.

In the Merina tribe in Madagascar, strong value is placed on speaking indirectly and avoiding open confrontation. Men are regarded as skillful at this type of speech; they use an illusive and formal style. Women are seen as norm-breakers, associated with a direct, straightforward, impolite manner of speech, blurting out what they mean and communicating anger and negative information. Men dominate situations where indirectness is desirable, such as ceremonial speech situations and inter-village relations.

KUHN, ELISABETH.

Geschlechtsspezifische Unterschiede in der Sprachverwendung (Sex-related differences in the use of speech). Trier, West Germany: L.A.U.T. Publications, Linguistic Agency of the Univ. of Trier, 1982.

In the first meeting of courses in a West Germany university women lecturers used more qualifying devices, such as weakening particles, emphatic particles, subjunctives, parenthetical verbs and tag questions, and directly addressed the students more often than men. Women also had a more cooperative discussion style, leaving more options to the students.

MARSHALL, LORNA.

Sharing, talking and giving: Relief of social tensions among !Kung Bushmen. In Joshua A. Fishman, eds., *Readings in the sociology of language*. The Hague: Mouton, pp. 179–84.

In this tribal, gathering-hunting society, men talk about past hunts. The women, who did not talk as much as the men, were more likely to talk about who did or did not give them food, and about women they considered very capable.

MILITANSKIJ, O.M.

Communicative dependence among children of middle school age upon age-sex characteristics. In A. A. Bodalev and B. D. Parygin, eds., *Socio-psychological and linguistic characteristics of forms of communication and the development of contact among people. Abstracts of an All-Union symposium*. Leningrad, 1970, pp. 109–10.

At Young Pioneer Camps, where boys and girls are kept separate, each group expresses low opinion of the other sex. When boys and girls are together, antagonism is low. [Translation and abstract by Susan Wobst]

TRÖMEL-PLÖTZ, SENTA.

The construction of conversational differences in women's and men's speech. Paper given at the Tenth World Congress of Sociology, Mexico City, 1982.

A study of discussions on German television found the women all used joining techniques to introduce their turns; their autonomous contributions did not succeed. Men used joinings (e.g., "yes," "but," and "I am in complete agreement with you" said before disagreeing), but far less often; their autonomous starts of turns succeeded.

WERNER, FRITJOF.
Gesprächsarbeit und Themenkontrolle, *Linguistische Berichte* 71 (1981), 26–46.

In this German study, groups with three male and female student members each were observed while they made decisions. Although there were initially no significant differences in the quality of individual solutions, and even though males and females did not differ significantly in their amount of talking, women were addressed significantly less often than the men, their suggestions had less influence on the group decision and were considered to be of much lower quality than the males', and subsequently they were chosen less frequently as partners for future cooperation. [Author's abstract]

Also see: VII-D: Fichtelius, Johansson, and Nordin; Jormakka.

VI. GENRE AND STYLE

A. Speech Genres

In a given social group, there may be specific types of speech genres, rituals, or expressive forms particular to either sex; the sexes may also use the same forms. Several writers have pointed to researchers' neglect of genres and verbal art created and used by women, which have been trivialized as "gossip" or "just talk," and which have been ignored because informants have so often been male. Marta Weigle, in "Women as verbal artists: Reclaiming the sisters of Enheduanna" (*Frontiers*, 3, no. 3 [1978], 1–9), provides an excellent review of women's folklore and verbal art; and Claire R. Farrer's "Women and folklore: Images and genres" (*Journal of American Folklore*, 88 [Jan.–March 1975]), reprinted as Claire R. Farrer, ed., *Women and folklore* (Austin: Univ. of Texas Press, 1975, pp. VII–XVII)), traces the history of folklore scholarship pertaining to women. See also Rosan A. Jordan and Susan J. Kalčik, eds., *Women's folklore, women's culture* (Philadelphia: Univ. of Pennsylvania Press, 1983). For a general bibliographic survey which includes humor, joking, verbal contests, obscenity, riddling, and narratives, see Barbara Kirshenblatt-Gimblett, ed., *Speech play* (Philadelphia: Univ. of Pennsylvania Press, 1976, pp. 179–223). A periodical, *Folklore Women's Communication,* edited by Carol Mitchell and Kathleen Manley (English Dept., Univ. of North Colorado, Greeley, CO 80639) reports ongoing work. The following genres have been studied in a gender-sensitive way:

1.   Verbal Dueling and Ritualized Joking

Among Black speakers in urban areas, there are forms of verbal dueling—*the dozens, signifying, sounding*—which may involve distinctions according to the sex of speakers and audience. Most studies of these speech forms have been based primarily on male informants, especially younger men, providing insight into the structure of male peer groups, beliefs about masculinity, social class and regional variation, and shifts in the use of Black vernacular over the life course. A sampling of this literature: Roger Abrahams, *Deep down in the jungle* (Chicago: Aldine, 1970) and *Talking Black* (Rowley, Mass.: Newbury House, 1976) [*Also see* Abrahams (two items), Sec. V-A]; essays in Thomas Kochman, ed., *Rappin' and stylin' out: Communication in urban Black America* (Urbana: Univ. of Illinois Press, 1972); and in Alan Dundes, ed., *Mother wit from the laughing barrel* (Englewood Cliffs, N.J.: Prentice-Hall, 1973); William Labov, "Rules for ritual insults" in *Language in the inner city* (Philadelphia: Univ. of Pennsylvania Press, 1972, pp. 297–353); and Ulf Hannerz, *Soulside* (New York: Columbia Univ. Press, 1969).

Edith Folb (*Runnin' down some lines*) [Sec IV-B] calls attention to the absence of research on Black women's expressive behavior and describes the skill of young Black women in using vernacular, including forms of verbal dueling; she also points to the greater constraint on females' use of these forms. Claudia Mitchell-Kernan ("Signifying," in Dundes, *op. cit.,* pp. 310–28; and

"Signifying, loud-talking and marking," in Kochman, *op. cit.,* pp. 315–35) collected data from Black women and observes that although women engage in speech acts like signifying and sounding, this is usually not in the context of verbal dueling. "Because verbal dueling permits a great deal of license (not absolute in any sense) women cannot be suitably competitive because other social norms require more circumspection in their verbal behavior" ("Signifying," p. 328). Roger Abrahams [*see* Abrahams (two items), Sec. V-A] also describes Black women's use of *smart talk* and *playing the dozens,* and argues that as women get older, they increasingly adopt respectability values and move away from the vernacular.

Ritualized, often obscene joking and insults have been described in other groups and settings. Millicent R. Ayoub and Stephen A. Barnett, in "Ritualized verbal insult in white high school culture" (*Journal of American Folklore,* 78 [1961], 337–44), describe the *sounding, burning, ranking, cutting down*—which escalated into *mother-sounding* (scurrilous comments on the sexual behavior of the opponent's mother)—played by white high school boys in Ohio. White boys sometimes sounded with Black male classmates, especially during sports events, and, the authors speculate, the genre may have originated in Afro-American culture. In an interview, most of the girls denied knowing the game, although one Black girl "jeered at this and said they certainly knew it well but were reluctant to say so." See also Simon J. Brommer, "A re-examining of white dozens" (*Western Folklore,* 37 [1978], 118–28). For analyses of similar types of verbal dueling played by boys and young men in other cultures, see Alan Dundes, Jerry W. Leach, and Bora Ozkok, "The strategy of Turkish boys' verbal dueling rhymes," in John J. Gumperz and Dell Hymes, eds., *Directions in sociolinguistics* (New York: Holt, Rinehart and Winston, 1972, pp. 130–60); and Gary H. Gossen, "Verbal dueling in Chamula," in Barbara Kirshenblatt-Gimblett, ed., *Speech play* (Philadelphia: Univ. of Pennsylvania Press, 1976, pp. 21–46).

Brenda Mann, in "Bar talk," in James P. Spradley and David W. McCurdy, eds., *Conformity and conflict* (Boston: Little, Brown, 1971, pp. 101–11), describes patterns of joking which expressed asymmetry between male bartenders and waitresses in a college bar in the midwest. See also James P. Spradley and Brenda J. Mann, *The cocktail waitress* (New York: John Wiley & Sons, 1973). Bartenders and waitresses *gave each other shit* and engaged in *slamming* (making personal digs at another's deficiencies). Bartenders had more latitude in these speech forms because of taboos on women using dirty words and because, as subordinates, waitresses had to be careful that their ritualized insults didn't derogate a male bartender. Ann Whitehead, in "Sexual antagonism in Hereforshire" [Sec. V-A], describes obscene, antagonistic joking in a working-class pub in England; joking relationships varied by gender, age, and sexual availability. A. J. M. Sikes, in "Joking relationships in an industrial setting" (*American Anthropologist,* 68 [1966], 188–93), analyzes joking relationships between women and men employees in a large printing factory in Glasgow. Obscene banter was reciprocal between older men and older women; between older men and younger women, it was always initiated by the men; and although younger men would initiate suggestive remarks to younger women, the convention was maintained that obscenity was shocking to the young women.

2. Joke-telling and Humor

In a review of cross-cultural research on obscene joking, "Obscene joking across cultures" (*Journal of Communication,* 26 [1976], 134–40), Gary Fine argues that sexual humor is primarily a male prerogative, used to justify excluding women from all-male domains; sexual joking bonds group members together. He cites his own research on pre-adolescent boys playing Little League baseball; they told sexual jokes only with good friends and never in the presence of adults. Fine argues that since men belong to and control more groups than women, they are more likely to joke. His argument is circular, and perpetuates a male bias in research on humor: all-women's groups have been virtually ignored by students of obscenity.

There is evidence of sexual joking and bawdy lore among women. Edith Folb (*Runnin' down some lines*) [*See* Sec. IV-B and VI-A-1] found that Black teenage girls were more likely to use vernacular and obscene joking with one another than in the presence of men or adults. Rayna Green, in "Magnolias grow in dirt: The bawdy lore of Southern women" (*Southern Exposure,* 4 [Winter 1977], 29–33), describes a tradition of obscene or bawdy lore—stories, jokes, sayings, expressions, songs—exchanged and passed on by Southern women of all social classes. As women become older, they take increased license to tell bawdy tales. In this covert tradition, obscured by the myth that women don't know obscene lore and by the fact that most scholars of obscenity have been male, women see themselves as comic artists and storytellers, roles rarely available to women in the public sphere. Another example, possibly from the same tradition, is "Miss Hilda," a Texas madam, described by Robbie Davis Johnson in "Folklore and women: A social interaction analysis of a Texas madam," (*Journal of American Folklore,* 86 [1973], 211–24). Miss Hilda told dirty stories and jokes, usually with men as the butt, as part of a verbal strategy for controlling customers and her women employees.

Comparisons have been made of the content and form of male and female humor. Carol Ann Mitchell, in "The differences between male and female joke telling as exemplified in a college community" (unpublished Ph.D. dissertation, Indiana Univ., 1976, in *Dissertation Abstracts,* 37 [1977], 5270A), collected over 1,000 jokes told by students and faculty at Colorado State Univ. and questioned tellers about their reasons for telling jokes. Male joke-telling was found to be more competitive and aggressive, while women's joke-telling often seemed to help develop intimacy. Men told more obscene, racial, ethnic, and religious jokes than women; women told more absurd, morbid, and Polack jokes than men. In two articles drawing on this research—"Damnation and stereotyping in joke telling" (in Dana V. Hiller and Robin Ann Sheets, eds., *Women and men: The consequences of power* [papers from Pioneers for Century II conference, Cincinnati Ohio, Univ. of Cincinnati Office of Women's Studies, 1977, pp. 298–310] and "Hostility and aggression toward males in female joke telling" [*Frontiers,* 3, no. 3 (1978), 19–23]—Mitchell describes ways in which joke-telling perpetuates gender stereotypes and is used by both women and men to embarrass, ridicule, and warn members of the other sex. For a review of some literature on sex differences in the use of jokes, storytelling, and insults, *see* Timothy B. Jay, "Sex roles and dirty word usage" [Sec. IV-B].

Rose Coser, in "Laughter among colleagues" [Sec. V-A], describes a hierarchy of joking in staff meetings of a mental hospital, with men making far more witticisms than women. Carole Edelsky, in "Who's got the floor?" [Sec. V-A], also found men told more jokes, in this case in meetings of a university faculty committee. In a study of routines of popular comedians, "The feminine routine" (*Journal of Communication,* 26 [1976], 173–75) Joan B. Levine found women used more self-deprecating humor than men did. Mary Jo Nietz, in "Humor, hierarchy, and the changing status of women" (*Psychiatry,* 43 [1980], 211–23), studied a radical feminist group and found the women rarely told formal or bawdy jokes; most joking took the form of informal witticisms, and the women refused to participate in anti-women jokes told by outsiders.

Dorothy Painter's "Lesbian humor as a normalization device," in Cynthia L. Berryman and Virginia A. Eman, eds., *Communication, language and sex* (Rowley, Mass.: Newbury House, 1980, pp. 132–48), analyzes the use of humor in a lesbian bar. Humor—often in the form of storytelling about past events—is part of the communicative work which helps constitute the social reality of a lesbian speech community. Julia Penelope Stanley and Susan Wolfe Robbins, in "Sexist slang and the gay community: Are you one too?" (*Michigan Occasional Papers in Women's Studies,* no. 14 [1979]), observe that *camp,* a frequent form of gay male humor, relies on pejorative terms for women (*pussy, bitch*), scapegoating women to elicit in-group laughter. Lesbian humor does not go outside the group for a scapegoat, is more participatory, and has a bonding function. A related article by the same authors: "Humor and bonding among lesbians" (*Regionalism and the Female Imagination* [special double issue on female humor], 3 [1977–78], 94–109).

A related topic concerns sex similarities and differences in perceptions of humor and humor preferences; references include: Cheris Kramarae, Chapter III ("Joking matters") in *Women and men speaking* [Sec. I-A]; Joanne R. Cantor, "What is funny to whom?" [Sec. III-C]; Alice Sheppard, "Humor and sex-role stereotypes" [Sec. III-C]; Dolf Zillman and Holly Stocking, "Putdown humor" [Sec. III-C]; and Paul E. McGhee, "The role of laughter and humor in growing up female" [Sec. VII-C]. On humor content, *see* Legman [Sec. II-E].

3. Storytelling

Storytelling (which overlaps joking) may figure centrally in the culture of same-sex or mixed-sex groups, and women and men may construct similar or different types of narrative. Susan Kalčik, in "... like Ann's gynecologist or the time I was almost raped" [Sec. V-A] describes the collectively constructed personal narratives in women's consciousness-raising groups. In a related study, "Stories women tell: An ethnographic study of personal experience narratives in a women's rap group" (paper given at the 10th World Congress of Sociology, Mexico City, 1982), Mercilee M. Jenkins contrasts patterns of cooperation, support, and joint participation in a women's rap group, with women's limited storytelling in mixed groups and with processes of storytelling in men's groups.

In an oral history of a white working-class lesbian who came out in New Orleans in the 1930s, "An old dyke's tale: An interview with Doris Lunden" (*Conditions Six*, 3 [Summer 1980], 26–44), Elly Bulkin describes a community network of white and Black lesbians in New York City during the 1960s; storytelling, Bulkin demonstrates, is central to the transmission of lesbian history. Storytelling and verbal art among women in a West Indian and Black American area of Brooklyn in the 1930s are beautifully conveyed in Paule Marshall's novel, *Brown Girl, Brownstones* (Old Westbury, New York: The Feminist Press, 1981).

James P. Leary, in "Fists and foul mouths: Fights and fight stories in contemporary rural American bars" (*Journal of American Folklore*, 89 [1976], 27–39), describes fight stories told by men in rural bars, storytelling marked by profanities, verbal modulation, and physical gesturing, and dependent on the presence of an active audience. In "The La Have Island general store: Sociability and verbal art in a Nova Scotia community" (*Journal of American Folklore*, 85 [1972], 330–43), Richard Bauman analyzes the *yarns* told by men who gathered at the general store in the evening, an occasion which both sexes recognized "as the premier speech situation of the community," even though women were excluded. Yarns, which were used in image building, were personal narratives mostly about fishing, the supernatural, and unusual local happenings. Barrie Thorne, in "Women in the draft resistance movement: A case study of sex roles and social movements" (*Sex Roles*, 1 [1975], 179–95), notes the prevalence in the draft resistance movement of the 1960s of storytelling about confrontations between draft resisters and draft and military officials. In Resistance storytelling sessions women listened while the men performed. Margaret C. McLaughlin, Michael J. Cody, Marjorie L. Kane, and Carl S. Robey, in "Sex differences in story receipt and story sequencing behaviors in dyadic conversations" (*Human Communication Research*, 7 [1981], 99–116), analyzed 30-minute conversations between unacquainted college students. Women were more often the recipients of storytelling, and the sexes differed in the ways they collaborated on the stories.

4. Gossip

Gossip is a derogatory term, more often applied to women's talk than to men's talk. Alexander Rysman's "How the 'gossip' became a woman" (*Journal of Communication*, 27 [1977], 176–80) traces the evolution of *gossip* from a positive term applied to both sexes into a negative term applied to women. Rysman observes that when social scientists such as James West (*Plainville, New York*: Columbia Univ. Press, 1945) and Max Gluckman ("Gossip and scandal," *Current Anthropology*, 4 [1963], 307–16) point to the use of gossiping to create group solidarity, they do not consider the undermining of female solidarity implicit in the inconsistent application of a derogatory stereotype. A patriarchal society, Rysman argues, resents female solidarity. James Faris illustrates this inconsistency in "The dynamics of verbal exchange: A Newfoundland example" (*Anthropologica*, 8 [1966], 235–48); he observes that when men gathered in the general store of a Newfoundland village to exchange information, it was called *news*, whereas women's talk, in smaller groups in homes and gardens, was called *gossip*.

Ruth Borker, in "Anthropology: Social and cultural perspectives" (in Sally McConnell-Ginet, Ruth Borker, and Nelly Furman, eds., *Women and language in literature and society*, New York:

Praeger, 1980, pp. 26–44) [Sec. I-A], reviews studies of gossip as a way of talking associated with women in villages in Portugal, Spain, Malta, France, Sicily, Italy, and Greece. In these cultures women and men live in separate worlds; women's talk is about people and takes place in more private places. One of the best of these studies is by Susan Harding, "Women and words in a Spanish village" (in Rayna Reiter, ed., *Towards an anthropology of women*, New York: Monthly Review Press, 1975, pp. 283–308). In the village which Harding studied, a division of verbal skills, topics, and genres of speech followed the division of labor between men and women. Women's world centered around home and family and the genres of chatting, storytelling, and gossip. Cut off from formal political power, women used gossip to help define what was or was not acceptable, and to subvert men's control; however, women were also controlled by gossip, and it was seen as wicked. Elinor Keenan, in "Norm-makers, norm-breakers" [Sec. V-H], notes the association of women with gossip, bargaining, and haggling in the Marina tribe in Madagascar.

Deborah Jones, in "Gossip: Notes on women's oral culture" (in Cheris Kramarae, ed., *The voices and words of women and men*, Oxford: Pergamon Press, 1980, pp. 193–98; also *Women's Studies International Quarterly*, 3, no. 2/3 [1980]), calls for a revaluation of women's gossip, for understanding the topics, forms, and functions of gossip from the vantage point of women's experiences and values. She argues that gossip is a language of intimacy and one of women's strengths. In a similar vein, Patricia Meyer Spacks ("In praise of gossip," *The Hudson Review*, 25 [1982], 19–38) describes gossip as the "resource of a deprived class," a means for concealing power and affirming alliances. Gossip expresses the position and experiences of women in its allegiance to personal facts and its penetration to the "human truth of things." On the process of gossiping, *see* Yerkovich [Sec. IV-A] and Marjorie Harness Goodwin, "He-said-she-said: Formal cultural procedures for the construction of a gossip dispute activity" (*American Ethnologist*, 7 [1980], 674–95), an analysis of gossip among urban Black girls, ages 7–13.

5. *Other Genres*

Riddling is another speech event in which sex differences have been found. Among the Dusun, in Southeast Asia, women prefer riddles using archaic words or syllables, while men use the more simply metaphoric type. See John W. Roberts and Michael L. Forman, "Riddles: Expressive models of interrogation," in John J. Gumperz and Dell Hymes, eds., *Directions in sociolinguistics* (New York: Holt, Rinehart and Winston, 1972, pp. 180–209).

Lamentations may be differentiated by sex. K. M. Tiwary, in "Tuneful weeping: A mode of communication" (*Frontiers*, 3, no. 3 [1978], 24–27), describes the tuneful weeping of girls and women in nothern India, who perform an organized set of wept statements—promises, regrets, memories—on well-defined situations: e.g., when a daughter leaves to be married or after a death. Men are essentially observers. Anna Caraveli-Chaves, in "Bridge between worlds: The Greek women's lament as communicative event" (*Journal of American Folklore*, 93 [1980], 129–57), analyzes ritual lamentations for the dead—a verbal genre used only by women—in a village on the island of Crete, pointing to ways in which the lament contributes to female bonding and strategies for survival. Men are ambivalent about women's lamentations. See also Margaret Alexiou, *The ritual lament in Greek tradition*, Cambridge: Cambridge Univ. Press, 1974.

Vocal music genres may vary by sex; see, for example, H. J. Ottenheimer, "Culture and contact and musical style: Ethnomusicology in the Comoro Islands" (*Ethnomusicology*, 14 [1970], 458–62), and Norma McLeod and Marcia Herndon, "The *Bormliza*: Maltese folksong style and women" (*Journal of American Folklore*, 88 [1975], 81–100).

B. Literary Style: Sexual Differentiation of Written Language

Analyses of gender and written language, including informal diaries and letters as well as more formal genres like the novel, raise issues which both parallel and depart from those in the study of speech. This section provides only a sampling of the large body of scholarship on gender and literature. It includes reviews and theoretical works, and specific studies which illustrate two areas of particular concern: the possible differentiation of women's writing styles from those of men, and depictions of female versus male speech within written literature.

BRUNER, EDWARD M. AND JANE PAIGE KELSO.

Gender differences in graffiti: A semiotic perspective. In Cheris Kramarae, ed., *The voices and words of women and men.* Oxford: Pergamon Press, 1980, pp. 239–52. Also *Women's Studies International Quarterly,* 3 no. 2/3 (1980), 239–52.

An analysis of female and male restroom graffiti, understood semiotically as texts and structures of meaning. Women's graffiti are more interactive and interpersonal, dealing with relationships; men's are more competitive and self-centered, focusing on isolated sex acts and organs. Fifty-four percent of the men's graffiti, compared with 15% of the women's, was derogatory. The article includes a good review of the literature on gender and graffiti.

COSTELLO, BONNIE.

The "feminine" language of Marianne Moore. In Sally McConnell-Ginet, Ruth Borker, and Nelly Furman, eds., *Women and language in literature and society.* New York: Praeger, 1980, 222–38.

Costello argues that a "conventional but redefined femininity" is a chief source of energy in Moore's poetry. For example, elongated, run-on lines and qualified statements express a humility which proves to be "more effective and durable than aggressive certitude."

DONOVAN, JOSEPHINE.

The silence is broken. In Sally McConnell-Ginet, Ruth Borker, and Nelly Furman, eds., *Women and language in literature and society.* New York: Praeger, 1980, pp. 205–18.

Dovovan explores women's contributions to literature beginning in the 17th century. Prior to the 19th century, women were denied adequate access to education, and they resorted to non-traditional forms of literature, such as the novel, to express themselves.

ELLMAN, MARY.

Thinking about women. New York: Harcourt Brace Jovanovich, 1968.

In this pioneering work of feminist criticism Ellman notes the stereotyped formlessness of women's speech as represented in the writing of men like Joyce, Sartre, Mailer, and Hemingway. She coins the term *phallic criticism* for men's criticisms of women's writing, in which books by women "are treated as though they themselves were women, and criticism embarks, at its happiest, upon an intellectual measuring of busts and hips."

FARRELL, THOMAS J.

The female and male modes of rhetoric. *College English,* 40 (1979), 909–21.

Farrell argues that there are distinguishable female and male modes of rhetoric. The female mode is more indirect and open, seeking to recreate the process of thinking and to avoid unnecessary antagonism; it tends to obfuscate boundaries between author, audience, and subject of discourse. The male mode tends to exaggerate these boundaries and to polarize; it is more contained and preselected. [*See also* Sheryl S. Pearson, "Rhetoric and organizational change: New applications of feminine style," in Barbara L. Forisha and Barbara H. Goldman, eds., *Outsiders on the inside.* Englewood Cliffs, N.J.: Prentice-Hall, 1981, pp. 55–74.]

FURMAN, NELLY.

Textual feminism. In Sally McConnell-Ginet, Ruth Borker, and Nelly Furman, eds., *Women and language in literature and society*. New York: Praeger, 1980, pp. 45–54.

Textual criticism can provide useful understanding of women's interaction with language since it attends to the interplay between "signifier and signified" and hence to construction by readers as well as authors. Textual criticism recognizes that "we speak, read, and write from a gender-marked place within our social and cultural context."

HIATT, MARY.

The way women write. New York: Teachers College Press, 1977.

To explore the recurring suggestion that there are "feminine" and "masculine" writing styles, Hiatt computerized 200,000 words from "mass audience" books written by an equal number of men and women. Among the findings: in non-fiction writing women's sentences are shorter than men's; in fiction women's and men's sentences are the same average length, but women's range of sentence length is less variable; there were few quantitative differences in women's and men's use of -*ly* adverbs; men writers use male pronouns three times more, and women writers use male pronouns 10% more, than female pronouns. [For important criticisms of this work—e.g., the assumption that gender-typed styles can be studied by the relative frequencies of formal features—see the book review by Sally McConnell-Ginet in *Language in Society*, 8 (1979), 466–69.]

HULL, GLORIA T., PATRICIA BELL SCOTT, AND BARBARA SMITH, EDS.

All the women are white, all the Blacks are men, but some of us are brave: Black women's studies. Old Westbury, N.Y.: The Feminist Press, 1982.

A very useful collection which includes review essays on Black women writers: Joan R. Sherman, "Afro-American women poets of the nineteenth century"; Rita B. Dandridge, "On the novels written by selected Black American women"; Jeanne-Marie A. Miller, "Black women playwrights from Grimké to Shange"; Barbara Smith, "Toward a Black feminist criticism" [this section separately annotated]; and Lorraine Bethel's essay on Zora Neal Hurston [Sec. VI-C].

JACOBUS, MARY, ED.

Women writing and writing about women. New York: Barnes & Noble, 1979.

An anthology of essays, mostly by British feminist writers, focused on the question: "What does writing as a woman mean, and to what extent does it involve a new theory and new practices?" Some articles are theoretical, e.g., Mary Jacobus explores "the rift experienced by women writers in a patriarchal society, where language itself may re-inscribe the structure by which they are oppressed." Other essays discuss specific writers such as Charlotte Brontë, Christina Rossetti, Emily Dickinson, and George Eliot.

KAMMER, JEANNE.

The art of silence and the forms of women's poetry. In Sandra M. Gilbert and Susan Gubar, eds., *Shakespeare's sisters: Feminist essays on women poets*. Bloomington: Indiana Univ. Press, 1979, pp. 153–64.

Kammer explores the "aesthetics of silence"—the use of linguistic compression, the diaphoric mode, and spatial appearance in poetry by Emily Dickinson, H. D., and Marianne Moore. Women poets have used tight modernist forms to express their cultural situation of "powerlessness and enforced containment," expressing, even as they deny, this condition.

KOLODNY, ANNETTE.

Dancing through the mine-field: Some observations on the theory, practice, and politics of a feminist literary criticism. In Dale Spender, ed., *Men's studies modified*. Oxford: Pergamon Press, 1981, pp. 23–42.

The consideration of language as a representative of oppressive power has drawn together feminist literary critics and linguists. Women writers, working with language and literary traditions appropriated for centuries for male expression, have become acutely aware of the need to remake language to express their concepts.

KOLODNY, ANNETTE.

Some notes on defining a feminist literary criticism. *Critical Inquiry*, 2 (1975), 75–92.

A careful discussion of a recurring question: What, if anything, makes women's writing different from that of men? Can one sum up the richness and variety of women's writing any more than that of men? Kolodny argues that rather than starting from a generalizing premise, each author and work should be treated as unique, with an eye for patterns. For example, she has noted the recurrence of stylistic devices such as reflexive perceptions in the writings of U.S. and Canadian women.

KOLODNY, ANNETTE.

The lady's not for spurning: Kate Millett and the critics. *Contemporary Literature*, 17 (1976), 541–67.

Critics such as Elinor Langer [this section separately annotated] have misread Kate Millett's *Flying*, which Kolodny sees as a daring experiment in altering traditional, largely male-defined genres of autobiography in order to describe previously unacknowledged aspects of women's experience.

LANGER, ELINOR.

Confessing. *Ms.*, 3 (Dec. 1974), 70–71.

Langer criticizes Kate Millett's *Flying* as "pointless, tangled self-revelation," rather than "disciplined autobiography" and as an example of a "confessional genre" encouraged by the women's movement and its rituals of disclosure. Langer regrets the "absence of a genuinely critical tradition in the women's movement." [For a response by Millett, see *Ms.*, 3 (Jan. 1975), 26–29.]

OATES, JOYCE CAROL.

Why is your writing so violent? *The New York Times Book Review*, March 29, 1981, pp. 15, 35.

Critics would limit a woman writer to the domestic, the "charming," "amusing," and "delightful." They would keep war, rape, murder, and other violence as topics only men can deal with.

REGISTER, CHERI.

Review essay: Literary criticism. *Signs*, 6 (1980), 268–82.

Feminist literary critics have asked if there is a female aesthetic (a question often confused with that of a feminist aesthetic). Some studies seek to describe distinctive features in the language of women writers, connecting them with women's experiences, e.g., compressed speech used by modernist women poets has been related to women's privacy and indirection. Others celebrate aspects of women's writing, e.g., the transformative possibilities in the poet H.D.'s "fusion of opposites." The article has a good bibliography.

Roberts, J. R.

Black lesbians: An annotated bibliography. P.O. Box 10543, Tallahassee, FL 32302: The Naiad Press, 1981.

This useful bibliographic source includes writings on the historic erasure of Black lesbians' lives and experiences, and the silencing and oppression experienced by Black lesbian writers/poets such as Angelina Ward Grimké (1880–1958). There are references to contemporary literature and literary criticism by Black lesbians.

Schulz, Muriel.

A style of one's own. In Douglas Butturff and Edmund L. Epstein, eds., Women's language and style. Akron, Ohio: L & S Books, 1978, pp. 75–83.

An analysis of Virginia Woolf's representation of female and male discourse in To the lighthouse. Women characters speak more unassertively (using more hedges, vague qualifiers, indirect commands), especially in discussing topics about which they lack expertise. Men have access to a wider intellectual sphere, and do not take women seriously. Women accept more responsibility for keeping mixed-sex conversation going, through solicitous questions and displays of enthusiasm.

Showalter, Elaine.

Feminist criticism in the wilderness. Critical Inquiry, 8 (1981), 179–206.

In this lead essay in an issue devoted to "writing and sexual difference," Showalter distinguishes the "feminist critique" of literature, which focuses on the feminist reader, from "gynocritics," centered on the woman writer. She argues that women's writing is a "double-voiced discourse," embodying traditions of both the muted and the dominant.

Showalter, Elaine.

Review essay: Literary criticism. Signs, 1 (1975), 435–60.

Showalter argues that since written language is more self-conscious and impersonal than speech, the methodology of linguistic analysis may not be adequate for understanding possible differences in the styles of women and men writers. Women poets and novelists have long worked with the concept of women's "bilinguality," and their history of trying to expand the boundaries of their language connects with contemporary women writers' "struggle against verbal repression and inhibition."

Smith, Barbara.

Toward a Black feminist criticism. Conditions Two, vol. 1, no. 2 (Oct. 1977), 25–44. Reprinted in Gloria T. Hull, Patricia Bell Scott, and Barbara Smith, eds., But some of us are brave. Old Westbury, N.Y.: The Feminist Press, 1982, pp. 157–175.

Black, feminist, lesbian writers have been both ignored and devalued; their work has been surrounded by a massive silence, which this essay seeks to break, connecting the politics of Black women's lives, their subject matter, and their situations as artists.

Taylor, Anne Robinson.

Male novelists and their female voices: Literary masquerades. Troy, N.Y.: Whitston Publishing, 1981.

A study of male novelists who have chosen to write in the first person as a woman for significant portions of their novels. When a man writes as a woman, Taylor argues, "he produces what Dickens called 'a fellow without breeches,' a man dressed up in woman's clothes. The female voice becomes a kind of psychic shorthand that leads us to the inner life of a male artist and to *his* fears, and fantasies, often in a more direct way than do his male narrators." [From author's abstract]

TODD, JANET, ED.

Gender and literary voice. New York: Holmes and Meier Publishers, 1980.

This first volume in a series on "Women and Literature" contains articles on American, British, and French literature, loosely organized under the general (and unresolved) question: "Is there a distinctive female style/tone/content?" Other issues concerning women characters and writers, and feminist criticism are also discussed.

TREICHLER, PAULA A.

The construction of ambiguity in *The Awakening*: A linguistic analysis. In Sally McConnell-Ginet, Ruth Borker, and Nelly Furman, eds., *Women and language in literature and society.* New York: Praeger, 1980, pp. 239–57.

Using detailed examples, Treichler analyzes the relationship between narrative meaning and grammatic patterns in Kate Chopin's novel. The syntactic interplay between active and passive voice, for example, forms a textual counterpart to Edna Pontellier's struggle to define herself as an active subject.

TREICHLER, PAULA A.

Verbal subversions in Dorothy Parker: "Trapped like a trap in a trap." *Language and Style*, 13, no. 4 (1980), 46–61.

In the short story "The Waltz" what the woman says to her dance partner is conventionally "feminine" but what she says to herself expresses comic savagery and malice toward her partner. A central feature of the story is the "verbal play on the notions of how women talk."

ZIMMERMAN, BONNIE.

What has never been: An overview of lesbian feminist literary criticism. *Feminist Studies*, 7 (1981), 451–75.

"Does a woman's sexual and affectional preference influence the way she writes, reads, thinks?" "Is there a lesbian aesthetic distinct from a feminist aesthetic?" These questions focus this useful review, which attends to problems of definition, silence and encoding, and experiments with literary form.

Also see: IV-E-2: Warshay.

C.   Seizing the Language

Women have been relatively silent in the history of literature and other forms of writing, and, in expressing themselves, women have to use a language that embodies their oppression. Feminists have written, often poetically, of experiences of silence, of being silenced, of women's use of silence as a subversive strategy, and of struggles to invent new language which can transcend patriarchy. These writings are attuned to the transformative power of the aesthetic, and differ from the more pragmatic, evidence-preoccupied efforts to change sexist language which are annotated in Sec. II.

ANZALDUA, GLORIA.

Speaking in tongues: A letter to Third World women writers. In Cherrié Moraga and Gloria Anzaldúa, eds., *This bridge called my back: Writings by radical women of color*. Watertown, Mass.: Persephone Press, 1981, pp. 165–73.

"For the Third World woman, who has, at best, one foot in the feminist literary world, the temptation is great to adopt the current feeling fads and theory fads, the latest half-truths in political thought, the half-digested new age psychological axioms that are preached by the white feminist establishment. Its followers are notorious for 'adopting' women of color as their 'cause' while still expecting us to adapt *their* expectations and *their* language" (p. 167). To write, "to assess the damage" (Cherrié Moraga) is a dangerous act, yet necessary for the survival of women of color.

BETHEL, LORRAINE.

"This infinity of conscious pain": Zora Neale Hurston and the Black female literary tradition. In Gloria T. Hull, Patricia Bell Scott, and Barbara Smith, eds., *But some of us are brave*. Old Westbury, N.Y.: The Feminist Press, 1982, pp. 157–75.

Hurston sought to capture the political and cultural realities of her experiences as a Black woman "while using literary forms created by and for white, upper-class men." Her work exemplifies a tradition of Black women writers who draw upon Afro-American folk culture—symbols, language, a legacy of Black women's storytelling and mythmaking.

BURKE, CAROLYN.

Becoming Mina Loy. *Women's studies*, 7 (1980), 137–50.

Mina Loy, an English expatriate poet living in France at the turn of the century, struggled to create new ways to speak as a woman, going through phases of self-discovery and self-naming and shattering taboos against the verbal expression of women's bodily experiences, for example, in a striking poem about childbirth.

CLIFF, MICHELLE.

The resonance of interruption. *Chrysalis*, no. 8 (Summer 1978), 29–37.

Cliff reflects upon connections between interruptions and silence in the lives and work of women writers and artists. Interruptions from serving the needs of others surround women's roles as mothers, daughters, sisters, wives. Cliff gives examples from the lives and writings of Simone Weil, Virginia Woolf, Olive Schreiner, and Assata Shakur.

DALY, MARY.

Beyond God the father: Toward a philosophy of women's liberation. Boston: Beacon Press, 1973.

Daly argues that "the symbolic and linguistic instruments for communication—which include essentially the whole theological tradition in world religions—have been formulated by males under the conditions of patriarchy." Women have had the power of naming stolen from them; feminist naming is a "deliberate confrontation with language structures of our heritage" and with "sexist language that has kept us from hearing our own word."

DALY, MARY.

Gyn/Ecology: The metaethics of radical feminism. Boston: Beacon Press, 1978.

A central theme in this bold and visionary feminist work is the exclusion of women from language—tied to the woman-hatred embedded in all institutions—and the need for women to reclaim their power of naming. Daly does such reclaiming through "gynocentric writing," drawing on the "obsolete" meanings of words like *spinster, crone,* and *hag*; inventing new words (*robotitude*); unmasking and inviting a different listening to old words (*gynecology* depends on "fixation and dismemberment"; *Gyn/Ecology* "affirms that everything is connected").

DIEHL, JOANNE FEIT.
"Cartographies of silence": Rich's *Common Language* and the woman poet. *Feminist Studies*, 6 (1980), 530–46.

Seeking a language which can free itself from its own patriarchial history, Rich draws upon the authority of women's unique experiences (e.g., of love between women). She uses a "gentle poetics" antithetical to patriarchal aggression, while, perhaps paradoxically, claiming "the bold, heroic nature of the enterprise."

ELSHTAIN, JEAN BETHKE.
Feminist discourse and its discontents: Language and power. *Signs*, 7 (1982), 603–21.

Searching for "speech that emancipates," Elshtain discusses relationships of language and domination, especially the silencing of women, in the work of classical political theorists such as Plato, Luther, Locke, and Marx. She suggests pitfalls in radical, liberal, Marxist, and psycho-analytic feminist discourses and offers ideas for constructing truly emancipatory feminist speech.

FARWELL, MARILYN R.
Adrienne Rich and an organic feminist criticism. *College English*, 39 (1977), 191–203.

Rich seeks to relate "ethics and language, text and artist, creation and relation, and ultimately art and life" and does so through belief that language is central to the condition of women and a basis for social change. A number of Rich's poems convey the experience of speaking within, while also seeking to transcend, an oppressive language.

GEARHART, SALLY MILLER.
The womanization of rhetoric. *Women's Studies International Quarterly*, 2 (1979), 195–201.

Gearhart argues that rhetoric (equated with persuasion) is part of a patriarchal, "con-quest/conversion mentality," and that "any intent to persuade is an act of violence." A "non-persuasive notion of communication," best described as a "womanization of rhetoric," has begun to emerge, a collective mode, emphasizing openness and dialogue.

GILBERT, SANDRA M.
Speaking in mother tongues. *Ms.*, 9 (June 1981), 39–40.

Gilbert contrasts the European vision of language which is basic to Homans's *Women writers and poetic identity* [this section] with perspectives in Dexter Fisher, ed., *The third woman: Minority women writers of the United States* (Boston: Houghton Mifflin, 1980). Black, Chicana, Native American, and Asian American women evoke poetic traditions inspired by the storytelling and strengths of their mothers and grandmothers. Gilbert asks what if contemporary theories about the "inevitably patriarchal ordering of language are also fantasies unconsciously designed to make grown-up little boys feel better about the fact that it is usually women who first confront babies with the powers of speech." "If language is really ours from the beginning, what poetic identities will we—do we—have?"

GILBERT, SANDRA.

What do feminist critics want? Or a postcard from the volcano. *ADE Bulletin*, no. 66 (Winter 1980), 16–24.

Writing that the personal, the authentic, the literary, and the rhetorical are all political, Gilbert argues that feminist criticism deals with questions about sexuality and textuality that are ontological. Many male colleagues reject or deny this new criticism, evidently alarmed or unnerved by the volcanic changes women have experienced.

GILBERT, SANDRA M. AND SUSAN GUBAR.

The madwoman in the attic: The woman writer and the nineteenth century imagination. New Haven, Conn.: Yale Univ. Press, 1979.

A much-lauded study of 19th-century women writers which emphasizes their struggle to break from patriarchy and create a legitimate voice. Some writers did this by confronting and reinterpreting male texts, and others by proclaiming new texts.

GOLDSMITH, ANDREA E.

Notes on the tyranny of language usage. In Cheris Kramarae, ed., *The voices and words of women and men*. Oxford: Pergamon Press, 1980, pp. 179–91. Also *Women's Studies International Quarterly*, 3, no. 2/3 (1980), 179–91.

Goldsmith draws on theories of symbolic interactionism to argue that there is a dialectical relationship between language and reality. Conventional language maintains and strengthens patriarchal society. A "radicalism of language" can help define alternative, emancipatory realities, a point she explores through writing by Virginia Woolf, Monique Wittig, Patti Smith.

GRIFFIN, SUSAN.

Thoughts on writing: A diary. In Janet Sternburg, ed., *The writer and her work*. New York: W. W. Norton, 1980, pp. 107–20.

Griffin describes a realization she came to in writing *Women and nature*: the need to use two voices, which continue inside her, posing conficting visions of reality. The voice of patriarchy is a voice of despair, hostile to intuition, fearful of loss of control. The voice of women and nature is a calm, rebellious voice of poetry, which sees the physical universe as embodying meaning.

GRIFFIN, SUSAN.

Women and nature: The roaring inside her. New York: Harper & Row, 1978.

In this prose/poetry exploration of connections between feminism and ecology, the patriarchal voices are represented by emotionless and objective statements which rarely contain a personal pronoun (e.g., "It is decided" or "The discovery was made"). The voices of women and nature are embodied and express feeling.

HALLIDAY, M.A.K.

Anti-languages. *American Anthropologist*, 78 (1976), 570–84.

Alternative societies set up within another society generate anti-languages. Halliday's discussion of "underworld" languages illustrates the role of language in defining the power structure of society and might be useful in analyzing patriarchal and feminist speaking and writing as counterposed language structures.

HOMANS, MARGARET.

Women writers and poetic identity: Dorothy Wordsworth, Emily Brontë, and Emily Dickinson. Princeton, N.J.: Princeton Univ. Press, 1980.

A study of the ways three 19th-century poets shaped their identities and work in response to a masculine literary tradition which places women on the side of the other, associated with nature and excluded from speaking subjectivity. Wordsworth wrote as "a docile daughter of nature," Brontë violated male authority as a "guilty Eve," and Dickinson escaped the patriarchal contraints of language by exploring "language's doubleness," with a poetic sense of the limits of language.

KRAMARAE, CHERIS, AND MERCILEE JENKINS.

Liberating language: Women's speech at a feminist conference. In Larry E. Larmer and Mary Kenny Padami, eds., *Proceedings of the 2nd and 3rd conferences on communication, language, and gender.* Madison: Univ. of Wisconsin—Extension, 1982, pp. 79–83.

At a 1978 feminist scholarship conference, women had difficulty pulling together female experiences and speaking of them in a coherent way because of their inability to be succinctly expressed in our language. They resorted to jokes, analogies, etc., to convey meanings for those experiences.

LORDE, AUDRE.

Poetry is not a luxury. In Hester Eisenstein and Alice Jardine, eds., *The future of difference.* Boston: G. K. Hall, 1980, pp. 125–27.

An evocative essay about the transformative powers of poetry, as "the way we help give name to the nameless so it can be thought."

MORA, GABRIELA AND KAREN S. VAN HOOFT, EDS.

Theory and practice of feminist literary criticism. Ypsilanti, Mich.: Bilingual Press/Editorial Bilingue, 1982.

The essays deal with Spanish, Spanish American, English, American, French, and Italian languages and literatures. Several discuss women writers' work to create a language free of phallocentric discourse, to write themselves into literature.

OLSEN, TILLIE.

Silences. New York: Delacorte Press, 1979.

A moving collection of essays on silences in the lives and work of writers, especially the "unnatural" silences caused by circumstances of social class, race, sex. Olsen asks why so many more women are silenced than men, and points to the "constriction to one dimension" (a form of censorship of one's full experience) entailed both in "writing like a man" and in "writing like a woman."

PENELOPE (STANLEY), JULIA AND SUSAN J. WOLFE.

Consciousness as style; Style as aesthetic. In this volume. Revision of Toward a feminist aesthetic. *Chrysalis,* no. 6 (Winter 1978), 57–71.

The authors describe a feminist aesthetic or "women's style," with examples from writings by Susan Griffin, Maud Haimson, Mary Daly, Marge Piercy, Gertrude Stein, Jill Johnston, Kate Millett, Ntozake Shange, Tillie Olsen, Toni Morrison, Bertha Harris, and Virginia Woolf. They contrast the epistemology of women's style, which perceives the world in terms of ambiguities, pluralities, processes, continuities, and complex relationships, with "patriarchal expressive modes," which perceive the world through categories, dichotomies, roles, stasis, and causation.

RICH, ADRIENNE.

On lies, secrets, and silence. New York: W. W. Norton, 1979.

This extraordinary collection of essays recurringly connects feminism and language, asking about relationships between language and power, the "theft of language" as part of the condition of powerlessness, problems of silence and speaking the unspeakable, and possibilities of women becoming "namers, definers, and shapers." In "When we dead awaken: Writing as revision" Rich traces her own changing relationships to language as her consciousness and poetry have evolved.

SARACHILD, KATIE.

"Who are we? The Redstockings position on names." In Redstockings of the women's liberation movement, *Feminist Revolution.* New York: Random House, 1978, pp. 53–55.

"Oppressed people have had even their names taken from them, been made nameless or given the names of others. They have wanted their own names and have fought for them." The article briefly traces various stances toward names taken by oppressors, and by different revolutionary movements.

SCHEMAN, NAOMI.

Anger and the politics of naming. In Sally McConnell-Ginet, Ruth Borker, and Nelly Furman, eds., *Women and language in literature and society.* New York: Praeger, 1980, pp. 174–87.

Traditional psychological interpretations of feelings tend to individualize, mask and discount female experience. Rather than being labeled as feeling states, emotions like anger should be understood as expressions which occur in environments which women share and which connect them politically.

SCHUSTER, MARILYN R.

Strategies for survival: The subtle subversion of Jane Rule. *Feminist Studies,* 7 (1981), 431–50.

Rule's writings are discussed within the context of efforts to invent texts compatible with lesbian sensibility and experience. Practicing "subtle subversion," Rule uses familiar language to construct new, unexpected meanings.

SMITH, DOROTHY E.

An analysis of ideological structures and how women are excluded: Considerations for academic women. *Canadian Review of Sociology and Anthropology,* 12, part 1 (1975), 353–69.

Smith uses a Marxist understanding of ideology in this provocative analysis of the exclusion of women from ideological structures (education, publishing, broadcasting) which order social relations. Since women are constituted as objects, not subjects, in established knowledges, they are confronted with the problem of reinventing the world of knowledge, thought, symbols, and images.

SPAFFORD, ROZ.

"Taking back the texts": Writing classes for re-entry women. Unpublished manuscript, 1982, Univ. of California, Santa Cruz.

Spafford reflects on her experiences in teaching writing to older, re-entry women students, whose writing tends to be associational, oblique, anecdotal, and circular, "somewhere between politeness and poetry"—a language perhaps anchored in years of homemaking. She describes methods for teaching more abstract, academic writing, while preserving and developing the strengths of "women's language."

SPENDER, DALE.

Man made language. London: Routledge & Kegan Paul, 1980.

Spender discusses the exclusion of women from the creation of cultural forms and from experiences of naming, including ways in which women writers have been devalued and consigned to the periphery. She also discusses, with varied examples, efforts by women writers to construct "woman-centered meanings," to create new symbolic systems. [*Also see* Spender, Sec. I-A]

STANLEY, JULIA PENELOPE, MARY DALY, AUDRE LORDE, JUDITH MCDANIEL, AND ADRIENNE RICH.

The transformation of silence into language and action. The lesbian literature panel of the annual Modern Language Assoc. convention, Chicago, Ill., 1977. *Sinister Wisdom,* 6 (Summer 1978), 4–25.

In this insightful discussion, the participants speak of "millenia of silence about our lives" (Stanley), silence caused by fear, contempt, annihilation (Lorde). Rich notes that "the unspoken, which we are afraid to name, becomes the unspeakable," including topics such as female anger, love between women, lesbian motherhood, the sexuality of older women, connections of "shame, manipulation, betrayal, contempt, hypocrisy, envy, love" between white and Black women. Daly writes of efforts to reclaim old women's words (*hag, crone*), and McDaniel, of breaking silence, especially around lesbianism, as a way of having access to an inner, defining reality.

Also see: I-A: Kramarae (*Women and men speaking*); III-A: Kramarae ("Perceptions and politics . . ."); Kramarae ("Proprietors of language"); IV-A: Kaplan.

A Note on French Feminisms

Within the last decade French feminists have developed an important theoretical tradition which attends centrally to language and is based upon, but is also seeking to transform, Lacanian psychoanalysis and structuralism. Writers such as Hélène Cixous, Julia Kristeva, and Luce Irigaray argue that women's repression is embedded in the Logos, or the Word, in subtle processes through which meaning is produced. In predominant "phallocentric" discourse women are absent, the unacknowledged different; their experience is systematically repressed. One group of French feminists, *l'écriture féminine,* seek to rupture this discourse, to inscribe the female in language and thought, partly through articulating connections between woman's body and woman's language. Among these writings which have been translated into English: Hélène Cixous, "The laugh of the Medusa," trans. by Keith Cohen and Paula Cohen (*Signs,* 1 [1976], 875–93); Luce Irigaray, "When our lips speak together," trans. and intro. by Carolyn Burke (*Signs,* 6 [1980], 66–79), and "And the one doesn't stir without the other," trans. by Hélène Vivienne Wenzel (*Signs,* 7 [1981], 56–67); Julia Kristeva, *Desire in language,* ed. by Leon Roudiez, trans. by Tom Gora, Alice

Jardine, and Leon Roudiez (New York: Columbia Univ. Press, 1980). Two journal issues—*Yale French Studies,* no. 62 (1982) and *Signs,* 7, no. 2 (1981)—focus on French feminism, with translated texts and commentaries. Elaine Marks and Isabelle de Courtrivron, *New French feminisms* (Amherst: Univ. of Mass., 1980), with texts and commentaries, conveys wide variation among writers in this tradition.

The future of difference, ed. by Hester Eisenstein and Alice Jardine (Boston: G. K. Hall, 1980), includes interesting papers which explore the work of French feminists and what Domna C. Stanton ("Language and revolution," pp. 73–87) calls "the Franco-American dis-connection." She observes that U.S. feminist criticism and studies of language tend to "pragmatic empiricism," while the French are more abstract and theoretical, more open to notions like "the female unconscious." Another excellent review for readers seeking access to this tradition is Ann Rosalind Jones, "Writing the body: Toward an understanding of *l'écriture féminine"* (*Feminist Studies,* 7 (1981), 247–63). Jones compares the approaches of Kristeva, Irigaray, and Cixous, and, while appreciating their contributions, offers incisive criticisms; e.g., of the positing of essential male/female dualism, and the flattening out of differences (such as social class) among women. Other useful essays which interpret the French tradition for English-speaking readers include: Elaine Marks, "Women and literature in France" (*Signs,* 3 [1978], 832–42); Carolyn Burke, "Report from Paris: Women's writing and the women's movement" (*Signs,* 3 [1978], 843–55); Michele Richman, "Sex and signs: The language of French feminist criticism" (*Language and Style,* 13 [1980], 62–80); and Gayatri Chakravorty Spivak, "French feminism in an international frame," (*Yale French Studies,* no. 62 [1982], 154–84).

Monique Wittig, also a French feminist, may be distinguished from the *l'écriture féminine* group. She is a lesbian-identified writer seeking to create women-centered language in her fiction, including *Les guerrillères* (New York: Avon, 1973), *The lesbian body* (New York: Avon, 1976), and, with Sande Zeig, *Lesbian peoples: Materials for a dictionary* (New York: Avon, 1979). Wittig, for example, breaks the subject and object *(j/e),* forms new words, modifies old ones, and breaks rules of gender to re-imagine relationships. See Hélène Vivienne Wenzel, "The text as body/politics: An appreciation of Monique Wittig's writings in context" (*Feminist Studies,* 7 [1981], 264–87), and Namascar Shaktini, "The politics of metaphor: Wittig's *'figuration de l'amour lesbien'"* (*Signs,* 8 [1982]). Wittig has been a vocal critic of Cixous, Irigaray, and Kristeva for their oppositional thinking and neglect of material reality. [*Also see* Wittig, Sec. II-J.]

A related current of work, influenced both by French and American feminisms, has been created by French feminist writers in Quebec, who have struggled against the image of women as linguistic purists, contending that male discourse has colonized women; they have sought to create new, women-centered language. See Karen Gould, "Setting words free: Feminist writing in Quebec" (*Signs,* 6 [1981], 617–42).

The relationship between a writer's sexuality and her or his literary practices is also a focus of contemporary French criticism and an issue which feminists have explored. *Homosexualities and French literature: Cultural contexts and critical texts,* ed. and intro. by George Sambolian and Elaine Marks (Ithaca: Cornell Univ. Press, 1979) provides an introduction, including an essay by Elaine Marks ("Lesbian intertextuality") on the lesbian imagination from Sappho to Monique Wittig, and an essay by Wittig ("Paradigm") which disentangles the semantics of "woman." Wittig writes: "Humankind must find another name for itself and another system of grammar that will do away with genders, the linguistic indicator of political oppositions."

VII. CHILDREN AND LANGUAGE

A. Language between Adults and Children

This section centers on two interrelated questions: Do adults speak differently to girls than to boys? When talking with children, do men speak differently than women? The second question has traditionally been eclipsed by emphasis upon the speech mothers use in addressing infants and young children, but recently researchers have begun to ask whether maternal speech to children is similar or different from that used by fathers, older children, or other caretakers of both sexes. [Items annotated in Sec. V-F-2, on teacher-student interaction, are also relevant to this topic.]

ALFGREN, SCOTT H., ELIZABETH J. ARIES, AND ROSE R. OLVER.

Sex differences in the interaction of adults and preschool children. *Psychological Reports,* 44 (1979), 115–18.

The authors studied the interaction of adults (17 to 22 years) and children (three to five years) at a summer camp. Boys received more attention from adults than did girls. Female adults gave proportionally more attention to boys than did male adults. Amount of attention was not correlated with amount of attention-seeking behavior by the child.

BERNSTEIN, BASIL, ED.

Class, codes and control, II: Applied studies towards a sociology of language. Boston: Routledge & Kegan Paul, 1973.

This book, reporting the sociolinguistic research of Bernstein and his colleagues, reflects their concern with class differences in "maternal language" (the language spoken by mothers to children). Among the topics explored: maternal orientations to communication; different strategies mothers use in controlling their children; interrelations among sex, class and hesitation phenomena.

BLOUNT, BEN G. AND ELISE J. PADGUG.

Mother and father speech distribution of parental speech features in English and Spanish. *Papers and Reports on Child Language Development.* Stanford, Calif: Stanford Univ., 1976, pp. 47–59.

Parents' speech to young children was taped in four English and four Spanish-speaking families in Texas. In both languages mothers used more baby-talk features than fathers. The English-speaking mothers' speech to children tended to be high pitched and to have lengthened vowels and special lexical items; fathers' speech was pitched lower and in creaky voice. In Spanish, mothers' speech was characterized by breathiness, exaggerated intonation, and lengthened vowels; fathers had more raised volume and fast tempo.

BOSSARD, JAMES.

Family modes of expression. *American Sociological Review,* 10 (1945), 226–37.

Commenting on transcripts of the talk of 35 different families at the dinner table, Bossard observes that there is a "sex appropriate language for boys and one for girls" evident in words used, habits of exclamation, subjects discussed, and phrases like "a lady never raises her voice" and "he sounds like a boy all right."

CHERRY, LOUISE AND MICHAEL LEWIS.

Differential socialization of girls and boys: Implications for sex differences in language development. In Natalie Waterson and Catherine Snow, eds., *The development of communication.* New York: John Wiley & Sons, 1978, pp. 189–97.

Extending the discussion of the speech of 12 two-year-olds and their mothers [*see* Cherry and Lewis, 1976, this section], the authors note that the mothers' speech varied according to sex of child, but there were no sex differences in the speech of the children. The mothers' speech was apparently affected by "a general sex role expectation that female children should be more verbally responsive."

CHERRY, LOUISE AND MICHAEL LEWIS.

Mothers and two-year-olds: A study of sex-differentiated aspects of verbal interaction. *Developmental Psychology,* 12 (1976), 278–82.

Six two-year-old girls and six two-year-old boys were taped interacting with their mothers in a laboratory playroom. Compared with mothers of boys, mothers of girls talked more, asked more questions, repeated their children's utterances more often, and used longer utterances. Mothers of boys used more directives than mothers of girls. In an article reviewing the same research ("Social behavior and language acquisition," in Michael Lewis and Leonard A. Rosenblum, eds., *Interaction, conversation, and the development of language.* New York: John Wiley & Sons, 1977, pp. 227–45), Lewis and Cherry suggest a connection between the mothers' speech and their physical distance from the children; boys were encouraged to move away, and girls to stay close to the mother.

CLARKE-STEWART, ALISON.

Interactions between mothers and their young children: Characteristics and consequences. *Monographs of the Society for Research in Child Development,* 38, nos. 6–7 (1973), 1–109.

A complex longitudinal study of 36 mothers and their children (nine to 18 months) observed over nine months at home. For both sexes, the child's language ability was related to the total amount and variety of maternal speech to the child. There was a trend for mothers of girls to score higher in the ratio of social to referential speech, the amount of time spent together, amount of eye contact, and the proportion of directive and restrictive behaviors. The author relates these patterns to greater maternal protectiveness and nurturance toward girls.

COHEN, SARALE E. AND LEILA BECKWITH.

Maternal language in infancy. *Developmental Psychology,* 12 (1976), 371–72.

The speech of 32 mothers to their infants (18 girls and 18 boys) was analyzed for total talk, positive comment, contingent vocalization, directives, criticism, and face-to-face vocalization. There was no difference in speech to boys and to girls; differences were related to infant age, birth order, and mother's level of education. There was dramatic variability between mothers.

COOK-GUMPERZ, JENNY.

Social control and socialization. London: Routledge & Kegan Paul, 1973.

Working-class, mixed (lower-middle-class and upper-working-class), and middle-class mothers were interviewed about problems of social control with their five-year-old children. Middle-class mothers tended to use strategies in the personal mode, the mixed group in the positional mode, and working-class mothers, the imperative mode of control. Middle-class mothers used more reasoning with boys, and working-class mothers used more emotional control with girls.

ENDSLEY, RICHARD C., M. ANN HUTCHERSON, ANITA P. GARNER, AND MICHAEL MARTIN.

Interrelationships among selected maternal behaviors, authoritarianism, and preschool children's verbal and nonverbal curiosity. *Child Development,* 50 (1979), 331–39.

Forty preschool children and their mothers were observed in a semi-structured play situation. Mothers of girls interacted more with their children and responded more often with affection and/or praise than did mothers of boys.

ENGLE, MARIANNE.

Family influences on the language development of young children. In Cheris Kramarae, ed., *The voices and words of women and men.* Oxford: Pergamon Press, 1980, pp. 259–66. Also *Women's Studies International Quarterly*, 3, no. 2/3 (1980), 259–66.

A study of language used by two- and three-year-olds and their parents found that both parents used simplified language to their young children, but while the mothers used more complex speech to three- than to two-year-olds, the fathers did not.

ENGLE, MARIANNE.

Language and play: A comparative analysis of parental initiatives. In Howard Giles, W. Peter Robinson, and Philip M. Smith, eds., *Language: Social psychological perspectives.* Oxford: Pergamon Press, 1980, pp. 29–34.

Analysis of interactions between four two-year-old boys and four three-year-old boys (all upper-middle-class) playing separately with each parent showed fathers used more directive specific initiatives ("Let's build a truck!") and mothers more non-specific initiatives ("What would you like to play now?").

ERVIN-TRIPP, SUSAN, CATHERINE O'CONNOR, AND JARRETT ROBENBERG.

Language and power in the family. In Cheris Kramarae, Muriel Schulz, and William O'Barr, eds., *Language and power.* Los Angeles: Sage, in press.

In natural interactions studied in four middle-class families, mothers *ignored* the control acts of sons and daughters at approximately the same rate, but mothers were more likely to *comply* with the control acts of girls. Boys were more likely to either comply or refuse requests, while girls more often ignored requests.

FERGUSON, CHARLES A.

Baby talk in six languages. *American Anthropologist,* 66, no. 6, part 2 (1964), 103–14.

Ferguson identifies the intonation patterns, lexical items, and recipients of baby talk (infants, pets, and adults in situations with "baby" aspects). There is little mention of speakers, but he notes that among Americans and Arabs baby talk is considered more appropriate for women to use than it is for men. (A related reference by the same author: "Baby talk as a simplified register," in Catherine E. Snow and Charles A. Ferguson, eds., *Talking to children,* New York: Cambridge Univ. Press, 1977.)

FIELD, TIFFANY.

Interaction behaviors of primary versus secondary caretaker fathers. *Developmental Psychology,* 14 (1978), 183–84.

Primary caretaker mothers and fathers (12 of each, interacting with their four-month-old infants) engaged in more smiling, imitative grimaces, and high-pitched imitative vocalizations than did secondary caretaker fathers, differences perhaps due to degree of familiarity with the infant. Fathers of sons engaged in less high-pitched vocalizing than fathers of daughters. There were no sex differences in amount of parent talk.

FRASER, COLIN AND NAOMI ROBERTS.

> Mothers' speech to children of four different ages. *Journal of Psycholinguistic Research,* 4 (1975), 9–16.

An experimental study of the speech of 32 middle- and upper-middle-class mothers interacting with their children, ages one and one half to six. Mothers' speech (total number of words, mean utterance length, grammatical complexity, number of different words) did not vary with sex or birth order of child; age of child and type of task did have strong effects.

FRIEDLANDER, BERNARD Z., A. C. JACOBS, B. B. DAVIS, AND H. S. WETSTONE.

> Time sampling analysis of infants' natural language environments in the home. *Child Development,* 43 (1972), 730–40.

For one week recordings were made of the home language environments of two 12-month-old infants. Fathers spoke less with infants than did mothers, and overall, the number of adult conversational turns with the boy was greater than with the girl. The authors suggest that parents expect girls to pay more attention to linguistic messages.

GARNICA, OLGA K.

> The boys have the muscles and the girls have the sexy legs: Adult-child speech and the use of generic person labels. In Olga Garnica and Martha King, eds., *Language, children and society.* Oxford: Pergamon Press, 1979.

The use of generic person words was analyzed in tapes of female day-care teachers, each playing with one of six girls (11 months to two years old). Adults used the sex-neutral term *baby* three times more often than sex-marked generics (*boy* or *girl*); *girl* and *baby* appeared in all but one of the elaborated sequences; *boy* appeared primarily in unelaborated sequences. The results are discussed in terms of adult teaching of gender categories, with associated stereotyped activities.

GLEASON, JEAN BERKO.

> Code switching in children's language. In Timothy E. Moore, ed., *Cognitive development and the acquisition of language.* New York: Academic Press, 1973, pp. 159–67.

Observations of adult-child communication in several families found boy babies were more often addressed in a "Hail-Baby-Well-Met style," especially by fathers, while girls were dealt with more gently, both physically and verbally.

GLEASON, JEAN BERKO AND ESTHER BLANK GREIF.

> Men's speech to young children. In this volume.

The authors summarize studies they have done finding differences and similarities in the speech of mothers and fathers to children, and finding the speech of male day-care teachers to be more similar to that of female teachers than to that of fathers at home. Some markers are generally more characteristic of men's speech to children, e.g., more use of imperatives and of the child's name. The paper includes material from Jean Berko Gleason, "Fathers and other strangers: Men's speech to young children" in D. P. Dato, ed., *Developmental psycholinguistics* (Washington, D.C.: Georgetown Univ. Press, 1975, pp. 289–97).

GOLDBERG, SUSAN AND MICHAEL LEWIS.

Play behavior in the year-old infant: Early sex differences. *Child Development,* 40 (1969), 21–32.

Analysis of 32 girls and 32 boys, 13 months old, interacting with their mothers in a free play situation revealed, among other things, that mothers vocalized to and touched their daughters more than their sons.

GOLINKOFF, ROBERTA MICHNICK AND GAIL JOHNSON AMES.

A comparison of fathers' and mothers' speech with their young children. *Child Development,* 50 (1979), 28–32.

Twelve parents with a traditional sexual division of labor were observed interacting with their 19-month-old girls and boys, separately and with both parents present. Fathers spoke less and took fewer conversational turns than mothers. Otherwise, the speech of mothers and fathers did not differ in mean length of turn, number of verbs per utterance, nor use of directives, questions, and repetitions. In the dyadic situation parents took more conversational turns with boys.

GREIF, ESTHER BLANK AND JEAN BERKO GLEASON.

Hi, thanks, and goodbye: More routine information. *Language in Society,* 9 (1980), 159–66.

Eleven girls and 11 boys, ages two to five, interacted separately with their father and mother in a playroom; a gift was used to solicit speech. Boys were more likely than girls to say *hi* to the researcher; parents were equally likely to prompt politeness routines from boys and girls, although mothers were more polite than fathers in saying *thank you* and *goodbye.*

GUNNAR, MEGAN R. AND MARGARET DONAHUE.

Sex differences in social responsiveness between six months and twelve months. *Child Development,* 51 (1980), 262–65.

Fourteen female and 14 male infants were observed interacting with their mothers in a free play situation at six, nine, and 12 months. There were no age or sex differences in either maternal responsiveness or number of attempts mothers made to initiate interaction with the infants. At all three ages girls initiated more interactions than did boys.

HALVERSON, CHARLES F. AND MARY F. WALDROP.

Maternal behavior toward own and other preschool children: The problem of "ownness." *Child Development,* 41 (1970), 839–45.

Forty-two mothers were observed interacting with their own and other two-and-a-half-year-olds in a structured situation. Maternal behavior tended to be consistent with both children, although mothers used more positive, encouraging statements with other versus their own children. Mothers of girls talked more than mothers with boys, and boys rated aggressive in nursery school had mothers who gave more negative, controlling statements to their sons than to other children.

LEWIS, MICHAEL.

Parents and children: Sex-role development. *School Review,* 80 (1972), 229–40.

Reviewing research, Lewis concludes that "mothers look at and talk to their girl infants more than to their boy infants. In fact, looking-at and talking-to behaviors are greater for girls over the entire first two years of life."

LEWIS, MICHAEL AND ROY FREEDLE.

Mother-infant dyad: The cradle of meaning. In P. Pliner, L. Krames, and T. Alloway, eds., *Communication and affect: Language and thought*. New York: Academic Press, 1973, pp. 127–55.

In a study of three-month-old infants and their mothers in a play situation, mothers of girls vocalized more to their children than mothers of boys, perhaps because girls vocalized more in response to their mothers than did boys.

LING, DANIEL AND AGNES H. LING.

Communication development in the first three years of life. *Journal of Speech and Hearing Research*, 17 (1974), 146–59.

Observations of 48 children (ages 11 to 36 months) interacting with their mothers revealed that the amount of verbal communication was affected neither by sex nor by age, but only by birth order; mothers of first-born babies communicated verbally more than mothers of last-born children.

MASUR, ELISE FRANK AND JEAN BERKO GLEASON.

Parent-child interaction and the acquisition of lexical information during play. *Developmental Psychology*, 16 (1980), 404–09.

Seven boys and seven girls, ages two and three (white and middle- or upper-middle-class), were taped playing separately with each parent; the play focused on a toy car. Fathers' speech contained more different terms than that of mothers; fathers were more cognitively and linguistically demanding, e.g., requesting labels from their children. Children produced more total vocabulary to fathers than mothers, especially girls, whose total vocabulary surpassed that of boys. The nature of the toy may have accentuated differences.

NOLLER, PATRICIA.

Cross-gender effects in two-child families. *Developmental Psychology*, 16 (1980), 159–60.

Twenty two-parent, two-child families with children of each sex were videotaped, and interactions between same-gender and cross-gender parent-child dyads were compared. There was more negative verbal behavior in same-gender parent-child interactions.

PHILLIPS, JULIET R.

Syntax and vocabulary of mothers' speech to young children: Age and sex comparisons. *Child Development*, 44 (1973), 182–85.

A comparison of 30 mother-son and 27 mother-daughter pairs, with children ranging from eight to 28 months, interacting in a free play situation, indicated no difference in speech addressed to girls compared with boys. There was some modification in mothers' speech according to age of the child addressed.

REBELSKY, FREDA AND CHERYL HANKS.

Fathers' verbal interaction with infants in the first three months of life. *Child Development*, 42 (1971), 63–68.

Microphones were attached to seven boys and three girls (white, lower-middle- and upper-middle-class) starting the second week of life, and interactions with parents were taped at intervals over a three-month period. The mean number of interactions per day between fathers and infants was 2.7, averaging 37.7 seconds per day. There were large individual differences. There was a decrease in vocalization during the last six weeks of the study, a decrease more marked for fathers of girls than boys.

SNOW, CATHERINE E. AND CHARLES A. FERGUSON, EDS.

    Talking to children. New York: Cambridge Univ. Press, 1977.

    A useful anthology of articles on maternal speech styles, baby-talk registers, and cross-cultural perspectives, including Catherine Snow's review essay which traces shifts in research on mothers' speech, and Ben G. Blount's cross-cultural review which describes the surprise of researchers who found that in other cultures the child's mother is not the major source of language input (other kin, non-kin, and older siblings also interact regularly with young children). [This point is also instructive for research in the U.S.; *see* Ward, this section.] The book includes an annotated bibliography.

STONEMAN, ZOLINDA AND GENE H. BRODY.

    Two's company, three makes a difference: An examination of mothers' and fathers' speech to their young children. *Child Development,* 52 (1981), 705–07.

    Eighteen two-year-old children were observed interacting with both parents present, and then in separate parent-child dyads. Fathers talked less in the triadic than the dyadic family grouping, a trend less apparent for mothers. Parental speech was influenced by gender of offspring, but there were no differences in children's speech by sex or type of situation.

WARD, MARTHA COONFIELD.

    Them children: A study in language learning. New York: Holt, Rinehart and Winston, 1971.

    Although she does not focus primarily on issues of gender, Ward observes that in the Black working-class community near New Orleans which she studied, mothers did not consider themselves to be language teachers for their children; reading and word games were more likely to be done between siblings.

Also see: II-D: Wilson; II-E: Lerner ("And what do little girls have?"); IV-B: Sause; IV-D-2: Lieberman; IV-E-2: Cherry; IV-F: Redlinger; V-A: Abrahams; Greif; Mishler; V-C: West and Zimmerman ("Woman's place in everyday talk"); V-F-2: Most of the section, on teacher-student interaction, is relevant.

B. Language among Children

DAWE, HELEN C.

    An analysis of 200 quarrels of preschool children. *Child Development,* 5 (1934), 139–57.

    Analysis of 200 quarrels of 19 girls and 21 boys in a nursery school showed that boys quarreled significantly more than girls; quarrels were most often between those of the same sex but different ages; boys threatened and forbade more often than girls, while girls cried more often than boys.

GARVEY, CATHERINE AND ELLEN DICKSTEIN.

    Levels of analysis and social class differences in language. *Language and Speech,* 15 (1972), 375–84.

    The speech of 48 status-homogeneous dyads (half female, half male; half low, half middle socioeconomic status; and half Black, half white) of fifth grade children performing three problem-solving tasks was analyzed for levels of linguistic construction. The grammatical form of construction differentiated between SES groups, sexes, and races; lexical choice within the construction differentiated between SES groups; use of the prediction type depended mainly on the task itself. Hence, status differences found at one level of linguistic analysis may not exist at another.

HAAS, ADELAIDE.

The acquisition of genderlect. In Judith Orsanu, Mariam K. Slater, and Leonore Loeb Adler, eds., *Language, sex and gender.* New York: New York Academy of Sciences, 1979, pp. 101–13.

Haas analyzed features of form, content, topic, and use in the talk of same and mixed-sex pairs of middle- and upper-class white children, ages four, eight, or twelve. There were sex differences in only 16 of the 45 features studied; only eight differences held across age and type of dyad. Among features associated with sex: boys talked more about sports and gave more information; girls talked more about school and sitting games, used fewer direct requests, laughed more, and showed more compliance. Boys made more direct requests and girls laughed more and used more compliant utterances in mixed than in same-sex groups.

LANGLOIS, JUDITH H., NATHAN W. GOTTFRIED, AND BILL SEAY.

The influence of sex of peer on the social behavior of preschool children. *Developmental Psychology*, 8 (1973), 93–98.

Thirty-two Black children, ages three and five, were observed playing in same-sex and cross-sex pairs. Girls talked with and touched their partners more frequently than did boys; three-year-old girls used more non-word vocalizations than boys; the reverse was true among five-year-olds. Children with same-sex partners displayed more hitting and touching and less talking than when with partners of the other sex.

LANGLOIS, JUDITH H., NATHAN W. GOTTFRIED, METTINA M. BARNES, AND DANIEL E. HENDRICKS.

The effect of peer age on the social behavior of preschool children. *The Journal of Genetic Psychology*, 132 (1978), 11–19.

An experimental study in which 16 boys and 16 girls (all white, ages three and five) were observed playing. Both three- and five-year-old boys talked more when in same than in mixed-age dyads; three-year-old girls talked the same amount regardless of age of play partner. In mixed-age pairs, five-year-old boys used verbal instructions to direct the three-year-old boys (who obeyed, but rarely responded verbally); the girls had a more reciprocal relationship.

MUELLER, EDWARD.

The maintenance of verbal exchanges between young children. *Child Development*, 43 (1972), 930–38.

Forty-eight children, ages three to five, were observed playing in same-sex pairs. Boys talked more than girls; there were no sex differences in number of successful or unsuccessful utterances, with success measured by whether the listener responded.

SGAN, MABEL L. AND SARAH M. PICKERT.

Cross-sex and same-sex assertive bids in a cooperative group task. *Child Development*, 51 (1980), 928–31.

The interactions of 108 children doing a cooperative task were analyzed for verbal indices of assertion, e.g., commands, instructions, and suggestions. Kindergarten and first grade boys made more assertive bids than girls, with bids mainly directed to other boys; with age, girls increased assertiveness to boys and other girls, and by third grade the girls' overall assertive bids equaled those of boys.

Also see: IV-C: Cheshire; IV-E-2: Brownell and Smith; IV-F: Patella and Kuvlesky; V-A: Dittman; Esposito; Goodwin; Maltz and Borker; Mishler; V-F-2: Elliott; V-H: Militanskij; VI-A-1: Abrahams; Ayoub and Barnett; Dundes; Folb; Kochman; Labov; VI-A-4: Goodwin.

C. Child Language Acquisition

This section includes studies of sex differences and similarities in the rate and process of language acquisition, and theoretical and empirical sources more specifically on the learning of sex-typed language.

ANDERSON, ELAINE.

Young children's knowledge of role-related speech differences: A mommy is not a daddy is not a baby. *Papers and Reports on Child Language Development,* 13 (1977), 83–90.

Twelve girls and 12 boys, ages three to seven, role-played with mother, father, and child puppets. The children portrayed the father's speech as straightfoward, unqualified, and forceful, and the mother as more talkative, polite, qualified, and higher pitched. Only girls used endearments, and only when they role-played parents.

BARTHOLOMEUS, BONNIE.

Voice identification by nursery school children. *Canadian Journal of Psychology/Révue Canadiènne de Psychologie,* 27 (1973), 464–73.

Voice identification scores varied widely among 36 nursery school children but did not differ significantly between girls and boys.

BATES, ELIZABETH AND LOUISE SILVERN.

Social adjustment and politeness in preschoolers. *Journal of Communication,* 27 (1977), 104–11.

Ninety-nine preschool children were each given a task which pressed for production of politeness forms (told to ask "really nice" for candy). There were no significant sex differences in production or comprehension of politeness forms.

BRANDIS, WALTER AND DOROTHY HENDERSON.

Social class, language, and communication. London: Routledge & Kegan Paul, 1970.

In a study of the speech of five-year-old working-class children in Britain, the authors found more adjectives used by girls than by boys, and they generalize that girls develop a "more differentiated, more individuated use of language in interpersonal contexts," which they explain as the result of older working-class girls being both in sibling and mothering roles.

CAHILL, SPENCER E.

Becoming boys and girls. Unpublished Ph.D. dissertation, Univ. of California, Santa Barbara, 1982.

Understanding peoples' "observational and tellable sex" as an "interactionally achieved event," Cahill develops a theory of the process of gender socialization, drawing upon observations of children's interactions in preschool settings, with attention to language.

EDELSKY, CAROLE.

Acquisition of an aspect of communicative competence: Learning what it means to talk like a lady. In Susan Ervin-Tripp and Claudia Mitchell-Kernan, eds., *Child discourse.* New York: Academic Press, 1977, pp. 225–43.

To study the acquisition of knowledge of sex-linked speech stereotypes, Edelsky had a large sample of adults and children attribute statements (with strong or weak expletives, polite requests or commands, intensifiers, and tag questions) to men or women or both. Adults agreed on the details of stereotypes and sixth graders' judgments resembled those of adults, with stronger stereotyping on some details. First graders' judgments were only minimally like those of adults. At different ages children used different strategies for making judgments. An earlier version of the paper: "The Acquisition of communicative competence: Recognition of linguistic correlates of sex roles." *Merrill-Palmer Quarterly,* 22 (1976), 47–59.

FILLMER, H. THOMPSON AND LESLIE HASWELL.

Sex-role stereotyping in English usage. *Sex Roles,* 3 (1977), 257–63.

First to fifth grade children from Southern, low-income inner-city schools were asked to identify statements that would be said by a woman or by a man (e.g., "It is a nice day"; "It is such a nice day"). More than 50% of the children chose the answer that reflected sex-stereotyped language usage.

GARCIA-ZAMOR, MARIE A.

Child awareness of sex role distinctions in language use. Paper given at Linguistic Society of America, San Diego, Calif., 1973.

Eight nursery school children, four boys and four girls (middle- and upper-middle-class) were interviewed to elicit overt attitudes toward sex roles (which were generally traditional) and were then asked to judge whether a girl or boy doll prop uttered various sentences. There was more agreement among male than female subjects about whether an item was uttered by a male or a female; "aggressive" and competitive expressions were associated with male dolls; tag questions tended to be female-associated; judgments for terms of endearments and for epithets were mixed.

GLEASON, JEAN BERKO.

Sex differences in the language of children and parents. In Olga Garnica and Martha King, eds., *Language, children and society.* Oxford: Pergamon Press, 1979, pp. 149–57.

Emphasizing sex differences in the process of language acquisition, Gleason discusses interactions between biology and enviroment, the reciprocal effects of adults and children on one another's speech, and differences in the speech of mothers and fathers. Questions are suggested for further research.

HARRIS, LAUREN JAY.

Sex differences in the growth and use of language. In Elaine Donelson and Jeanne Gullahorn, eds., *Women: A psychological perspective.* New York: John Wiley & Sons, 1977.

In a careful review of the literature on language acquisition, Harris concludes that girls acquire language earlier than boys according to a variety of measures—acquisition of phonemes, amount of vocalization in infancy, the age of use of the first words, vocabulary size (at least in early childhood), articulation, comprehensibility, and fluency. Neurological, genetic, and environmental factors probably interact from the first days of a child's life to produce the differences.

KLANN-DELIUS, GISELA.

Sex and language acquisition—Is there any influence? *Journal of Pragmatics*, 5 (1981), 1–25.

An excellent, thorough review, emphasizing the mixed nature of empirical findings (the stereotype of girls' verbal superiority can empirically be neither confirmed nor refuted; possible difference, not deficit is the issue). The author concludes that sex differences are more likely in the semantic-pragmatic than in the phonological and syntactic dimensions of language acquisition. She also discusses methodological problems in this field of research, e.g., the scarcity of longitudinal studies and the skew to middle-class children and to quantifiable data. [*Also see* Klann-Delius, Sec. IV-E-1.]

LAKOFF, ROBIN.

Language and woman's place. New York: Harper & Row, 1975.

Lakoff speculates that both boys and girls first learn "women's language" and that between the ages of five and ten boys learn male speech, e.g., going through a stage of rough talk; thus boys adopt new forms, while girls retain their original speech. While most of the phonological, syntactic, and semantic structure of language is in active use by four or five, social-contextual factors are not learned until much later. [*Also see* Lakoff, Sec. I-A.]

MCCARTHY, DOROTHEA.

Language development of the preschool child. Minneapolis: Univ. of Minnesota Press, 1930.

An influential early study of the language development of 140 children, ages one-and-a-half to four-and-a-half who were observed talking in natural settings. McCarthy found girls produced longer and more comprehensible and complete responses than boys of the same chronological age; she found no consistent sex differences in vocabulary or lexical diversity.

MCGHEE, PAUL E.

The role of laughter and humor in growing up female. In Claire Kopp, ed., *Becoming female*. New York: Plenum, 1979, pp. 183–206.

In this review essay McGhee concludes that after age six boys are more likely to initiate, and girls to respond, to verbal humor; the laughter of both girls and women seems to be more strongly influenced by the presence and reactions of others; there is little evidence of a distinctively female sense of humor.

MEDITCH, ANDREA.

The development of sex-specific speech patterns in young children. *Anthropological Linguistics*, 17 (1975), 421–33.

Guessing the sex of children (ages three to five) on the basis of taped voices, college students were more accurate in identifying the boys than the girls. Since there are few or no physiological differences in the vocal mechanisms of girls and boys, Meditch explains the results by arguing that children learn sex-specific speech markers at an early age, boys earlier than girls.

MENYUK, PAULA.

Syntactic structures in the language of children. *Child Development*, 18 (1963), 407–22.

Analysis of spontaneous speech of 24 girls and 24 boys of nursery school age, talking in three different settings, revealed no sex differences in syntactic transformations nor amount of verbalization.

NUNEZ-WORMACK, ELSA.

Sex differences in the acquisition of English and Spanish. Paper given at the 9th World Congress of Sociology, Uppsala, Sweden, 1978.

Most studies focusing on the acquisiton of English syntactic competence have found trends of female superiority. However, Paul Betancourt (Sex differences in language proficiency of Mexican-American third and fourth graders, *Journal of Education*, 158, no. 2 [1976], 55–65) found males scored significantly higher on Spanish proficiency tests. The Nunez-Wormack study of Puerto Rican bilingual first, second, and third graders demonstrated that, on the majority of assigned tasks, the males had a more rapid development of morphological competence than the females.

RAMER, ANDRYA L.

Syntactic styles in emerging language. *Journal of Child Language*, 3 (1976), 49–62.

A longitudinal study of the emerging grammar of three girls and four boys, all white and middle-class. The girls developed language more rapidly than boys. Two, sex and speed-related, styles of syntactic acquisition were identified: rapidly developing girls employed few, if any presyntactic forms; slower developing boys depended heavily on presyntactic forms.

STEWART, WILLIAM A.

Urban Negro speech: Sociolinguistic factors affecting English teaching. In Roger W. Shuy, ed., *Social dialects and language learning*. Champaign, Ill.: National Council of Teachers of English, 1964, pp. 10–18.

Among Blacks in Washington, D.C., the least "standard" dialect is largely restricted to young children. At ages seven or eight there is (at least for boys) a noticeable shift to more "standard" speech, coinciding with the shift from "small-boy" to "big-boy" in the peer group. In a footnote, Stewart adds that this rapid dialect shift is less frequent among girls, who are less rigidly age graded; their dialect change is more the result of formal education.

TIEDT, PAMELA LYNN.

Possible sources of linguistic input for the acquisition of sex appropriate language by children. Unpublished M.A. thesis, Linguistics Dept., Stanford University, Stanford, Calif., 1975.

Tiedt discusses theories of how children may learn sex differentiated language: children may model their speech on the parent of the same sex; parents may speak differently to girls and boys; boys and girls may learn women's speech first and later differentiate.

Also see: II-D: DeStefano, Kuhner, and Pepinsky; Eberhart; Harrison; Harrison and Passero; II-E: Mamola; Montemayor; III-B: Centineo; Edwards; III-C: Bennett and Weinberg; Fillmer and Haswell; IV-A: Kaplan; Silverman; IV-C: Cheshire; Fischer; Hartford; IV-D-1: Sachs; Sachs, Lieberman, and Erickson; IV-D-3: Key; IV-E-1: Garai and Scheinfeld; Gunderson; Klann-Delius; Macaulay; Maccoby and Jacklin; Nelson; Plomin and Foch; Rousey and Moriarty; Strauch; IV-E-2: Brownell and Smith; Winitz; IV-E-3: McCarthy; IV-F: Patella and Kuvlesky; IV-G: Schneiderman; V-B: Cowan, Weber, Hoddinott, and Klein; VII-B: Haas.

D.   Other Languages

BURROWS, PHYLLIS BRONSTEIN.

Mexican parental roles: Differences between mothers' and fathers' behavior to children. Paper given at meeting of the Society for Cross-Cultural Research, Philadelphia, 1980.

Interactions between 78 parent-child (ages 7 to 12) dyads, residents of a city in Mexico, were observed and coded. Both parents (fathers much more than mothers) used more direct control (scolding, acting hostile, threatening, interrogating) with boys, and more indirect control (correcting, manipulating, belittling) with girls. Fathers directed more attention toward sons, and more interrupting, disagreeing, and short answers toward daughters. (Based on Burrows, *Parent-child behavior in a sample of Mexican families*. Unpublished Ph.D. dissertation, Harvard Univ., Cambridge, Mass., 1979.)

DEBLAUW, AKKE, CLARA DUBBER, GHISLAINE VON ROSSMALEN, AND CATHERINE E. SNOW.

Sex and social class differences in early mother-child interaction. In Olga Garnica and Martha King, eds., *Language, children and society*. Oxford: Pergamon Press, 1979, pp. 53–64.

Sixteen Dutch mother-infant pairs were observed interacting. No significant sex or social class differences were found in frequency of infant vocalization or smiles nor in number or length of episodes of maternal vocalization. Boys produced more negative vocalizations at three months.

FICHTELIUS, ANNA, IRENE JOHANSSON, AND KERSTIN NORDIN.

Three investigations of sex-associated speech variations in day school. In Cheris Kramarae, ed., *The voices and words of women and men*. Oxford: Pergamon Press, 1980, pp. 219–25. Also *Women's Studies International Quarterly*, 3, no. 2/3 (1980), 219–25.

Tapes of the speech of 20 Swedish children (ages three to seven) were played to adults and to second graders who guessed the sex of the speakers. The adult respondents averaged 67.3% correct guesses and the children, 61.5%. The children tended to be more attentive and correct in assigning the speech of the other sex. In an analysis of the speech of teachers talking to day-school children, the researchers found that teachers directed more *yes/no* questions to girls and younger children, and used more exclamations and a "brisker" style with boys. Boys received more affirmations in response to their utterances.

JORMAKKA, LEA.

The behavior of children during a first encounter. *Scandinavian Journal of Psychology*, 17 (1976), 15–22.

In this study by a Finnish researcher, children six to seven years of age were divided into unacquainted pairs, 14 each. Personal talk (talking about self and asking questions about the other) was more common among unacquainted children, especially girls.

LARSON, KAREN.

Role-playing and the real thing: Socialization and standard speech in Norway. *Journal of anthropological research*, 38 (1982), 401–10.

In this study of talk among family members in Norway, speech is examined in the context of the range of communicative skills and assets available to speakers as occupants of specific social groups. Through temporarily switching to standard speech, speakers can establish social distance;

girls learn to switch to standard to have an impact on others since the more direct verbal strategies used frequently by males are not considered appropriate for the girls.

MARTENS, KARIN.

Sprachliche Kommunikation in der Familie. Kronberg Ts.: Scriptor Verlag, 1974.

An analysis of the communication of a woman and a man talking to each other and talking to their children.

SCHNEIDERMAN, ETA I.

Sex differences in the development of children's ethnic and language attitudes. *International Journal of Social Languages,* 38 (1982), 37–44.

A puppet show, using French- and English-speaking characters, was shown to French-Canadian children, 3–12 years of age. Girls preferred the French puppet at all age levels, boys in nursery school were pro-English but began to favor the French puppet from grade one on. Schneiderman comments on our limited understanding of the development of language attitudes—including their relationship to gender—and how children's attitudes are related to those of adults.

WINTERMANTEL, MARGRET.

Geschlechtstypische Unterschiede im Sprachverhalten. In Heidi Keller, ed., *Geschlechts-unterschiede. Psychologische und Physiologische Grundlagen der Geschlechter-differen-zierung.* Weinheim: Beltz Verlag, 1979, pp. 140–53.

This review article deals with sex differences in the speech of children.

VIII.   LANGUAGE VARIETIES IN AMERICAN ENGLISH

The speech of dominant groups—men, whites, heterosexuals, those with class privilege—is often assumed as the norm, and that of subordinate groups marked off, or treated as a special case. Our purpose in cross-listing all items which deal with the speech of groups subordinate on the basis of race, social class, and sexuality, is not to further mark them off, but to call attention to their relative invisibility, to challenge the equation of the speech of dominant groups with the norm, and to encourage further research on interactions between gender, race, ethnicity, sexuality, and social class.

A.   Race and Ethnic Variation

1.   Blacks

See: I-A: Moraga and Anzuldúa; II-A: Scott; III-A: Broderick; III-C: Abrahams; Lass, Mertz, and Kimmel; IV-A: Nichols; IV-B: Folb; Garcia and Frosch; Nichols; IV-C: Anshen; Fasold; Labov; Wolfram; IV-F: Hannerz; V-A: Abrahams ("Black talking on the streets"); Abrahams ("Negotiating respect"); Goodwin; Kochman; Stanback; VI-A-1: Abrahams ("Deep down in the jungle"); Abrahams ("Talking Black"); Ayoub and Barnett; Dundes; Folb; Hannerz; Kochman; Labov; Mitchell-Kernan ("Signifying"); Mitchell-Kernan ("Signifying, loud talking, and marking"); VI-A-2: Folb; VI-A-3: Bulkin; Marshall; VI-A-4: Goodwin; VI-B: Hull, Scott, and Smith; Roberts; Smith; VI-C: Anzaldúa; Gilbert ("Speaking in mother tongues"); Stanley, Daly, Lorde, McDaniel, and Rich; VII-A: Ward; VII-B: Garvey and Dickstein; Langlois, Gottfried, and Seay; VII-C: Nunez-Wormack; Stewart; IX: Johnson.

2. Chicanas/os and Puerto Ricans

See: I-A: Moraga and Anzaldúa; IV-B: Garcia and Frosch; IV-C: Hartford; IV-F: Patella and Kuvlesky; Redlinger; Sole; Valdéz-Fallis; V-D: Vigil and Elsasser; VI-C: Anzaldúa; Gilbert ("Speaking in mother tongues"); Mora and Van Hooft; VII-A: Blount and Padgug; VII-C: Nunez-Wormack.

3. Native Americans

See II-F: Fiske; IV-F: John-Steiner and Irvine; IV-G: Bodine; Flannery; Haas; Taylor.

B. Lesbian and Gay Male Speech

In addition to items cross-referenced below, there are useful sources with additional bibliography: James W. Chesebro, ed., *Gayspeak: Gay male and lesbian communication* (New York: Pilgrim Press, 1981) is a collection of 25 articles on spoken and nonverbal language used in lesbian and gay male subcultures, the labeling of lesbians and gay men by themselves and others, and the rhetoric and political dilemmas of gay liberation. Joseph J. Hayes's "Language behavior of lesbian women and gay men: A selected bibliography (Part 1)" (*Journal of Homosexuality,* 4 [1978], 201–12), provides an annotated bibliography on slang, labels, interaction in gay male and lesbian subcultures, rhetoric and style, and an introductory discussion of methodological issues.

See: I-A: Moraga and Anzaldúa; II-E: Hayes; Lesher; Rudes and Healy; Stanley ("When we say 'Out of the closets!' "); II-I: Darsey; Nogle; II-J: Wittig; III-A: Hayes; III-C: Newton; IV-B: Hayes; V-A: Painter; VI-A-2: Painter; Stanley and Robbins; VI-A-3: Bulkin; VI-B: Roberts; Smith; Zimmerman; VI-C: Anzaldúa; Rich; Shaktini; Sambolian and Marks; Penelope (Stanley) and Wolfe; Schuster; Stanley, Daly, Lorde, McDaniel, and Rich; Wittig; IX: Hayes; Painter.

C. Social Class

These items are sensitive to possible speech variation by social class.

See: III-B: Edwards; O'Barr and Atkins; III-D: Philipsen; Rubin; IV-A: Nichols (both items); Trudgill; IV-B: Bisseret; IV-C: Fasold; Fischer; Levine and Crockett; Shuy, Wolfram, and Riley; Wolfram; V-A: Komarovsky; V-B: Moreau; V-D: Klein; VII-A: Bernstein; Cook-Gumperz; Ward; VII-B: Garvey and Dickstein; VII-C: Brandis and Henderson.

IX. NONVERBAL ASPECTS OF COMMUNICATION

Only comprehensive sources and ones directly concerned with gender are included here. There are now many references on specific aspects and modalities of nonverbal communication and gender. For these, and for other related sources, see the references in the sources listed below and the many books now available on nonverbal communication.

BIRDWHISTELL, RAY.

Masculinity and femininity as display. In *Kinesics and context.* Philadelphia: Univ. of Pennsylvania Press, 1970, pp. 39–46.

Birdwhistell points out that human beings are weakly differentiated by sex, compared with other animal species, thus "necessarily organize much of gender display and recognition at the level of position, movement, and expression." He discusses origins of gender-differentiated behavior, U.S. gender display, cross-cultural views of gender-associated movement, "inappropriate" gender display, contexts of behavior, division of labor, and childhood learning of gender display.

FRANCES, SUSAN J.

Sex differences in nonverbal behavior. *Sex Roles,* 5 (1979), 519–35.

An exploratory search for sex differences in eight nonverbal channels, using 54 behavioral variables, was conducted using videotapes of 88 same-sex and mixed-sex dyadic conversations. Subject sex significantly affected behavior (e.g., men spoke longer and used more filled pauses, women smiled and laughed more), but sex of partner did not.

FRIEZE, IRENE H. AND RAMSEY, SHEILA J.

Nonverbal maintenance of traditional sex roles. *Journal of Social Issues,* 32 (1976), 133–41.

This paper reviews studies documenting nonverbal behaviors which indicate either dominance and status or liking and warmth, and compares them with studies finding nonverbal sex differences. Sex differences perpetuate sex-role stereotypes, are resistant to change, and serve to maintain traditional roles.

GOFFMAN, ERVING.

Gender advertisements. New York: Harper & Row, 1979.

An analysis of the depiction of gender in U.S. print advertising, with photographs of illustrative ads. Goffman's thesis is that advertising tends to "hyper-ritualize" gender display, i.e., to emphasize and further abstract it, to give an imbalanced and distorted view of the arrangement between the sexes. He uncovers themes of relative size, feminine touch, function ranking, the family, the ritualization of subordination, and licensed withdrawal. [For a review, see Nancy M. Henley, Gender hype, in Cheris Kramarae, ed., *The voices and words of women and men.* Oxford: Pergamon Press, 1980, pp. 305–12. Also *Women's Studies International Quarterly*, 3, no. 2/3 (1980), 305–12.]

HALL, JUDITH A.

Gender effects in decoding nonverbal cues. *Psychological Bulletin,* 85 (1978), 845–57.

This is a summary of 75 studies that reported nonverbal decoding accuracy for females and males, with attention to the size, direction, and significance level of effects. Female advantage, consistent but of moderate magnitude, is demonstrated in the studies, which span the years from 1923 to 1978 and cover all age groups. [It is a more detailed and statistically oriented review than Hall, 1979 (this section) but there is much overlap.]

HALL, JUDITH A.

Gender, gender-roles and nonverbal communication skills. In R. Rosenthal, ed., *Skill in nonverbal communication: Individual differences.* Cambridge, Mass.: Oelgeschlager, Gunn & Hain, 1979.

A review of the literature on sex differences in ability to decode and encode nonverbal cues, with a discussion of various explanations for the finding of moderate female advantage: empathy; gender stereotypes and roles; adaptation to asymmetrical power; practice effects; accommodatingness; innate capacity; cognitive strategies; gender differences in the use of verbal codes. Tests of several of the hypotheses are reported and reviewed. The portion on decoding in this paper overlaps with that of Hall, 1978 [this section].

HAYDEN, DOLORES.

Social space, women's labor, and socialist feminism. Paper presented at Berkshire Conference on the History of Women, Vassar College, Poughkeepsie, N.Y., 1981.

Hayden presents a socialist feminist synthesis of microspace and macrospace theory (Henley and Lefebvre). See also her book, *The grand domestic revolution* (Cambridge, Mass.: M.I.T. Press, 1981), on the attempts of earlier feminists to transform the spatial design and material culture of American urban life.

HAYES, JOSEPH.

Lesbians, gay men, and their "languages." In James W. Chesebro, ed., *Gayspeak: Gay male and lesbian communication.* New York: Pilgrim Press, 1981.

A section on "Nonverbal behavior (Paralanguage)" discusses nonverbal signaling systems among gay males and stereotypes of lesbian and gay male nonverbal behavior. [*Also see* Sec. III-A.]

HENLEY, NANCY M.

Body politics: Power, sex, and nonverbal communication. Englewood Cliffs, N.J.: Prentice-Hall, 1977.

A review of the research on power (status, dominance) and on sex differences in nonverbal communication, in various modalities. The main theses presented are that nonverbal forms follow the pattern described by Roger Brown for terms of address; that nonverbal communication is an important avenue of social control; that the nonverbal signals of dominance and submission parallel those of males and females, respectively; and that females' adoption of male-associated gestures of dominance may be interpreted by observers as sexual rather than dominant.

HENLEY, NANCY M.

Changing the body power structure. *Women: A Journal of Liberation,* 6, 1 (1978), 34–38.

A brief review of knowledge about gender and nonverbal communication, with suggestions for feminist change and a call to reconsider positive values expressed in women's behavior rather than blindly assume power lies in changing to male-associated forms.

HENLEY, NANCY M.

Power, sex and nonverbal communication. *Berkeley Review of Sociology,* 18 (1973/74), 1–26. Also in Barrie Thorne and Nancy Henley, eds., *Language and sex: Difference and dominance* (Rowley, Mass.: Newbury House, 1975, pp. 185–203); and in Zick Rubin, ed., *Doing unto others* (Englewood Cliffs, N.J.: Prentice-Hall, 1974, pp. 48–60).

A survey of nonverbal behaviors of women and men, compared to those of persons of low and high power, with the thesis that nonverbal behavior reflects and shapes sexual power relationships. [*See also:* Nancy Henley and Jo Freeman, The sexual politics of interpersonal behavior. In Jo Freeman, ed., *Women: A feminist perspective* (3rd ed.). Palo Alto, Calif.: Mayfield, 1983.]

HENLEY, NANCY M.

Women's nonverbal behavior: Underlying assumptions in the admonition to change. Paper presented at the International Interdisciplinary Congress on Women, Haifa, Israel, 1981.

The author argues for a reassessment of the admonition for women to change their nonverbal behavior, on the basis that we know little about women's behavior and its source, and that such an admonition often unwittingly attaches greater value to the supposed behavior of men.

HERESIES 2 (Special issue).

Patterns of communication and space among women. *Heresies 2*, May 1977.

This feminist publication on art and politics includes in this issue various articles relevant to women in space: e.g., Sherry Markovitz, Body, space and personal ritual; Elizabeth Weatherford, Women's traditional architecture; Ann Marie Rousseau, Homeless women; Dolores Hayden, Skyscraper seduction, skyscraper rape; Noel Phyllis Birkby and Leslie Kanes Weisman, Women's fantasy environments.

JOHNSON, KENNETH R.

Black kinesics—Some nonverbal communication patterns in the Black culture. *Florida FL Reporter,* Spring/Fall 1971, 17–20.

The author surveys patterns of nonverbal communication among U.S. Blacks, suggesting possible African influences on certain forms, as well as the influence of U.S. Blacks' cultural isolation. Differences in eye behavior and posture are described in detail to illustrate Black-white differences and male-female differences among Blacks, particularly in encounters with authority or in courtship.

LAFRANCE, MARIANNE AND CLARA MAYO.

A review of nonverbal behaviors of women and men. *Western Journal of Speech Communication,* 43 (1979), 96–107.

A review of the literature on gender-linked aspects of nonverbal communication, finding that sex differences are in line with societal expectations calling for women to be reactive and men to be proactive.

MAYO, CLARA AND NANCY M. HENLEY, EDS.

Gender and nonverbal behavior. New York: Springer-Verlag, 1981.

An edited collection covering topics of touching, visual behavior, body movements and positions, leadership, dyadic interaction, androgyny, conversational assertiveness, child development, advertising images, lesbian/gay orientation, feminist therapy, and change.

PAINTER, DOROTHY S.

Recognition among lesbians in straight settings. In James. W. Chesebro, ed., *Gayspeak: Gay male and lesbian communication.* New York: Pilgrim Press, 1981.

This paper has a section on "Nonverbal and verbal cues." The author and her informants are unable to name or describe any nonverbal behaviors specific to or carrying specific meaning to lesbians in these settings, but they believe they must exist; the author sees no value in identifying gay/straight differences through research. [*Also see* Sec. V-A.]

PUTNAM, LINDA L. AND LINDA MCALLISTER.

Situational effects of task and gender on nonverbal display. In Dan Nimmo, ed., *Communication Yearbook 4.* New Brunswick, N.J.: Transaction Books, 1980, pp. 679–97.

This study examines the impact of sex, psychological gender, and task on ten nonverbal conversational dominance and listener attentiveness cues. Subjects in general use more warmth-attentiveness cues on the feminine task and more conversational control cues on the masculine one; however, there is also variation by psychological gender.

ROSENTHAL, ROBERT AND BELLA M. DEPAULO.

Sex differences in accommodation in nonverbal communication. In Robert Rosenthal, ed., *Skill in nonverbal communication*. Cambridge, Mass.: Oelgeschlager, Gunn & Hain, 1979.

A review of past studies and presentation of the authors' own research on nonverbal decoding abilities of women and men. Women's advantage over men was less when visual cues were of very brief duration and when cues were least controllable (most "leaky") by the sender. Women were less likely than men to eavesdrop on leaky nonverbal channels; women tended more to see positive behavior; and women who tended to focus on the positive tended to decrease in accuracy as they matured.

ROSENTHAL, ROBERT, JUDITH A. HALL, M. ROBIN DiMATTEO, PETER L. ROGERS, AND DANE ARCHER.

Sensitivity to nonverbal communication: The PONS test. Baltimore: Johns Hopkins Univ. Press, 1979.

A presentation of the authors' comprehensive research on ability to decode nonverbal messages, conducted with subjects of all ages and from a variety of occupations and cultures, finding a consistent sex difference favoring females.

UMIKER-SEBEOK, JEAN.

Nature's way? Visual images of childhood in American culture. *Semiotica*, 27 (1979), 173–220.

A survey and semiotic analysis of the depiction of girls and boys in advertising—alone, together, and in various family groups. The ads demonstrate a stereotypically biased selection of cultural values for children.

WEITZ, SHIRLEY.

Sex differences in nonverbal communication. *Sex Roles,* 2 (1976), 175–84.

In a laboratory experiment using videotaped interactions of women and men in same-sex and mixed-sex dyads, women were found to elicit more warmth and men more anxiety from their partners. Weitz posits the existence of a monitoring mechanism whereby women adjust their nonverbal behavior to accommodate to men in interaction.

WEX, MARIANNE.

Let's take back our space. "Female" and "male" body language as a result of patriarchal structures. Hamburg: Frauenliteraturverlag Hermine Fees, 1979. (Also available in German.)

Photographs and text by the author, a sculptor and artist, illustrating typical postures, gestures, and facial expressions of women and men, from candid shots and advertising. There is also a section on depiction of the body in sculpture of the last 3,000–4,000 years; Wex concludes that the ideals of body language and form have never been so different for the sexes as they are today.

AUTHOR INDEX TO THE BIBLIOGRAPHY